ABOUT THE
TREATMENT OF
THE DETAINEES
AT GUANTÁNAMO
AND ABU GHRAIB

THE "TAGUBA REPORT,"
GENEVA CONVENTION RELATIVE TO THE TREATMENT OF
PRISONERS OF WAR,
GENEVA CONVENTION RELATIVE TO THE PROTECTION OF CIVILIAN
PERSONS IN TIME OF WAR,
RASUL V. BUSH, HAMDI V. RUMSFELD, RUMSFELD V. PADILLA

FIRST EDITION, JULY 2004
EDITED BY W. FREDERICK ZIMMERMAN

NIMBLE BOOKS
ANN ARBOR, MICHIGAN

NIMBLE BOOKS

Library of Congress Cataloging Information

Library of Congress Control Number: 2004109247

ISBN

0-9754479-0-4

Change History

Version 1.02

Cover Design

Kelsey Zimmerman

Copyright Notice

The documents included in this volume were published by the United States government.

The front matter, table of contents, and index were prepared by W. Frederick Zimmerman and are copyright 2004 W. Frederick Zimmerman.

BASIC DOCUMENTS ABOUT THE DETAINEES

Table of Contents

Items in UPPER CASE are from the original documents; items in Title Case were prepared by the editor.

Readers and Reviewers, Set Your Expectations Here v
   Read This Book If v
   Don't Bother If v
   Look on the Bright Side! v
   Understand How This Book Is Organized vi
   How to Read This Book vi
Read the Acknowledgements So That You Can Be Properly Appreciative of the Author's Colleagues, Friends, and Family vii
Read about the Publisher So That You Can Be Either Baffled or Impressed, or Both viii
ARTICLE 15-6 INVESTIGATION OF THE 800th MILITARY POLICE BRIGADE 1
   BACKGROUND 1
   ASSESSMENT OF DoD COUNTER-TERRORISM INTERROGATION AND DETENTION OPERATIONS IN IRAQ (MG MILLER'S ASSESSMENT) 2
   IO COMMENTS ON MG MILLER'S ASSESSMENT 3
   REPORT ON DETENTION AND CORRECTIONS IN IRAQ (MG RYDER'S REPORT) 4
   PRELIMINARY INVESTIGATIVE ACTIONS 6
   FINDINGS AND RECOMMENDATIONS (PART ONE) 7
   RECOMMENDATIONS AS TO PART ONE OF THE INVESTIGATION: 12
   FINDINGS AND RECOMMENDATIONS (PART TWO) 13
   FINDINGS AND RECOMMENDATIONS (PART THREE) 21
   RECOMMENDATIONS AS TO PART THREE OF THE INVESTIGATION: 28
   OTHER FINDINGS/OBSERVATIONS 33
   CONCLUSION 34
   ANNEXES 34
   REFERENCES 37
GENEVA CONVENTION RELATIVE TO THE TREATMENT OF PRISONERS OF WAR OF AUGUST 12, 1949 (GENEVA CONVENTION III) 39
   PART I: GENERAL PROVISIONS 39
   PART II: GENERAL PROTECTION OF PRISONERS OF WAR 42
   PART III: CAPTIVITY 43
   PART IV: TERMINATION OF CAPTIVITY 72
GENEVA CONVENTION (IV) RELATIVE TO THE PROTECTION OF CIVILIAN PERSONS IN TIME OF WAR (GENEVA CONVENTION IV) 77
   PART I: GENERAL PROVISIONS 77

NIMBLE BOOKS

PART II: GENERAL PROTECTION OF POPULATIONS AGAINST CERTAIN CONSEQUENCES OF WAR 82
PART III: STATUS AND TREATMENT OF PROTECTED PERSONS 86
PART IV: EXECUTION OF THE CONVENTION 123
RASUL V. BUSH 133
HAMDI V. RUMSFELD 181
RUMSFELD V. PADILLA 283

BASIC DOCUMENTS ABOUT THE DETAINEES

Readers and Reviewers, Set Your Expectations Here

This book is something of an experiment. I thought it would be useful to publish selected public domain documents related to the Abu Ghraib prison scandal and the internment of detainees at Guantánamo Bay in a handy book format for reference. The selection of content is based on the premise that responsible citizens of the United States and the world need to inform themselves about the details of these issues. This is *not* intended to be an academic volume that meets the needs of scholars by providing dozens of noteworthy documents. I wanted to keep the page count, and the price, at a point where the purchase makes sense for active-minded citizens.

If the price is right, the documents are interesting and the book is convenient to read, then I have achieved my objectives! Since this is my first time as a publisher, I am keenly aware that there will be opportunities for improvement, and I welcome suggestions via e-mail to nimblebooks@wfzimmerman.com.

Read This Book If …

You are interested in understanding the treatment of detainees at Guantánamo Bay during the war on terror that began 9/11/2001 and the prisoner abuse scandal at Abu Ghraib following the U.S. invasion of Iraq. The book contains six basic substantive documents which provide essential information and context:

- Major General Antonio M. Taguba's summary of his initial investigation of reported abuses at Abu Ghraib (the "Taguba Report");
- The Geneva Convention Relative to the Treatment of Prisoners of War;
- The Geneva Convention Relative to the Protection of Civilian Persons in Time of War;
- The opinions by the Supreme Court of the United States in Rasul v. Bush;
- The opinions by the Supreme Court of the United States in Hamdi v. Rumsfeld; and
- The opinions by the Supreme Court of the United States in Rumsfeld v. Padilla.

These are what historians call "primary" documents, i.e. they are the original documents written at the time of the events by the people who made the key decisions.

Don't Bother If …

You want everything explained to you. The documents in this book are technical in nature and assume that the reader will make the necessary effort to read them. But …

Look on the Bright Side!

These documents were written with broader public audiences, and the public interest, in mind. They will readily reward thoughtful reading.

NIMBLE BOOKS

Understand How This Book Is Organized
A series of documents, following one after another.

How to Read This Book
There is no substitute for actually reading complex substantive documents in their entirety. Accordingly, I recommend that you proceed front to back and left to right.

If you are a high school or undergraduate student, I recommend that you read slowly and thoroughly, take careful notes, and re-read the entire document at least once. Always try to understand who is writing the document and for what purpose – what is being decided, recommended, or agreed upon?

Supreme Court cases are presented in their original format so as to preserve the pagination, which is important for making legal citations.

Read the Acknowledgements So That You Can Be Properly Appreciative of the Author's Colleagues, Friends, and Family

First, last, and always, my lovely wife, Cheryl, and our great kids, Kelsey and Parker, who more or less patiently stood by as I devoted many, many hours to editing and producing this book.

Morris Rosenthal, who answered many of my early questions about Print-Quantity-Needed publishing and introduced me to pod_publishers@yahoogroups.com.

Specialist Joseph C. Darby, who had the moral courage to come forward, forcing the investigation of the Abu Ghraib prison scandal. He should be receiving the Silver Star.

NIMBLE BOOKS

Read about the Publisher So That You Can Be Either Baffled or Impressed, or Both

W. Frederick Zimmerman is a Research Scientist for ISciences, L.L.C, an information sciences consulting firm located in Ann Arbor, Michigan. Previously, Fred directed emerging technology strategy for legal market products at LexisNexis, one of four major business units of Reed Elsevier PLC, one of the world's largest professional publishers. He has led teams in the development of products and prototypes using a wide variety of emerging technologies, including visualization, voice ⇔ Web, wireless & synchronization, e-books, "custom publishing," browser plug-ins, point of view searching, Tablet PC, XML/XQUERY search, and geospatial vulnerability assessment. Fred is the author of Complete Guide to OneNote (Apress), a Microsoft MVP, and editor of OneNoteInfoCenter.com. He has been a member of the State of Michigan Bar and a PMI-certified Project Management Professional. He earned a B.A. with Honors from Swarthmore College and a J.D. from Wayne State University.

BASIC DOCUMENTS ABOUT THE DETAINEES

ARTICLE 15-6 INVESTIGATION OF THE 800th MILITARY POLICE BRIGADE

by Maj. Gen. Antonio M. Taguba

BACKGROUND

1. On 19 January 2004, Lieutenant General (LTG) Ricardo S. Sanchez, Commander, Combined Joint Task Force Seven (CJTF-7) requested that the Commander, US Central Command, appoint an Investigating Officer (IO) in the grade of Major General (MG) or above to investigate the conduct of operations within the 800th Military Police (MP) Brigade. LTG Sanchez requested an investigation of detention and internment operations by the Brigade from 1 November 2003 to present. LTG Sanchez cited recent reports of detainee abuse, escapes from confinement facilities, and accountability lapses, which indicated systemic problems within the brigade and suggested a lack of clear standards, proficiency, and leadership. LTG Sanchez requested a comprehensive and all-encompassing inquiry to make findings and recommendations concerning the fitness and performance of the 800th MP Brigade. (**ANNEX 2**)[1]

2. On 24 January 2003, the Chief of Staff of US Central Command (CENTCOM), MG R. Steven Whitcomb, on behalf of the CENTCOM Commander, directed that the Commander, Coalition Forces Land Component Command (CFLCC), LTG David D. McKiernan, conduct an investigation into the 800th MP Brigade's detention and internment operations from 1 November 2003 to present. CENTCOM directed that the investigation should inquire into all facts and circumstances surrounding recent reports of suspected detainee abuse in Iraq. It also directed that the investigation inquire into detainee escapes and accountability lapses as reported by CJTF-7, and to gain a more comprehensive and all-encompassing inquiry into the fitness and performance of the 800th MP Brigade. (**ANNEX 3**)

3. On 31 January 2004, the Commander, CFLCC, appointed MG Antonio M. Taguba, Deputy Commanding General Support, CFLCC, to conduct this investigation. MG Taguba was directed to conduct an informal investigation under AR 15-6 into the 800th MP Brigade's detention and internment operations. Specifically, MG Taguba was tasked to:

    a. Inquire into all the facts and circumstances surrounding recent allegations of detainee abuse, specifically allegations of maltreatment at the Abu Ghraib Prison (Baghdad Central Confinement Facility (BCCF));

    b. Inquire into detainee escapes and accountability lapses as reported by CJTF-7, specifically allegations concerning these events at the Abu Ghraib Prison;

    c. Investigate the training, standards, employment, command policies, internal procedures, and command climate in the 800th MP Brigade, as appropriate;

    d. Make specific findings of fact concerning all aspects of the investigation, and make any recommendations for corrective action, as appropriate. (**ANNEX 4**)

---

[1] **Bolding** and <u>underlining</u> in the Taguba report are as in the source document.

4. LTG Sanchez's request to investigate the 800th MP Brigade followed the initiation of a criminal investigation by the US Army Criminal Investigation Command (USACIDC) into specific allegations of detainee abuse committed by members of the 372nd MP Company, 320th MP Battalion in Iraq. These units are part of the 800th MP Brigade. The Brigade is an Iraq Theater asset, TACON to CJTF-7, but OPCON to CFLCC at the time this investigation was initiated. In addition, CJTF-7 had several reports of detainee escapes from US/Coalition Confinement Facilities in Iraq over the past several months. These include Camp Bucca, Camp Ashraf, Abu Ghraib, and the High Value Detainee (HVD) Complex/Camp Cropper. The 800th MP Brigade operated these facilities. In addition, four Soldiers from the 320th MP Battalion had been formally charged under the Uniform Code of Military Justice (UCMJ) with detainee abuse in May 2003 at the Theater Internment Facility (TIF) at Camp Bucca, Iraq. (**ANNEXES 5-18, 34 and 35**)

5. I began assembling my investigation team prior to the actual appointment by the CFLCC Commander. I assembled subject matter experts from the CFLCC Provost Marshal (PM) and the CFLCC Staff Judge Advocate (SJA). I selected COL Kinard J. La Fate, CFLCC Provost Marshal to be my Deputy for this investigation. I also contacted the Provost Marshal General of the Army, MG Donald J. Ryder, to enlist the support of MP subject matter experts in the areas of detention and internment operations. (**ANNEXES 4 and 19**)

6. The Investigating Team also reviewed the Assessment of DoD Counter-Terrorism Interrogation and Detention Operations in Iraq conducted by MG Geoffrey D. Miller, Commander, Joint Task Force Guantánamo (JTF-GTMO). From 31 August to 9 September 2003, MG Miller led a team of personnel experienced in strategic interrogation to HQ, CJTF-7 and the Iraqi Survey Group (ISG) to review current Iraqi Theater ability to rapidly exploit internees for actionable intelligence. MG Miller's team focused on three areas: intelligence integration, synchronization, and fusion; interrogation operations; and detention operations. MG Miller's team used JTF-GTMO procedures and interrogation authorities as baselines. (**ANNEX 20**)

7. The Investigating Team began its inquiry with an in-depth analysis of the Report on Detention and Corrections in Iraq, dated 5 November 2003, conducted by MG Ryder and a team of military police, legal, medical, and automation experts. The CJTF-7 Commander, LTG Sanchez, had previously requested a team of subject matter experts to assess, and make specific recommendations concerning detention and corrections operations. From 13 October to 6 November 2003, MG Ryder personally led this assessment/assistance team in Iraq. (**ANNEX 19**)

ASSESSMENT OF DoD COUNTER-TERRORISM INTERROGATION AND DETENTION OPERATIONS IN IRAQ (MG MILLER'S ASSESSMENT)

1. (S/NF)[2] The principal focus of MG Miller's team was on the strategic interrogation of detainees/internees in Iraq. Among its conclusions in its Executive Summary were that CJTF-7 did not

---

[2] Some paragraphs in the source document, which was obtained from the public Internet, were marked with classification prefixes (U). It is assumed that since the document has been widely available to the public since the

BASIC DOCUMENTS ABOUT THE DETAINEES

have authorities and procedures in place to affect a unified strategy to detain, interrogate, and report information from detainees/internees in Iraq. The Executive Summary also stated that detention operations must act as an enabler for interrogation. **(ANNEX 20)**

2. (S/NF) With respect to interrogation, MG Miller's Team recommended that CJTF-7 dedicate and train a detention guard force subordinate to the Joint Interrogation Debriefing Center (JIDC) Commander that "sets the conditions for the successful interrogation and exploitation of internees/detainees." Regarding Detention Operations, MG Miller's team stated that the function of Detention Operations is to provide a safe, secure, and humane environment that supports the expeditious collection of intelligence. However, it also stated "it is essential that the guard force be actively engaged in setting the conditions for successful exploitation of the internees." **(ANNEX 20)**

3. (S/NF) MG Miller's team also concluded that Joint Strategic Interrogation Operations (within CJTF-7) are hampered by lack of active control of the internees within the detention environment. The Miller Team also stated that establishment of the Theater Joint Interrogation and Detention Center (JIDC) at Abu Ghraib (BCCF) will consolidate both detention and strategic interrogation operations and result in synergy between MP and MI resources and an integrated, synchronized, and focused strategic interrogation effort. **(ANNEX 20)**

4. (S/NF) MG Miller's team also observed that the application of emerging strategic interrogation strategies and techniques contain new approaches and operational art. The Miller Team also concluded that a legal review and recommendations on internee interrogation operations by a dedicated Command Judge Advocate is required to maximize interrogation effectiveness. **(ANNEX 20)**

IO COMMENTS ON MG MILLER'S ASSESSMENT

1. (S/NF) MG Miller's team recognized that they were using JTF-GTMO operational procedures and interrogation authorities as baselines for its observations and recommendations. There is a strong argument that the intelligence value of detainees held at JTF-Guantánamo (GTMO) is different than that of the detainees/internees held at Abu Ghraib (BCCF) and other detention facilities in Iraq. Currently, there are a large number of Iraqi criminals held at Abu Ghraib (BCCF). These are not believed to be international terrorists or members of Al Qaida, Anser Al Islam, Taliban, and other international terrorist organizations. **(ANNEX 20)**

2. (S/NF) The recommendations of MG Miller's team that the "guard force" be actively engaged in setting the conditions for successful exploitation of the internees would appear to be in conflict with the recommendations of MG Ryder's Team and AR 190-8 that military police "do not participate in military intelligence supervised interrogation sessions." The Ryder Report concluded that the OEF template whereby military police actively set the favorable conditions for subsequent interviews runs counter to the smooth operation of a detention facility. **(ANNEX 20)**

Senate hearings on the matter, these classification prefixes are no longer operative. Unfortunately, the source document leaves many paragraphs unmarked.

NIMBLE BOOKS

REPORT ON DETENTION AND CORRECTIONS IN IRAQ (MG RYDER'S REPORT)

1. MG Ryder and his assessment team conducted a comprehensive review of the entire detainee and corrections system in Iraq and provided recommendations addressing each of the following areas as requested by the Commander CJTF-7:

   a. Detainee and corrections system management
   b. Detainee management, including detainee movement, segregation, and accountability
   c. Means of command and control of the detention and corrections system
   d. Integration of military detention and corrections with the Coalition Provisional Authority (CPA) and adequacy of plans for transition to an Iraqi-run corrections system
   e. Detainee medical care and health management
   f. Detention facilities that meet required health, hygiene, and sanitation standards
   g. Court integration and docket management for criminal detainees
   h. Detainee legal processing
   i. Detainee databases and records, including integration with law enforcement and court databases **(ANNEX 19)**

2. Many of the findings and recommendations of MG Ryder's team are beyond the scope of this investigation. However, several important findings are clearly relevant to this inquiry and are summarized below (emphasis is added in certain areas):

   A. **Detainee Management (including movement, segregation, and accountability)**

   1. There is a wide variance in standards and approaches at the various detention facilities. Several Division/Brigade collection points and US monitored Iraqi prisons had flawed or insufficiently detailed use of force and other standing operating procedures or policies (e.g. weapons in the facility, improper restraint techniques, detainee management, etc.) Though, there were no military police units purposely applying inappropriate confinement practices. **(ANNEX 19)**

   2. Currently, due to lack of adequate Iraqi facilities, Iraqi criminals (generally Iraqi-on-Iraqi crimes) are detained with security internees (generally Iraqi-on-Coalition offenses) and EPWs in the same facilities, though segregated in different cells/compounds. **(ANNEX 19)**

   3. The management of multiple disparate groups of detained people in a single location by members of the same unit invites confusion about handling, processing, and treatment, and typically facilitates the transfer of information between different categories of detainees. **(ANNEX 19)**

   4. The 800th MP (I/R) units did not receive Internment/Resettlement (I/R) and corrections specific training during their mobilization period. Corrections training is only on the METL of two MP (I/R) Confinement Battalions throughout the Army, one currently serving in Afghanistan, and elements of the other are at Camp Arifjan, Kuwait. MP units supporting JTF-GTMO received ten days of training in detention facility operations, to include two days of unarmed self-defense, training in interpersonal communication skills, forced cell moves, and correctional officer safety. **(ANNEX 19)**

   B. **Means of Command and Control of the Detention and Corrections System**

   1. The 800th MP Brigade was originally task organized with eight MP (I/R) Battalions consisting of both MP Guard and Combat Support companies. Due to force rotation plans, the 800th redeployed two

Basic Documents about the Detainees

Battalion HHCs in December 2003, the 115th MP Battalion and the 324th MP Battalion. In December 2003, the 400th MP Battalion was relieved of its mission and redeployed in January 2004. The 724th MP Battalion redeployed on 11 February 2004 and the remainder is scheduled to redeploy in March and April 2004. They are the 310th MP Battalion, 320th MP Battalion, 530th MP Battalion, and 744th MP Battalion. The units that remain are generally understrength, as Reserve Component units do not have an individual personnel replacement system to mitigate medical losses or the departure of individual Soldiers that have reached 24 months of Federal active duty in a five-year period. (**ANNEX 19**)

2. The 800th MP Brigade (I/R) is currently a CFLCC asset, TACON to CJTF-7 to conduct Internment/Resettlement (I/R) operations in Iraq. All detention operations are conducted in the CJTF-7 AO; Camps Ganci, Vigilant, Bucca, TSP Whitford, and a separate High Value Detention (HVD) site. (**ANNEX 19**)

3. The 800th MP Brigade has experienced challenges adapting its task organizational structure, training, and equipment resources from a unit designed to conduct standard EPW operations in the COMMZ (Kuwait). Further, the doctrinally trained MP Soldier-to-detainee population ratio and facility layout templates are predicated on a compliant, self-disciplining EPW population, and not criminals or high-risk security internees. (**ANNEX 19**)

4. EPWs and Civilian Internees should receive the full protections of the Geneva Conventions, unless the denial of these protections is due to specifically articulated military necessity (e.g., no visitation to preclude the direction of insurgency operations). (**ANNEXES 19 and 24**)

5. AR 190-8, *Enemy Prisoners of War, Retained Personnel, Civilian Internees, and other Detainees*, FM 3-19.40, *Military Police Internment and Resettlement Operations,* and FM 34-52, *Intelligence Interrogations*, require military police to provide an area for intelligence collection efforts within EPW facilities. Military Police, though adept at passive collection of intelligence within a facility, do not participate in Military Intelligence supervised interrogation sessions. Recent intelligence collection in support of Operation Enduring Freedom posited a template whereby military police actively set favorable conditions for subsequent interviews. Such actions generally run counter to the smooth operation of a detention facility, attempting to maintain its population in a compliant and docile state. <u>The 800th MP Brigade has not been directed to change its facility procedures to set the conditions for MI interrogations, nor participate in those interrogations.</u> (**ANNEXES 19 and 21-23**)

6. MG Ryder's Report also made the following, inter alia, near-term and mid-term recommendations regarding the command and control of detainees:

a. Align the release process for security internees with DoD Policy. The process of screening security internees should include intelligence findings, interrogation results, and current threat assessment.

b. Determine the scope of intelligence collection that will occur at Camp Vigilant. Refurbish the Northeast Compound to separate the screening operation from the Iraqi run Baghdad Central Correctional Facility. <u>Establish procedures that define the role of military police Soldiers securing the compound, clearly separating the actions of the guards from those of the military intelligence personnel.</u>

c. Consolidate all Security Internee Operations, except the MEK security mission, under a single Military Police Brigade Headquarters for OIF 2.

d. **Insist that all units identified to rotate into the Iraqi Theater of Operations (ITO) to conduct internment and confinement operations in support of OIF 2 be organic to CJTF-7.** (ANNEX 19)

IO COMMENTS REGARDING MG RYDER'S REPORT

1. The objective of MG Ryder's Team was to observe detention and prison operations, identify potential systemic and human rights issues, and provide near-term, mid-term, and long-term recommendations to improve CJTF-7 operations and transition of the Iraqi prison system from US military control/oversight to the Coalition Provisional Authority and eventually to the Iraqi Government. The Findings and Recommendations of MG Ryder's Team are thorough and precise and should be implemented immediately. (ANNEX 19)

2. **Unfortunately, many of the systemic problems that surfaced during MG Ryder's Team's assessment are the very same issues that are the subject of this investigation. In fact, many of the abuses suffered by detainees occurred during, or near to, the time of that assessment.** As will be pointed out in detail in subsequent portions of this report, I disagree with the conclusion of MG Ryder's Team in one critical aspect, that being its conclusion that the 800th MP Brigade had not been asked to change its facility procedures to set the conditions for MI interviews. **While clearly the 800th MP Brigade and its commanders were not tasked to set conditions for detainees for subsequent MI interrogations, it is obvious from a review of comprehensive CID interviews of suspects and witnesses that this was done at lower levels.** (ANNEX 19)

3. I concur fully with MG Ryder's conclusion regarding the effect of AR 190-8. Military Police, though adept at passive collection of intelligence within a facility, should not participate in Military Intelligence supervised interrogation sessions. Moreover, Military Police should not be involved with setting **"favorable conditions"** for subsequent interviews. These actions, as will be outlined in this investigation, clearly run counter to the smooth operation of a detention facility. (ANNEX 19)

PRELIMINARY INVESTIGATIVE ACTIONS

1. Following our review of MG Ryder's Report and MG Miller's Report, my investigation team immediately began an in-depth review of all available documents regarding the 800th MP Brigade. We reviewed in detail the voluminous CID investigation regarding alleged detainee abuses at detention facilities in Iraq, particularly the Abu Ghraib (BCCF) Detention Facility. We analyzed approximately fifty witness statements from military police and military intelligence personnel, potential suspects, and detainees. We reviewed numerous photos and videos of actual detainee abuse taken by detention facility personnel, which are now in the custody and control of the US Army Criminal Investigation Command and the CJTF-7 prosecution team. The photos and videos are not contained in this investigation. We obtained copies of the 800th MP Brigade roster, rating chain, and assorted internal investigations and disciplinary actions involving that command for the past several months. **(All ANNEXES Reviewed by Investigation Team)**

2. In addition to military police and legal officers from the CFLCC PMO and SJA Offices we also obtained the services of two individuals who are experts in military police detention practices and training. These were LTC Timothy Weathersbee, Commander, 705th MP Battalion, United States Disciplinary Barracks, Fort Leavenworth, and SFC Edward Baldwin, Senior Corrections Advisor, US Army Military

BASIC DOCUMENTS ABOUT THE DETAINEES

Police School, Fort Leonard Wood. I also requested and received the services of Col (Dr) Henry Nelson, a trained US Air Force psychiatrist assigned to assist my investigation team. (**ANNEX 4**)

3. In addition to MG Ryder's and MG Miller's Reports, the team reviewed numerous reference materials including the 12 October 2003 CJTF-7 Interrogation and Counter-Resistance Policy, the AR 15-6 Investigation on Riot and Shootings at Abu Ghraib on 24 November 2003, the 205th MI Brigade's Interrogation Rules of Engagement (IROE), facility staff logs/journals and numerous records of AR 15-6 investigations and Serious Incident Reports (SIRs) on detainee escapes/shootings and disciplinary matters from the 800th MP Brigade. (**ANNEXES 5-20, 37, 93, and 94**)

4. On 2 February 2004, I took my team to Baghdad for a one-day inspection of the Abu Ghraib Prison (BCCF) and the High Value Detainee (HVD) Complex in order to become familiar with those facilities. We also met with COL Jerry Mocello, Commander, 3rd MP Criminal Investigation Group (CID), COL Dave Quantock, Commander, 16th MP Brigade, COL Dave Phillips, Commander, 89th MP Brigade, and COL Ed Sannwaldt, CJTF-7 Provost Marshal. On 7 February 2004, the team visited the Camp Bucca Detention Facility to familiarize itself with the facility and operating structure. In addition, on 6 and 7 February 2004, at Camp Doha, Kuwait, we conducted extensive training sessions on approved detention practices. We continued our preparation by reviewing the ongoing CID investigation and were briefed by the Special Agent in Charge, CW2 Paul Arthur. We refreshed ourselves on the applicable reference materials within each team member's area of expertise, and practiced investigative techniques. I met with the team on numerous occasions to finalize appropriate witness lists, review existing witness statements, arrange logistics, and collect potential evidence. We also coordinated with CJTF-7 to arrange witness attendance, force protection measures, and general logistics for the team's move to Baghdad on 8 February 2004. (**ANNEXES 4 and 25**)

5. At the same time, due to the Transfer of Authority on 1 February 2004 between III Corps and V Corps, and the upcoming demobilization of the 800th MP Brigade Command, I directed that several critical witnesses who were preparing to leave the theater remain at Camp Arifjan, Kuwait until they could be interviewed (**ANNEX 29**). My team deployed to Baghdad on 8 February 2004 and conducted a series of interviews with a variety of witnesses (**ANNEX 30**). We returned to Camp Doha, Kuwait on 13 February 2004. On 14 and 15 February we interviewed a number of witnesses from the 800th MP Brigade. On 17 February we returned to Camp Bucca, Iraq to complete interviews of witnesses at that location. From 18 February thru 28 February we collected documents, compiled references, did follow-up interviews, and completed a detailed analysis of the volumes of materials accumulated throughout our investigation. On 29 February we finalized our executive summary and out-briefing slides. On 9 March we submitted the AR 15-6 written report with findings and recommendations to the CFLCC Deputy SJA, LTC Mark Johnson, for a legal sufficiency review. The out-brief to the appointing authority, LTG McKiernan, took place on 3 March 2004. (**ANNEXES 26 and 45-91**)

FINDINGS AND RECOMMENDATIONS (PART ONE)

(U) **The investigation should inquire into all of the facts and circumstances surrounding recent allegations of detainee abuse, specifically, allegations of maltreatment at the Abu Ghraib Prison (Baghdad Central Confinement Facility).**

Nimble Books

1. The US Army Criminal Investigation Command (CID), led by COL Jerry Mocello, and a team of highly trained professional agents have done a superb job of investigating several complex and extremely disturbing incidents of detainee abuse at the Abu Ghraib Prison. They conducted over 50 interviews of witnesses, potential criminal suspects, and detainees. They also uncovered numerous photos and videos portraying in graphic detail detainee abuse by Military Police personnel on numerous occasions from October to December 2003. Several potential suspects rendered full and complete confessions regarding their personal involvement and the involvement of fellow Soldiers in this abuse. Several potential suspects invoked their rights under Article 31 of the Uniform Code of Military Justice (UCMJ) and the 5th Amendment of the U.S. Constitution. **(ANNEX 25)**

2. In addition to a comprehensive and exhaustive review of all of these statements and documentary evidence, we also interviewed numerous officers, NCOs, and junior enlisted Soldiers in the 800th MP Brigade, as well as members of the 205th Military Intelligence Brigade working at the prison. We did not believe it was necessary to re-interview all the numerous witnesses who had previously provided comprehensive statements to CID, and I have adopted those statements for the purposes of this investigation. **(ANNEXES 26, 34, 35, and 45-91)**

REGARDING PART ONE OF THE INVESTIGATION, I MAKE THE FOLLOWING SPECIFIC FINDINGS OF FACT:

1. That Forward Operating Base (FOB) Abu Ghraib (BCCF) provides security of both criminal and security detainees at the Baghdad Central Correctional Facility, facilitates the conducting of interrogations for CJTF-7, supports other CPA operations at the prison, and enhances the force protection/quality of life of Soldiers assigned in order to ensure the success of ongoing operations to secure a free Iraq. **(ANNEX 31)**

2. That the Commander, 205th Military Intelligence Brigade, was designated by CJTF-7 as the Commander of FOB Abu Ghraib (BCCF) effective 19 November 2003. That the 205th MI Brigade conducts operational and strategic interrogations for CJTF-7. That from 19 November 2003 until Transfer of Authority (TOA) on 6 February 2004, COL Thomas M. Pappas was the Commander of the 205th MI Brigade and the Commander of FOB Abu Ghraib (BCCF). **(ANNEX 31)**

3. That the 320th Military Police Battalion of the 800th MP Brigade is responsible for the Guard Force at Camp Ganci, Camp Vigilant, & Cellblock 1 of FOB Abu Ghraib (BCCF). That from February 2003 to until he was suspended from his duties on 17 January 2004, LTC Jerry Phillabaum served as the Battalion Commander of the 320th MP Battalion. That from December 2002 until he was suspended from his duties, on 17 January 2004, CPT Donald Reese served as the Company Commander of the 372nd MP Company, which was in charge of guarding detainees at FOB Abu Ghraib. I further find that both the 320th MP Battalion and the 372nd MP Company were located within the confines of FOB Abu Ghraib. **(ANNEXES 32 and 45)**

4. That from July of 2003 to the present, BG Janis L. Karpinski was the Commander of the 800th MP Brigade. **(ANNEX 45)**

5. (S) That between October and December 2003, at the Abu Ghraib Confinement Facility (BCCF), numerous incidents of sadistic, blatant, and wanton criminal abuses were inflicted on several detainees. This systemic and illegal abuse of detainees was intentionally perpetrated by several members of the military police guard force (372nd Military Police Company, 320th Military Police Battalion, 800th MP Brigade), in

Basic Documents about the Detainees

Tier (section) 1-A of the Abu Ghraib Prison (BCCF). The allegations of abuse were substantiated by detailed witness statements (**ANNEX 26**) and the discovery of extremely graphic photographic evidence. Due to the extremely sensitive nature of these photographs and videos, the ongoing CID investigation, and the potential for the criminal prosecution of several suspects, the photographic evidence is not included in the body of my investigation. The pictures and videos are available from the Criminal Investigative Command and the CTJF-7 prosecution team. In addition to the aforementioned crimes, there were also abuses committed by members of the 325th MI Battalion, 205th MI Brigade, and Joint Interrogation and Debriefing Center (JIDC). Specifically, on 24 November 2003, SPC Luciana Spencer, 205th MI Brigade, sought to degrade a detainee by having him strip and returned to cell naked. (**ANNEXES 26 and 53**)

6. (S) I find that the intentional abuse of detainees by military police personnel included the following acts:

   a. (S) Punching, slapping, and kicking detainees; jumping on their naked feet;
   b. (S) Videotaping and photographing naked male and female detainees;
   c. (S) Forcibly arranging detainees in various sexually explicit positions for photographing;
   d. (S) Forcing detainees to remove their clothing and keeping them naked for several days at a time;
   e. (S) Forcing naked male detainees to wear women's underwear;
   f. (S) Forcing groups of male detainees to masturbate themselves while being photographed and videotaped;
   g. (S) Arranging naked male detainees in a pile and then jumping on them;
   h. (S) Positioning a naked detainee on a MRE Box, with a sandbag on his head, and attaching wires to his fingers, toes, and penis to simulate electric torture;
   i. (S) Writing "I am a Rapest" (sic) on the leg of a detainee alleged to have forcibly raped a 15-year old fellow detainee, and then photographing him naked;
   j. (S) Placing a dog chain or strap around a naked detainee's neck and having a female Soldier pose for a picture;
   k. (S) A male MP guard having sex with a female detainee;
   l. (S) Using military working dogs (without muzzles) to intimidate and frighten detainees, and in at least one case biting and severely injuring a detainee;
   m. (S) Taking photographs of dead Iraqi detainees.

(**ANNEXES 25 and 26**)

7. (U) These findings are amply supported by written confessions provided by several of the suspects, written statements provided by detainees, and witness statements. In reaching my findings, I have carefully considered the pre-existing statements of the following witnesses and suspects (**ANNEX 26**):

   a. SPC Jeremy Sivits, 372nd MP Company - **Suspect**
   b. SPC Sabrina Harman, 372nd MP Company – **Suspect**
   c. SGT Javal S. Davis, 372nd MP Company - **Suspect**
   c. PFC Lynndie R. England, 372nd MP Company - **Suspect**
   d. Adel Nakhla, Civilian Translator, Titan Corp., Assigned to the 205th MI Brigade- **Suspect**
   (Names deleted)

8. In addition, several detainees also described the following acts of abuse, which under the circumstances, I find credible based on the clarity of their statements and supporting evidence provided by other witnesses (**ANNEX 26**):

   a. Breaking chemical lights and pouring the phosphoric liquid on detainees;
   b. Threatening detainees with a charged 9mm pistol;
   c. Pouring cold water on naked detainees;
   d. Beating detainees with a broom handle and a chair;
   e. Threatening male detainees with rape;
   f. (U) Allowing a military police guard to stitch the wound of a detainee who was injured after being slammed against the wall in his cell;
   g. Sodomizing a detainee with a chemical light and perhaps a broom stick.
   h. Using military working dogs to frighten and intimidate detainees with threats of attack, and in one instance actually biting a detainee.

9. I have carefully considered the statements provided by the following detainees, which under the circumstances I find credible based on the clarity of their statements and supporting evidence provided by other witnesses:

   a. Amjed Isail Waleed, Detainee # 151365
   b. Hiadar Saber Abed Miktub-Aboodi, Detainee # 13077
   c. Huessin Mohssein Al-Zayiadi, Detainee # 19446
   d. Kasim Mehaddi Hilas, Detainee # 151108
   e. Mohanded Juma Juma (sic), Detainee # 152307
   f. (U) Mustafa Jassim Mustafa, Detainee # 150542
   g. Shalan Said Alsharoni, Detainee, # 150422
   h. Abd Alwhab Youss, Detainee # 150425
   i. (U) Asad Hamza Hanfosh, Detainee # 152529
   j. (U) Nori Samir Gunbar Al-Yasseri, Detainee # 7787
   k. Thaar Salman Dawod, Detainee # 150427
   l. (U) Ameen Sa'eed Al-Sheikh, Detainee # 151362
   m. (U) Abdou Hussain Saad Faleh, Detainee # 18470 (**ANNEX 26**)

10. I find that contrary to the provision of AR 190-8, and the findings found in MG Ryder's Report, Military Intelligence (MI) interrogators and Other US Government Agency's (OGA) interrogators actively requested that MP guards set physical and mental conditions for favorable interrogation of witnesses. Contrary to the findings of MG Ryder's Report, I find that personnel assigned to the 372nd MP Company, 800th MP Brigade were directed to change facility procedures to "set the conditions" for MI interrogations. I find no direct evidence that MP personnel actually participated in those MI interrogations. (**ANNEXES 19, 21, 25, and 26**).

11. I reach this finding based on the actual proven abuse that I find was inflicted on detainees and by the following witness statements. (**ANNEXES 25 and 26**):

   a. **SPC Sabrina Harman, 372nd MP Company,** stated in her sworn statement regarding the incident where a detainee was placed on a box with wires attached to his fingers, toes, and penis, "that her job was to keep detainees awake." She stated that MI was talking to CPL Grainer. She stated: "MI wanted to get them to talk. It is Grainer and Frederick's job to do things for MI and OGA to get these people to talk."

b. <u>SGT Javal S. Davis</u>, 372nd MP Company, stated in his sworn statement as follows: "I witnessed prisoners in the MI hold section, wing 1A being made to do various things that I would question morally. In Wing 1A we were told that they had different rules and different SOP for treatment. I never saw a set of rules or SOP for that section just word of mouth. The Soldier in charge of 1A was Corporal Granier. He stated that the Agents and MI Soldiers would ask him to do things, but nothing was ever in writing he would complain (sic)." When asked why the rules in 1A/1B were different than the rest of the wings, SGT Davis stated: **"The rest of the wings are regular prisoners and 1A/B are Military Intelligence (MI) holds."** When asked why he did not inform his chain of command about this abuse, SGT Davis stated: **" Because I assumed that if they were doing things out of the ordinary or outside the guidelines, someone would have said something. Also the wing belongs to MI and it appeared MI personnel approved of the abuse."** SGT Davis also stated that he had heard MI insinuate to the guards to abuse the inmates. When asked what MI said he stated: **"Loosen this guy up for us." Make sure he has a bad night." "Make sure he gets the treatment."** He claimed these comments were made to CPL Granier and SSG Frederick. Finally, SGT Davis stated that (sic): **"the MI staffs to my understanding have been giving Granier compliments on the way he has been handling the MI holds. Example being statements like, "Good job, they're breaking down real fast. They answer every question. They're giving out good information, Finally, and Keep up the good work . Stuff like that."**

c. <u>SPC Jason Kennel</u>, 372nd MP Company, was asked if he were present when any detainees were abused. He stated: **"I saw them nude, but MI would tell us to take away their mattresses, sheets, and clothes."** He could not recall who in MI had instructed him to do this, but commented that, "if they wanted me to do that they needed to give me paperwork." He was later informed that "we could not do anything to embarrass the prisoners."

d. <u>Mr. Adel L. Nakhla</u>, a US civilian contract translator was questioned about several detainees accused of rape. He observed (sic): **"They (detainees) were all naked, a bunch of people from MI, the MP were there that night and the inmates were ordered by SGT Granier and SGT Frederick ordered the guys while questioning them to admit what they did. They made them do strange exercises by sliding on their stomach, jump up and down, throw water on them and made them some wet, called them all kinds of names such as "gays" do they like to make love to guys, then they handcuffed their hands together and their legs with shackles and started to stack them on top of each other by insuring that the bottom guys penis will touch the guy on tops butt."**

e. <u>SPC Neil A Wallin,</u> 109th Area Support Medical Battalion, a medic testified that: **"Cell 1A was used to house high priority detainees and cell 1B was used to house the high risk or trouble making detainees. During my tour at the prison I observed that when the male detainees were first brought to the facility, some of them were made to wear female underwear, which I think was to somehow break them down."**

12. I find that prior to its deployment to Iraq for Operation Iraqi Freedom, the 320th MP Battalion and the 372nd MP Company had received no training in detention/internee operations. I also find that very little instruction or training was provided to MP personnel on the applicable rules of the Geneva

NIMBLE BOOKS

Convention Relative to the Treatment of Prisoners of War, FM 27-10, AR 190-8, or FM 3-19.40. Moreover, I find that few, if any, copies of the Geneva Conventions were ever made available to MP personnel or detainees. **(ANNEXES 21-24, 33, and multiple witness statements)**

    13.(U) Another obvious example of the Brigade Leadership not communicating with its Soldiers or ensuring their tactical proficiency concerns the incident of detainee abuse that occurred at Camp Bucca, Iraq, on May 12, 2003. Soldiers from the 223rd MP Company reported to the 800th MP Brigade Command at Camp Bucca, that four Military Police Soldiers from the 320th MP Battalion had abused a number of detainees during in processing at Camp Bucca. An extensive CID investigation determined that four soldiers from the 320th MP Battalion had kicked and beaten these detainees following a transport mission from Talil Air Base. **(ANNEXES 34 and 35)**

    14. Formal charges under the UCMJ were preferred against these Soldiers and an Article-32 Investigation conducted by LTC Gentry. He recommended a general court martial for the four accused, which BG Karpinski supported. Despite this documented abuse, there is no evidence that BG Karpinski ever attempted to remind 800th MP Soldiers of the requirements of the Geneva Conventions regarding detainee treatment or took any steps to ensure that such abuse was not repeated. Nor is there any evidence that LTC(P) Phillabaum, the commander of the Soldiers involved in the Camp Bucca abuse incident, took any initiative to ensure his Soldiers were properly trained regarding detainee treatment. **(ANNEXES 35 and 62)**

RECOMMENDATIONS AS TO PART ONE OF THE INVESTIGATION:

    1. Immediately deploy to the Iraq Theater an integrated multi-discipline Mobile Training Team (MTT) comprised of subject matter experts in internment/resettlement operations, international and operational law, information technology, facility management, interrogation and intelligence gathering techniques, chaplains, Arab cultural awareness, and medical practices as it pertains to I/R activities. This team needs to oversee and conduct comprehensive training in all aspects of detainee and confinement operations.

    2. That all military police and military intelligence personnel involved in any aspect of detainee operations or interrogation operations in CJTF-7, and subordinate units, be immediately provided with training by an international/operational law attorney on the specific provisions of The Law of Land Warfare FM 27-10, specifically the Geneva Convention Relative to the Treatment of Prisoners of War, Enemy Prisoners of War, Retained Personnel, Civilian Internees, and Other Detainees, and AR 190-8.

    3. **That a single commander in CJTF-7 be responsible for overall detainee operations throughout the Iraq Theater of Operations**. I also recommend that the Provost Marshal General of the Army assign a minimum of two (2) subject matter experts, one officer and one NCO, to assist CJTF-7 in coordinating detainee operations.

    4. That detention facility commanders and interrogation facility commanders ensure that appropriate copies of the Geneva Convention Relative to the Treatment of Prisoners of War and notice of protections be made available in both English and the detainees' language and be prominently displayed in all detention facilities. Detainees with questions regarding their treatment should be given the full opportunity to read the Convention.

BASIC DOCUMENTS ABOUT THE DETAINEES

5. That each detention facility commander and interrogation facility commander publish a complete and comprehensive set of Standing Operating Procedures (SOPs) regarding treatment of detainees, and that all personnel be required to read the SOPs and sign a document indicating that they have read and understand the SOPs.

6. That in accordance with the recommendations of MG Ryder's Assessment Report, and my findings and recommendations in this investigation, all units in the Iraq Theater of Operations conducting internment/confinement/detainment operations in support of Operation Iraqi Freedom be OPCON for all purposes, to include action under the UCMJ, to CJTF-7.

7. Appoint the C3, CJTF as the staff proponent for detainee operations in the Iraq Joint Operations Area (JOA). (MG Tom Miller, C3, CJTF-7, has been appointed by COMCJTF-7).

8. That an inquiry UP AR 381-10, Procedure 15 be conducted to determine the extent of culpability of Military Intelligence personnel, assigned to the 205th MI Brigade and the Joint Interrogation and Debriefing Center (JIDC) regarding abuse of detainees at Abu Ghraib (BCCF).

9. That it is critical that the proponent for detainee operations is assigned a dedicated Senior Judge Advocate, with specialized training and knowledge of international and operational law, to assist and advise on matters of detainee operations.

FINDINGS AND RECOMMENDATIONS (PART TWO)

The Investigation inquire into detainee escapes and accountability lapses as reported by CJTF-7, specifically allegations concerning these events at the Abu Ghraib Prison:

REGARDING PART TWO OF THE INVESTIGATION,
I MAKE THE FOLLOWING SPECIFIC FINDINGS OF FACT:

1. The 800th MP Brigade was responsible for theater-wide Internment and Resettlement (I/R) operations. (**ANNEXES 45 and 95**)

2. The 320th MP Battalion, 800th MP Brigade was tasked with detainee operations at the Abu Ghraib Prison Complex during the time period covered in this investigation. (**ANNEXES 41, 45, and 59**)

3. The 310th MP Battalion, 800th MP Brigade was tasked with detainee operations and Forward Operating Base (FOB) Operations at the Camp Bucca Detention Facility until TOA on 26 February 2004. (**ANNEXES 41 and 52**)

4. The 744th MP Battalion, 800th MP Brigade was tasked with detainee operations and FOB Operations at the HVD Detention Facility until TOA on 4 March 2004. (**ANNEXES 41 and 55**)

5. The 530th MP Battalion, 800th MP Brigade was tasked with detainee operations and FOB Operations at the MEK holding facility until TOA on 15 March 2004. (**ANNEXES 41 and 97**)

6. Detainee operations include accountability, care, and well being of Enemy Prisoners of War, Retained Person, Civilian Detainees, and Other Detainees, as well as Iraqi criminal prisoners. (**ANNEX 22**)

7. The accountability for detainees is doctrinally an MP task IAW FM 3-19.40. (**ANNEX 22**)

8. There is a general lack of knowledge, implementation, and emphasis of basic legal, regulatory, doctrinal, and command requirements within the 800th MP Brigade and its subordinate units. (**Multiple witness statements in ANNEXES 45-91**).

9. The handling of detainees and criminal prisoners after in-processing was inconsistent from detention facility to detention facility, compound to compound, encampment to encampment, and even shift to shift throughout the 800th MP Brigade AOR. (**ANNEX 37**)

10. Camp Bucca, operated by the 310th MP Battalion, had a "Criminal Detainee In-Processing SOP" and a "Training Outline" for transferring and releasing detainees, which appears to have been followed. (**ANNEXES 38 and 52**)

11. Incoming and outgoing detainees are being documented in the National Detainee Reporting System (NDRS) and Biometric Automated Toolset System (BATS) as required by regulation at all detention facilities. However, it is underutilized and often does not give a "real time" accurate picture of the detainee population due to untimely updating. (**ANNEX 56**)

12. There was a severe lapse in the accountability of detainees at the Abu Ghraib Prison Complex. The 320th MP Battalion used a self-created "change sheet" to document the transfer of a detainee from one location to another. For proper accountability, it is imperative that these change sheets be processed and the detainee manifest be updated within 24 hours of movement. At Abu Ghraib, this process would often take as long as 4 days to complete. This lag-time resulted in inaccurate detainee Internment Serial Number (ISN) counts, gross differences in the detainee manifest and the actual occupants of an individual compound, and significant confusion of the MP Soldiers. The 320th MP Battalion S-1, CPT Theresa Delbalso, and the S-3, MAJ David DiNenna, explained that this breakdown was due to the lack of manpower to process change sheets in a timely manner. (**ANNEXES 39 and 98**)

13. The 320th Battalion TACSOP requires detainee accountability at least 4 times daily at Abu Ghraib. However, a detailed review of their operational journals revealed that these accounts were often not done or not documented by the unit. Additionally, there is no indication that accounting errors or the loss of a detainee in the accounting process triggered any immediate corrective action by the Battalion TOC. (**ANNEX 44**)

14. There is a lack of standardization in the way the 320th MP Battalion conducted physical counts of their detainees. Each compound within a given encampment did their headcounts differently. Some compounds had detainees line up in lines of 10, some had them sit in rows, and some moved all the detainees to one end of the compound and counted them as they passed to the other end of the compound. (**ANNEX 98**)

15. FM 3-19.40 outlines the need for 2 roll calls (100% ISN band checks) per day. The 320th MP Battalion did this check only 2 times per week. Due to the lack of real-time updates to the system, these checks were regularly inaccurate. (**ANNEXES 22 and 98**)

16. The 800th MP Brigade and subordinate units adopted non-doctrinal terms such as "band checks," "roll-ups," and "call-ups," which contributed to the lapses in accountability and confusion at the soldier level. (**ANNEXES 63, 88, and 98**)

17. Operational journals at the various compounds and the 320th Battalion TOC contained numerous unprofessional entries and flippant comments, which highlighted the lack of discipline within the unit. There was no indication that the journals were ever reviewed by anyone in their chain of command. (**Annex 37**)

BASIC DOCUMENTS ABOUT THE DETAINEES

18. Accountability SOPs were not fully developed and standing TACSOPs were widely ignored. Any SOPs that did exist were not trained on, and were never distributed to the lowest level. Most procedures were shelved at the unit TOC, rather than at the subordinate units and guards mount sites. (**ANNEXES 44, 67, 71, and 85**)

19. Accountability and facility operations SOPs lacked specificity, implementation measures, and a system of checks and balances to ensure compliance. (**ANNEXES 76 and 82**)

20. Basic Army Doctrine was not widely referenced or utilized to develop the accountability practices throughout the 800th MP Brigade's subordinate units. Daily processing, accountability, and detainee care appears to have been made up as the operations developed with reliance on, and guidance from, junior members of the unit who had civilian corrections experience. (**Annex 21**)

21. Soldiers were poorly prepared and untrained to conduct I/R operations prior to deployment, at the mobilization site, upon arrival in theater, and throughout their mission. (**ANNEXES 62, 63, and 69**)

22. The documentation provided to this investigation identified 27 escapes or attempted escapes from the detention facilities throughout the 800th MP Brigade's AOR. Based on my assessment and detailed analysis of the substandard accountability process maintained by the 800th MP Brigade, it is highly likely that there were several more unreported cases of escape that were probably "written off" as administrative errors or otherwise undocumented. 1LT Lewis Raeder, Platoon Leader, 372nd MP Company, reported knowing about at least two additional escapes (one from a work detail and one from a window) from Abu Ghraib (BCCF) that were not documented. LTC Dennis McGlone, Commander, 744th MP Battalion, detailed the escape of one detainee at the High Value Detainee Facility who went to the latrine and then outran the guards and escaped. Lastly, BG Janis Karpinski, Commander, 800th MP Brigade, stated that there were more than 32 escapes from her holding facilities, which does not match the number derived from the investigation materials. (**ANNEXES 5-10, 45, 55, and 71**)

23. The Abu Ghraib and Camp Bucca detention facilities are significantly over their intended maximum capacity while the guard force is undermanned and under resourced. This imbalance has contributed to the poor living conditions, escapes, and accountability lapses at the various facilities. The overcrowding of the facilities also limits the ability to identify and segregate leaders in the detainee population who may be organizing escapes and riots within the facility. (**ANNEXES 6, 22, and 92**)

24. The screening, processing, and release of detainees who should not be in custody takes too long and contributes to the overcrowding and unrest in the detention facilities. There are currently three separate release mechanisms in the theater-wide internment operations. First, the apprehending unit can release a detainee if there is a determination that their continued detention is not warranted. Secondly, a criminal detainee can be released after it has been determined that the detainee has no intelligence value, and that their release would not be detrimental to society. BG Karpinski had signature authority to release detainees in this second category. Lastly, detainees accused of committing "Crimes Against the Coalition," who are held throughout the separate facilities in the CJTF-7 AOR, can be released upon a determination that they are of no intelligence value and no longer pose a significant threat to Coalition Forces. The release process for this category of detainee is a screening by the local US Forces Magistrate Cell and a review by a Detainee Release Board consisting of BG Karpinski, COL Marc Warren, SJA, CJTF-7, and MG Barbara Fast, C-2, CJTF-7. MG Fast is the "Detainee Release Authority" for detainees being held for committing crimes against the coalition. According to BG Karpinski, this category of detainee makes up more than 60% of the

total detainee population, and is the fastest growing category. However, MG Fast, according to BG Karpinski, routinely denied the board's recommendations to release detainees in this category who were no longer deemed a threat and clearly met the requirements for release. According to BG Karpinski, the extremely slow and ineffective release process has significantly contributed to the overcrowding of the facilities. **(ANNEXES 40, 45, and 46)**

25. After Action Reviews (AARs) are not routinely being conducted after an escape or other serious incident. No lessons learned seem to have been disseminated to subordinate units to enable corrective action at the lowest level. The Investigation Team requested copies of AARs, and none were provided. **(Multiple Witness Statements)**

26. Lessons learned (i.e. Findings and Recommendations from various 15-6 Investigations concerning escapes and accountability lapses) were rubber stamped as approved and ordered implemented by BG Karpinski. There is no evidence that the majority of her orders directing the implementation of substantive changes were ever acted upon. Additionally, there was no follow-up by the command to verify the corrective actions were taken. Had the findings and recommendations contained within their own investigations been analyzed and actually implemented by BG Karpinski, many of the subsequent escapes, accountability lapses, and cases of abuse may have been prevented. **(ANNEXES 5-10)**

27. The perimeter lighting around Abu Ghraib and the detention facility at Camp Bucca is inadequate and needs to be improved to illuminate dark areas that have routinely become avenues of escape. **(ANNEX 6)**

28. Neither the camp rules nor the provisions of the Geneva Conventions are posted in English or in the language of the detainees at any of the detention facilities in the 800th MP Brigade's AOR, even after several investigations had annotated the lack of this critical requirement. **(Multiple Witness Statements and the Personal Observations of the Investigation Team)**

29. The Iraqi guards at Abu Ghraib BCCF) demonstrate questionable work ethics and loyalties, and are a potentially dangerous contingent within the Hard-Site. These guards have furnished the Iraqi criminal inmates with contraband, weapons, and information. Additionally, they have facilitated the escape of at least one detainee. **(ANNEX 8 and 26-SPC Polak's Statement)**

30. In general, US civilian contract personnel (Titan Corporation, CACI, etc...), third country nationals, and local contractors do not appear to be properly supervised within the detention facility at Abu Ghraib. During our on-site inspection, they wandered about with too much unsupervised free access in the detainee area. Having civilians in various outfits (civilian and DCUs) in and about the detainee area causes confusion and may have contributed to the difficulties in the accountability process and with detecting escapes. **(ANNEX 51, Multiple Witness Statements, and the Personal Observations of the Investigation Team)**

31. SGM Marc Emerson, Operations SGM, 320th MP Battalion, contended that the Detainee Rules of Engagement (DROE) and the general principles of the Geneva Convention were briefed at every guard mount and shift change on Abu Ghraib. However, none of our witnesses, nor our personal observations, support his contention. I find that SGM Emerson was not a credible witness. **(ANNEXES 45, 80, and the Personal Observations of the Investigation Team)**

BASIC DOCUMENTS ABOUT THE DETAINEES

32. Several interviewees insisted that the MP and MI Soldiers at Abu Ghraib (BCCF) received regular training on the basics of detainee operations; however, they have been unable to produce any verifying documentation, sign-in rosters, or soldiers who can recall the content of this training. **(ANNEXES 59, 80, and the Absence of any Training Records)**

33. The various detention facilities operated by the 800th MP Brigade have routinely held persons brought to them by Other Government Agencies (OGAs) without accounting for them, knowing their identities, or even the reason for their detention. The Joint Interrogation and Debriefing Center (JIDC) at Abu Ghraib called these detainees "ghost detainees." On at least one occasion, the 320th MP Battalion at Abu Ghraib held a handful of "ghost detainees" (6-8) for OGAs that they moved around within the facility to hide them from a visiting International Committee of the Red Cross (ICRC) survey team. This maneuver was deceptive, contrary to Army Doctrine, and in violation of international law. **(Annex 53)**

34. The following riots, escapes, and shootings have been documented and reported to this Investigation Team. Although there is no data from other missions of similar size and duration to compare the number of escapes with, the most significant factors derived from these reports are twofold. First, investigations and SIRs lacked critical data needed to evaluate the details of each incident. Second, each investigation seems to have pointed to the same types of deficiencies; however, little to nothing was done to correct the problems and to implement the recommendations as was ordered by BG Karpinski, nor was there any command emphasis to ensure these deficiencies were corrected:

a. 4 June 03- This escape was mentioned in the 15-6 Investigation covering the 13 June 03 escape, recapture, and shootings of detainees at Camp Vigilant (320th MP Battalion). However, no investigation or additional information was provided as requested by this investigation team. **(ANNEX 7)**

b. 9 June 03- Riot and shootings of five detainees at Camp Cropper. (115th MP Battalion) Several detainees allegedly rioted after a detainee was subdued by MPs of the 115th MP Battalion after striking a guard in compound B of Camp Cropper. A 15-6 investigation by 1LT Magowan (115th MP Battalion, Platoon Leader) concluded that a detainee had acted up and hit an MP. After being subdued, one of the MPs took off his DCU top and flexed his muscles to the detainees, which further escalated the riot. The MPs were overwhelmed and the guards fired lethal rounds to protect the life of the compound MPs, whereby 5 detainees were wounded. Contributing factors were poor communications, no clear chain of command, facility-obstructed views of posted guards, the QRF did not have non-lethal equipment, and the SOP was inadequate and outdated. **(ANNEX 5)**

c. 12 June 03- Escape and recapture of detainee #8399, escape and shooting of detainee # 7166, and attempted escape of an unidentified detainee from Camp Cropper Holding Area (115th MP Battalion). Several detainees allegedly made their escape in the nighttime hours prior to 0300. A 15-6 investigation by CPT Wendlandt (115th MP Battalion, S-2) concluded that the detainees allegedly escaped by crawling under the wire at a location with inadequate lighting. One detainee was stopped prior to escape. An MP of the 115th MP Battalion search team recaptured detainee # 8399, and detainee # 7166 was shot and killed by a Soldier during the recapture process. Contributing factors were overcrowding, poor lighting, and the nature of the hardened criminal detainees at that location. It is of particular note that the command was informed at least 24 hours in advance of the upcoming escape attempt and started doing amplified announcements in Arabic stating the camp rules. The investigation pointed out that rules and guidelines were not posted in the camps in the detainees' native languages. **(ANNEX 6)**

d. **13 June 03- Escape and recapture of detainee # 8968 and the shooting of eight detainees at Abu Ghraib (BCCF) (320th MP Battalion).** Several detainees allegedly attempted to escape at about 1400 hours from the Camp Vigilant Compound, Abu Ghraib (BCCF). A 15-6 investigation by CPT Wyks (400th MP Battalion, S-1) concluded that the detainee allegedly escaped by sliding under the wire while the tower guard was turned in the other direction. This detainee was subsequently apprehended by the QRF. At about 1600 the same day, 30-40 detainees rioted and pelted three interior MP guards with rocks. One guard was injured and the tower guards fired lethal rounds at the rioters injuring 7 and killing 1 detainee. (ANNEX 7)

e. **05 November 03- Escape of detainees # 9877 and # 10739 from Abu Ghraib (320th MP Battalion).** Several detainees allegedly escaped at 0345 from the Hard-Site, Abu Ghraib (BCCF). An SIR was initiated by SPC Warner (320th MP Battalion, S-3 RTO). The SIR indicated that 2 criminal prisoners escaped through their cell window in tier 3A of the Hard-Site. No information on findings, contributing factors, or corrective action has been provided to this investigation team. (ANNEX 11)

f. **07 November 03- Escape of detainee # 14239 from Abu Ghraib (320th MP Battalion).** A detainee allegedly escaped at 1330 from Compound 2 of the Ganci Encampment, Abu Ghraib (BCCF). An SIR was initiated by SSG Hydro (320th MP Battalion, S-3 Asst. NCOIC). The SIR indicated that a detainee escaped from the North end of the compound and was discovered missing during distribution of the noon meal, but there is no method of escape listed in the SIR. No information on findings, contributing factors, or corrective action has been provided to this investigation team. (ANNEX 12)

g. **08 November 03- Escape of detainees # 115089, # 151623, # 151624, # 116734, # 116735, and # 116738 from Abu Ghraib (320th MP Battalion).** Several detainees allegedly escaped at 2022 from Compound 8 of the Ganci encampment, Abu Ghraib. An SIR was initiated by MAJ DiNenna (320th MP Battalion, S-3). The SIR indicated that 5-6 prisoners escaped from the North end of the compound, but there is no method of escape listed in the SIR. No information on findings, contributing factors, or corrective action has been provided to this investigation team. (ANNEX 13)

h. **24 November 03- Riot and shooting of 12 detainees # 150216, #150894, #153096, 153165, #153169, #116361, #153399, #20257, #150348, #152616, #116146, and #152156 at Abu Ghraib(320th MP Battalion).** Several detainees allegedly began to riot at about 1300 in all of the compounds at the Ganci encampment. This resulted in the shooting deaths of 3 detainees, 9 wounded detainees, and 9 injured US Soldiers. A 15-6 investigation by COL Bruce Falcone (220th MP Brigade, Deputy Commander) concluded that the detainees rioted in protest of their living conditions, that the riot turned violent, the use of non-lethal force was ineffective, and, after the 320th MP Battalion CDR executed "Golden Spike," the emergency containment plan, the use of deadly force was authorized. Contributing factors were lack of comprehensive training of guards, poor or non-existent SOPs, no formal guard-mount conducted prior to shift, no rehearsals or ongoing training, the mix of less than lethal rounds with lethal rounds in weapons, no AARs being conducted after incidents, ROE not posted and not understood, overcrowding, uniforms not standardized, and poor communication between the command and Soldiers. (ANNEX 8)

i. **24 November 03- Shooting of detainee at Abu Ghraib (320th MP Battalion).** A detainee allegedly had a pistol in his cell and around 1830 an extraction team shot him with less than lethal and lethal rounds

BASIC DOCUMENTS ABOUT THE DETAINEES

in the process of recovering the weapon. A 15-6 investigation by COL Bruce Falcone (220th Brigade, Deputy Commander) concluded that one of the detainees in tier 1A of the Hard Site had gotten a pistol and a couple of knives from an Iraqi Guard working in the encampment. Immediately upon receipt of this information, an ad-hoc extraction team consisting of MP and MI personnel conducted what they called a routine cell search, which resulted in the shooting of an MP and the detainee. Contributing factors were a corrupt Iraqi Guard, inadequate SOPs, the Detention ROE in place at the time was ineffective due to the numerous levels of authorization needed for use of lethal force, poorly trained MPs, unclear lanes of responsibility, and ambiguous relationship between the MI and MP assets. (**ANNEX 8**)

    j. **13 December 03- Shooting by non-lethal means into crowd at Abu Ghraib (320th MP Battalion).** Several detainees allegedly got into a detainee-on-detainee fight around 1030 in Compound 8 of the Ganci encampment, Abu Ghraib. An SIR was initiated by SSG Matash (320th MP Battalion, S-3 Section). The SIR indicated that there was a fight in the compound and the MPs used a non-lethal crowd-dispersing round to break up the fight, which was successful. No information on findings, contributing factors, or corrective action has been provided to this investigation team. (**ANNEX 14**)

    k. **13 December 03- Shooting by non-lethal means into crowd at Abu Ghraib (320th MP Battalion).** Several detainees allegedly got into a detainee-on-detainee fight around 1120 in Compound 2 of the Ganci encampment, Abu Ghraib. An SIR was initiated by SSG Matash (320th MP Battalion, S-3 Section). The SIR indicated that there was a fight in the compound and the MPs used two non-lethal shots to disperse the crowd, which was successful. No information on findings, contributing factors, or corrective action has been provided to this investigation team. (**ANNEX 15**)

    l. **13 December 03- Shooting by non-lethal means into crowd at Abu Ghraib (320th MP Battalion).** Approximately 30-40 detainees allegedly got into a detainee-on-detainee fight around 1642 in Compound 3 of the Ganci encampment, Abu Ghraib (BCCF). An SIR was initiated by SSG Matash (320th MP Battalion, S-3 Section). The SIR indicates that there was a fight in the compound and the MPs used a non-lethal crowd-dispersing round to break up the fight, which was successful. No information on findings, contributing factors, or corrective action has been provided to this investigation team. (**ANNEX 16**)

    m. **17 December 03- Shooting by non-lethal means of detainee from Abu Ghraib (320th MP Battalion).** Several detainees allegedly assaulted an MP at 1459 inside the Ganci Encampment, Abu Ghraib (BCCF). An SIR was initiated by SSG Matash (320th MP BRIGADE, S-3 Section). The SIR indicated that three detainees assaulted an MP, which resulted in the use of a non-lethal shot that calmed the situation. No information on findings, contributing factors, or corrective action has been provided to this investigation team. (**ANNEX 17**)

    n. **07 January 04- Escape of detainee #115032 from Camp Bucca (310th MP Battalion).** A detainee allegedly escaped between the hours of 0445 and 0640 from Compound 12, of Camp Bucca. Investigation by CPT Kaires (310th MP Battalion S-3) and CPT Holsombeck (724th MP Battalion S-3) concluded that the detainee escaped through an undetected weakness in the wire. Contributing factors were inexperienced guards, lapses in accountability, complacency, lack of leadership presence, poor visibility, and lack of clear and concise communication between the guards and the leadership. (**ANNEX 9**)

    o. **12 January 04- Escape of Detainees #115314 and #109950 as well as the escape and recapture of 5 unknown detainees at the Camp Bucca Detention Facility (310th MP Battalion).** Several detainees allegedly escaped around 0300 from Compound 12, of Camp Bucca. An AR 15-6 Investigation by LTC

Leigh Coulter (800th MP Brigade, OIC Camp Arifjan Detachment) concluded that three of the detainees escaped through the front holding cell during conditions of limited visibility due to fog. One of the detainees was noticed, shot with a non-lethal round, and returned to his holding compound. That same night, 4 detainees exited through the wire on the South side of the camp and were seen and apprehended by the QRF. Contributing factors were the lack of a coordinated effort for emplacement of MPs during implementation of the fog plan, overcrowding, and poor communications. (**ANNEX 10**)

    p. **14 January 04- Escape of detainee #12436 and missing Iraqi guard from Hard-Site, Abu Ghraib (320th MP Battalion).** A detainee allegedly escaped at 1335 from the Hard Site at Abu Ghraib (BCCF). An SIR was initiated by SSG Hydro (320th MP Battalion, S-3 Asst. NCOIC). The SIR indicates that an Iraqi guard assisted a detainee to escape by signing him out on a work detail and disappearing with him. At the time of the second SIR, neither missing person had been located. No information on findings, contributing factors, or corrective action has been provided to this investigation team. (**ANNEX 99**)

    q. **26 January 04- Escape of detainees #s 115236, 116272, and 151933 from Camp Bucca(310th MP Battalion).** Several Detainees allegedly escaped between the hours of 0440 and 0700 during a period of intense fog. Investigation by CPT Kaires (310th MP Battalion S-3) concluded that the detainees crawled under a fence when visibility was only 10-15 meters due to fog. Contributing factors were the limited visibility (darkness under foggy conditions), lack of proper accountability reporting, inadequate number of guards, commencement of detainee feeding during low visibility operations, and poorly rested MPs. (**ANNEX 18**)

    36. As I have previously indicated, this investigation determined that there was virtually a complete lack of detailed SOPs at any of the detention facilities. Moreover, despite the fact that there were numerous reported escapes at detention facilities throughout Iraq (in excess of 35), AR 15-6 Investigations following these escapes were simply forgotten or ignored by the Brigade Commander with no dissemination to other facilities. After-Action Reports and Lessons Learned, if done at all, remained at individual facilities and were not shared among other commanders or soldiers throughout the Brigade. The Command never issued standard TTPs for handling escape incidents. (**ANNEXES 5-10, Multiple Witness Statements, and the Personal Observations of the Investigation Team**)

RECOMMENDATIONS REGARDING PART TWO OF THE INVESTIGATION:

    ANNEX 100 of this investigation contains a detailed and referenced series of recommendations for improving the detainee accountability practices throughout the OIF area of operations. Accountability practices throughout any particular detention facility must be standardized and in accordance with applicable regulations and international law. The NDRS and BATS accounting systems must be expanded and used to their fullest extent to facilitate real time updating when detainees are moved and or transferred from one location to another.

    (U) "Change sheets," or their doctrinal equivalent must be immediately processed and updated into the system to ensure accurate accountability. The detainee roll call or ISN counts must match the manifest provided to the compound guards to ensure proper accountability of detainees. Develop, staff, and implement comprehensive and detailed SOPs utilizing the lessons learned from this investigation as well as any previous findings, recommendations, and reports. SOPs must be written, disseminated, trained on, and understood at the lowest level.

BASIC DOCUMENTS ABOUT THE DETAINEES

(U) Iraqi criminal prisoners must be held in separate facilities from any other category of detainee. All of the compounds should be wired into the master manifest whereby MP Soldiers can account for their detainees in real time and without waiting for their change sheets to be processed. This would also have the change sheet serve as a way to check up on the accuracy of the manifest as updated by each compound. The BATS and NDRS system can be utilized for this function.

(U) Accountability lapses, escapes, and disturbances within the detainment facilities must be immediately reported through both the operational and administrative Chain of Command via a Serious Incident Report (SIR). The SIRs must then be tracked and followed by daily SITREPs until the situation is resolved. Detention Rules of Engagement (DROE), Interrogation Rules of Engagement (IROE), and the principles of the Geneva Conventions need to be briefed at every shift change and guard mount.

(U) AARs must be conducted after serious incidents at any given facility. The observations and corrective actions that develop from the AARs must be analyzed by the respective MP Battalion S-3 section, developed into a plan of action, shared with the other facilities, and implemented as a matter of policy.

(U) There must be significant structural improvements at each of the detention facilities. The needed changes include significant enhancement of perimeter lighting, additional chain link fencing, staking down of all concertina wire, hard site development, and expansion of Abu Ghraib (BCCF). The Geneva Conventions and the facility rules must be prominently displayed in English and the language of the detainees at each compound and encampment at every detention facility IAW AR 190-8.

(U) Further restrict US civilians and other contractors' access throughout the facility. Contractors and civilians must be in an authorized and easily identifiable uniform to be more easily distinguished from the masses of detainees in civilian clothes. Facilities must have a stop movement/transfer period of at least 1 hour prior to every 100% detainee roll call and ISN counts to ensure accurate accountability.

(U) The method for doing head counts of detainees within a given compound must be standardized. Those military units conducting I/R operations must know of, train on, and constantly reference the applicable Army Doctrine and CJTF command policies. The references provided in this report cover nearly every deficiency I have enumerated. Although they do not, and cannot, make up for leadership shortfalls, all soldiers, at all levels, can use them to maintain standardized operating procedures and efficient accountability practices.

FINDINGS AND RECOMMENDATIONS (PART THREE)

Investigate the training, standards, employment, command policies, internal procedures, and command climate in the 800th MP Brigade, as appropriate:

(Names deleted)
(ANNEXES 45-91)

REGARDING PART THREE OF THE INVESTIGATION, I MAKE THE FOLLOWING SPECIFIC FINDINGS OF FACT:

1. I find that BG Janis Karpinski took command of the 800th MP Brigade on 30 June 2003 from BG Paul Hill. BG Karpinski has remained in command since that date. The 800th MP Brigade is comprised of eight MP battalions in the Iraqi TOR: 115th MP Battalion, 310th MP Battalion, 320th MP Battalion, 324th MP Battalion, 400th MP Battalion, 530th MP Battalion, 724th MP Battalion, and 744th MP Battalion.

(ANNEXES 41 and 45)

2. Prior to BG Karpinski taking command, members of the 800th MP Brigade believed they would be allowed to go home when all the detainees were released from the Camp Bucca Theater Internment Facility following the cessation of major ground combat on 1 May 2003. At one point, approximately 7,000 to 8,000 detainees were held at Camp Bucca. Through Article-5 Tribunals and a screening process, several thousand detainees were released. Many in the command believed they would go home when the detainees were released. In late May-early June 2003 the 800th MP Brigade was given a new mission to manage the Iraqi penal system and several detention centers. This new mission meant Soldiers would not redeploy to CONUS when anticipated. Morale suffered, and over the next few months there did not appear to have been any attempt by the Command to mitigate this morale problem. (ANNEXES 45 and 96)

3. There is abundant evidence in the statements of numerous witnesses that soldiers throughout the 800th MP Brigade were not proficient in their basic MOS skills, particularly regarding internment/resettlement operations. Moreover, there is no evidence that the command, although aware of these deficiencies, attempted to correct them in any systemic manner other than ad hoc training by individuals with civilian corrections experience. (Multiple Witness Statements and the Personal Observations of the Investigation Team)

4. I find that the 800th MP Brigade was not adequately trained for a mission that included operating a prison or penal institution at Abu Ghraib Prison Complex. As the Ryder Assessment found, I also concur that units of the 800th MP Brigade did not receive corrections-specific training during their mobilization period. MP units did not receive pinpoint assignments prior to mobilization and during the post mobilization training, and thus could not train for specific missions. The training that was accomplished at the mobilization sites were developed and implemented at the company level with little or no direction or supervision at the Battalion and Brigade levels, and consisted primarily of common tasks and law enforcement training. However, I found no evidence that the Command, although aware of this deficiency, ever requested specific corrections training from the Commandant of the Military Police School, the US Army Confinement Facility at Mannheim, Germany, the Provost Marshal General of the Army, or the US Army Disciplinary Barracks at Fort Leavenworth, Kansas. (ANNEXES 19 and 76)

5. I find that without adequate training for a civilian internee detention mission, Brigade personnel relied heavily on individuals within the Brigade who had civilian corrections experience, including many who worked as prison guards or corrections officials in their civilian jobs. Almost every witness we interviewed had no familiarity with the provisions of AR 190-8 or FM 3-19.40. It does not appear that a Mission Essential Task List (METL) based on in-theater missions was ever developed nor was a training plan implemented throughout the Brigade. (ANNEXES 21, 22, 67, and 81)

6. I also find, as did MG Ryder's Team, that the 800th MP Brigade as a whole, was understrength for the mission for which it was tasked. Army Doctrine dictates that an I/R Brigade can be organized with between 7 and 21 battalions, and that the average battalion size element should be able to handle approximately 4000 detainees at a time. This investigation indicates that BG Karpinski and her staff did a poor job allocating resources throughout the Iraq JOA. Abu Ghraib (BCCF) normally housed between 6000 and 7000 detainees, yet it was operated by only one battalion. In contrast, the HVD Facility maintains only about 100 detainees, and is also run by an entire battalion. (ANNEXES 19, 22, and 96)

Basic Documents about the Detainees

7. Reserve Component units do not have an individual replacement system to mitigate medical or other losses. Over time, the 800th MP Brigade clearly suffered from personnel shortages through release from active duty (REFRAD) actions, medical evacuation, and demobilization. In addition to being severely undermanned, the quality of life for Soldiers assigned to Abu Ghraib (BCCF) was extremely poor. There was no DFAC, PX, barbershop, or MWR facilities. There were numerous mortar attacks, random rifle and RPG attacks, and a serious threat to Soldiers and detainees in the facility. The prison complex was also severely overcrowded and the Brigade lacked adequate resources and personnel to resolve serious logistical problems. Finally, because of past associations and familiarity of Soldiers within the Brigade, it appears that friendship often took precedence over appropriate leader and subordinate relationships. **(ANNEX 101, Multiple Witness Statements, and the Personal Observations of the Investigation Team)**

8. With respect to the 800th MP Brigade mission at Abu Ghraib (BCCF), I find that there was clear friction and lack of effective communication between the Commander, 205th MI Brigade, who controlled FOB Abu Ghraib (BCCF) after 19 November 2003, and the Commander, 800th MP Brigade, who controlled detainee operations inside the FOB. There was no clear delineation of responsibility between commands, little coordination at the command level, and no integration of the two functions. Coordination occurred at the lowest possible levels with little oversight by commanders. **(ANNEXES 31, 45, and 46)**

9. I find that this ambiguous command relationship was exacerbated by a CJTF-7 Fragmentary Order (FRAGO) 1108 issued on 19 November 2003. Paragraph 3.C.8, Assignment of 205th MI Brigade Commander's Responsibilities for the Baghdad Central Confinement Facility, states as follows:

3.C.8. A.205 MI BRIGADE.

3.C.8. A. 1. EFFECTIVE IMMEDIATELY COMMANDER 205 MI BRIGADE ASSUMES RESPONSIBILITY FOR THE BAGHDAD CONFINEMENT FACILITY (BCCF) AND IS APPOINTED THE FOB COMMANDER. UNITS CURRENTLY AT ABU GHRAIB (BCCF) ARE TACON TO 205 MI BRIGADE FOR "SECURITY OF DETAINEES AND FOB PROTECTION."

Although not supported by BG Karpinski, FRAGO 1108 made all of the MP units at Abu Ghraib TACON to the Commander, 205th MI Brigade. This effectively made an MI Officer, rather than an MP Officer, responsible for the MP units conducting detainee operations at that facility. This is not doctrinally sound due to the different missions and agendas assigned to each of these respective specialties. **(ANNEX 31)**

10. Joint Publication 0-2, Unified Action Armed Forces (UNAAF), 10 July 2001 defines Tactical Control (TACON) as the detailed direction and control of movements or maneuvers within the operational area necessary to accomplish assigned missions or tasks. **(ANNEX 42)**

"TACON is the command authority over assigned or attached forces or commands or military capability made available for tasking that is limited to the detailed direction and control of movements or maneuvers within the operational area necessary to accomplish assigned missions or tasks. TACON is inherent in OPCON and may be delegated to and exercised by commanders at any echelon at or below the level of combatant commander."

11. Based on all the facts and circumstances in this investigation, I find that there was little, if any, recognition of this TACON Order by the 800th MP Brigade or the 205th MI Brigade. Further, there was no evidence if the Commander, 205th MI Brigade clearly informed the Commander, 800th MP Brigade,

and specifically the Commander, 320th MP Battalion assigned at Abu Ghraib (BCCF), on the specific requirements of this TACON relationship. (**ANNEXES 45 and 46**)

12. It is clear from a comprehensive review of witness statements and personal interviews that the 320th MP Battalion and 800th MP Brigade continued to function as if they were responsible for the security, health and welfare, and overall security of detainees within Abu Ghraib (BCCF) prison. Both BG Karpinski and COL Pappas clearly behaved as if this were still the case. (**ANNEXES 45 and 46**)

13. With respect to the 320th MP Battalion, I find that the Battalion Commander, LTC (P) Jerry Phillabaum, was an extremely ineffective commander and leader. Numerous witnesses confirm that the Battalion S-3, MAJ David W. DiNenna, basically ran the battalion on a day-to-day basis. At one point, BG Karpinski sent LTC (P) Phillabaum to Camp Arifjan, Kuwait for approximately two weeks, apparently to give him some relief from the pressure he was experiencing as the 320th Battalion Commander. This movement to Camp Arifjan immediately followed a briefing provided by LTC (P) Phillabaum to the CJTF-7 Commander, LTG Sanchez, near the end of October 2003. BG Karpinski placed LTC Ronald Chew, Commander of the 115th MP Battalion, in charge of the 320th MP Battalion for a period of approximately two weeks. LTC Chew was also in command of the 115th MP Battalion assigned to Camp Cropper, BIAP, Iraq. I could find no orders, either suspending or relieving LTC (P) Phillabaum from command, nor any orders placing LTC Chew in command of the 320th. In addition, there was no indication this removal and search for a replacement was communicated to the Commander CJTF-7, the Commander 377th TSC, or to Soldiers in the 320th MP Battalion. Temporarily removing one commander and replacing him with another serving Battalion Commander without an order and without notifying superior or subordinate commands is without precedent in my military career. LTC (P) Phillabaum was also reprimanded for lapses in accountability that resulted in several escapes. The 320th MP Battalion was stigmatized as a unit due to previous detainee abuse which occurred in May 2003 at the Bucca Theater Internment Facility (TIF), while under the command of LTC (P) Phillabaum. Despite his proven deficiencies as both a commander and leader, BG Karpinski allowed LTC (P) Phillabaum to remain in command of her most troubled battalion guarding, by far, the largest number of detainees in the 800th MP Brigade. LTC (P) Phillabaum was suspended from his duties by LTG Sanchez, CJTF-7 Commander on 17 January 2004. (**ANNEXES 43, 45, and 61**)

14. During the course of this investigation I conducted a lengthy interview with BG Karpinski that lasted over four hours, and is included verbatim in the investigation Annexes. BG Karpinski was extremely emotional during much of her testimony. What I found particularly disturbing in her testimony was her complete unwillingness to either understand or accept that many of the problems inherent in the 800th MP Brigade were caused or exacerbated by poor leadership and the refusal of her command to both establish and enforce basic standards and principles among its soldiers. (**ANNEX 45 and the Personal Observations of the Interview Team**)

15. BG Karpinski alleged that she received no help from the Civil Affairs Command, specifically, no assistance from either BG John Kern or COL Tim Regan. She blames much of the abuse that occurred in Abu Ghraib (BCCF) on MI personnel and stated that MI personnel had given the MPs "ideas" that led to detainee abuse. In addition, she blamed the 372nd Company Platoon Sergeant, SFC Snider, the Company Commander, CPT Reese, and the First Sergeant, MSG Lipinski, for the abuse. She argued that problems in

BASIC DOCUMENTS ABOUT THE DETAINEES

Abu Ghraib were the fault of COL Pappas and LTC Jordan because COL Pappas was in charge of FOB Abu Ghraib. **(ANNEX 45)**

16. BG Karpinski also implied during her testimony that the criminal abuses that occurred at Abu Ghraib (BCCF) might have been caused by the ultimate disposition of the detainee abuse cases that originally occurred at Camp Bucca in May 2003. She stated that **"about the same time those incidents were taking place out of Baghdad Central, the decisions were made to give the guilty people at Bucca plea bargains. So, the system communicated to the soldiers, the worst that's gonna happen is, you're gonna go home."** I think it important to point out that almost every witness testified that the serious criminal abuse of detainees at Abu Ghraib (BCCF) occurred in late October and early November 2003. The photographs and statements clearly support that the abuses occurred during this time period. The Bucca cases were set for trial in January 2004 and were not finally disposed of until 29 December 2003. There is entirely no evidence that the decision of numerous MP personnel to intentionally abuse detainees at Abu Ghraib (BCCF) was influenced in any respect by the Camp Bucca cases. **(ANNEXES 25, 26, and 45)**

17. Numerous witnesses stated that the 800th MP Brigade S-1, MAJ Hinzman and S-4, MAJ Green, were essentially dysfunctional, but that despite numerous complaints, these officers were not replaced. This had a detrimental effect on the Brigade Staff's effectiveness and morale. Moreover, the Brigade Command Judge Advocate, LTC James O'Hare, appears to lack initiative and was unwilling to accept responsibility for any of his actions. LTC Gary Maddocks, the Brigade XO did not properly supervise the Brigade staff by failing to lay out staff priorities, take overt corrective action when needed, and supervise their daily functions. **(ANNEXES 45, 47, 48, 62, and 67)**

18. In addition to poor morale and staff inefficiencies, I find that the 800th MP Brigade did not articulate or enforce clear and basic Soldier and Army standards. I specifically found these examples of unenforced standards:

   a. There was no clear uniform standard for any MP Soldiers assigned detention duties. Despite the fact that hundreds of former Iraqi soldiers and officers were detainees, MP personnel were allowed to wear civilian clothes in the FOB after duty hours while carrying weapons. **(ANNEXES 51 and 74)**

   b. Some Soldiers wrote poems and other sayings on their helmets and soft caps. **(ANNEXES 51 and 74)**

   c. In addition, numerous officers and senior NCOs have been reprimanded/disciplined for misconduct during this period. Those disciplined include; **(ANNEXES 43 and 102)**

   1). BG Janis Karpinski, Commander, 800th MP Brigade

   - Memorandum of Admonishment by LTG Sanchez, Commander, CJTF-7, on 17 January 2004.

   2). LTC (P) Jerry Phillabaum, Commander, 320th MP Battalion

   - GOMOR from BG Karpinski, Commander 800th MP Brigade, on 10 November 2003, for lack of leadership and for failing to take corrective security measures as ordered by the Brigade Commander; filed locally

   - Suspended by BG Karpinski, Commander 800th MP Brigade, 17 January 2004; Pending Relief for Cause, for dereliction of duty

3). LTC Dale Burtyk, Commander, 400th MP Battalion
- GOMOR from BG Karpinski, Commander 800th MP Brigade, on 20 August 2003, for failure to properly train his Soldiers. (Soldier had negligent discharge of M-16 while exiting his vehicle, round went into fuel tank); filed locally.

4). MAJ David DiNenna, S-3, 320th MP Battalion
- GOMOR from LTG McKiernan, Commander CFLCC, on 25 May 2003, for dereliction of duty for failing to report a violation of CENTCOM General Order #1 by a subordinate Field Grade Officer and Senior Noncommissioned Officer, which he personally observed; returned to soldier unfiled.
- GOMOR from BG Karpinski, Commander 800th MP Brigade, on 10 November 03, for failing to take corrective security measures as ordered by the Brigade Commander; filed locally.

5). MAJ Stacy Garrity, Finance Officer, 800th MP Brigade
- GOMOR from LTG McKiernan, Commander CFLCC, on 25 May 2003, for violation of CENTCOM General Order #1, consuming alcohol with an NCO; filed locally.

6). CPT Leo Merck, Commander, 870th MP Company
- Court-Martial Charges Preferred, for Conduct Unbecoming an Officer and Unauthorized Use of Government Computer in that he was alleged to have taken nude pictures of his female Soldiers without their knowledge; Trial date to be announced.

7). CPT Damaris Morales, Commander, 770th MP Company
- GOMOR from BG Karpinski, Commander 800th MP Brigade, on 20 August 2003, for failing to properly train his Soldiers (Soldier had negligent discharge of M-16 while exiting his vehicle, round went into fuel tank); filed locally.

8) CSM Roy Clement, Command Sergeant Major, 800th MP Brigade
- GOMOR and Relief for Cause from BG Janis Karpinski, Commander 800th MP Brigade, for fraternization and dereliction of duty for fraternizing with junior enlisted soldiers within his unit; GOMOR officially filed and he was removed from the CSM list.

9). CSM Edward Stotts, Command Sergeant Major, 400th MP Battalion
- GOMOR from BG Karpinski, Commander 800th MP Brigade, on 20 August 2003, for failing to properly train his Soldiers (Soldier had negligent discharge of M-16 while exiting his vehicle, round went into fuel tank); filed locally.

10). 1SG Carlos Villanueva, First Sergeant, 770th MP Company
- GOMOR from BG Karpinski, Commander 800th MP Brigade, on 20 August 2003, for failing to properly train his Soldiers (Soldier had negligent discharge of M-16 while exiting his vehicle, round went into fuel tank); filed locally.

Basic Documents about the Detainees

11). MSG David Maffett, NBC NCO, 800th MP Brigade,

- GOMOR from LTG McKiernan, Commander CFLCC, on 25 May 2003, for violation of CENTCOM General Order #1, consuming alcohol; filed locally.

12) SGM Marc Emerson, Operations SGM, 320th MP Battalion,

- Two GO Letters of Concern and a verbal reprimand from BG Karpinski, Commander 800th MP Brigade, for failing to adhere to the guidance/directives given to him by BG Karpinski; filed locally.

d. Saluting of officers was sporadic and not enforced. LTC Robert P. Walters, Jr., Commander of the 165th Military Intelligence Battalion (Tactical Exploitation), testified that the saluting policy was enforced by COL Pappas for all MI personnel, and that BG Karpinski approached COL Pappas to reverse the saluting policy back to a no-saluting policy as previously existed. (**ANNEX 53**)

19. I find that individual Soldiers within the 800th MP Brigade and the 320th Battalion stationed throughout Iraq had very little contact during their tour of duty with either LTC (P) Phillabaum or BG Karpinski. BG Karpinski claimed, during her testimony, that she paid regular visits to the various detention facilities where her Soldiers were stationed. However, the detailed calendar provided by her Aide-de-Camp, 1LT Mabry, does not support her contention. Moreover, numerous witnesses stated that they rarely saw BG Karpinski or LTC (P) Phillabaum. (**Multiple Witness Statements**)

20. In addition I find that psychological factors, such as the difference in culture, the Soldiers' quality of life, the real presence of mortal danger over an extended time period, and the failure of commanders to recognize these pressures contributed to the pervasive atmosphere that existed at Abu Ghraib (BCCF) Detention Facility and throughout the 800th MP Brigade. (**ANNEX 1**).

21. As I have documented in other parts of this investigation, I find that there was no clear emphasis by BG Karpinski to ensure that the 800th MP Brigade Staff, Commanders, and Soldiers were trained to standard in detainee operations and proficiency or that serious accountability lapses that occurred over a significant period of time, particularly at Abu Ghraib (BCCF), were corrected. AR 15-6 Investigations regarding detainee escapes were not acted upon, followed up with corrective action, or disseminated to subordinate commanders or Soldiers. Brigade and unit SOPs for dealing with detainees if they existed at all, were not read or understood by MP Soldiers assigned the difficult mission of detainee operations. Following the abuse of several detainees at Camp Bucca in May 2003, I could find no evidence that BG Karpinski ever directed corrective training for her soldiers or ensured that MP Soldiers throughout Iraq clearly understood the requirements of the Geneva Conventions relating to the treatment of detainees. (**Multiple Witness Statements and the Personal Observations of the Investigation Team**)

22. On 17 January 2004 BG Karpinski was formally admonished in writing by LTG Sanchez regarding the serious deficiencies in her Brigade. LTG Sanchez found that the performance of the 800th MP Brigade had not met the standards set by the Army or by CJTF-7. He found that incidents in the preceding six months had occurred that reflected a lack of clear standards, proficiency and leadership within the Brigade. LTG Sanchez also cited the recent detainee abuse at Abu Ghraib (BCCF) as the most recent example of a poor leadership climate that "permeates the Brigade." I totally concur with LTG Sanchez' opinion regarding the performance of BG Karpinski and the 800th MP Brigade. (**ANNEX 102 and the Personal Observations of the Investigating Officer**)

RECOMMENDATIONS AS TO PART THREE OF THE INVESTIGATION:

1. That **BG Janis L. Karpinski, Commander, 800th MP Brigade** be Relieved from Command and given a General Officer Memorandum of Reprimand for the following acts which have been previously referred to in the aforementioned findings:

- Failing to ensure that MP Soldiers at theater-level detention facilities throughout Iraq had appropriate SOPs for dealing with detainees and that Commanders and Soldiers had read, understood, and would adhere to these SOPs.

- Failing to ensure that MP Soldiers in the 800th MP Brigade knew, understood, and adhered to the protections afforded to detainees in the Geneva Convention Relative to the Treatment of Prisoners of War.

- Making material misrepresentations to the Investigation Team as to the frequency of her visits to her subordinate commands.

- Failing to obey an order from the CFLCC Commander, LTG McKiernan, regarding the withholding of disciplinary authority for Officer and Senior Noncommissioned Officer misconduct.

- Failing to take appropriate action regarding the ineffectiveness of a subordinate Commander, LTC (P) Jerry Phillabaum.

- Failing to take appropriate action regarding the ineffectiveness of numerous members of her Brigade Staff including her XO, S-1, S-3, and S-4.

- Failing to properly ensure the results and recommendations of the AARs and numerous 15-6 Investigation reports on escapes and shootings (over a period of several months) were properly disseminated to, and understood by, subordinate commanders.

- Failing to ensure and enforce basic Soldier standards throughout her command.

- Failing to establish a Brigade METL.

- Failing to establish basic proficiency in assigned tasks for Soldiers throughout the 800th MP Brigade.

- Failing to ensure that numerous and reported accountability lapses at detention facilities throughout Iraq were corrected.

2. That **COL Thomas M. Pappas, Commander, 205th MI Brigade**, be given a General Officer Memorandum of Reprimand and Investigated UP Procedure 15, AR 381-10, US Army Intelligence Activities for the following acts which have been previously referred to in the aforementioned findings:

- Failing to ensure that Soldiers under his direct command were properly trained in and followed the IROE.

BASIC DOCUMENTS ABOUT THE DETAINEES

- Failing to ensure that Soldiers under his direct command knew, understood, and followed the protections afforded to detainees in the Geneva Convention Relative to the Treatment of Prisoners of War.

- Failing to properly supervise his soldiers working and "visiting" Tier 1 of the Hard-Site at Abu Ghraib (BCCF).

3. That **LTC (P) Jerry L. Phillabaum, Commander, 320th MP Battalion,** be Relieved from Command, be given a General Officer Memorandum of Reprimand, and be removed from the Colonel/O-6 Promotion List for the following acts which have been previously referred to in the aforementioned findings:

- Failing to properly ensure the results, recommendations, and AARs from numerous reports on escapes and shootings over a period of several months were properly disseminated to, and understood by, subordinates.

- Failing to implement the appropriate recommendations from various 15-6 Investigations as specifically directed by BG Karpinski.

- Failing to ensure that Soldiers under his direct command were properly trained in Internment and Resettlement Operations.

- Failing to ensure that Soldiers under his direct command knew and understood the protections afforded to detainees in the Geneva Convention Relative to the Treatment of Prisoners of War.

- Failing to properly supervise his soldiers working and "visiting" Tier 1 of the Hard-Site at Abu Ghraib (BCCF).

- Failing to properly establish and enforce basic soldier standards, proficiency, and accountability.

- Failure to conduct an appropriate Mission Analysis and to task organize to accomplish his mission.

4. That **LTC Steven L. Jordan, Former Director, Joint Interrogation and Debriefing Center and Liaison Officer to 205th Military Intelligence Brigade,** be relieved from duty and be given a General Officer Memorandum of Reprimand for the following acts which have been previously referred to in the aforementioned findings:

- Making material misrepresentations to the Investigating Team, including his leadership roll at Abu Ghraib (BCCF).

- Failing to ensure that Soldiers under his direct control were properly trained in and followed the IROE.

- Failing to ensure that Soldiers under his direct control knew, understood, and followed the protections afforded to detainees in the Geneva Convention Relative to the Treatment of Prisoners of War.

- Failing to properly supervise soldiers under his direct authority working and "visiting" Tier 1 of the Hard-Site at Abu Ghraib (BCCF).

5. That **MAJ David W. DiNenna, Sr., S-3, 320th MP Battalion,** be Relieved from his position as the Battalion S-3 and be given a General Officer Memorandum of Reprimand for the following acts which have been previously referred to in the aforementioned findings:

- Received a GOMOR from LTG McKiernan, Commander CFLCC, on 25 May 2003, for dereliction of duty for failing to report a violation of CENTCOM General Order #1 by a subordinate Field Grade Officer and Senior Noncommissioned Officer, which he personally observed; GOMOR was returned to Soldier and not filed.

- Failing to take corrective action and implement recommendations from various 15-6 investigations even after receiving a GOMOR from BG Karpinski, Commander 800th MP Brigade, on 10 November 03, for failing to take corrective security measures as ordered; GOMOR was filed locally.

- Failing to take appropriate action and report an incident of detainee abuse, whereby he personally witnessed a Soldier throw a detainee from the back of a truck.

6. That **CPT Donald J. Reese, Commander, 372nd MP Company,** be Relieved from Command and be given a General Officer Memorandum of Reprimand for the following acts which have been previously referred to in the aforementioned findings:

- Failing to ensure that Soldiers under his direct command knew and understood the protections afforded to detainees in the Geneva Convention Relative to the Treatment of Prisoners of War.

- Failing to properly supervise his Soldiers working and "visiting" Tier 1 of the Hard-Site at Abu Ghraib (BCCF).

- Failing to properly establish and enforce basic soldier standards, proficiency, and accountability.

- Failing to ensure that Soldiers under his direct command were properly trained in Internment and Resettlement Operations.

7. That **1LT Lewis C. Raeder, Platoon Leader, 372nd MP Company,** be Relieved from his duties as Platoon Leader and be given a General Officer Memorandum of Reprimand for the following acts which have been previously referred to in the aforementioned findings:

- Failing to ensure that Soldiers under his direct command knew and understood the protections afforded to detainees in the Geneva Convention Relative to the Treatment of Prisoners of War.

Basic Documents about the Detainees

- Failing to properly supervise his soldiers working and "visiting" Tier 1 of the Hard-Site at Abu Ghraib (BCCF).

- Failing to properly establish and enforce basic Soldier standards, proficiency, and accountability.

- Failing to ensure that Soldiers under his direct command were properly trained in Internment and Resettlement Operations.

8. That **SGM Marc Emerson, Operations SGM, 320th MP Battalion,** be Relieved from his duties and given a General Officer Memorandum of Reprimand for the following acts which have been previously referred to in the aforementioned findings:

- Making a material misrepresentation to the Investigation Team stating that he had "never" been admonished or reprimanded by BG Karpinski, when in fact he had been admonished for failing to obey an order from BG Karpinski to "stay out of the towers" at the holding facility.

- Making a material misrepresentation to the Investigation Team stating that he had attended every shift change/guard-mount conducted at the 320th MP Battalion, and that he personally briefed his Soldiers on the proper treatment of detainees, when in fact numerous statements contradict this assertion.

- Failing to ensure that Soldiers in the 320th MP Battalion knew and understood the protections afforded to detainees in the Geneva Convention Relative to the Treatment of Prisoners of War.

- Failing to properly supervise his soldiers working and "visiting" Tier 1 of the Hard-Site at Abu Ghraib (BCCF).

- Failing to properly establish and enforce basic soldier standards, proficiency, and accountability.

- Failing to ensure that his Soldiers were properly trained in Internment and Resettlement Operations.

9. That **1SG Brian G. Lipinski, First Sergeant, 372nd MP Company,** be Relieved from his duties as First Sergeant of the 372nd MP Company and given a General Officer Memorandum of Reprimand for the following acts which have been previously referred to in the aforementioned findings:

- Failing to ensure that Soldiers in the 372nd MP Company knew and understood the protections afforded to detainees in the Geneva Convention Relative to the Treatment of Prisoners of War.

- Failing to properly supervise his soldiers working and "visiting" Tier 1 of the Hard-Site at Abu Ghraib (BCCF).

- Failing to properly establish and enforce basic soldier standards, proficiency, and accountability.

- Failing to ensure that his Soldiers were properly trained in Internment and Resettlement Operations.

10. That **SFC Shannon K. Snider, Platoon Sergeant, 372nd MP Company**, be Relieved from his duties, receive a General Officer Memorandum of Reprimand, and receive action under the Uniform Code of Military Justice for the following acts which have been previously referred to in the aforementioned findings:

- Failing to ensure that Soldiers in his platoon knew and understood the protections afforded to detainees in the Geneva Convention Relative to the Treatment of Prisoners of War.

- Failing to properly supervise his soldiers working and "visiting" Tier 1 of the Hard-Site at Abu Ghraib (BCCF).

- Failing to properly establish and enforce basic soldier standards, proficiency, and accountability.

- Failing to ensure that his Soldiers were properly trained in Internment and Resettlement Operations.

- Failing to report a Soldier, who under his direct control, abused detainees by stomping on their bare hands and feet in his presence.

11. That **Mr. Steven Stephanowicz, Contract US Civilian Interrogator, CACI, 205th Military Intelligence Brigade**, be given an Official Reprimand to be placed in his employment file, termination of employment, and generation of a derogatory report to revoke his security clearance for the following acts which have been previously referred to in the aforementioned findings:

- Made a false statement to the investigation team regarding the locations of his interrogations, the activities during his interrogations, and his knowledge of abuses.

- Allowed and/or instructed MPs, who were not trained in interrogation techniques, to facilitate interrogations by "setting conditions" which were neither authorized and in accordance with applicable regulations/policy. He clearly knew his instructions equated to physical abuse.

12. That **Mr. John Israel, Contract US Civilian Interpreter, CACI, 205th Military Intelligence Brigade,** be given an Official Reprimand to be placed in his employment file and have his security clearance reviewed by competent authority for the following acts or concerns which have been previously referred to in the aforementioned findings:

- Denied ever having seen interrogation processes in violation of the IROE, which is contrary to several witness statements.

- Did not have a security clearance.

13. I find that there is sufficient credible information to warrant an Inquiry UP Procedure 15, AR 381-10, US Army Intelligence Activities, be conducted to determine the extent of culpability of MI personnel, assigned to the 205th MI Brigade and the Joint Interrogation and Debriefing Center (JIDC) at Abu Ghraib (BCCF). Specifically, I suspect that **COL Thomas M. Pappas, LTC Steve L. Jordan, Mr. Steven Stephanowicz,** and **Mr. John Israel** were either directly or indirectly responsible for the abuses at Abu

BASIC DOCUMENTS ABOUT THE DETAINEES

Ghraib (BCCF) and strongly recommend immediate disciplinary action as described in the preceding paragraphs as well as the initiation of a Procedure 15 Inquiry to determine the full extent of their culpability. **(Annex 36)**

OTHER FINDINGS/OBSERVATIONS

1. Due to the nature and scope of this investigation, I acquired the assistance of Col (Dr.) Henry Nelson, a USAF Psychiatrist, to analyze the investigation materials from a psychological perspective. He determined that there was evidence that the horrific abuses suffered by the detainees at Abu Ghraib (BCCF) were wanton acts of select soldiers in an unsupervised and dangerous setting. There was a complex interplay of many psychological factors and command insufficiencies. A more detailed analysis is contained in **ANNEX 1** of this investigation.

2. During the course of this investigation I conducted a lengthy interview with BG Karpinski that lasted over four hours, and is included verbatim in the investigation Annexes. BG Karpinski was extremely emotional during much of her testimony. What I found particularly disturbing in her testimony was her complete unwillingness to either understand or accept that many of the problems inherent in the 800th MP Brigade were caused or exacerbated by poor leadership and the refusal of her command to both establish and enforce basic standards and principles among its Soldiers. **(ANNEX 45)**

3. Throughout the investigation, we observed many individual Soldiers and some subordinate units under the 800th MP Brigade that overcame significant obstacles, persevered in extremely poor conditions, and upheld the Army Values. We discovered numerous examples of Soldiers and Sailors taking the initiative in the absence of leadership and accomplishing their assigned tasks.

   a. The 744th MP Battalion, commanded by LTC Dennis McGlone, efficiently operated the HVD Detention Facility at Camp Cropper and met mission requirements with little to no guidance from the 800th MP Brigade. The unit was disciplined, proficient, and appeared to understand their basic tasks.

   b. The 530th MP Battalion, commanded by LTC Stephen J. Novotny, effectively maintained the MEK Detention Facility at Camp Ashraf. His Soldiers were proficient in their individual tasks and adapted well to this highly unique and non-doctrinal operation.

   c. The 165th MI Battalion excelled in providing perimeter security and force protection at Abu Ghraib (BCCF). LTC Robert P. Walters, Jr., demanded standards be enforced and worked endlessly to improve discipline throughout the FOB.

4. The individual Soldiers and Sailors that we observed and believe should be favorably noted include:

   a. Master-at-Arms First Class William J. Kimbro, US Navy Dog Handler, knew his duties and refused to participate in improper interrogations despite significant pressure from the MI personnel at Abu Ghraib.

   b. SPC Joseph M. Darby, 372nd MP Company discovered evidence of abuse and turned it over to military law enforcement.

   c. 1LT David O. Sutton, 229th MP Company, took immediate action and stopped an abuse, then reported the incident to the chain of command.

CONCLUSION

1. Several US Army Soldiers have committed egregious acts and grave breaches of international law at Abu Ghraib/BCCF and Camp Bucca, Iraq. Furthermore, key senior leaders in both the 800th MP Brigade and the 205th MI Brigade failed to comply with established regulations, policies, and command directives in preventing detainee abuses at Abu Ghraib (BCCF) and at Camp Bucca during the period August 2003 to February 2004.

2. Approval and implementation of the recommendations of this AR 15-6 Investigation and those highlighted in previous assessments are essential to establish the conditions with the resources and personnel required to prevent future occurrences of detainee abuse.

ANNEXES

1. Psychological Assessment
2. Request for investigation from CJTF-7 to CENTCOM
3. Directive to CFLCC from CENTCOM directing investigation
4. Appointment Memo from CFLCC CDR to MG Taguba
5. 15-6 Investigation 9 June 2003
6. 15-6 Investigation 12 June 2003
7. 15-6 Investigation 13 June 2003
8. 15-6 Investigation 24 November 2003
9. 15-6 Investigation 7 January 2004
10. 15-6 Investigation 12 January 2004
11. SIR 5 November 2003
12. SIR 7 November 2003
13. SIR 8 November 2003
14. SIR 13 December 2003
15. SIR 13 December 2003
16. SIR 13 December 2003
17. SIR 17 December 2003
18. Commander's Inquiry 26 January 2004
19. MG Ryder's Report, 6 November 2003
20. MG Miller's Report, 9 September 2003
21. AR 190-8, Enemy Prisoners of War, Retained Personnel, Civilian Internees, and Other Detainees, 1 October 1997
22. FM 3-19.40, Military Police Internment/Resettlement Operations, 1 August 2001
23. FM 34-52, Intelligence Interrogation, 28 September 1992
24. Fourth Geneva Convention, 12 August 1949
25. CID Report on criminal abuses at Abu Ghraib, 28 January 2004
26. CID Interviews, 10-25 January 2004
27. 800th MP Brigade Roster, 29 January 2004
28. 205th MI Brigade's IROE, Undated

BASIC DOCUMENTS ABOUT THE DETAINEES

29. TOA Order (800th MP Brigade) and letter holding witnesses
30. Investigation Team's witness list
31. FRAGO #1108
32. Letters suspending several key leaders in the 800th MP Brigade and Rating Chain with suspensions annotated
33. FM 27-10, Military Justice, 6 September 2002
34. CID Report on abuse of detainees at Camp Bucca, 8 June 2003
35. Article 32 Findings on abuse of detainees at Camp Bucca, 26 August 2003
36. AR 381-10, 1 July 1984
37. Excerpts from log books, 320th MP Battalion
38. 310th MP Battalion's Inprocessing SOP
39. 320th MP Battalion's "Change Sheet"
40. Joint Interrogation and Debriefing Center's (JIDC) Slides, Undated
41. Order of Battle Slides, 12 January 2004
42. Joint Publication 0-2, Unified Actions Armed Forces, 10 July 2001
43. General Officer Memorandums of Reprimand
44. 800th MP Battalion's TACSOP
45. BG Janis Karpinski, Commander, 800th MP Brigade
46. COL Thomas Pappas, Commander, 205th MI Brigade
47. COL Ralph Sabatino, CFLCC Judge Advocate, CPA Ministry of Justice
48. LTC Gary W. Maddocks, S-5 and Executive Officer, 800th MP Brigade
49. LTC James O'Hare, Command Judge Advocate, 800th MP Brigade
50. LTC Robert P. Walters Jr., Commander, 165th MI Battalion (Tactical exploitation)
51. LTC James D. Edwards, Commander, 202nd MI Battalion
52. LTC Vincent Montera, Commander 310th MP Battalion
53. LTC Steve Jordan, former Director, Joint Interrogation and Debriefing Center/LNO to the 205th MI Brigade
54. LTC Leigh A. Coulter, Commander 724th MP Battalion and OIC Arifjan Detachment, 800th MP Brigade
55. LTC Dennis McGlone, Commander, 744th MP Battalion
56. MAJ David Hinzman, S-1, 800th MP Brigade
57. MAJ William D. Proietto, Deputy CJA, 800th MP Brigade
58. MAJ Stacy L. Garrity, S-1 (FWD), 800th MP Brigade
59. MAJ David W. DiNenna, S-3, 320th MP Battalion
60. MAJ Michael Sheridan, XO, 320th MP Battalion
61. MAJ Anthony Cavallaro, S-3, 800th MP Brigade
62. CPT Marc C. Hale, Commander, 670th MP Company
63. CPT Donald Reese, Commander, 372nd MP Company
64. CPT Darren Hampton, Assistant S-3, 320th MP Battalion
65. CPT John Kaires, S-3, 310th MP Battalion
66. CPT Ed Diamantis, S-2, 800th MP Brigade

Nimble Books

67. LTC Jerry L. Phillabaum, Commander, 320th MP Battalion
68. CPT James G. Jones, Commander, 229th MP Company
69. CPT Michael A. Mastrangelo, Jr., Commander, 310th MP Company
70. CPT Lawrence Bush, IG, 800th MP Brigade
71. 1LT Lewis C. Raeder, Platoon Leader, 372nd MP Company
72. 1LT Elvis Mabry, Aide-de-Camp to Brigade Commander, 800th MP Brigade
73. 1LT Warren E. Ford, II, Commander, HHC 320th MP Battalion
74. 2LT David O. Sutton, Platoon Leader, 229th MP Company
75. CW2 Edward J. Rivas, 205th MI Brigade
76. CSM Joseph P. Arrison, Command Sergeant Major, 320th MP Battalion
77. SGM Pascual Cartagena, Command Sergeant Major, 800th MP Brigade
78. CSM Timothy L. Woodcock, Command Sergeant Major, 310th MP Battalion
79. 1SG Dawn J. Rippelmeyer, First Sergeant, 977th MP Company
80. SGM Mark Emerson, Operations SGM, 320th MP Battalion
81. MSG Brian G. Lipinski, First Sergeant, 372nd MP Company
82. MSG Andrew J. Lombardo, Operations Sergeant, 310th MP Battalion
83. SFC Daryl J. Plude, Platoon Sergeant, 229th MP Company
84. SFC Shannon K. Snider, Platoon SGT, 372nd MP Company
85. SFC Keith A. Comer, 372nd MP Company
86. SSG Robert Elliot, Squad Leader, 372nd MP Company
87. SSG Santos A. Cardona, Army Dog Handler
88. SGT Michael Smith, Army Dog Handler
89. MA1 William J. Kimbro, USN Dog Handler
90. Mr. Steve Stephanowicz, US civilian contract Interrogator, CACI, 205th MI Brigade
91. Mr. John Israel, US civilian contract Interpreter, Titan Corporation, 205th MI Brigade
92. FM 3-19.1, Military Police Operations, 22 March 2001
93. CJTF-7 IROE and DROE, Undated
94. CJTF-7 Interrogation and Counter Resistance Policy, 12 October 2003
95. 800th MP Brigade Mobilization Orders
96. Sample Detainee Status Report, 13 March 2004
97. 530th MP Battalion Mission Brief, 11 February 2004
98. Memorandum for Record, CPT Ed Ray, Chief of Military Justice, CFLCC, 9 March 2004
99. SIR 14 January 2004
100. Accountability Plan Recommendations, 9 March 2004
101. 2LT Michael R. Osterhout, S-2, 320th MP Battalion
102. Memorandum of Admonishment from LTG Sanchez to BG Karpinski, 17 January 2004
103. Various SIRs from the 800th MP Brigade/320th MP Battalion
104. 205th MI Brigade SITREP to MG Miller, 12 December 2003
105. SGT William A. Cathcart, 372nd MP Company
106. 1LT Michael A. Drayton, Commander, 870th MP Company

Basic Documents about the Detainees

REFERENCES

1. Geneva Convention Relative to the Treatment of Prisoners of War, 12 August 1949
2. Geneva Convention for the Amelioration of the Condition of the Wounded and Sick in the Armed Forces in the Field, 12 August 1949
3. Geneva Convention for the Amelioration of the Condition of the Wounded, Sick and Shipwrecked Members of Armed Forces at Sea, 12 August 1949
4. Geneva Convention Protocol Relative to the Status of Refugees, 1967
5. Geneva Convention Relative to the Status of Refugees, 1951
6. Geneva Convention for the Protection of War Victims, 12 August 1949
7. Geneva Convention Relative to the Protection of Civilian Persons in Time of War, 12 August 1949
8. DOD Directive 5100.69, "DOD Program for Prisoners of War and other Detainees," 27 December 1972
9. DOD Directive 5100.77 "DOD Law of War Program," 10 July 1979
10. STANAG No. 2044, Procedures for Dealing with Prisoners of War (PW) (Edition 5), 28 June 1994
11. STANAG No. 2033, Interrogation of Prisoners of War (PW) (Edition 6), 6 December 1994
12. AR 190-8, Enemy Prisoners of War, Retained Personnel, Civilian Internees, and Other Detainees, 1 October 1997
13. AR 190-47, The Army Corrections System, 15 August 1996
14. AR 190-14, Carrying of Firearms and Use of Force for Law Enforcement and Security Duties, 12 March 1993
15. AR 195-5, Evidence Procedures, 28 August 1992
16. AR 190-11, Physical Security of Arms, Ammunition and Explosives, 12 February 1998
17. AR 190-12, Military Police Working Dogs, 30 September 1993
18. AR 190-13, The Army Physical Security Program, 30 September 1993
19. AR 380-67, Personnel Security Program, 9 September 1988
20. AR 380-5, Department of the Army Information Security, 31 September 2000
21. AR 670-1, Wear and Appearance of Army Uniforms and Insignia, 5 September 2003
22. AR 190-40, Serious Incident Report, 30 November 1993
23. AR 15-6, Procedures for Investigating Officers and Boards of Officers, 11 May 1988
24. AR 27-10, Military Justice, 6 September 2002
25. AR 635-200, Enlisted Personnel, 1 November 2000
26. AR 600-8-24, Officer Transfers and Discharges, 29 June 2002
27. AR 500-5, Army Mobilization, 6 July 1996
28. AR 600-20, Army Command Policy, 13 May 2002
29. AR 623-105, Officer Evaluation Reports, 1 April 1998
30. AR 175-9, Contractors Accompanying the Force, 29 October 1999
31. FM 3-19.40, Military Police Internment/Resettlement Operations, 1 August 2001
32. FM 3-19.1, Military Police Operations, 22 March 2001
33. FM 3-19.4, Military Police Leaders' Handbook, 4 March 2002
34. FM 3-05.30, Psychological Operations, 19 June 2000

NIMBLE BOOKS

35. FM 33-1-1, Psychological Operations Techniques and Procedures, 5 May 1994
36. FM 34-52, Intelligence Interrogation, 28 September 1992
37. FM 19-15, Civil Disturbances, 25 November 198538.
38. FM 3-0, Operations, 14 June 2001
39. FM 101-5, Staff Organizations and Functions, 23 May 1984
40. FM 3-19.30, Physical Security, 8 January 2001
41. FM 3-21.5, Drill and Ceremonies, 7 July 2003
42. ARTEP 19-546-30 MTP, Mission Training Plan for Military Police Battalion (IR)
43. ARTEP 19-667-30 MTP, Mission Training Plan for Military Police Guard Company
44. ARTEP 19-647-30 MTP, Mission Training Plan for Military Police Escort Guard Company
45. STP 19-95B1-SM, Soldier's Manual, MOS 95B, Military Police, Skill Level 1, 6 August 2002
46. STP 19-95C14-SM-TG, Soldier's Manual and Trainer's Guide for MOS 95C Internment/Resettlement Specialist, Skill Levels 1/2/3/4, 26 March 1999
47. STP 19-95C1-SM MOS 95C, Corrections Specialist, Skill Level 1, Soldier's Manual, 30 September 2003
48. STP 19-95C24-SM-TG MOS 95C, Corrections Specialist, Skill Levels 2/3/4, Soldier's Manual and Trainer's Guide, 30 September 2003
49. Assessment of DOD Counter-Terrorism Interrogation and Detention Operations in Iraq, (MG Geoffrey D. Miller, Commander JTF-GTMO, Guantánamo Bay, Cuba), 9 September 2003
50. Assessment of Detention and Corrections Operations in Iraq, (MG Donald J. Ryder, Provost Marshal General), 6 November 2003
51. CJTF-7 FRAGO #1108, Subject: *includes* para 3.C.8 & 3.C.8.A.1, Assignment of 205 MI BDE CDR Responsibilities for the Baghdad Central Confinement Facility (BCCF), 19 November 2003
52. CJTF-7 FRAGO #749, Subject: Intelligence and Evidence-Led Detention Operations Relating to Detainees, 24 August 2003
53. 800th MP BDE FRAGO # 89, Subject: Rules of Engagement, 26 December 2003
54. CG CJTF-7 Memo: CJTF-7 Interrogation and Counter-Resistance Policy, 12 October 2003
55. CG CJTF-7 Memo: Dignity and Respect While Conducting Operations, 13 December 2003
56. Uniform Code of Military Justice and Manual for Courts Martial, 2002 Edition

BASIC DOCUMENTS ABOUT THE DETAINEES

GENEVA CONVENTION RELATIVE TO THE TREATMENT OF PRISONERS OF WAR OF AUGUST 12, 1949 (GENEVA CONVENTION III)

Entry into Force: 21 October 1950

The undersigned Plenipotentiaries of the Governments represented at the Diplomatic Conference held at Geneva from April 21 to August 12, 1949, for the purpose of revising the Convention concluded at Geneva on July 27, 1929 relative to the Treatment of Prisoners of War, have agreed as follows:

PART I: GENERAL PROVISIONS

Article 1

The High Contracting Parties undertake to respect and to ensure respect for the present Convention in all circumstances.

Article 2

In addition to the provisions which shall be implemented in peace time, the present Convention shall apply to all cases of declared war or of any other armed conflict which may arise between two or more of the High Contracting Parties, even if the state of war is not recognized by one of them.

The Convention shall also apply to all cases of partial or total occupation of the territory of a High Contracting Party, even if the said occupation meets with no armed resistance.

Although one of the Powers in conflict may not be a party to the present Convention, the Powers who are parties thereto shall remain bound by it in their mutual relations. They shall furthermore be bound by the Convention in relation to the said Power, if the latter accepts and applies the provisions thereof.

Article 3

In the case of armed conflict not of an international character occurring in the territory of one of the High Contracting Parties, each Party to the conflict shall be bound to apply, as a minimum, the following provisions:

(1) Persons taking no active part in the hostilities, including members of armed forces who have laid down their arms and those placed hors de combat by sickness, wounds, detention, or any other cause, shall in all circumstances be treated humanely, without any adverse distinction founded on race, colour, religion or faith, sex, birth or wealth, or any other similar criteria.

To this end the following acts are and shall remain prohibited at any time and in any place whatsoever with respect to the above-mentioned persons:

(a) violence to life and person, in particular murder of all kinds, mutilation, cruel treatment and torture;

(b) taking of hostages;

(c) outrages upon personal dignity, in particular, humiliating and degrading treatment;

(d) the passing of sentences and the carrying out of executions without previous judgment pronounced by a regularly constituted court affording all the judicial guarantees which are recognized as indispensable by civilized peoples.

(2) The wounded and sick shall be collected and cared for.

An impartial humanitarian body, such as the International Committee of the Red Cross, may offer its services to the Parties to the conflict.

The Parties to the conflict should further endeavour to bring into force, by means of special agreements, all or part of the other provisions of the present Convention.

The application of the preceding provisions shall not affect the legal status of the Parties to the conflict.

Article 4

A. Prisoners of war, in the sense of the present Convention, are persons belonging to one of the following categories, who have fallen into the power of the enemy:

(1) Members of the armed forces of a Party to the conflict, as well as members of militias or volunteer corps forming part of such armed forces.

(2) Members of other militias and members of other volunteer corps, including those of organized resistance movements, belonging to a Party to the conflict and operating in or outside their own territory, even if this territory is occupied, provided that such militias or volunteer corps, including such organized resistance movements, fulfil the following conditions:

(a) that of being commanded by a person responsible for his subordinates;

(b) that of having a fixed distinctive sign recognizable at a distance;

(c) that of carrying arms openly;

(d) that of conducting their operations in accordance with the laws and customs of war.

(3) Members of regular armed forces who profess allegiance to a government or an authority not recognized by the Detaining Power.

(4) Persons who accompany the armed forces without actually being members thereof, such as civilian members of military aircraft crews, war correspondents, supply contractors, members of labour units or of services responsible for the welfare of the armed forces, provided that they have received authorization, from the armed forces which they accompany, who shall provide them for that purpose with an identity card similar to the annexed model.

(5) Members of crews, including masters, pilots and apprentices, of the merchant marine and the crews of civil aircraft of the Parties to the conflict, who do not benefit by more favourable treatment under any other provisions of international law.

(6) Inhabitants of a non-occupied territory, who on the approach of the enemy spontaneously take up arms to resist the invading forces, without having had time to form themselves into regular armed units, provided they carry arms openly and respect the laws and customs of war.

B. The following shall likewise be treated as prisoners of war under the present Convention:

(1) Persons belonging, or having belonged, to the armed forces of the occupied country, if the occupying Power considers it necessary by reason of such allegiance to intern them, even though it has originally liberated them while hostilities were going on outside the territory it occupies, in particular where such persons have made an unsuccessful attempt to rejoin the armed forces to which they belong and which are engaged in combat, or where they fail to comply with a summons made to them with a view to internment.

(2) The persons belonging to one of the categories enumerated in the present Article, who have been received by neutral or non-belligerent Powers on their territory and whom these Powers are required to intern under international law, without prejudice to any more favourable treatment which these Powers may choose to give and with the exception of Articles 8, 10, 15, 30, fifth paragraph, 58-67, 92, 126 and, where diplomatic relations exist between the Parties to the conflict and the neutral or non-belligerent Power concerned, those Articles concerning the Protecting Power. Where such diplomatic relations exist, the Parties to a conflict on whom these persons depend shall be allowed to perform towards them the functions of a Protecting Power as provided in the present Convention, without prejudice to the functions which these Parties normally exercise in conformity with diplomatic and consular usage and treaties.

C. This Article shall in no way affect the status of medical personnel and chaplains as provided for in Article 33 of the present Convention.

Article 5

The present Convention shall apply to the persons referred to in Article 4 from the time they fall into the power of the enemy and until their final release and repatriation.

Should any doubt arise as to whether persons, having committed a belligerent act and having fallen into the hands of the enemy, belong to any of the categories enumerated in Article 4, such persons shall enjoy the protection of the present Convention until such time as their status has been determined by a competent tribunal.

* * *

Article 7

Prisoners of war may in no circumstances renounce in part or in entirety the rights secured to them by the present Convention, and by the special agreements referred to in the foregoing Article, if such there be.

* * *

PART II: GENERAL PROTECTION OF PRISONERS OF WAR

Article 12

Prisoners of war are in the hands of the enemy Power, but not of the individuals or military units who have captured them. Irrespective of the individual responsibilities that may exist, the Detaining Power is responsible for the treatment given them.

Prisoners of war may only be transferred by the Detaining Power to a Power which is a party to the Convention and after the Detaining Power has satisfied itself of the willingness and ability of such transferee Power to apply the Convention. When prisoners of war are transferred under such circumstances, responsibility for the application of the Convention rests on the Power accepting them while they are in its custody.

Nevertheless, if that Power fails to carry out the provisions of the Convention in any important respect, the Power by whom the prisoners of war were transferred shall, upon being notified by the Protecting Power, take effective measures to correct the situation or shall request the return of the prisoners of war. Such requests must be complied with.

Article 13

Prisoners of war must at all times be humanely treated. Any unlawful act or omission by the Detaining Power causing death or seriously endangering the health of a prisoner of war in its custody is prohibited, and will be regarded as a serious breach of the present Convention. In particular, no prisoner of war may be subjected to physical mutilation or to medical or scientific experiments of any kind which are not justified by the medical, dental or hospital treatment of the prisoner concerned and carried out in his interest.

Likewise, prisoners of war must at all times be protected, particularly against acts of violence or intimidation and against insults and public curiosity.

Measures of reprisal against prisoners of war are prohibited.

Article 14

Prisoners of war are entitled in all circumstances to respect for their persons and their honour.

Women shall be treated with all the regard due to their sex and shall in all cases benefit by treatment as favourable as that granted to men.

Prisoners of war shall retain the full civil capacity which they enjoyed at the time of their capture. The Detaining Power may not restrict the exercise, either within or without its own territory, of the rights such capacity confers except in so far as the captivity requires.

Article 15

The Power detaining prisoners of war shall be bound to provide free of charge for their maintenance and for the medical attention required by their state of health.

Article 16

Taking into consideration the provisions of the present Convention relating to rank and sex, and subject to any privileged treatment which may be accorded to them by reason of their state of health, age or professional qualifications, all prisoners of war shall be treated alike by the Detaining Power, without any adverse distinction based on race, nationality, religious belief or political opinions, or any other distinction founded on similar criteria.

PART III: CAPTIVITY

SECTION I: BEGINNING OF CAPTIVITY

Article 17

Every prisoner of war, when questioned on the subject, is bound to give only his surname, first names and rank, date of birth, and army, regimental, personal or serial number, or failing this, equivalent information.

If he wilfully infringes this rule, he may render himself liable to a restriction of the privileges accorded to his rank or status.

Each Party to a conflict is required to furnish the persons under its jurisdiction who are liable to become prisoners of war, with an identity card showing the owner's surname, first names, rank, army, regimental, personal or serial number or equivalent information, and date of birth. The identity card may, furthermore, bear the signature or the fingerprints, or both, of the owner, and may bear, as well, any other information the Party to the conflict may wish to add concerning persons belonging to its armed forces. As far as possible the card shall measure 6.5 x 10 cm. and shall be issued in duplicate. The identity card shall be shown by the prisoner of war upon demand, but may in no case be taken away from him.

No physical or mental torture, nor any other form of coercion, may be inflicted on prisoners of war to secure from them information of any kind whatever. Prisoners of war who refuse to answer may not be threatened, insulted, or exposed to unpleasant or disadvantageous treatment of any kind.

Prisoners of war who, owing to their physical or mental condition, are unable to state their identity, shall be handed over to the medical service. The identity of such prisoners shall be established by all possible means, subject to the provisions of the preceding paragraph.

The questioning of prisoners of war shall be carried out in a language which they understand.

Article 18

All effects and articles of personal use, except arms, horses, military equipment and military documents, shall remain in the possession of prisoners of war, likewise their metal helmets and gas masks and like articles issued for personal protection. Effects and articles used for their clothing or feeding shall likewise remain in their possession, even if such effects and articles belong to their regulation military equipment.

At no time should prisoners of war be without identity documents. The Detaining Power shall supply such documents to prisoners of war who possess none.

Badges of rank and nationality, decorations and articles having above all a personal or sentimental value may not be taken from prisoners of war.

Sums of money carried by prisoners of war may not be taken away from them except by order of an officer, and after the amount and particulars of the owner have been recorded in a special register and an itemized receipt has been given, legibly inscribed with the name, rank and unit of the person issuing the said receipt. Sums in the currency of the Detaining Power, or which are changed into such currency at the prisoner's request, shall be placed to the credit of the prisoner's account as provided in Article 64.

The Detaining Power may withdraw articles of value from prisoners of war only for reasons of security; when such articles are withdrawn, the procedure laid down for sums of money impounded shall apply.

Such objects, likewise sums taken away in any currency other than that of the Detaining Power and the conversion of which has not been asked for by the owners, shall be kept in the custody of the Detaining Power and shall be returned in their initial shape to prisoners of war at the end of their captivity.

Article 19

Prisoners of war shall be evacuated, as soon as possible after their capture, to camps situated in an area far enough from the combat zone for them to be out of danger.

Only those prisoners of war who, owing to wounds or sickness, would run greater risks by being evacuated than by remaining where they are, may be temporarily kept back in a danger zone.

Prisoners of war shall not be unnecessarily exposed to danger while awaiting evacuation from a fighting zone.

Article 20

The evacuation of prisoners of war shall always be effected humanely and in conditions similar to those for the forces of the Detaining Power in their changes of station.

The Detaining Power shall supply prisoners of war who are being evacuated with sufficient food and potable water, and with the necessary clothing and medical attention. The Detaining Power shall take all suitable precautions to ensure their safety during evacuation, and shall establish as soon as possible a list of the prisoners of war who are evacuated.

If prisoners of war must, during evacuation, pass through transit camps, their stay in such camps shall be as brief as possible.

SECTION II: INTERNMENT OF PRISONERS OF WAR

CHAPTER I: GENERAL OBSERVATIONS

Article 21

The Detaining Power may subject prisoners of war to internment. It may impose on them the obligation of not leaving, beyond certain limits, the camp where they are interned, or if the said camp is fenced in, of not going outside its perimeter. Subject to the provisions of the present Convention relative to penal and disciplinary sanctions, prisoners of war may not be held in close confinement except where necessary to safeguard their health and then only during the continuation of the circumstances which make such confinement necessary.

Prisoners of war may be partially or wholly released on parole or promise, in so far as is allowed by the laws of the Power on which they depend. Such measures shall be taken particularly in cases where this may contribute to the improvement of their state of health. No prisoner of war shall be compelled to accept liberty on parole or promise.

Upon the outbreak of hostilities, each Party to the conflict shall notify the adverse Party of the laws and regulations allowing or forbidding its own nationals to accept liberty on parole or promise. Prisoners of war who are paroled or who have given their promise in conformity with the laws and regulations so notified, are bound on their personal honour scrupulously to fulfil, both towards the Power on which they depend and towards the Power which has captured them, the engagements of their paroles or promises. In such cases, the Power on which they depend is bound neither to require nor to accept from them any service incompatible with the parole or promise given.

Article 22

Prisoners of war may be interned only in premises located on land and affording every guarantee of hygiene and healthfulness. Except in particular cases which are justified by the interest of the prisoners themselves, they shall not be interned in penitentiaries.

Prisoners of war interned in unhealthy areas, or where the climate is injurious for them, shall be removed as soon as possible to a more favourable climate.

The Detaining Power shall assemble prisoners of war in camps or camp compounds according to their nationality, language and customs, provided that such prisoners shall not be separated from prisoners of war belonging to the armed forces with which they were serving at the time of their capture, except with their consent.

Article 23

No prisoner of war may at any time be sent to, or detained in areas where he may be exposed to the fire of the combat zone, nor may his presence be used to render certain points or areas immune from military operations.

Prisoners of war shall have shelters against air bombardment and other hazards of war, to the same extent as the local civilian population. With the exception of those engaged in the protection of their quarters against the aforesaid hazards, they may enter such shelters as soon as possible after the giving of the alarm. Any other protective measure taken in favour of the population shall also apply to them.

Detaining Powers shall give the Powers concerned, through the intermediary of the Protecting Powers, all useful information regarding the geographical location of prisoner of war camps.

Whenever military considerations permit, prisoner of war camps shall be indicated in the day-time by the letters PW or PG, placed so as to be clearly visible from the air. The Powers concerned may, however, agree upon any other system of marking. Only prisoner of war camps shall be marked as such.

Article 24

Transit or screening camps of a permanent kind shall be fitted out under conditions similar to those described in the present Section, and the prisoners therein shall have the same treatment as in other camps.

CHAPTER II: QUARTERS, FOOD AND CLOTHING OF PRISONERS OF WAR

Article 25

Prisoners of war shall be quartered under conditions as favourable as those for the forces of the Detaining Power who are billeted in the same area. The said conditions shall make allowance for the habits and customs of the prisoners and shall in no case be prejudicial to their health.

The foregoing provisions shall apply in particular to the dormitories of prisoners of war as regards both total surface and minimum cubic space, and the general installations, bedding and blankets.

The premises provided for the use of prisoners of war individually or collectively, shall be entirely protected from dampness and adequately heated and lighted, in particular between dusk and lights out. All precautions must be taken against the danger of fire.

In any camps in which women prisoners of war, as well as men, are accommodated, separate dormitories shall be provided for them.

Article 26

The basic daily food rations shall be sufficient in quantity, quality and variety to keep prisoners of war in good health and to prevent loss of weight or the development of nutritional deficiencies. Account shall also be taken of the habitual diet of the prisoners.

The Detaining Power shall supply prisoners of war who work with such additional rations as are necessary for the labour on which they are employed.

Sufficient drinking water shall be supplied to prisoners of war. The use of tobacco shall be permitted.

Prisoners of war shall, as far as possible, be associated with the preparation of their meals; they may be employed for that purpose in the kitchens. Furthermore, they shall be given the means of preparing, themselves, the additional food in their possession.

Adequate premises shall be provided for messing.

Collective disciplinary measures affecting food are prohibited.

Article 27

Clothing, underwear and footwear shall be supplied to prisoners of war in sufficient quantities by the Detaining Power, which shall make allowance for the climate of the region where the prisoners are detained. Uniforms of enemy armed forces captured by the Detaining Power should, if suitable for the climate, be made available to clothe prisoners of war.

The regular replacement and repair of the above articles shall be assured by the Detaining Power. In addition, prisoners of war who work shall receive appropriate clothing, wherever the nature of the work demands.

Article 28

Canteens shall be installed in all camps, where prisoners of war may procure foodstuffs, soap and tobacco and ordinary articles in daily use. The tariff shall never be in excess of local market prices.

The profits made by camp canteens shall be used for the benefit of the prisoners; a special fund shall be created for this purpose. The prisoners' representative shall have the right to collaborate in the management of the canteen and of this fund.

When a camp is closed down, the credit balance of the special fund shall be handed to an international welfare organization, to be employed for the benefit of prisoners of war of the same nationality as those who have contributed to the fund. In case of a general repatriation, such profits shall be kept by the Detaining Power, subject to any agreement to the contrary between the Powers concerned.

CHAPTER III: HYGIENE AND MEDICAL ATTENTION

Article 29

The Detaining Power shall be bound to take all sanitary measures necessary to ensure the cleanliness and healthfulness of camps and to prevent epidemics.

Prisoners of war shall have for their use, day and night, conveniences which conform to the rules of hygiene and are maintained in a constant state of cleanliness. In any camps in which women prisoners of war are accommodated, separate conveniences shall be provided for them.

Also, apart from the baths and showers with which the camps shall be furnished prisoners of war shall be provided with sufficient water and soap for their personal toilet and for washing their personal laundry; the necessary installations, facilities and time shall be granted them for that purpose.

BASIC DOCUMENTS ABOUT THE DETAINEES

Article 30

Every camp shall have an adequate infirmary where prisoners of war may have the attention they require, as well as appropriate diet. Isolation wards shall, if necessary, be set aside for cases of contagious or mental disease.

Prisoners of war suffering from serious disease, or whose condition necessitates special treatment, a surgical operation or hospital care, must be admitted to any military or civilian medical unit where such treatment can be given, even if their repatriation is contemplated in the near future. Special facilities shall be afforded for the care to be given to the disabled, in particular to the blind, and for their rehabilitation, pending repatriation.

Prisoners of war shall have the attention, preferably, of medical personnel of the Power on which they depend and, if possible, of their nationality.

Prisoners of war may not be prevented from presenting themselves to the medical authorities for examination. The detaining authorities shall, upon request, issue to every prisoner who has undergone treatment, an official certificate indicating the nature of his illness or injury, and the duration and kind of treatment received. A duplicate of this certificate shall be forwarded to the Central Prisoners of War Agency.

The costs of treatment, including those of any apparatus necessary for the maintenance of prisoners of war in good health, particularly dentures and other artificial appliances, and spectacles, shall be borne by the Detaining Power.

Article 31

Medical inspections of prisoners of war shall be held at least once a month. They shall include the checking and the recording of the weight of each prisoner of war.

Their purpose shall be, in particular, to supervise the general state of health, nutrition and cleanliness of prisoners and to detect contagious diseases, especially tuberculosis, malaria and venereal disease. For this purpose the most efficient methods available shall be employed, e.g. periodic mass miniature radiography for the early detection of tuberculosis.

Article 32

Prisoners of war who, though not attached to the medical service of their armed forces, are physicians, surgeons, dentists, nurses or medical orderlies, may be required by the Detaining Power to exercise their medical functions in the interests of prisoners of war dependent on the same Power. In that case they shall continue to be prisoners of war, but shall receive the same treatment as corresponding medical personnel retained by the Detaining Power. They shall be exempted from any other work under Article 49.

* * *

CHAPTER V: RELIGIOUS, INTELLECTUAL AND PHYSICAL ACTIVITIES

Article 34

Prisoners of war shall enjoy complete latitude in the exercise of their religious duties, including attendance at the service of their faith, on condition that they comply with the disciplinary routine prescribed by the military authorities.

Adequate premises shall be provided where religious services may be held.

* * *

Article 38

While respecting the individual preferences of every prisoner, the Detaining Power shall encourage the practice of intellectual, educational, and recreational pursuits, sports and games amongst prisoners, and shall take the measures necessary to ensure the exercise thereof by providing them with adequate premises and necessary equipment.

Prisoners shall have opportunities for taking physical exercise, including sports and games, and for being out of doors. Sufficient open spaces shall be provided for this purpose in all camps.

CHAPTER VI: DISCIPLINE

Article 39

Every prisoner of war camp shall be put under the immediate authority of a responsible commissioned officer belonging to the regular armed forces of the Detaining Power. Such officer shall have in his possession a copy of the present Convention; he shall ensure that its provisions are known to the camp staff and the guard and shall be responsible, under the direction of his government, for its application.

Prisoners of war, with the exception of officers, must salute and show to all officers of the Detaining Power the external marks of respect provided for by the regulations applying in their own forces.

Officer prisoners of war are bound to salute only officers of a higher rank of the Detaining Power; they must, however, salute the camp commander regardless of his rank.

Article 40

The wearing of badges of rank and nationality, as well as of decorations, shall be permitted.

Basic Documents about the Detainees

Article 41

In every camp the text of the present Convention and its Annexes and the contents of any special agreement provided for in Article 6, shall be posted, in the prisoners' own language, in places where all may read them. Copies shall be supplied, on request, to the prisoners who cannot have access to the copy which has been posted.

Regulations, orders, notices and publications of every kind relating to the conduct of prisoners of war shall be issued to them in a language which they understand. Such regulations, orders and publications shall be posted in the manner described above and copies shall be handed to the prisoners' representative. Every order and command addressed to prisoners of war individually must likewise be given in a language which they understand.

Article 42

The use of weapons against prisoners of war, especially against those who are escaping or attempting to escape, shall constitute an extreme measure, which shall always be preceded by warnings appropriate to the circumstances.

CHAPTER VII: RANK OF PRISONERS OF WAR

Article 43

Upon the outbreak of hostilities, the Parties to the conflict shall communicate to one another the titles and ranks of all the persons mentioned in Article 4 of the present Convention, in order to ensure equality of treatment between prisoners of equivalent rank. Titles and ranks which are subsequently created shall form the subject of similar communications.

The Detaining Power shall recognize promotions in rank which have been accorded to prisoners of war and which have been duly notified by the Power on which these prisoners depend.

Article 44

Officers and prisoners of equivalent status shall be treated with the regard due to their rank and age.

In order to ensure service in officers' camps, other ranks of the same armed forces who, as far as possible, speak the same language, shall be assigned in sufficient numbers, account being taken of the rank of officers and prisoners of equivalent status. Such orderlies shall not be required to perform any other work.

Supervision of the mess by the officers themselves shall be facilitated in every way.

Article 45

Prisoners of war other than officers and prisoners of equivalent status shall be treated with the regard due to their rank and age.

Supervision of the mess by the prisoners themselves shall be facilitated in every way.

* * *

SECTION III: LABOUR OF PRISONERS OF WAR

Article 49

The Detaining Power may utilize the labour of prisoners of war who are physically fit, taking into account their age, sex, rank and physical aptitude, and with a view particularly to maintaining them in a good state of physical and mental health.

Non-commissioned officers who are prisoners of war shall only be required to do supervisory work. Those not so required may ask for other suitable work which shall, so far as possible, be found for them.

If officers or persons of equivalent status ask for suitable work, it shall be found for them, so far as possible, but they may in no circumstances be compelled to work.

Article 50

Besides work connected with camp administration, installation or maintenance, prisoners of war may be compelled to do only such work as is included in the following classes:

(a) agriculture;

(b) industries connected with the production or the extraction of raw materials, and manufacturing industries, with the exception of metallurgical, machinery and chemical industries; public works and building operations which have no military character or purpose;

(c) transport and handling of stores which are not military in character or purpose;

(d) commercial business, and arts and crafts;

(e) domestic service;

(f) public utility services having no military character or purpose.

Should the above provisions be infringed, prisoners of war shall be allowed to exercise their right of complaint, in conformity with Article 78.

Article 51

Prisoners of war must be granted suitable working conditions, especially as regards accommodation, food, clothing and equipment; such conditions shall not be inferior to those enjoyed by nationals of the Detaining Power employed in similar work; account shall also be taken of climatic conditions.

The Detaining Power, in utilizing the labour of prisoners of war, shall ensure that in areas in which such prisoners are employed, the national legislation concerning the protection of labour, and, more particularly, the regulations for the safety of workers, are duly applied.

Prisoners of war shall receive training and be provided with the means of protection suitable to the work they will have to do and similar to those accorded to the nationals of the Detaining Power. Subject to the provisions of Article 52, prisoners may be submitted to the normal risks run by these civilian workers.

Conditions of labour shall in no case be rendered more arduous by disciplinary measures.

Article 52

Unless he be a volunteer, no prisoner of war may be employed on labour which is of an unhealthy or dangerous nature.

No prisoner of war shall be assigned to labour which would be looked upon as humiliating for a member of the Detaining Power's own forces.

The removal of mines or similar devices shall be considered as dangerous labour.

Article 53

The duration of the daily labour of prisoners of war, including the time of the journey to and from, shall not be excessive, and must in no case exceed that permitted for civilian workers in the district, who are nationals of the Detaining Power and employed on the same work.

Prisoners of war must be allowed, in the middle of the day's work, a rest of not less than one hour. This rest will be the same as that to which workers of the Detaining Power are entitled, if the latter is of longer duration. They shall be allowed in addition a rest of twenty-four consecutive hours every week, preferably on Sunday or the day of rest in their country of origin. Furthermore, every prisoner who has worked for one year shall be granted a rest of eight consecutive days, during which his working pay shall be paid him.

If methods of labour such as piece work are employed, the length of the working period shall not be rendered excessive thereby.

Article 54

The working pay due to prisoners of war shall be fixed in accordance with the provisions of Article 62 of the present Convention.

Prisoners of war who sustain accidents in connection with work, or who contract a disease in the course, or in consequence of their work, shall receive all the care their condition may require. The Detaining Power shall furthermore deliver to such prisoners of war a medical certificate enabling them to submit their claims to the Power on which they depend, and shall send a duplicate to the Central Prisoners of War Agency provided for in Article 123.

Article 55

The fitness of prisoners of war for work shall be periodically verified by medical examinations at least once a month. The examinations shall have particular regard to the nature of the work which prisoners of war are required to do.

If any prisoner of war considers himself incapable of working, he shall be permitted to appear before the medical authorities of his camp. Physicians or surgeons may recommend that the prisoners who are, in their opinion, unfit for work, be exempted therefrom.

Article 56

The organization and administration of labour detachments shall be similar to those of prisoner of war camps.

Every labour detachment shall remain under the control of and administratively part of a prisoner of war camp. The military authorities and the commander of the said camp shall be responsible, under the direction of their government, for the observance of the provisions of the present Convention in labour detachments.

The camp commander shall keep an up-to-date record of the labour detachments dependent on his camp, and shall communicate it to the delegates of the Protecting Power, of the International Committee of the Red Cross, or of other agencies giving relief to prisoners of war, who may visit the camp.

Article 57

The treatment of prisoners of war who work for private persons, even if the latter are responsible for guarding and protecting them, shall not be inferior to that which is provided for by the present Convention. The Detaining Power, the military authorities and the commander of the camp to which such prisoners belong shall be entirely responsible for the maintenance, care, treatment, and payment of the working pay of such prisoners of war.

Such prisoners of war shall have the right to remain in communication with the prisoners' representatives in the camps on which they depend.

Basic Documents about the Detainees

SECTION IV: FINANCIAL RESOURCES OF PRISONERS OF WAR

Article 58

Upon the outbreak of hostilities, and pending an arrangement on this matter with the Protecting Power, the Detaining Power may determine the maximum amount of money in cash or in any similar form, that prisoners may have in their possession. Any amount in excess, which was properly in their possession and which has been taken or withheld from them, shall be placed to their account, together with any monies deposited by them, and shall not be converted into any other currency without their consent.

If prisoners of war are permitted to purchase services or commodities outside the camp against payment in cash, such payments shall b~ made by the prisoner himself or by the camp administration who will charge them to the accounts of the prisoners concerned. The Detaining Power will establish the necessary rules in this respect.

Article 59

Cash which was taken from prisoners of war, in accordance with Article 18, at the time of their capture, and which is in the currency of the Detaining Power, shall be placed to their separate accounts, in accordance with the provisions of Article 64 of the present Section.

The amounts, in the currency of the Detaining Power, due to the conversion of sums in other currencies that are taken from the prisoners of war at the same time, shall also be credited to their separate accounts.

Article 60

The Detaining Power shall grant all prisoners of war a monthly advance of pay, the amount of which shall be fixed by conversion, into the currency of the said Power, of the following amounts:

Category I : Prisoners ranking below sergeants: eight Swiss francs.

Category II : Sergeants and other non-commissioned officers, or prisoners of equivalent rank: twelve Swiss francs.

Category III: Warrant officers and commissioned officers below the rank of major or prisoners of equivalent rank: fifty Swiss francs.

Category IV : Majors, lieutenant-colonels, colonels or prisoners of equivalent rank: sixty Swiss francs.

Category V : General officers or prisoners of war of equivalent rank: seventy-five Swiss francs.

However, the Parties to the conflict concerned may by special agreement modify the amount of advances of pay due to prisoners of the preceding categories.

Furthermore, if the amounts indicated in the first paragraph above would be unduly high compared with the pay of the Detaining Power's armed forces or would, for any reason, seriously embarrass the Detaining Power, then, pending the conclusion of a special agreement with the Power on which the prisoners depend to vary the amounts indicated above, the Detaining Power:

(a) shall continue to credit the accounts of the prisoners with the amounts indicated in the first paragraph above;

(b) may temporarily limit the amount made available from these advances of pay to prisoners of war for their own use, to sums which are reasonable, but which, for Category I, shall never be inferior to the amount that the Detaining Power gives to the members of its own armed forces.

The reasons for any limitations will be given without delay to the Protecting Power.

Article 61

The Detaining Power shall accept for distribution as supplementary pay to prisoners of war sums which the Power on which the prisoners depend may forward to them, on condition that the sums to be paid shall be the same for each prisoner of the same category, shall be payable to all prisoners of that category depending on that Power, and shall be placed in their separate accounts, at the earliest opportunity, in accordance with the provisions of Article 64. Such supplementary pay shall not relieve the Detaining Power of any obligation under this Convention.

Article 62

Prisoners of war shall be paid a fair working rate of pay by the detaining authorities direct. The rate shall be fixed by the said authorities, but shall at no time be less than one-fourth of one Swiss franc for a full working day. The Detaining Power shall inform prisoners of war, as well as the Power on which they depend, through the intermediary of the Protecting Power, of the rate of daily working pay that it has fixed.

Working pay shall likewise be paid by the detaining authorities to prisoners of war permanently detailed to duties or to a skilled or semi-skilled occupation in connection with the administration, installation or maintenance of camps, and to the prisoners who are required to carry out spiritual or medical duties on behalf of their comrades.

The working pay of the prisoners' representative, of his advisers, if any, and of his assistants, shall be paid out of the fund maintained by canteen profits. The scale of this working pay shall be fixed by the prisoners' representative and approved by the camp commander. If there is no such fund, the detaining authorities shall pay these prisoners a fair working rate of pay.

Article 63

Prisoners of war shall be permitted to receive remittances of money addressed to them individually or collectively.

Every prisoner of war shall have at his disposal the credit balance of his account as provided for in the following Article, within the limits fixed by the Detaining Power, which shall make such payments as are requested. Subject to financial or monetary restrictions which the Detaining Power regards as essential, prisoners of war may also have payments made abroad. In this case payments addressed by prisoners of war to dependents shall be given priority.

In any event, and subject to the consent of the Power on which they depend, prisoners may have payments made in their own country, as follows: the Detaining Power shall send to the aforesaid Power through the Protecting Power, a notification giving all the necessary particulars concerning the prisoners of war, the beneficiaries of the payments, and the amount of the sums to be paid, expressed in the Detaining Power's currency. The said notification shall be signed by the prisoners and countersigned by the camp commander. The Detaining Power shall debit the prisoners' account by a corresponding amount; the sums thus debited shall be placed by it to the credit of the Power on which the prisoners depend.

To apply the foregoing provisions, the Detaining Power may usefully consult the Model Regulations in Annex V of the present Convention.

Article 64

The Detaining Power shall hold an account for each prisoner of war, showing at least the following:

(1) The amounts due to the prisoner or received by him as advances of pay, as working pay or derived from any other source; the sums in the currency of the Detaining Power which were taken from him; the sums taken from him and converted at his request into the currency of the said Power.

(2) The payments made to the prisoner in cash, or in any other similar form; the payments made on his behalf and at his request; the sums transferred under Article 63, third paragraph.

Article 65

Every item entered in the account of a prisoner of war shall be countersigned or initialled by him, or by the prisoners' representative acting on his behalf.

Prisoners of war shall at all times be afforded reasonable facilities for consulting and obtaining copies of their accounts, which may likewise be inspected by the representatives of the Protecting Powers at the time of visits to the camp.

When prisoners of war are transferred from one camp to another, their personal accounts will follow them. In case of transfer from one Detaining Power to another, the monies which are their property and are not in the currency of the Detaining Power will follow them. They shall be given certificates for any other monies standing to the credit of their accounts.

The Parties to the conflict concerned may agree to notify to each other at specific intervals through the Protecting Power, the amount of the accounts of the prisoners of war.

Article 66

On the termination of captivity, through the release of a prisoner of war or his repatriation, the Detaining Power shall give him a statement, signed by an authorized officer of that Power, showing the credit balance then due to him. The Detaining Power shall also send through the Protecting Power to the government upon which the prisoner of war depends, lists giving all appropriate particulars of all prisoners of war whose captivity has been terminated by repatriation, release, escape, death or any other means, and showing the amount of their credit balances. Such lists shall be certified on each sheet by an authorized representative of the Detaining Power.

Any of the above provisions of this Article may be varied by mutual agreement between any two Parties to the conflict.

The Power on which the prisoner of war depends shall be responsible for settling with him any credit balance due to him from the Detaining Power on the termination of his captivity.

Article 67

Advances of pay, issued to prisoners of war in conformity with Article 60, shall be considered as made on behalf of the Power on which they depend. Such advances of pay, as well as all payments made by the said Power under Article 63, third paragraph, and Article 68, shall form the subject of arrangements between the Powers concerned, at the close of hostilities.

Article 68

Any claim by a prisoner of war for compensation in respect of any injury or other disability arising out of work shall be referred to the Power on which he depends, through the Protecting Power. In accordance with Article 54, the Detaining Power will, in all cases, provide the prisoner of war concerned with a statement showing the nature of the injury or disability, the circumstances in which it arose and particulars of medical or hospital treatment given for it. This statement will be signed by a responsible officer of the Detaining Power and the medical particulars certified by a medical officer.

Any claim by a prisoner of war for compensation in respect of personal effects monies or valuables impounded by the Detaining Power under Article 18 and not forthcoming on his repatriation, or in respect of loss alleged to be due to the fault of the Detaining Power or any of its servants, shall likewise be referred to the Power on which he depends. Nevertheless, any such personal effects required for use by the prisoners of war whilst in captivity shall be replaced at the expense of the Detaining Power. The Detaining

BASIC DOCUMENTS ABOUT THE DETAINEES

Power will, in all cases, provide the prisoner of war with a statement, signed by a responsible officer, showing all available information regarding the reasons why such effects, monies or valuables have not been restored to him. A copy of this statement will be forwarded to the Power on which he depends through the Central Prisoners of War Agency provided for in Article 123.

SECTION V: RELATIONS OF PRISONERS OF WAR WITH THE EXTERIOR

Article 69

Immediately upon prisoners of war falling into its power, the Detaining Power shall inform them and the Powers on which they depend, through the Protecting Power, of the measures taken to carry out the provisions of the present Section. They shall likewise inform the parties concerned of any subsequent modifications of such measures.

Article 70

Immediately upon capture, or not more than one week after arrival at a camp, even if it is a transit camp, likewise in case of sickness or transfer to hospital or to another camp, every prisoner of war shall be enabled to write direct to his family, on the one hand, and to the Central Prisoners of War Agency provided for in Article 123, on the other hand, a card similar, if possible, to the model annexed to the present Convention, informing his relatives of his capture, address and state of health. The said cards shall be forwarded as rapidly as possible and may not be delayed in any manner.

Article 71

Prisoners of war shall be allowed to send and receive letters and cards. If the Detaining Power deems it necessary to limit the number of letters and cards sent by each prisoner of war, the said number shall not be less than two letters and four cards monthly, exclusive of the capture cards provided for in Article 70, and conforming as closely as possible to the models annexed to the present Convention. Further limitations may be imposed only if the Protecting Power is satisfied that it would be in the interests of the prisoners of war concerned to do so owing to difficulties of translation caused by the Detaining Power's inability to find sufficient qualified linguists to carry out the necessary censorship. If limitations must be placed on the correspondence addressed to prisoners of war, they may be ordered only by the Power on which the prisoners depend, possibly at the request of the Detaining Power. Such letters and cards must be conveyed by the most rapid method at the disposal of the Detaining Power; they may not be delayed or retained for disciplinary reasons.

Prisoners of war who have been without news for a long period, or who are unable to receive news from their next of kin or to give them news by the ordinary postal route, as well as those who are at a great distance from their homes, shall be permitted to send telegrams, the fees being charged against the prisoners of war's accounts with the Detaining Power or paid in the currency at their disposal. They shall likewise benefit by this measure in cases of urgency.

As a general rule, the correspondence of prisoners of war shall be written in their native language. The Parties to the conflict may allow correspondence in other languages.

Sacks containing prisoner of war mail must be securely sealed and labelled so as clearly to indicate their contents, and must be addressed to offices of destination.

Article 72

Prisoners of war shall be allowed to receive by post or by any other means individual parcels or collective shipments containing, in particular, foodstuffs, clothing, medical supplies and articles of a religious, educational or recreational character which may meet their needs, including books, devotional articles, scientific equipment, examination papers, musical instruments, sports outfits and materials allowing prisoners of war to pursue their studies or their cultural activities.

Such shipments shall in no way free the Detaining Power from the obligations imposed upon it by virtue of the present Convention.

The only limits which may be placed on these shipments shall be those proposed by the Protecting Power in the interest of the prisoners themselves, or by the International Committee of the Red Cross or any other organization giving assistance to the prisoners, in respect of their own shipments only, on account of exceptional strain on transport or communications.

The conditions for the sending of individual parcels and collective relief shall, if necessary, be the subject of special agreements between the Powers concerned, which may in no case delay the receipt by the prisoners of relief supplies. Books may not be included in parcels of clothing and foodstuffs. Medical supplies shall, as a rule, be sent in collective parcels.

* * *

Article 76

The censoring of correspondence addressed to prisoners of war or despatched by them shall be done as quickly as possible. Mail shall be censored only by the despatching State and the receiving State, and once only by each.

The examination of consignments intended for prisoners of war shall not be carried out under conditions that will expose the goods contained in them to deterioration; except in the case of written or printed matter, it shall be done in the presence of the addressee, or of a fellow-prisoner duly delegated by him. The delivery to prisoners of individual or collective consignments shall not be delayed under the pretext of difficulties of censorship.

Any prohibition of correspondence ordered by Parties to the conflict, either for military or political reasons, shall be only temporary and its duration shall be as short as possible.

* * *

SECTION VI: RELATIONS BETWEEN PRISONERS OF WAR AND THE AUTHORITIES

CHAPTER I: COMPLAINTS OF PRISONERS OF WAR RESPECTING THE CONDITIONS OF CAPTIVITY

Article 78

Prisoners of war shall have the right to make known to the military authorities in whose power they are, their requests regarding the conditions of captivity to which they are subjected.

They shall also have the unrestricted right to apply to the representatives of the Protecting Powers either through their prisoners' representative or, if they consider it necessary, direct, in order to draw their attention to any points on which they may have complaints to make regarding their conditions of captivity.

These requests and complaints shall not be limited nor considered to be a part of the correspondence quota referred to in Article 71. They must be transmitted immediately. Even if they are recognized to be unfounded, they may not give rise to any punishment.

Prisoners' representatives may send periodic reports on the situation in the camps and the needs of the prisoners of war to the representatives of the Protecting Powers.

CHAPTER II: PRISONER OF WAR REPRESENTATIVES

Article 79

In all places where there are prisoners of war, except in those where there are officers, the prisoners shall freely elect by secret ballot, every six months, and also in case of vacancies, prisoners' representatives entrusted with representing them before the military authorities, the Protecting Powers, the International Committee of the Red Cross and any other organization which may assist them. These prisoners' representatives shall be eligible for re-election.

In camps for officers and persons of equivalent status or in mixed camps, the senior officer among the prisoners of war shall be recognized as the camp prisoners' representative. In camps for officers, he shall be assisted by one or more advisers chosen by the officers; in mixed camps, his assistants shall be chosen from among the prisoners of war who are not officers and shall be elected by them.

Officer prisoners of war of the same nationality shall be stationed in labour camps for prisoners of war, for the purpose of carrying out the camp administration duties for which the prisoners of war are responsible. These officers may be elected as prisoners' representatives under the first paragraph of this Article. In such a case the assistants to the prisoners' representatives shall be chosen from among those prisoners of war who are not officers.

Every representative elected must be approved by the Detaining Power before he has the right to commence his duties. Where the Detaining Power refuses to approve a prisoner of war elected by his fellow prisoners of war, it must inform the Protecting Power of the reason for such refusal.

In all cases the prisoners' representative must have the same nationality, language and customs as the prisoners of war whom he represents. Thus, prisoners of war distributed in different sections of a camp, according to their nationality, language or customs, shall have for each section their own prisoners' representative, in accordance with the foregoing paragraphs.

Article 80

Prisoners' representatives shall further the physical, spiritual and intellectual well-being of prisoners of war.

In particular, where the prisoners decide to organize amongst themselves a system of mutual assistance, this organization will be within the province of the prisoners' representative, in addition to the special duties entrusted to him by other provisions of the present Convention.

Prisoners' representatives shall not be held responsible, simply by reason of their duties, for any offences committed by prisoners of war.

Article 81

Prisoners' representatives shall not be required to perform any other work, if the accomplishment of their duties is thereby made more difficult.

Prisoners' representatives may appoint from amongst the prisoners such assistants as they may require. All material facilities shall be granted them, particularly a certain freedom of movement necessary for the accomplishment of their duties (inspection of labour detachments, receipt of supplies, etc.).

Prisoners' representatives shall be permitted to visit premises where prisoners of war are detained, and every prisoner of war shall have the right to consult freely his prisoners' representative.

All facilities shall likewise be accorded to the prisoners' representatives for communication by post and telegraph with the detaining authorities, the Protecting Powers, the International Committee of the Red Cross and their delegates, the Mixed Medical Commissions and the bodies which give assistance to prisoners of war. Prisoners' representatives of labour detachments shall enjoy the same facilities for communication with the prisoners' representatives of the principal camp. Such communications shall not be restricted, nor considered as forming a part of the quota mentioned in Article 71.

Prisoners' representatives who are transferred shall be allowed a reasonable time to acquaint their successors with current affairs.

In case of dismissal, the reasons therefor shall be communicated to the Protecting Power.

CHAPTER III: PENAL AND DISCIPLINARY SANCTIONS

I. General Provisions

Article 82

A prisoner of war shall be subject to the laws, regulations and orders in force in the armed forces of the Detaining Power; the Detaining Power shall be justified in taking judicial or disciplinary measures in respect of any offence committed by a prisoner of war against such laws, regulations or orders. However, no proceedings or punishments contrary to the provisions of this Chapter shall be allowed.

If any law, regulation or order of the Detaining Power shall declare acts committed by a prisoner of war to be punishable, whereas the same acts would not be punishable if committed by a member of the forces of the Detaining Power, such acts shall entail disciplinary punishments only.

Article 83

In deciding whether proceedings in respect of an offence alleged to have been committed by a prisoner of war shall be judicial or disciplinary, the Detaining Power shall ensure that the competent authorities exercise the greatest leniency and adopt, wherever possible, disciplinary rather than judicial measures.

Article 84

A prisoner of war shall be tried only by a military court, unless the existing laws of the Detaining Power expressly permit the civil courts to try a member of the armed forces of the Detaining Power in respect of the particular offence alleged to have been committed by the prisoner of war.

In no circumstances whatever shall a prisoner of war be tried by a court of any kind which does not offer the essential guarantees of independence and impartiality as generally recognized, and, in particular, the procedure of which does not afford the accused the rights and means of defence provided for in Article 105.

Article 85

Prisoners of war prosecuted under the laws of the Detaining Power for acts committed prior to capture shall retain, even if convicted, the benefits of the present Convention.

Article 86

No prisoner of war may be punished more than once for the same act or on the same charge.

Article 87

Prisoners of war may not be sentenced by the military authorities and courts of the Detaining Power to any penalties except those provided for in respect of members of the armed forces of the said Power who have committed the same acts.

When fixing the penalty, the courts or authorities of the Detaining Power shall take into consideration, to the widest extent possible, the fact that the accused, not being a national of the Detaining Power, is not bound to it by any duty of allegiance, and that he is in its power as the result of circumstances independent of his own will. The said courts or authorities shall be at liberty to reduce the penalty provided for the violation of which the prisoner of war is accused, and shall therefore not be bound to apply the minimum penalty prescribed.

Collective punishment for individual acts, corporal punishment, imprisonment in premises without daylight and, in general, any form of torture or cruelty, are forbidden.

No prisoner of war may be deprived of his rank by the Detaining Power, or prevented from wearing his badges.

Article 88

Officers, non-commissioned officers and men who are prisoners of war undergoing a disciplinary or judicial punishment, shall not be subjected to more severe treatment than that applied in respect of the same punishment to members of the armed forces of the Detaining Power of equivalent rank.

A woman prisoner of war shall not be awarded or sentenced to a punishment more severe, or treated whilst undergoing punishment more severely, than a woman member of the armed forces of the Detaining Power dealt with for a similar offence.

In no case may a woman prisoner of war be awarded or sentenced to a punishment more severe, or treated whilst undergoing punishment more severely, than a male member of the armed forces of the Detaining Power dealt with for a similar offence.

Prisoners of war who have served disciplinary or judicial sentences may not be treated differently from other prisoners of war.

BASIC DOCUMENTS ABOUT THE DETAINEES

II. Disciplinary Sanctions

Article 89

The disciplinary punishments applicable to prisoners of war are the following:

(1) A fine which shall not exceed 50 per cent of the advances of pay and working pay which the prisoner of war would otherwise receive under the provisions of Articles 60 and 62 during a period of not more than thirty days.

(2) Discontinuance of privileges granted over and above the treatment provided for by the present Convention.

(3) Fatigue duties not exceeding two hours daily.

(4) Confinement.

The punishment referred to under (3) shall not be applied to officers.

In no case shall disciplinary punishments be inhuman, brutal or dangerous to the health of prisoners of war.

Article 90

The duration of any single punishment shall in no case exceed thirty days. Any period of confinement awaiting the hearing of a disciplinary offence or the award of disciplinary punishment shall be deducted from an award pronounced against a prisoner of war.

The maximum of thirty days provided above may not be exceeded, even if the prisoner of war is answerable for several acts at the same time when he is awarded punishment, whether such acts are related or not.

The period between the pronouncing of an award of disciplinary punishment and its execution shall not exceed one month.

When a prisoner of war is awarded a further disciplinary punishment, a period of at least three days shall elapse between the execution of any two of the punishments, if the duration of one of these is ten days or more.

Article 91

The escape of a prisoner of war shall be deemed to have succeeded when:

(1) he has joined the armed forces of the Power on which he depends, or those of an allied Power;

(2) he has left the territory under the control of the Detaining Power, or of an ally of the said Power;

(3) he has joined a ship flying the flag of the Power on which he depends, or of an allied Power, in the territorial waters of the Detaining Power, the said ship not being under the control of the last named Power.

Prisoners of war who have made good their escape in the sense of this Article and who are recaptured, shall not be liable to any punishment in respect of their previous escape.

Article 92

A prisoner of war who attempts to escape and is recaptured before having made good his escape in the sense of Article 91 shall be liable only to a disciplinary punishment in respect of this act, even if it is a repeated offence.

A prisoner of war who is recaptured shall be handed over without delay to the competent military authority.

Article 88, fourth paragraph, notwithstanding, prisoners of war punished as a result of an unsuccessful escape may be subjected to special surveillance. Such surveillance must not affect the state of their health, must be undergone in a prisoner of war camp, and must not entail the suppression of any of the safeguards granted them by the present Convention.

Article 93

Escape or attempt to escape, even if it is a repeated offence, shall not be deemed an aggravating circumstance if the prisoner of war is subjected to trial by judicial proceedings in respect of an offence committed during his escape or attempt to escape.

In conformity with the principle stated in Article 83, offences committed by prisoners of war with the sole intention of facilitating their escape and which do not entail any violence against life or limb, such as offences against public property, theft without intention of self-enrichment, the drawing up or use of false papers, or the wearing of civilian clothing, shall occasion disciplinary punishment only.

Prisoners of war who aid or abet an escape or an attempt to escape shall be liable on this count to disciplinary punishment only.

Article 94

If an escaped prisoner of war is recaptured, the Power on which he depends shall be notified thereof in the manner defined in Article 122, provided notification of his escape has been made.

Article 95

A prisoner of war accused of an offence against discipline shall not be kept in confinement pending the hearing unless a member of the armed forces of the Detaining Power would be so kept if he were accused of a similar offence, or if it is essential in the interests of camp order and discipline.

Any period spent by a prisoner of war in confinement awaiting the disposal of an offence against discipline shall be reduced to an absolute minimum and shall not exceed fourteen days.

The provisions of Articles 97 and 98 of this Chapter shall apply to prisoners of war who are in confinement awaiting the disposal of offences against discipline.

Article 96

Acts which constitute offences against discipline shall be investigated immediately.

Without prejudice to the competence of courts and superior military authorities, disciplinary punishment may be ordered only by an officer having disciplinary powers in his capacity as camp commander, or by a responsible officer who replaces him or to whom he has delegated his disciplinary powers.

In no case may such powers be delegated to a prisoner of war or be exercised by a prisoner of war.

Before any disciplinary award is pronounced, the accused shall be given precise information regarding the offences of which he is accused, and given an opportunity of explaining his conduct and of defending himself. He shall be permitted, in particular, to call witnesses and to have recourse, if necessary, to the services of a qualified interpreter. The decision shall be announced to the accused prisoner of war and to the prisoners' representative.

A record of disciplinary punishments shall be maintained by the camp commander and shall be open to inspection by representatives of the Protecting Power.

Article 97

Prisoners of war shall not in any case be transferred to penitentiary establishments (prisons, penitentiaries, convict prisons, etc.) to undergo disciplinary punishment therein.

All premises in which disciplinary punishments are undergone shall conform to the sanitary requirements set forth in Article 25. A prisoner of war undergoing punishment shall be enabled to keep himself in a state of cleanliness, in conformity with Article 29.

Officers and persons of equivalent status shall not be lodged in the same quarters as non-commissioned officers or men.

Women prisoners of war undergoing disciplinary punishment shall be confined in separate quarters from male prisoners of war and shall be under the immediate supervision of women.

Article 98

A prisoner of war undergoing confinement as a disciplinary punishment, shall continue to enjoy the benefits of the provisions of this Convention except in so far as these are necessarily rendered inapplicable by the mere fact that he is confined. In no case may he be deprived of the benefits of the provisions of Articles 78 and 126.

A prisoner of war awarded disciplinary punishment may not be deprived of the prerogatives attached to his rank.

Prisoners of war awarded disciplinary punishment shall be allowed to exercise and to stay in the open air at least two hours daily.

They shall be allowed, on their request, to be present at the daily medical inspections. They shall receive the attention which their state of health requires and, if necessary, shall be removed to the camp infirmary or to a hospital.

They shall have permission to read and write, likewise to send and receive letters. Parcels and remittances of money however, may be withheld from them until the completion of the punishment; they shall meanwhile be entrusted to the prisoners' representative, who will hand over to the infirmary the perishable goods contained in such parcels.

III. Judicial Proceedings

Article 99

No prisoner of war may be tried or sentenced for an act which is not forbidden by the law of the Detaining Power or by international law, in force at the time the said act was committed.

No moral or physical coercion may be exerted on a prisoner of war in order to induce him to admit himself guilty of the act of which he is accused.

No prisoner of war may be convicted without having had an opportunity to present his defence and the assistance of a qualified advocate or counsel.

Article 100

Prisoners of war and the Protecting Powers shall be informed as soon as possible of the offences which are punishable by the death sentence under the laws of the Detaining Power.

Other offences shall not thereafter be made punishable by the death penalty without the concurrence of the Power on which the prisoners of war depend.

The death sentence cannot be pronounced on a prisoner of war unless the attention of the court has, in accordance with Article 87, second paragraph, been particularly called to the fact that since the accused is not a national of the Detaining Power, he is not bound to it by any duty of allegiance, and that he is in its power as the result of circumstances independent of his own will.

Basic Documents about the Detainees

Article 101

If the death penalty is pronounced on a prisoner of war, the sentence shall not be executed before the expiration of a period of at least six months from the date when the Protecting Power receives, at an indicated address, the detailed communication provided for in Article 107.

Article 102

A prisoner of war can be validly sentenced only if the sentence has been pronounced by the same courts according to the same procedure as in the case of members of the armed forces of the Detaining Power, and if, furthermore, the provisions of the present Chapter have been observed.

Article 103

Judicial investigations relating to a prisoner of war shall be conducted as rapidly as circumstances permit and so that his trial shall take place as soon as possible. A prisoner of war shall not be confined while awaiting trial unless a member of the armed forces of the Detaining Power would be so confined if he were accused of a similar offence, or if it is essential to do so in the interests of national security. In no circumstances shall this confinement exceed three months.

Any period spent by a prisoner of war in confinement awaiting trial shall be deducted from any sentence of imprisonment passed upon him and taken into account in fixing any penalty.

The provisions of Articles 97 and 98 of this Chapter shall apply to a prisoner of war whilst in confinement awaiting trial.

Article 104

In any case in which the Detaining Power has decided to institute judicial proceedings against a prisoner of war, it shall notify the Protecting Power as soon as possible and at least three weeks before the opening of the trial. This period of three weeks shall run as from the day on which such notification reaches the Protecting Power at the address previously indicated by the latter to the Detaining Power.

The said notification shall contain the following information:

(1) Surname and first names of the prisoner of war, his rank, his army, regimental, personal or serial number, his date of birth, and his profession or trade, if any;

(2) Place of internment or confinement;

(3) Specification of the charge or charges on which the prisoner of war is to be arraigned, giving the legal provisions applicable;

(4) Designation of the court which will try the case, likewise the date and place fixed for the opening of the trial.

The same communication shall be made by the Detaining Power to the prisoners' representative.

If no evidence is submitted, at the opening of a trial, that the notification referred to above was received by the Protecting Power, by the prisoner of war and by the prisoners' representative concerned, at least three weeks before the opening of the trial, then the latter cannot take place and must be adjourned.

Article 105

The prisoner of war shall be entitled to assistance by one of his prisoner comrades, to defence by a qualified advocate or counsel of his own choice, to the calling of witnesses and, if he deems necessary, to the services of a competent interpreter. He shall be advised of these rights by the Detaining Power in due time before the trial.

Failing a choice by the prisoner of war, the Protecting Power shall find him an advocate or counsel, and shall have at least one week at its disposal for the purpose. The Detaining Power shall deliver to the said Power, on request, a list of persons qualified to present the defence. Failing a choice of an advocate or counsel by the prisoner of war or the Protecting Power, the Detaining Power shall appoint a competent advocate or counsel to conduct the defence.

The advocate or counsel conducting the defence on behalf of the prisoner of war shall have at his disposal a period of two weeks at least before the opening of the trial, as well as the necessary facilities to prepare the defence of the accused. He may, in particular, freely visit the accused and interview him in private. He may also confer with any witnesses for the defence, including prisoners of war. He shall have the benefit of these facilities until the term of appeal or petition has expired.

Particulars of the charge or charges on which the prisoner of war is to be arraigned, as well as the documents which are generally communicated to the accused by virtue of the laws in force in the armed forces of the Detaining Power, shall be communicated to the accused prisoner of war in a language which he understands, and in good time before the opening of the trial. The same communication in the same circumstances shall be made to the advocate or counsel conducting the defence on behalf of the prisoner of war.

The representatives of the Protecting Power shall be entitled to attend the trial of the case, unless, exceptionally, this is held in camera in the interest of State security. In such a case the Detaining Power shall advise the Protecting Power accordingly.

Article 106

Every prisoner of war shall have, in the same manner as the members of the armed forces of the Detaining Power, the right of appeal or petition from any sentence pronounced upon him, with a view to the quashing or revising of the sentence or the reopening of the trial. He shall be fully informed of his right to appeal or petition and of the time limit within which he may do so.

Article 107

Any judgment and sentence pronounced upon a prisoner of war shall be immediately reported to the Protecting Power in the form of a summary communication, which shall also indicate whether he has the right of appeal with a view to the quashing of the sentence or the reopening of the trial. This communication shall likewise be sent to the prisoners' representative concerned. It shall also be sent to the accused prisoner of war in a language he understands, if the sentence was not pronounced in his presence. The Detaining Power shall also immediately communicate to the Protecting Power the decision of the prisoner of war to use or to waive his right of appeal.

Furthermore, if a prisoner of war is finally convicted or if a sentence pronounced on a prisoner of war in the first instance is a death sentence, the Detaining Power shall as soon as possible address to the Protecting Power a detailed communication containing:

(1) the precise wording of the finding and sentence;

(2) a summarized report of any preliminary investigation and of the trial, emphasizing in particular the elements of the prosecution and the defence;

(3) notification, where applicable, of the establishment where the sentence will be served.

The communications provided for in the foregoing sub-paragraphs shall be sent to the Protecting Power at the address previously made known to the Detaining Power.

Article 108

Sentences pronounced on prisoners of war after a conviction has become duly enforceable, shall be served in the same establishments and under the same conditions as in the case of members of the armed forces of the Detaining Power. These conditions shall in all cases conform to the requirements of health and humanity.

A woman prisoner of war on whom such a sentence has been pronounced shall be confined in separate quarters and shall be under the supervision of women.

In any case, prisoners of war sentenced to a penalty depriving them of their liberty shall retain the benefit of the provisions of Articles 78 and 126 of the present Convention. Furthermore, they shall be entitled to receive and despatch correspondence, to receive at least one relief parcel monthly, to take regular exercise in the open air, to have the medical care required by their state of health, and the spiritual assistance they may desire. Penalties to which they may be subjected shall be in accordance with the provisions of Article 87, third paragraph.

PART IV: TERMINATION OF CAPTIVITY

SECTION I: DIRECT REPATRIATION AND ACCOMMODATION IN NEUTRAL COUNTRIES

Article 109

Subject to the provisions of the third paragraph of this Article, Parties to the conflict are bound to send back to their own country, regardless of number or rank, seriously wounded and seriously sick prisoners of war, after having cared for them until they are fit to travel, in accordance with the first paragraph of the following Article.

Throughout the duration of hostilities, Parties to the conflict shall endeavour, with the cooperation of the neutral Powers concerned, to make arrangements for the accommodation in neutral countries of the sick and wounded prisoners of war referred to in the second paragraph of the following Article. They may, in addition, conclude agreements with a view to the direct repatriation or internment in a neutral country of able-bodied prisoners of war who have undergone a long period of captivity.

No sick or injured prisoner of war who is eligible for repatriation under the first paragraph of this Article, may be repatriated against his will during hostilities.

Article 110

The following shall be repatriated direct:

(1) Incurably wounded and sick whose mental or physical fitness seems to have been gravely diminished.

(2) Wounded and sick who, according to medical opinion, are not likely to recover within one year, whose condition requires treatment and whose mental or physical fitness seems to have been gravely diminished.

(3) Wounded and sick who have recovered, but whose mental or physical fitness seems to have been gravely and permanently diminished.

The following may be accommodated in a neutral country:

(1) Wounded and sick whose recovery may be expected within one year of the date of the wound or the beginning of the illness, if treatment in a neutral country might increase the prospects of a more certain and speedy recovery.

(2) Prisoners of war whose mental or physical health, according to medical opinion, is seriously threatened by continued captivity, but whose accommodation in a neutral country might remove such a threat.

The conditions which prisoners of war accommodated in a neutral country must fulfil in order to permit their repatriation shall be fixed, as shall likewise their status, by agreement between the Powers concerned. In general, prisoners of war who have been accommodated in a neutral country, and who belong to the following categories, should be repatriated:

(1) Those whose state of health has deteriorated so as to fulfil the condition laid down for direct repatriation;

(2) Those whose mental or physical powers remain, even after treatment, considerably impaired.

If no special agreements are concluded between the Parties to the conflict concerned, to determine the cases of disablement or sickness entailing direct repatriation or accommodation in a neutral country, such cases shall be settled in accordance with the principles laid down in the Model Agreement concerning direct repatriation and accommodation in neutral countries of wounded and sick prisoners of war and in the Regulations concerning Mixed Medical Commissions annexed to the present Convention.

* * *

Article 115

No prisoner of war on whom a disciplinary punishment has been imposed and who is eligible for repatriation or for accommodation in a neutral country, may be kept back on the plea that he has not undergone his punishment.

Prisoners of war detained in connection with a judicial prosecution or conviction, and who are designated for repatriation or accommodation in a neutral country, may benefit by such measures before the end of the proceedings or the completion of the punishment, if the Detaining Power consents.

Parties to the conflict shall communicate to each other the names of those who will be detained until the end of the proceedings or the completion of the punishment.

* * *

Article 117

No repatriated person may be employed on active military service.

SECTION II: RELEASE AND REPATRIATION OF PRISONERS OF WAR AT THE CLOSE OF HOSTILITIES

Article 118

Prisoners of war shall be released and repatriated without delay after the cessation of active hostilities.

SECTION III: DEATH OF PRISONERS OF WAR

Article 120

Wills of prisoners of war shall be drawn up so as to satisfy the conditions of validity required by the legislation of their country of origin, which will take steps to inform the Detaining Power of its requirements in this respect. At the request of the prisoner of war and, in all cases, after death, the will shall be transmitted without delay to the Protecting Power; a certified copy shall be sent to the Central Agency.

Death certificates, in the form annexed to the present Convention, or lists certified by a responsible officer, of all persons who die as prisoners of war shall be forwarded as rapidly as possible to the Prisoner of War Information Bureau established in accordance with Article 122. The death certificates or certified lists shall show particulars of identity as set out in the third paragraph of Article 17, and also the date and place of death, the cause of death, the date and place of burial and all particulars necessary to identify the graves.

The burial or cremation of a prisoner of war shall be preceded by a medical examination of the body with a view to confirming death and enabling a report to be made and, where necessary, establishing identity.

The detaining authorities shall ensure that prisoners of war who have died in captivity are honourably buried, if possible according to the rites of the religion to which they belonged, and that their graves are respected, suitably maintained and marked so as to be found at any time. Wherever possible, deceased prisoners of war who depended on the same Power shall be interred in the same place.

Deceased prisoners of war shall be buried in individual graves unless unavoidable circumstances require the use of collective graves. Bodies may be cremated only for imperative reasons of hygiene, on account of the religion of the deceased or in accordance with his express wish to this effect. In case of cremation, the fact shall be stated and the reasons given in the death certificate of the deceased.

In order that graves may always be found, all particulars of burials and graves shall be recorded with a Graves Registration Service established by the Detaining Power. Lists of graves and particulars of the prisoners of war interred in cemeteries and elsewhere shall be transmitted to the Power on which such prisoners of war depended. Responsibility for the care of these graves and for records of any subsequent moves of the bodies shall rest on the Power controlling the territory, if a Party to the present Convention. These provisions shall also apply to the ashes, which shall be kept by the Graves Registration Service until proper disposal thereof in accordance with the wishes of the home country.

Basic Documents about the Detainees

Article 121

Every death or serious injury of a prisoner of war caused or suspected to have been caused by a sentry, another prisoner of war, or any other person, as well as any death the cause of which is unknown, shall be immediately followed by an official enquiry by the Detaining Power.

A communication on this subject shall be sent immediately to the Protecting Power. Statements shall be taken from witnesses, especially from those who are prisoners of war, and a report including such statements shall be forwarded to the Protecting Power.

If the enquiry indicates the guilt of one or more persons, the Detaining Power shall take all measures for the prosecution of the person or persons responsible.

NIMBLE BOOKS

GENEVA CONVENTION (IV) RELATIVE TO THE PROTECTION OF CIVILIAN PERSONS IN TIME OF WAR (GENEVA CONVENTION IV)

Signed at Geneva, 12 August 1949

The undersigned Plenipotentiaries of the Governments represented at the Diplomatic Conference held at Geneva from 21 April to 12 August 1949, for the purpose of establishing a Convention for the Protection of Civilians in Time of War, have agreed as follows:

PART I: GENERAL PROVISIONS

Article 1

The High Contracting Parties undertake to respect and to ensure respect for the present Convention in all circumstances.

Article 2

In addition to the provisions which shall be implemented in peace-time, the present Convention shall apply to all cases of declared war or of any other armed conflict which may arise between two or more of the High Contracting Parties, even if the state of war is not recognized by one of them.

The Convention shall also apply to all cases of partial or total occupation of the territory of a High Contracting Party, even if the said occupation meets with no armed resistance.

Although one of the Powers in conflict may not be a party to the present Convention, the Powers who are parties thereto shall remain bound by it in their mutual relations. They shall furthermore be bound by the Convention in relation to the said Power, if the latter accepts and applies the provisions thereof.

Article 3

In the case of armed conflict not of an international character occurring in the territory of one of the High Contracting Parties, each Party to the conflict shall be bound to apply, as a minimum, the following provisions:

(1) Persons taking no active part in the hostilities, including members of armed forces who have laid down their arms and those placed hors de combat by sickness, wounds, detention, or any other cause, shall in all circumstances be treated humanely, without any adverse distinction founded on race, colour, religion or faith, sex, birth or wealth, or any other similar criteria.

To this end the following acts are and shall remain prohibited at any time and in any place whatsoever with respect to the above-mentioned persons:

(a) violence to life and person, in particular murder of all kinds, mutilation, cruel treatment and torture;

(b) taking of hostages;

(c) outrages upon personal dignity, in particular humiliating and degrading treatment;

(d) the passing of sentences and the carrying out of executions without previous judgment pronounced by a regularly constituted court, affording all the judicial guarantees which are recognized as indispensable by civilized peoples.

(2) The wounded and sick shall be collected and cared for.

An impartial humanitarian body, such as the International Committee of the Red Cross, may offer its services to the Parties to the conflict.

The Parties to the conflict should further endeavour to bring into force, by means of special agreements, all or part of the other provisions of the present Convention.

The application of the preceding provisions shall not affect the legal status of the Parties to the conflict.

Article 4

Persons protected by the Convention are those who, at a given moment and in any manner whatsoever, find themselves, in case of a conflict or occupation, in the hands of a Party to the conflict or Occupying Power of which they are not nationals.

Nationals of a State which is not bound by the Convention are not protected by it. Nationals of a neutral State who find themselves in the territory of a belligerent State, and nationals of a co-belligerent State, shall not be regarded as protected persons while the State of which they are nationals has normal diplomatic representation in the State in whose hands they are.

The provisions of Part II are, however, wider in application, as defined in Article 13.

Persons protected by the Geneva Convention for the Amelioration of the Condition of the Wounded and Sick in Armed Forces in the Field of 12 August 1949, or by the Geneva Convention for the Amelioration of the Condition of Wounded, Sick and Shipwrecked Members of Armed Forces at Sea of 12 August 1949, or by the Geneva Convention relative to the Treatment of Prisoners of War of 12 August 1949, shall not be considered as protected persons within the meaning of the present Convention.

Basic Documents about the Detainees

Article 5

Where in the territory of a Party to the conflict, the latter is satisfied that an individual protected person is definitely suspected of or engaged in activities hostile to the security of the State, such individual person shall not be entitled to claim such rights and privileges under the present Convention as would, if exercised in the favour of such individual person, be prejudicial to the security of such State.

Where in occupied territory an individual protected person is detained as a spy or saboteur, or as a person under definite suspicion of activity hostile to the security of the Occupying Power, such person shall, in those cases where absolute military security so requires, be regarded as having forfeited rights of communication under the present Convention.

In each case, such persons shall nevertheless be treated with humanity and, in case of trial, shall not be deprived of the rights of fair and regular trial prescribed by the present Convention. They shall also be granted the full rights and privileges of a protected person under the present Convention at the earliest date consistent with the security of the State or Occupying Power, as the case may be.

Article 6

The present Convention shall apply from the outset of any conflict or occupation mentioned in Article 2.

In the territory of Parties to the conflict, the application of the present Convention shall cease on the general close of military operations.

In the case of occupied territory, the application of the present Convention shall cease one year after the general close of military operations; however, the Occupying Power shall be bound, for the duration of the occupation, to the extent that such Power exercises the functions of government in such territory, by the provisions of the following Articles of the present Convention: 1 to 12, 27, 29 to 34, 47, 49, 51, 52, 53, 59, 61 to 77, 143.

Protected persons whose release, repatriation or re-establishment may take place after such dates shall meanwhile continue to benefit by the present Convention.

Article 7

In addition to the agreements expressly provided for in Articles 11, 14, 15, 17, 36, 108, 109, 132, 133 and 149, the High Contracting Parties may conclude other special agreements for all matters concerning which they may deem it suitable to make separate provision. No special agreement shall adversely affect the situation of protected persons, as defined by the present Convention, not restrict the rights which it confers upon them.

Protected persons shall continue to have the benefit of such agreements as long as the Convention is applicable to them, except where express provisions to the contrary are contained in the aforesaid or in subsequent agreements, or where more favourable measures have been taken with regard to them by one or other of the Parties to the conflict.

Article 8

Protected persons may in no circumstances renounce in part or in entirety the rights secured to them by the present Convention, and by the special agreements referred to in the foregoing Article, if such there be.

Article 9

The present Convention shall be applied with the cooperation and under the scrutiny of the Protecting Powers whose duty it is to safeguard the interests of the Parties to the conflict. For this purpose, the Protecting Powers may appoint, apart from their diplomatic or consular staff, delegates from amongst their own nationals or the nationals of other neutral Powers. The said delegates shall be subject to the approval of the Power with which they are to carry out their duties.

The Parties to the conflict shall facilitate to the greatest extent possible the task of the representatives or delegates of the Protecting Powers.

The representatives or delegates of the Protecting Powers shall not in any case exceed their mission under the present Convention.

They shall, in particular, take account of the imperative necessities of security of the State wherein they carry out their duties.

Article 10

The provisions of the present Convention constitute no obstacle to the humanitarian activities which the International Committee of the Red Cross or any other impartial humanitarian organization may, subject to the consent of the Parties to the conflict concerned, undertake for the protection of civilian persons and for their relief.

Article 11

The High Contracting Parties may at any time agree to entrust to an international organization which offers all guarantees of impartiality and efficacy the duties incumbent on the Protecting Powers by virtue of the present Convention.

When persons protected by the present Convention do not benefit or cease to benefit, no matter for what reason, by the activities of a Protecting Power or of an organization provided for in the first paragraph above, the Detaining Power shall request a neutral State, or such an organization, to undertake the functions performed under the present Convention by a Protecting Power designated by the Parties to a conflict.

If protection cannot be arranged accordingly, the Detaining Power shall request or shall accept, subject to the provisions of this Article, the offer of the services of a humanitarian organization, such as the International Committee of the Red Cross, to assume the humanitarian functions performed by Protecting Powers under the present Convention.

Any neutral Power or any organization invited by the Power concerned or offering itself for these purposes, shall be required to act with a sense of responsibility towards the Party to the conflict on which persons protected by the present Convention depend, and shall be required to furnish sufficient assurances that it is in a position to undertake the appropriate functions and to discharge them impartially.

No derogation from the preceding provisions shall be made by special agreements between Powers one of which is restricted, even temporarily, in its freedom to negotiate with the other Power or its allies by reason of military events, more particularly where the whole, or a substantial part, of the territory of the said Power is occupied.

Whenever in the present Convention mention is made of a Protecting Power, such mention applies to substitute organizations in the sense of the present Article.

The provisions of this Article shall extend and be adapted to cases of nationals of a neutral State who are in occupied territory or who find themselves in the territory of a belligerent State in which the State of which they are nationals has not normal diplomatic representation.

Article 12

In cases where they deem it advisable in the interest of protected persons, particularly in cases of disagreement between the Parties to the conflict as to the application or interpretation of the provisions of the present Convention, the Protecting Powers shall lend their good offices with a view to settling the disagreement.

For this purpose, each of the Protecting Powers may, either at the invitation of one Party or on its own initiative, propose to the Parties to the conflict a meeting of their representatives, and in particular of the authorities responsible for protected persons, possibly on neutral territory suitably chosen. The Parties to the conflict shall be bound to give effect to the proposals made to them for this purpose. The Protecting Powers may, if necessary, propose for approval by the Parties to the conflict a person belonging to a neutral Power, or delegated by the International Committee of the Red Cross, who shall be invited to take part in such a meeting.

PART II: GENERAL PROTECTION OF POPULATIONS AGAINST CERTAIN CONSEQUENCES OF WAR

Article 13

The provisions of Part II cover the whole of the populations of the countries in conflict, without any adverse distinction based, in particular, on race, nationality, religion or political opinion, and are intended to alleviate the sufferings caused by war.

Article 14

In time of peace, the High Contracting Parties and, after the outbreak of hostilities, the Parties thereto, may establish in their own territory and, if the need arises, in occupied areas, hospital and safety zones and localities so organized as to protect from the effects of war, wounded, sick and aged persons, children under fifteen, expectant mothers and mothers of children under seven.

Upon the outbreak and during the course of hostilities, the Parties concerned may conclude agreements on mutual recognition of the zones and localities they have created. They may for this purpose implement the provisions of the Draft Agreement annexed to the present Convention, with such amendments as they may consider necessary.

The Protecting Powers and the International Committee of the Red Cross are invited to lend their good offices in order to facilitate the institution and recognition of these hospital and safety zones and localities.

Article 15

Any Party to the conflict may, either direct or through a neutral State or some humanitarian organization, propose to the adverse Party to establish, in the regions where fighting is taking place, neutralized zones intended to shelter from the effects of war the following persons, without distinction:

  (a) wounded and sick combatants or non-combatants;

  (b) civilian persons who take no part in hostilities, and who, while they reside in the zones, perform no work of a military character.

When the Parties concerned have agreed upon the geographical position, administration, food supply and supervision of the proposed neutralized zone, a written agreement shall be concluded and signed by the representatives of the Parties to the conflict. The agreement shall fix the beginning and the duration of the neutralization of the zone.

Article 16

The wounded and sick, as well as the infirm, and expectant mothers, shall be the object of particular protection and respect.

As far as military considerations allow, each Party to the conflict shall facilitate the steps taken to search for the killed and wounded, to assist the shipwrecked and other persons exposed to grave danger, and to protect them against pillage and ill-treatment.

Article 17

The Parties to the conflict shall endeavour to conclude local agreements for the removal from besieged or encircled areas, of wounded, sick, infirm, and aged persons, children and maternity cases, and for the passage of ministers of all religions, medical personnel and medical equipment on their way to such areas.

Article 18

Civilian hospitals organized to give care to the wounded and sick, the infirm and maternity cases, may in no circumstances be the object of attack but shall at all times be respected and protected by the Parties to the conflict.

States which are Parties to a conflict shall provide all civilian hospitals with certificates showing that they are civilian hospitals and that the buildings which they occupy are not used for any purpose which would deprive these hospitals of protection in accordance with Article 19.

Civilian hospitals shall be marked by means of the emblem provided for in Article 38 of the Geneva Convention for the Amelioration of the Condition of the Wounded and Sick in Armed Forces in the Field of 12 August 1949, but only if so authorized by the State.

The Parties to the conflict shall, in so far as military considerations permit, take the necessary steps to make the distinctive emblems indicating civilian hospitals clearly visible to the enemy land, air and naval forces in order to obviate the possibility of any hostile action.

In view of the dangers to which hospitals may be exposed by being close to military objectives, it is recommended that such hospitals be situated as far as possible from such objectives.

Article 19

The protection to which civilian hospitals are entitled shall not cease unless they are used to commit, outside their humanitarian duties, acts harmful to the enemy. Protection may, however, cease only after due warning has been given, naming, in all appropriate cases, a reasonable time limit and after such warning has remained unheeded. The fact that sick or wounded members of the armed forces are nursed in these hospitals, or the presence of small arms and ammunition taken from such combatants which have not yet been handed to the proper service, shall not be considered to be acts harmful to the enemy.

Article 20

Persons regularly and solely engaged in the operation and administration of civilian hospitals, including the personnel engaged in the search for, removal and transporting of and caring for wounded and sick civilians, the infirm and maternity cases shall be respected and protected.

In occupied territory and in zones of military operations, the above personnel shall be recognizable by means of an identity card certifying their status, bearing the photograph of the holder and embossed with the stamp of the responsible authority, and also by means of a stamped, water-resistant armlet which they shall wear on the left arm while carrying out their duties. This armlet shall be issued by the State and shall bear the emblem provided for in Article 38 of the Geneva Convention for the Amelioration of the Condition of the Wounded and Sick in Armed Forces in the Field of 12 August 1949.

Other personnel who are engaged in the operation and administration of civilian hospitals shall be entitled to respect and protection and to wear the armlet, as provided in and under the conditions prescribed in this Article, while they are employed on such duties. The identity card shall state the duties on which they are employed.

The management of each hospital shall at all times hold at the disposal of the competent national or occupying authorities an up-to-date list of such personnel.

Article 21

Convoys of vehicles or hospital trains on land or specially provided vessels on sea, conveying wounded and sick civilians, the infirm and maternity cases, shall be respected and protected in the same manner as the hospitals provided for in Article 18, and shall be marked, with the consent of the State, by the display of the distinctive emblem provided for in Article 38 of the Geneva Convention for the Amelioration of the Condition of the Wounded and Sick in Armed Forces in the Field of 12 August 1949.

Article 22

Aircraft exclusively employed for the removal of wounded and sick civilians, the infirm and maternity cases or for the transport of medical personnel and equipment, shall not be attacked, but shall be respected while flying at heights, times and on routes specifically agreed upon between all the Parties to the conflict concerned.

They may be marked with the distinctive emblem provided for in Article 38 of the Geneva Convention for the Amelioration of the Condition of the Wounded and Sick in Armed Forces in the Field of 12 August 1949.

Unless agreed otherwise, flights over enemy or enemy occupied territory are prohibited.

Such aircraft shall obey every summons to land. In the event of a landing thus imposed, the aircraft with its occupants may continue its flight after examination, if any.

Article 23

Each High Contracting Party shall allow the free passage of all consignments of medical and hospital stores and objects necessary for religious worship intended only for civilians of another High Contracting Party, even if the latter is its adversary. It shall likewise permit the free passage of all consignments of essential foodstuffs, clothing and tonics intended for children under fifteen, expectant mothers and maternity cases.

The obligation of a High Contracting Party to allow the free passage of the consignments indicated in the preceding paragraph is subject to the condition that this Party is satisfied that there are no serious reasons for fearing:

(a) that the consignments may be diverted from their destination,

(b) that the control may not be effective, or

(c) that a definite advantage may accrue to the military efforts or economy of the enemy through the substitution of the above-mentioned consignments for goods which would otherwise be provided or produced by the enemy or through the release of such material, services or facilities as would otherwise be required for the production of such goods.

The Power which allows the passage of the consignments indicated in the first paragraph of this Article may make such permission conditional on the distribution to the persons benefited thereby being made under the local supervision of the Protecting Powers.

Such consignments shall be forwarded as rapidly as possible, and the Power which permits their free passage shall have the right to prescribe the technical arrangements under which such passage is allowed.

Article 24

The Parties to the conflict shall take the necessary measures to ensure that children under fifteen, who are orphaned or are separated from their families as a result of the war, are not left to their own resources, and that their maintenance, the exercise of their religion and their education are facilitated in all circumstances. Their education shall, as far as possible, be entrusted to persons of a similar cultural tradition.

The Parties to the conflict shall facilitate the reception of such children in a neutral country for the duration of the conflict with the consent of the Protecting Power, if any, and under due safeguards for the observance of the principles stated in the first paragraph.

They shall, furthermore, endeavour to arrange for all children under twelve to be identified by the wearing of identity discs, or by some other means.

Article 25

All persons in the territory of a Party to the conflict, or in a territory occupied by it, shall be enabled to give news of a strictly personal nature to members of their families, wherever they may be, and to receive news from them. This correspondence shall be forwarded speedily and without undue delay.

If, as a result of circumstances, it becomes difficult or impossible to exchange family correspondence by the ordinary post, the Parties to the conflict concerned shall apply to a neutral intermediary, such as the Central Agency provided for in Article 140, and shall decide in consultation with it how to ensure the fulfilment of their obligations under the best possible conditions, in particular with the cooperation of the National Red Cross (Red Crescent, Red Lion and Sun) Societies.

If the Parties to the conflict deem it necessary to restrict family correspondence, such restrictions shall be confined to the compulsory use of standard forms containing twenty-five freely chosen words, and to the limitation of the number of these forms despatched to one each month.

Article 26

Each Party to the conflict shall facilitate enquiries made by members of families dispersed owing to the war, with the object of renewing contact with one another and of meeting, if possible. It shall encourage, in particular, the work of organizations engaged on this task provided they are acceptable to it and conform to its security regulations.

PART III: STATUS AND TREATMENT OF PROTECTED PERSONS

SECTION I: Provisions Common to the Territories of the Parties to the Conflict and to Occupied Territories

Article 27

Protected persons are entitled, in all circumstances, to respect for their persons, their honour, their family rights, their religious convictions and practices, and their manners and customs. They shall at all times be humanely treated, and shall be protected especially against all acts of violence or threats thereof and against insults and public curiosity.

Women shall be especially protected against any attack on their honour, in particular against rape, enforced prostitution, or any form of indecent assault.

Without prejudice to the provisions relating to their state of health, age and sex, all protected persons shall be treated with the same consideration by the Party to the conflict in whose power they are, without any adverse distinction based, in particular, on race, religion or political opinion.

However, the Parties to the conflict may take such measures of control and security in regard to protected persons as may be necessary as a result of the war.

Article 28

The presence of a protected person may not be used to render certain points or areas immune from military operations.

Article 29

The Party to the conflict in whose hands protected persons may be, is responsible for the treatment accorded to them by its agents, irrespective of any individual responsibility which may be incurred.

Article 30

Protected persons shall have every facility for making application to the Protecting Powers, the International Committee of the Red Cross, the National Red Cross (Red Crescent, Red Lion and Sun) Society of the country where they may be, as well as to any organization that might assist them.

These several organizations shall be granted all facilities for that purpose by the authorities, within the bounds set by military or security considerations.

Apart from the visits of the delegates of the Protecting Powers and of the International Committee of the Red Cross, provided for by Article 143, the Detaining or Occupying Powers shall facilitate, as much as possible, visits to protected persons by the representatives of other organizations whose object is to give spiritual aid or material relief to such persons.

Article 31

No physical or moral coercion shall be exercised against protected persons, in particular to obtain information from them or from third parties.

Article 32

The High Contracting Parties specifically agree that each of them is prohibited from taking any measure of such a character as to cause the physical suffering or extermination of protected persons in their hands. This prohibition applies not only to murder, torture, corporal punishments, mutilation and medical or scientific experiments not necessitated by the medical treatment of a protected person, but also to any other measures of brutality whether applied by civilian or military agents.

Article 33

No protected person may be punished for an offence he or she has not personally committed. Collective penalties and likewise all measures of intimidation or of terrorism are prohibited.

Pillage is prohibited.

Reprisals against protected persons and their property are prohibited.

Article 34

The taking of hostages is prohibited.

SECTION II: Aliens in the Territory of a Party to the Conflict

Article 35

All protected persons who may desire to leave the territory at the outset of, or during a conflict, shall be entitled to do so, unless their departure is contrary to the national interests of the State. The applications of such persons to leave shall be decided in accordance with regularly established procedures and the decision shall be taken as rapidly as possible. Those persons permitted to leave may provide themselves with the necessary funds for their journey and take with them a reasonable amount of their effects and articles of personal use.

If any such person is refused permission to leave the territory, he shall be entitled to have refusal reconsidered, as soon as possible by an appropriate court or administrative board designated by the Detaining Power for that purpose.

Upon request, representatives of the Protecting Power shall, unless reasons of security prevent it, or the persons concerned object, be furnished with the reasons for refusal of any request for permission to leave the territory and be given, as expeditiously as possible, the names of all persons who have been denied permission to leave.

Article 36

Departures permitted under the foregoing Article shall be carried out in satisfactory conditions as regards safety, hygiene, sanitation and food. All costs in connection therewith, from the point of exit in the territory of the Detaining Power, shall be borne by the country of destination, or, in the case of accommodation in a neutral country, by the Power whose nationals are benefited. The practical details of such movements may, if necessary, be settled by special agreements between the Powers concerned.

The foregoing shall not prejudice such special agreements as may be concluded between Parties to the conflict concerning the exchange and repatriation of their nationals in enemy hands.

Article 37

Protected persons who are confined pending proceedings or subject to a sentence involving loss of liberty, shall during their confinement be humanely treated.

As soon as they are released, they may ask to leave the territory in conformity with the foregoing Articles.

Article 38

With the exception of special measures authorized by the present Convention, in particularly by Article 27 and 41 thereof, the situation of protected persons shall continue to be regulated, in principle, by the provisions concerning aliens in time of peace. In any case, the following rights shall be granted to them:

(1) they shall be enabled to receive the individual or collective relief that may be sent to them.

(2) they shall, if their state of health so requires, receive medical attention and hospital treatment to the same extent as the nationals of the State concerned.

(3) they shall be allowed to practise their religion and to receive spiritual assistance from ministers of their faith.

(4) if they reside in an area particularly exposed to the dangers of war, they shall be authorized to move from that area to the same extent as the nationals of the State concerned.

(5) children under fifteen years, pregnant women and mothers of children under seven years shall benefit by any preferential treatment to the same extent as the nationals of the State concerned.

Article 39

Protected persons who, as a result of the war, have lost their gainful employment, shall be granted the opportunity to find paid employment. That opportunity shall, subject to security considerations and to the provisions of Article 40, be equal to that enjoyed by the nationals of the Power in whose territory they are.

Where a Party to the conflict applies to a protected person methods of control which result in his being unable to support himself, and especially if such a person is prevented for reasons of security from finding paid employment on reasonable conditions, the said Party shall ensure his support and that of his dependents.

Protected persons may in any case receive allowances from their home country, the Protecting Power, or the relief societies referred to in Article 30.

Article 40

Protected persons may be compelled to work only to the same extent as nationals of the Party to the conflict in whose territory they are.

If protected persons are of enemy nationality, they may only be compelled to do work which is normally necessary to ensure the feeding, sheltering, clothing, transport and health of human beings and which is not directly related to the conduct of military operations.

In the cases mentioned in the two preceding paragraphs, protected persons compelled to work shall have the benefit of the same working conditions and of the same safeguards as national workers in particular as regards wages, hours of labour, clothing and equipment, previous training and compensation for occupational accidents and diseases.

If the above provisions are infringed, protected persons shall be allowed to exercise their right of complaint in accordance with Article 30.

Article 41

Should the Power, in whose hands protected persons may be, consider the measures of control mentioned in the present Convention to be inadequate, it may not have recourse to any other measure of control more severe than that of assigned residence or internment, in accordance with the provisions of Articles 42 and 43.

In applying the provisions of Article 39, second paragraph, to the cases of persons required to leave their usual places of residence by virtue of a decision placing them in assigned residence, by virtue of a decision placing them in assigned residence, elsewhere, the Detaining Power shall be guided as closely as possible by the standards of welfare set forth in Part III, Section IV of this Convention.

Article 42

The internment or placing in assigned residence of protected persons may be ordered only if the security of the Detaining Power makes it absolutely necessary.

If any person, acting through the representatives of the Protecting Power, voluntarily demands internment, and if his situation renders this step necessary, he shall be interned by the Power in whose hands he may be.

Article 43

Any protected person who has been interned or placed in assigned residence shall be entitled to have such action reconsidered as soon as possible by an appropriate court or administrative board designated by the Detaining Power for that purpose. If the internment or placing in assigned residence is maintained, the court or administrative board shall periodically, and at least twice yearly, give consideration to his or her case, with a view to the favourable amendment of the initial decision, if circumstances permit.

Unless the protected persons concerned object, the Detaining Power shall, as rapidly as possible, give the Protecting Power the names of any protected persons who have been interned or subjected to assigned residence, or who have been released from internment or assigned residence. The decisions of the courts or boards mentioned in the first paragraph of the present Article shall also, subject to the same conditions, be notified as rapidly as possible to the Protecting Power.

Article 44

In applying the measures of control mentioned in the present Convention, the Detaining Power shall not treat as enemy aliens exclusively on the basis of their nationality de jure of an enemy State, refugees who do not, in fact, enjoy the protection of any government.

Article 45

Protected persons shall not be transferred to a Power which is not a party to the Convention.

This provision shall in no way constitute an obstacle to the repatriation of protected persons, or to their return to their country of residence after the cessation of hostilities.

Protected persons may be transferred by the Detaining Power only to a Power which is a party to the present Convention and after the Detaining Power has satisfied itself of the willingness and ability of such transferee Power to apply the present Convention. If protected persons are transferred under such circumstances, responsibility for the application of the present Convention rests on the Power accepting them, while they are in its custody. Nevertheless, if that Power fails to carry out the provisions of the present Convention in any important respect, the Power by which the protected persons were transferred shall, upon being so notified by the Protecting Power, take effective measures to correct the situation or shall request the return of the protected persons. Such request must be complied with.

In no circumstances shall a protected person be transferred to a country where he or she may have reason to fear persecution for his or her political opinions or religious beliefs.

The provisions of this Article do not constitute an obstacle to the extradition, in pursuance of extradition treaties concluded before the outbreak of hostilities, of protected persons accused of offences against ordinary criminal law.

Article 46

In so far as they have not been previously withdrawn, restrictive measures taken regarding protected persons shall be cancelled as soon as possible after the close of hostilities.

Restrictive measures affecting their property shall be cancelled, in accordance with the law of the Detaining Power, as soon as possible after the close of hostilities.

SECTION III: Occupied Territories

Article 47

Protected persons who are in occupied territory shall not be deprived, in any case or in any manner whatsoever, of the benefits of the present Convention by any change introduced, as the result of the occupation of a territory, into the institutions or government of the said territory, nor by any agreement concluded between the authorities of the occupied territories and the Occupying Power, nor by any annexation by the latter of the whole or part of the occupied territory.

Article 48

Protected persons who are not nationals of the Power whose territory is occupied, may avail themselves of the right to leave the territory subject to the provisions of Article 35, and decisions thereon shall be taken in accordance with the procedure which the Occupying Power shall establish in accordance with the said Article.

Article 49

Individual or mass forcible transfers, as well as deportations of protected persons from occupied territory to the territory of the Occupying Power or to that of any other country, occupied or not, are prohibited, regardless of their motive.

Nevertheless, the Occupying Power may undertake total or partial evacuation of a given area if the security of the population or imperative military reasons so demand. Such evacuations may not involve the displacement of protected persons outside the bounds of the occupied territory except when for material reasons it is impossible to avoid such displacement. Persons thus evacuated shall be transferred back to their homes as soon as hostilities in the area in question have ceased.

The Occupying Power undertaking such transfers or evacuations shall ensure, to the greatest practicable extent, that proper accommodation is provided to receive the protected persons, that the removals are effected in satisfactory conditions of hygiene, health, safety and nutrition, and that members of the same family are not separated.

The Protecting Power shall be informed of any transfers and evacuations as soon as they have taken place.

The Occupying Power shall not detain protected persons in an area particularly exposed to the dangers of war unless the security of the population or imperative military reasons so demand.

The Occupying Power shall not deport or transfer parts of its own civilian population into the territory it occupies.

Basic Documents about the Detainees

Article 50

The Occupying Power shall, with the cooperation of the national and local authorities, facilitate the proper working of all institutions devoted to the care and education of children.

The Occupying Power shall take all necessary steps to facilitate the identification of children and the registration of their parentage. It may not, in any case, change their personal status, nor enlist them in formations or organizations subordinate to it.

Should the local institutions be inadequate for the purpose, the Occupying Power shall make arrangements for the maintenance and education, if possible by persons of their own nationality, language and religion, of children who are orphaned or separated from their parents as a result of the war and who cannot be adequately cared for by a near relative or friend.

A special section of the Bureau set up in accordance with Article 136 shall be responsible for taking all necessary steps to identify children whose identity is in doubt. Particulars of their parents or other near relatives should always be recorded if available.

The Occupying Power shall not hinder the application of any preferential measures in regard to food, medical care and protection against the effects of war which may have been adopted prior to the occupation in favour of children under fifteen years, expectant mothers, and mothers of children under seven years.

Article 51

The Occupying Power may not compel protected persons to serve in its armed or auxiliary forces. No pressure or propaganda which aims at securing voluntary enlistment is permitted.

The Occupying Power may not compel protected persons to work unless they are over eighteen years of age, and then only on work which is necessary either for the needs of the army of occupation, or for the public utility services, or for the feeding, sheltering, clothing, transportation or health of the population of the occupied country. Protected persons may not be compelled to undertake any work which would involve them in the obligation of taking part in military operations. The Occupying Power may not compel protected persons to employ forcible means to ensure the security of the installations where they are performing compulsory labour.

The work shall be carried out only in the occupied territory where the persons whose services have been requisitioned are. Every such person shall, so far as possible, be kept in his usual place of employment. Workers shall be paid a fair wage and the work shall be proportionate to their physical and intellectual capacities. The legislation in force in the occupied country concerning working conditions, and safeguards as regards, in particular, such matters as wages, hours of work, equipment, preliminary training and compensation for occupational accidents and diseases, shall be applicable to the protected persons assigned to the work referred to in this Article.

In no case shall requisition of labour lead to a mobilization of workers in an organization of a military or semi-military character.

Article 52

No contract, agreement or regulation shall impair the right of any worker, whether voluntary or not and wherever he may be, to apply to the representatives of the Protecting Power in order to request the said Power's intervention.

All measures aiming at creating unemployment or at restricting the opportunities offered to workers in an occupied territory, in order to induce them to work for the Occupying Power, are prohibited.

Article 53

Any destruction by the Occupying Power of real or personal property belonging individually or collectively to private persons, or to the State, or to other public authorities, or to social or cooperative organizations, is prohibited, except where such destruction is rendered absolutely necessary by military operations.

Article 54

The Occupying Power may not alter the status of public officials or judges in the occupied territories, or in any way apply sanctions to or take any measures of coercion or discrimination against them, should they abstain from fulfilling their functions for reasons of conscience.

This prohibition does not prejudice the application of the second paragraph of Article 51. It does not affect the right of the Occupying Power to remove public officials from their posts.

Article 55

To the fullest extent of the means available to it, the Occupying Power has the duty of ensuring the food and medical supplies of the population; it should, in particular, bring in the necessary foodstuffs, medical stores and other articles if the resources of the occupied territory are inadequate.

The Occupying Power may not requisition foodstuffs, articles or medical supplies available in the occupied territory, except for use by the occupation forces and administration personnel, and then only if the requirements of the civilian population have been taken into account. Subject to the provisions of other international Conventions, the Occupying Power shall make arrangements to ensure that fair value is paid for any requisitioned goods.

The Protecting Power shall, at any time, be at liberty to verify the state of the food and medical supplies in occupied territories, except where temporary restrictions are made necessary by imperative military requirements.

BASIC DOCUMENTS ABOUT THE DETAINEES

Article 56

To the fullest extent of the means available to it, the public Occupying Power has the duty of ensuring and maintaining, with the cooperation of national and local authorities, the medical and hospital establishments and services, public health and hygiene in the occupied territory, with particular reference to the adoption and application of the prophylactic and preventive measures necessary to combat the spread of contagious diseases and epidemics. Medical personnel of all categories shall be allowed to carry out their duties.

If new hospitals are set up in occupied territory and if the competent organs of the occupied State are not operating there, the occupying authorities shall, if necessary, grant them the recognition provided for in Article 18. In similar circumstances, the occupying authorities shall also grant recognition to hospital personnel and transport vehicles under the provisions of Articles 20 and 21.

In adopting measures of health and hygiene and in their implementation, the Occupying Power shall take into consideration the moral and ethical susceptibilities of the population of the occupied territory.

Article 57

The Occupying Power may requisition civilian hospitals of hospitals only temporarily and only in cases of urgent necessity for the care of military wounded and sick, and then on condition that suitable arrangements are made in due time for the care and treatment of the patients and for the needs of the civilian population for hospital accommodation.

The material and stores of civilian hospitals cannot be requisitioned so long as they are necessary for the needs of the civilian population.

Article 58

The Occupying Power shall permit ministers of religion to give spiritual assistance to the members of their religious communities.

The Occupying Power shall also accept consignments of books and articles required for religious needs and shall facilitate their distribution in occupied territory.

Article 59

If the whole or part of the population of an occupied territory is inadequately supplied, the Occupying Power shall agree to relief schemes on behalf of the said population, and shall facilitate them by all the means at its disposal.

Such schemes, which may be undertaken either by States or by impartial humanitarian organizations such as the International Committee of the Red Cross, shall consist, in particular, of the provision of consignments of foodstuffs, medical supplies and clothing.

All Contracting Parties shall permit the free passage of these consignments and shall guarantee their protection.

A Power granting free passage to consignments on their way to territory occupied by an adverse Party to the conflict shall, however, have the right to search the consignments, to regulate their passage according to prescribed times and routes, and to be reasonably satisfied through the Protecting Power that these consignments are to be used for the relief of the needy population and are not to be used for the benefit of the Occupying Power.

Article 60

Relief consignments shall in no way relieve the Occupying Power of any of its responsibilities under Articles 55, 56 and 59. The Occupying Power shall in no way whatsoever divert relief consignments from the purpose for which they are intended, except in cases of urgent necessity, in the interests of the population of the occupied territory and with the consent of the Protecting Power.

Article 61

The distribution of the relief consignments referred to in the foregoing Articles shall be carried out with the cooperation and under the supervision of the Protecting Power. This duty may also be delegated, by agreement between the Occupying Power and the Protecting Power, to a neutral Power, to the International Committee of the Red Cross or to any other impartial humanitarian body.

Such consignments shall be exempt in occupied territory from all charges, taxes or customs duties unless these are necessary in the interests of the economy of the territory. The Occupying Power shall facilitate the rapid distribution of these consignments.

All Contracting Parties shall endeavour to permit the transit and transport, free of charge, of such relief consignments on their way to occupied territories.

Article 62

Subject to imperative reasons of security, protected persons in occupied territories shall be permitted to receive the individual relief consignments sent to them.

Article 63

Subject to temporary and exceptional measures imposed for urgent reasons of security by the Occupying Power:

   (a) recognized National Red Cross (Red Crescent, Red Lion and Sun) Societies shall be able to pursue their activities in accordance with Red Cross principles, as defined by the International Red Cross

Conferences. Other relief societies shall be permitted to continue their humanitarian activities under similar conditions;

(b) the Occupying Power may not require any changes in the personnel or structure of these societies, which would prejudice the aforesaid activities.

The same principles shall apply to the activities and personnel of special organizations of a non-military character, which already exist or which may be established, for the purpose of ensuring the living conditions of the civilian population by the maintenance of the essential public utility services, by the distribution of relief and by the organization of rescues.

Article 64

The penal laws of the occupied territory shall remain in force, with the exception that they may be repealed or suspended by the Occupying Power in cases where they constitute a threat to its security or an obstacle to the application of the present Convention.

Subject to the latter consideration and to the necessity for ensuring the effective administration of justice, the tribunals of the occupied territory shall continue to function in respect of all offences covered by the said laws.

The Occupying Power may, however, subject the population of the occupied territory to provisions which are essential to enable the Occupying Power to fulfil its obligations under the present Convention, to maintain the orderly government of the territory, and to ensure the security of the Occupying Power, of the members and property of the occupying forces or administration, and likewise of the establishments and lines of communication used by them.

Article 65

The penal provisions enacted by the Occupying Power shall not come into force before they have been published and brought to the knowledge of the inhabitants in their own language. The effect of these penal provisions shall not be retroactive.

Article 66

In case of a breach of the penal provisions promulgated by it by virtue of the second paragraph of Article 64 the Occupying Power may hand over the accused to its properly constituted, non-political military courts, on condition that the said courts sit in the occupied country. Courts of appeal shall preferably sit in the occupied country.

Article 67

The courts shall apply only those provisions of law which were applicable prior to the offence, and which are in accordance with general principles of law, in particular the principle that the penalty shall be proportionate to the offence. They shall take into consideration the fact the accused is not a national of the Occupying Power.

Article 68

Protected persons who commit an offence which is solely intended to harm the Occupying Power, but which does not constitute an attempt on the life or limb of members of the occupying forces or administration, nor a grave collective danger, nor seriously damage the property of the occupying forces or administration or the installations used by them, shall be liable to internment or simple imprisonment, provided the duration of such internment or imprisonment is proportionate to the offence committed. Furthermore, internment or imprisonment shall, for such offences, be the only measure adopted for depriving protected persons of liberty. The courts provided for under Article 66 of the present Convention may at their discretion convert a sentence of imprisonment to one of internment for the same period.

The penal provisions promulgated by the Occupying Power in accordance with Articles 64 and 65 may impose the death penalty on a protected person only in cases where the person is guilty of espionage, of serious acts of sabotage against the military installations of the Occupying Power or of intentional offences which have caused the death of one or more persons, provided that such offences were punishable by death under the law of the occupied territory in force before the occupation began.

The death penalty may not be pronounced on a protected person unless the attention of the court has been particularly called to the fact that since the accused is not a national of the Occupying Power, he is not bound to it by any duty of allegiance.

In any case, the death penalty may not be pronounced on a protected person who was under eighteen years of age at the time of the offence.

Article 69

In all cases the duration of the period during which a protected person accused of an offence is under arrest awaiting trial or punishment shall be deducted from any period of imprisonment of awarded.

Article 70

Protected persons shall not be arrested, prosecuted or convicted by the Occupying Power for acts committed or for opinions expressed before the occupation, or during a temporary interruption thereof, with the exception of breaches of the laws and customs of war.

Nationals of the occupying Power who, before the outbreak of hostilities, have sought refuge in the territory of the occupied State, shall not be arrested, prosecuted, convicted or deported from the occupied territory, except for offences committed after the outbreak of hostilities, or for offences under common law committed before the outbreak of hostilities which, according to the law of the occupied State, would have justified extradition in time of peace.

Article 71

No sentence shall be pronounced by the competent courts of the Occupying Power except after a regular trial.

Accused persons who are prosecuted by the Occupying Power shall be promptly informed, in writing, in a language which they understand, of the particulars of the charges preferred against them, and shall be brought to trial as rapidly as possible. The Protecting Power shall be informed of all proceedings instituted by the Occupying Power against protected persons in respect of charges involving the death penalty or imprisonment for two years or more; it shall be enabled, at any time, to obtain information regarding the state of such proceedings. Furthermore, the Protecting Power shall be entitled, on request, to be furnished with all particulars of these and of any other proceedings instituted by the Occupying Power against protected persons.

The notification to the Protecting Power, as provided for in the second paragraph above, shall be sent immediately, and shall in any case reach the Protecting Power three weeks before the date of the first hearing. Unless, at the opening of the trial, evidence is submitted that the provisions of this Article are fully complied with, the trial shall not proceed. The notification shall include the following particulars:

(a) description of the accused;

(b) place of residence or detention;

(c) specification of the charge or charges (with mention of the penal provisions under which it is brought);

(d) designation of the court which will hear the case;

(e) place and date of the first hearing.

Article 72

Accused persons shall have the right to present evidence necessary to their defence and may, in particular, call witnesses. They shall have the right to be assisted by a qualified advocate or counsel of their own choice, who shall be able to visit them freely and shall enjoy the necessary facilities for preparing the defence.

Failing a choice by the accused, the Protecting Power may provide him with an advocate or counsel. When an accused person has to meet a serious charge and the Protecting Power is not functioning, the Occupying Power, subject to the consent of the accused, shall provide an advocate or counsel.

Accused persons shall, unless they freely waive such assistance, be aided by an interpreter, both during preliminary investigation and during the hearing in court. They shall have at any time the right to object to the interpreter and to ask for his replacement.

Article 73

A convicted person shall have the right of appeal provided for by the laws applied by the court. He shall be fully informed of his right to appeal or petition and of the time limit within which he may do so.

The penal procedure provided in the present Section shall apply, as far as it is applicable, to appeals. Where the laws applied by the Court make no provision for appeals, the convicted person shall have the right to petition against the finding and sentence to the competent authority of the Occupying Power.

Article 74

Representatives of the Protecting Power shall have the right to attend the trial of any protected person, unless the hearing has, as an exceptional measure, to be held in camera in the interests of the security of the Occupying Power, which shall then notify the Protecting Power. A notification in respect of the date and place of trial shall be sent to the Protecting Power.

Any judgement involving a sentence of death, or imprisonment for two years or more, shall be communicated, with the relevant grounds, as rapidly as possible to the Protecting Power. The notification shall contain a reference to the notification made under Article 71 and, in the case of sentences of imprisonment, the name of the place where the sentence is to be served. A record of judgements other than those referred to above shall be kept by the court and shall be open to inspection by representatives of the Protecting Power. Any period allowed for appeal in the case of sentences involving the death penalty, or imprisonment of two years or more, shall not run until notification of judgement has been received by the Protecting Power.

Article 75

In no case shall persons condemned to death be deprived of the right of petition for pardon or reprieve.

No death sentence shall be carried out before the expiration of a period of a least six months from the date of receipt by the Protecting Power of the notification of the final judgment confirming such death sentence, or of an order denying pardon or reprieve.

The six months period of suspension of the death sentence herein prescribed may be reduced in individual cases in circumstances of grave emergency involving an organized threat to the security of the Occupying Power or its forces, provided always that the Protecting Power is notified of such reduction and is given reasonable time and opportunity to make representations to the competent occupying authorities in respect of such death sentences.

Article 76

Protected persons accused of offences shall be detained in the occupied country, and if convicted they shall serve their sentences therein. They shall, if possible, be separated from other detainees and shall enjoy conditions of food and hygiene which will be sufficient to keep them in good health, and which will be at least equal to those obtaining in prisons in the occupied country.

They shall receive the medical attention required by their state of health.

They shall also have the right to receive any spiritual assistance which they may require.

Women shall be confined in separate quarters and shall be under the direct supervision of women.

Proper regard shall be paid to the special treatment due to minors.

Protected persons who are detained shall have the right to be visited by delegates of the Protecting Power and of the International Committee of the Red Cross, in accordance with the provisions of Article 143.

Such persons shall have the right to receive at least one relief parcel monthly.

Article 77

Protected persons who have been accused of offences or convicted by the courts in occupied territory, shall be handed over at the close of occupation, with the relevant records, to the authorities of the liberated territory.

Article 78

If the Occupying Power considers it necessary, for imperative reasons of security, to take safety measures concerning protected persons, it may, at the most, subject them to assigned residence or to internment.

Decisions regarding such assigned residence or internment shall be made according to a regular procedure to be prescribed by the Occupying Power in accordance with the provisions of the present Convention. This procedure shall include the right of appeal for the parties concerned. Appeals shall be decided with the least possible delay. In the event of the decision being upheld, it shall be subject to periodical review, if possible every six months, by a competent body set up by the said Power.

Protected persons made subject to assigned residence and thus required to leave their homes shall enjoy the full benefit of Article 39 of the present Convention.

SECTION IV: Regulations for the Treatment of Internees

CHAPTER I: General Provisions

Article 79

The Parties to the conflict shall not intern protected persons, except in accordance with the provisions of Articles 41, 42, 43, 68 and 78.

Article 80

Internees shall retain their full civil capacity and shall exercise such attendant rights as may be compatible with their status.

Article 81

Parties to the conflict who intern protected persons shall be bound to provide free of charge for their maintenance, and to grant them also the medical attention required by their state of health.

No deduction from the allowances, salaries or credits due to the internees shall be made for the repayment of these costs.

The Detaining Power shall provide for the support of those dependent on the internees, if such dependents are without adequate means of support or are unable to earn a living.

Article 82

The Detaining Power shall, as far as possible, accommodate the internees according to their nationality, language and customs. Internees who are nationals of the same country shall not be separated merely because they have different languages.

Throughout the duration of their internment, members of the same family, and in particular parents and children, shall be lodged together in the same place of internment, except when separation of a temporary nature is necessitated for reasons of employment or health or for the purposes of enforcement of the provisions of Chapter IX of the present Section. Internees may request that their children who are left at liberty without parental care shall be interned with them.

Wherever possible, interned members of the same family shall be housed in the same premises and given separate accommodation from other internees, together with facilities for leading a proper family life.

Basic Documents about the Detainees

CHAPTER II: PLACES OF INTERNMENT

Article 83

The Detaining Power shall not set up places of internment in areas particularly exposed to the dangers of war.

The Detaining Power shall give the enemy Powers, through the intermediary of the Protecting Powers, all useful information regarding the geographical location of places of internment.

Whenever military considerations permit, internment camps shall be indicated by the letters IC, placed so as to be clearly visible in the daytime from the air. The Powers concerned may, however, agree upon any other system of marking. No place other than an internment camp shall be marked as such.

Article 84

Internees shall be accommodated and administered separately from prisoners of war and from persons deprived of liberty for any other reason.

Article 85

The Detaining Power is bound to take all necessary and possible measures to ensure that protected persons shall, from the outset of their internment, be accommodated in buildings or quarters which afford every possible safeguard as regards hygiene and health, and provide efficient protection against the rigours of the climate and the effects of the war. In no case shall permanent places of internment be situated in unhealthy areas or in districts, the climate of which is injurious to the internees. In all cases where the district, in which a protected person is temporarily interned, is an unhealthy area or has a climate which is harmful to his health, he shall be removed to a more suitable place of internment as rapidly as circumstances permit.

The premises shall be fully protected from dampness, adequately heated and lighted, in particular between dusk and lights out. The sleeping quarters shall be sufficiently spacious and well ventilated, and the internees shall have suitable bedding and sufficient blankets, account being taken of the climate, and the age, sex, and state of health of the internees.

Internees shall have for their use, day and night, sanitary conveniences which conform to the rules of hygiene, and are constantly maintained in a state of cleanliness. They shall be provided with sufficient water and soap for their daily personal toilet and for washing their personal laundry; installations and facilities necessary for this purpose shall be granted to them. Showers or baths shall also be available. The necessary time shall be set aside for washing and for cleaning.

Whenever it is necessary, as an exceptional and temporary measure, to accommodate women internees who are not members of a family unit in the same place of internment as men, the provision of separate sleeping quarters and sanitary conveniences for the use of such women internees shall be obligatory.

Article 86

The Detaining Power shall place at the disposal of interned persons, of whatever denomination, premises suitable for the holding of their religious services.

Article 87

Canteens shall be installed in every place of internment, except where other suitable facilities are available. Their purpose shall be to enable internees to make purchases, at prices not higher than local market prices, of foodstuffs and articles of everyday use, including soap and tobacco, such as would increase their personal well-being and comfort.

Profits made by canteens shall be credited to a welfare fund to be set up for each place of internment, and administered for the benefit of the internees attached to such place of internment. The Internee Committee provided for in Article 102 shall have the right to check the management of the canteen and of the said fund.

When a place of internment is closed down, the balance of the welfare fund shall be transferred to the welfare fund of a place of internment for internees of the same nationality, or, if such a place does not exist, to a central welfare fund which shall be administered for the benefit of all internees remaining in the custody of the Detaining Power. In case of a general release, the said profits shall be kept by the Detaining Power, subject to any agreement to the contrary between the Powers concerned.

Article 88

In all places of internment exposed to air raids and other hazards of war, shelters adequate in number and structure to ensure the necessary protection shall be installed. In case of alarms, the measures internees shall be free to enter such shelters as quickly as possible, excepting those who remain for the protection of their quarters against the aforesaid hazards. Any protective measures taken in favour of the population shall also apply to them.

All due precautions must be taken in places of internment against the danger of fire.

CHAPTER III: FOOD AND CLOTHING

Article 89

Daily food rations for internees shall be sufficient in quantity, quality and variety to keep internees in a good state of health and prevent the development of nutritional deficiencies. Account shall also be taken of the customary diet of the internees.

Internees shall also be given the means by which they can prepare for themselves any additional food in their possession.

Sufficient drinking water shall be supplied to internees. The use of tobacco shall be permitted.

Internees who work shall receive additional rations in proportion to the kind of labour which they perform.

Expectant and nursing mothers and children under fifteen years of age, shall be given additional food, in proportion to their physiological needs.

Article 90

When taken into custody, internees shall be given all facilities to provide themselves with the necessary clothing, footwear and change of underwear, and later on, to procure further supplies if required. Should any internees not have sufficient clothing, account being taken of the climate, and be unable to procure any, it shall be provided free of charge to them by the Detaining Power.

The clothing supplied by the Detaining Power to internees and the outward markings placed on their own clothes shall not be ignominious nor expose them to ridicule.

Workers shall receive suitable working outfits, including protective clothing, whenever the nature of their work so requires.

CHAPTER IV: HYGIENE AND MEDICAL ATTENTION

Article 91

Every place of internment shall have an adequate infirmary, under the direction of a qualified doctor, where internees may have the attention they require, as well as appropriate diet. Isolation wards shall be set aside for cases of contagious or mental diseases.

Maternity cases and internees suffering from serious diseases, or whose condition requires special treatment, a surgical operation or hospital care, must be admitted to any institution where adequate treatment can be given and shall receive care not inferior to that provided for the general population.

Internees shall, for preference, have the attention of medical personnel of their own nationality.

Internees may not be prevented from presenting themselves to the medical authorities for examination. The medical authorities of the Detaining Power shall, upon request, issue to every internee who has undergone treatment an official certificate showing the nature of his illness or injury, and the duration and nature of the treatment given. A duplicate of this certificate shall be forwarded to the Central Agency provided for in Article 140.

Treatment, including the provision of any apparatus necessary for the maintenance of internees in good health, particularly dentures and other artificial appliances and spectacles, shall be free of charge to the internee.

Article 92

Medical inspections of internees shall be made at least once a month. Their purpose shall be, in particular, to supervise the general state of health, nutrition and cleanliness of internees, and to detect contagious diseases, especially tuberculosis, malaria, and venereal diseases. Such inspections shall include, in particular, the checking of weight of each internee and, at least once a year, radioscopic examination.

CHAPTER V: RELIGIOUS, INTELLECTUAL AND PHYSICAL ACTIVITIES

Article 93

Internees shall enjoy complete latitude in the exercise of their religious duties, including attendance at the services of their faith, on condition that they comply with the disciplinary routine prescribed by the detaining authorities.

Ministers of religion who are interned shall be allowed to minister freely to the members of their community. For this purpose the Detaining Power shall ensure their equitable allocation amongst the various places of internment in which there are internees speaking the same language and belonging to the same religion. Should such ministers be too few in number, the Detaining Power shall provide them with the necessary facilities, including means of transport, for moving from one place to another, and they shall be authorized to visit any internees who are in hospital. Ministers of religion shall be at liberty to correspond on matters concerning their ministry with the religious authorities in the country of detention and, as far as possible, with the international religious organizations of their faith. Such correspondence shall not be considered as forming a part of the quota mentioned in Article 107. It shall, however, be subject to the provisions of Article 112.

When internees do not have at their disposal the assistance of ministers of their faith, or should these latter be too few in number, the local religious authorities of the same faith may appoint, in agreement with the Detaining Power, a minister of the internees' faith or, if such a course is feasible from a denominational point of view, a minister of similar religion or a qualified layman. The latter shall enjoy the facilities granted to the ministry he has assumed. Persons so appointed shall comply with all regulations laid down by the Detaining Power in the interests of discipline and security.

Basic Documents about the Detainees

Article 94

The Detaining Power shall encourage intellectual, educational and recreational pursuits, sports and games amongst internees, whilst leaving them free to take part in them or not. It shall take all practicable measures to ensure the exercise thereof, in particular by providing suitable premises.

All possible facilities shall be granted to internees to continue their studies or to take up new subjects. The education of children and young people shall be ensured; they shall be allowed to attend schools either within the place of internment or outside.

Internees shall be given opportunities for physical exercise, sports and outdoor games. For this purpose, sufficient open spaces shall be set aside in all places of internment. Special playgrounds shall be reserved for children and young people.

Article 95

The Detaining Power shall not employ internees as workers, unless they so desire. Employment which, if undertaken under compulsion by a protected person not in internment, would involve a breach of Articles 40 or 51 of the present Convention, and employment on work which is of a degrading or humiliating character are in any case prohibited.

After a working period of six weeks, internees shall be free to give up work at any moment, subject to eight days' notice.

These provisions constitute no obstacle to the right of the Detaining Power to employ interned doctors, dentists and other medical personnel in their professional capacity on behalf of their fellow internees, or to employ internees for administrative and maintenance work in places of internment and to detail such persons for work in the kitchens or for other domestic tasks, or to require such persons to undertake duties connected with the protection of internees against aerial bombardment or other war risks. No internee may, however, be required to perform tasks for which he is, in the opinion of a medical officer, physically unsuited.

The Detaining Power shall take entire responsibility for all working conditions, for medical attention, for the payment of wages, and for ensuring that all employed internees receive compensation for occupational accidents and diseases. The standards prescribed for the said working conditions and for compensation shall be in accordance with the national laws and regulations, and with the existing practice; they shall in no case be inferior to those obtaining for work of the same nature in the same district. Wages for work done shall be determined on an equitable basis by special agreements between the internees, the Detaining Power, and, if the case arises, employers other than the Detaining Power to provide for free maintenance of internees and for the medical attention which their state of health may require. Internees permanently detailed for categories of work mentioned in the third paragraph of this Article, shall be paid fair wages by the Detaining Power. The working conditions and the scale of compensation for occupational accidents and diseases to internees, thus detailed, shall not be inferior to those applicable to work of the same nature in the same district.

Article 96

All labour detachments shall remain part of and dependent upon a place of internment. The competent authorities of the Detaining Power and the commandant of a place of internment shall be responsible for the observance in a labour detachment of the provisions of the present Convention. The commandant shall keep an up-to-date list of the labour detachments subordinate to him and shall communicate it to the delegates of the Protecting Power, of the International Committee of the Red Cross and of other humanitarian organizations who may visit the places of internment.

CHAPTER VI: PERSONAL PROPERTY AND FINANCIAL RESOURCES

Article 97

Internees shall be permitted to retain articles of personal use. Monies, cheques, bonds, etc., and valuables in their possession may not be taken from them except in accordance with established procedure. Detailed receipts shall be given therefor.

The amounts shall be paid into the account of every internee as provided for in Article 98. Such amounts may not be converted into any other currency unless legislation in force in the territory in which the owner is interned so requires or the internee gives his consent.

Articles which have above all a personal or sentimental value may not be taken away.

A woman internee shall not be searched except by a woman.

On release or repatriation, internees shall be given all articles, monies or other valuables taken from them during internment and shall receive in currency the balance of any credit to their accounts kept in accordance with Article 98, with the exception of any articles or amounts withheld by the Detaining Power by virtue of its legislation in force. If the property of an internee is so withheld, the owner shall receive a detailed receipt.

Family or identity documents in the possession of internees may not be taken away without a receipt being given. At no time shall internees be left without identity documents. If they have none, they shall be issued with special documents drawn up by the detaining authorities, which will serve as their identity papers until the end of their internment.

Internees may keep on their persons a certain amount of money, in cash or in the shape of purchase coupons, to enable them to make purchases.

Article 98

All internees shall receive regular allowances, sufficient to enable them to purchase goods and articles, such as tobacco, toilet requisites, etc. Such allowances may take the form of credits or purchase coupons.

Furthermore, internees may receive allowances from the Power to which they owe allegiance, the Protecting Powers, the organizations which may assist them, or their families, as well as the income on their property in accordance with the law of the Detaining Power. The amount of allowances granted by the Power to which they owe allegiance shall be the same for each category of internees (infirm, sick, pregnant women, etc.)

but may not be allocated by that Power or distributed by the Detaining Power on the basis of discriminations between internees which are prohibited by Article 27 of the present Convention.

The Detaining Power shall open a regular account for every internee, to which shall be credited the allowances named in the present Article, the wages earned and the remittances received, together with such sums taken from him as may be available under the legislation in force in the territory in which he is interned. Internees shall be granted all facilities consistent with the legislation in force in such territory to make remittances to their families and to other dependents. They may draw from their accounts the amounts necessary for their personal expenses, within the limits fixed by the Detaining Power. They shall at all times be afforded reasonable facilities for consulting and obtaining copies of their accounts. A statement of accounts shall be furnished to the Protecting Power, on request, and shall accompany the internee in case of transfer.

CHAPTER VII: ADMINISTRATION AND DISCIPLINE

Article 99

Every place of internment shall be put under the authority of a responsible officer, chosen from the regular military forces or the regular civil administration of the Detaining Power. The officer in charge of the place of internment must have in his possession a copy of the present Convention in the official language, or one of the official languages, of his country and shall be responsible for its application. The staff in control of internees shall be instructed in the provisions of the present Convention and of the administrative measures adopted to ensure its application.

The text of the present Convention and the texts of special agreements concluded under the said Convention shall be posted inside the place of internment, in a language which the internees understand, or shall be in the possession of the Internee Committee.

Regulations, orders, notices and publications of every kind shall be communicated to the internees and posted inside the places of internment, in a language which they understand.

Every order and command addressed to internees individually must, likewise, be given in a language which they understand.

Article 100

The disciplinary regime in places of internment shall be consistent with humanitarian principles, and shall in no circumstances include regulations imposing on internees any physical exertion dangerous to their health or involving physical or moral victimization. Identification by tattooing or imprinting signs or markings on the body, is prohibited.

In particular, prolonged standing and roll-calls, punishment drill, military drill and manoeuvres, or the reduction of food rations, are prohibited.

Article 101

Internees shall have the right to present to the authorities in whose power they are, any petition with regard to the conditions of internment to which they are subjected.

They shall also have the right to apply without restriction through the Internee Committee or, if they consider it necessary, direct to the representatives of the Protecting Power, in order to indicate to them any points on which they may have complaints to make with regard to the conditions of internment.

Such petitions and complaints shall be transmitted forthwith and without alteration, and even if the latter are recognized to be unfounded, they may not occasion any punishment.

Periodic reports on the situation in places of internment and as to the needs of the internees may be sent by the Internee Committees to the representatives of the Protecting Powers.

Article 102

In every place of internment, the internees shall freely elect by secret ballot every six months, the members of a Committee empowered to represent them before the Detaining and the Protecting Powers, the International Committee of the Red Cross and any other organization which may assist them. The members of the Committee shall be eligible for re-election.

Internees so elected shall enter upon their duties after their election has been approved by the detaining authorities. The reasons for any refusals or dismissals shall be communicated to the Protecting Powers concerned.

Article 103

The Internee Committees shall further the physical, spiritual and intellectual well-being of the internees.

In case the internees decide, in particular, to organize a system of mutual assistance amongst themselves, this organization would be within the competence of the Committees in addition to the special duties entrusted to them under other provisions of the present Convention.

Article 104

Members of Internee Committees shall not be required to perform any other work, if the accomplishment of their duties is rendered more difficult thereby.

Members of Internee Committees may appoint from amongst the internees such assistants as they may require. All material facilities shall be granted to them, particularly a certain freedom of movement necessary for the accomplishment of their duties (visits to labour detachments, receipt of supplies, etc.).

All facilities shall likewise be accorded to members of Internee Committees for communication by post and telegraph with the detaining authorities, the Protecting Powers, the International Committee of the Red Cross and their delegates, and with the organizations which give assistance to internees. Committee members in labour detachments shall enjoy similar facilities for communication with their Internee Committee in the principal place of internment. Such communications shall not be limited, nor considered as forming a part of the quota mentioned in Article 107.

Members of Internee Committees who are transferred shall be allowed a reasonable time to acquaint their successors with current affairs.

CHAPTER VIII: RELATIONS WITH THE EXTERIOR

Article 105

Immediately upon interning protected persons, the Detaining Powers shall inform them, the Power to which they owe allegiance and their Protecting Power of the measures taken for executing the provisions of the present Chapter. The Detaining Powers shall likewise inform the Parties concerned of any subsequent modifications of such measures.

Article 106

As soon as he is interned, or at the latest not more than one week after his arrival in a place of internment, and likewise in cases of sickness or transfer to another place of internment or to a hospital, every internee shall be enabled to send direct to his family, on the one hand, and to the Central Agency provided for by Article 140, on the other, an internment card similar, if possible, to the model annexed to the present Convention, informing his relatives of his detention, address and state of health. The said cards shall be forwarded as rapidly as possible and may not be delayed in any way.

Article 107

Internees shall be allowed to send and receive letters and cards. If the Detaining Power deems it necessary to limit the number of letters and cards sent by each internee, the said number shall not be less than two letters and four cards monthly; these shall be drawn up so as to conform as closely as possible to the models annexed to the present Convention. If limitations must be placed on the correspondence addressed to internees, they may be ordered only by the Power to which such internees owe allegiance, possibly at the request of the Detaining Power. Such letters and cards must be conveyed with reasonable despatch; they may not be delayed or retained for disciplinary reasons.

Internees who have been a long time without news, or who find it impossible to receive news from their relatives, or to give them news by the ordinary postal route, as well as those who are at a considerable distance from their homes, shall be allowed to send telegrams, the charges being paid by them in the currency at their disposal. They shall likewise benefit by this provision in cases which are recognized to be urgent.

As a rule, internees' mail shall be written in their own language. The Parties to the conflict may authorize correspondence in other languages.

Article 108

Internees shall be allowed to receive, by post or by any other means, individual parcels or collective shipments containing in particular foodstuffs, clothing, medical supplies, as well as books and objects of a devotional, educational or recreational character which may meet their needs. Such shipments shall in no way free the Detaining Power from the obligations imposed upon it by virtue of the present Convention.

Should military necessity require the quantity of such shipments to be limited, due notice thereof shall be given to the Protecting Power and to the International Committee of the Red Cross, or to any other organization giving assistance to the internees and responsible for the forwarding of such shipments.

The conditions for the sending of individual parcels and collective shipments shall, if necessary, be the subject of special agreements between the Powers concerned, which may in no case delay the receipt by the internees of relief supplies. Parcels of clothing and foodstuffs may not include books. Medical relief supplies shall, as a rule, be sent in collective parcels.

Article 109

In the absence of special agreements between Parties to the conflict regarding the conditions for the receipt and distribution of collective relief shipments, the regulations concerning collective relief which are annexed to the present Convention shall be applied.

The special agreements provided for above shall in no case restrict the right of Internee Committees to take possession of collective relief shipments intended for internees, to undertake their distribution and to dispose of them in the interests of the recipients. Nor shall such agreements restrict the right of representatives of the Protecting Powers, the International Committee of the Red Cross, or any other organization giving assistance to internees and responsible for the forwarding of collective shipments, to supervise their distribution to the recipients.

Article 110

An relief shipments for internees shall be exempt from import, customs and other dues.

All matter sent by mail, including relief parcels sent by parcel post and remittances of money, addressed from other countries to internees or despatched by them through the post office, either direct or through the Information Bureaux provided for in Article 136 and the Central Information Agency provided for in Article 140, shall be exempt from all postal dues both in the countries of origin and destination and in intermediate countries. To this effect, in particular, the exemption provided by the Universal Postal Convention of 1947 and by the agreements of the Universal Postal Union in favour of civilians of enemy nationality detained in camps or civilian prisons, shall be extended to the other interned persons protected by the present Convention. The countries not signatory to the above-mentioned agreements shall be bound to grant freedom from charges in the same circumstances.

The cost of transporting relief shipments which are intended for internees and which, by reason of their weight or any other cause, cannot be sent through the post office, shall be borne by the Detaining Power in all the territories under its control. Other Powers which are Parties to the present Convention shall bear the cost of transport in their respective territories.

Costs connected with the transport of such shipments, which are not covered by the above paragraphs, shall be charged to the senders.

The High Contracting Parties shall endeavour to reduce, so far as possible, the charges for telegrams sent by internees, or addressed to them.

Article 111

Should military operations prevent the Powers concerned from fulfilling their obligation to ensure the conveyance of the mail and relief shipments provided for in Articles 106, 107, 108 and 113, the Protecting Powers concerned, the International Committee of the Red Cross or any other organization duly approved by the Parties to the conflict may undertake to ensure the conveyance of such shipments by suitable means (rail, motor vehicles, vessels or aircraft, etc.). For this purpose, the High Contracting Parties shall endeavour to supply them with such transport, and to allow its circulation, especially by granting the necessary safe-conducts.

Such transport may also be used to convey:

(a) correspondence, lists and reports exchanged between the Central Information Agency referred to in Article 140 and the National Bureaux referred to in Article 136;

(b) correspondence and reports relating to internees which the Protecting Powers, the International Committee of the Red Cross or any other organization assisting the internees exchange either with their own delegates or with the Parties to the conflict.

These provisions in no way detract from the right of any Party to the conflict to arrange other means of transport if it should so prefer, nor preclude the granting of safe-conducts, under mutually agreed conditions, to such means of transport.

The costs occasioned by the use of such means of transport shall be borne, in proportion to the importance of the shipments, by the Parties to the conflict whose nationals are benefited thereby.

Article 112

The censoring of correspondence addressed to internees or despatched by them shall be done as quickly as possible.

The examination of consignments intended for internees shall not be carried out under conditions that will expose the goods contained in them to deterioration. It shall be done in the presence of the addressee, or of a fellow-internee duly delegated by him. The delivery to internees of individual or collective consignments shall not be delayed under the pretext of difficulties of censorship.

Any prohibition of correspondence ordered by the Parties to the conflict either for military or political reasons, shall be only temporary and its duration shall be as short as possible.

Article 113

The Detaining Powers shall provide all reasonable execution facilities for the transmission, through the Protecting Power or the Central Agency provided for in Article 140, or as otherwise required, of wills, powers of attorney, letters of authority, or any other documents intended for internees or despatched by them.

In all cases the Detaining Powers shall facilitate the execution and authentication in due legal form of such documents on behalf of internees, in particular by allowing them to consult a lawyer.

Article 114

The Detaining Power shall afford internees all facilities to enable them to manage their property, provided this is not incompatible with the conditions of internment and the law which is applicable. For this purpose, the said Power may give them permission to leave the place of internment in urgent cases and if circumstances allow.

Article 115

In all cases where an internee is a party to proceedings in any court, the Detaining Power shall, if he so requests, cause the court to be informed of his detention and shall, within legal limits, ensure that all necessary steps are taken to prevent him from being in any way prejudiced, by reason of his internment, as regards the preparation and conduct of his case or as regards the execution of any judgment of the court.

Article 116

Every internee shall be allowed to receive visitors, especially near relatives, at regular intervals and as frequently as possible.

As far as is possible, internees shall be permitted to visit their homes in urgent cases, particularly in cases of death or serious illness of relatives.

CHAPTER IX: PENAL AND DISCIPLINARY SANCTIONS

Article 117

Subject to the provisions of the present Chapter, the laws in force in the territory in which they are detained will continue to apply to internees who commit offences during internment.

If general laws, regulations or orders declare acts committed by internees to be punishable, whereas the same acts are not punishable when committed by persons who are not internees, such acts shall entail disciplinary punishments only.

No internee may be punished more than once for the same act, or on the same count.

Article 118

The courts or authorities shall in passing sentence take as far as possible into account the fact that the defendant is not a national of the Detaining Power. They shall be free to reduce the penalty prescribed for the offence with which the internee is charged and shall not be obliged, to this end, to apply the minimum sentence prescribed.

Imprisonment in premises without daylight, and, in general, all forms of cruelty without exception are forbidden.

Internees who have served disciplinary or judicial sentences shall not be treated differently from other internees.

The duration of preventive detention undergone by an internee shall be deducted from any disciplinary or judicial penalty involving confinement to which he may be sentenced.

Internee Committees shall be informed of all judicial proceedings instituted against internees whom they represent, and of their result.

Article 119

The disciplinary punishments applicable to internees shall be the following:

(1) a fine which shall not exceed 50 per cent of the wages which the internee would otherwise receive under the provisions of Article 95 during a period of not more than thirty days.

(2) discontinuance of privileges granted over and above the treatment provided for by the present Convention

(3) fatigue duties, not exceeding two hours daily, in connection with the maintenance of the place of internment.

(4) confinement.

In no case shall disciplinary penalties be inhuman, brutal or dangerous for the health of internees. Account shall be taken of the internee's age, sex and state of health.

The duration of any single punishment shall in no case exceed a maximum of thirty consecutive days, even if the internee is answerable for several breaches of discipline when his case is dealt with, whether such breaches are connected or not.

Article 120

Internees who are recaptured after having escaped or when attempting to escape, shall be liable only to disciplinary punishment in respect of this act, even if it is a repeated offence.

Article 118, paragraph 3, notwithstanding, internees punished as a result of escape or attempt to escape, may be subjected to special surveillance, on condition that such surveillance does not affect the state of their health, that it is exercised in a place of internment and that it does not entail the abolition of any of the safeguards granted by the present Convention.

Internees who aid and abet an escape or attempt to escape, shall be liable on this count to disciplinary punishment only.

Article 121

Escape, or attempt to escape, even if it is a repeated offence, shall not be deemed an aggravating circumstance in cases where an internee is prosecuted for offences committed during his escape.

The Parties to the conflict shall ensure that the competent authorities exercise leniency in deciding whether punishment inflicted for an offence shall be of a disciplinary or judicial nature, especially in respect of acts committed in connection with an escape, whether successful or not.

Article 122

Acts which constitute offences against discipline shall be investigated immediately. This rule shall be applied, in particular, in cases of escape or attempt to escape. Recaptured internees shall be handed over to the competent authorities as soon as possible.

In cases of offences against discipline, confinement awaiting trial shall be reduced to an absolute minimum for all internees, and shall not exceed fourteen days. Its duration shall in any case be deducted from any sentence of confinement.

The provisions of Articles 124 and 125 shall apply to internees who are in confinement awaiting trial for offences against discipline.

Article 123

Without prejudice to the competence of courts and higher authorities, disciplinary punishment may be ordered only by the commandant of the place of internment, or by a responsible officer or official who replaces him, or to whom he has delegated his disciplinary powers.

Before any disciplinary punishment is awarded, the accused internee shall be given precise information regarding the offences of which he is accused, and given an opportunity of explaining his conduct and of defending himself. He shall be permitted, in particular, to call witnesses and to have recourse, if necessary, to the services of a qualified interpreter. The decision shall be announced in the presence of the accused and of a member of the Internee Committee.

The period elapsing between the time of award of a disciplinary punishment and its execution shall not exceed one month.

When an internee is awarded a further disciplinary punishment, a period of at least three days shall elapse between the execution of any two of the punishments, if the duration of one of these is ten days or more.

A record of disciplinary punishments shall be maintained by the commandant of the place of internment and shall be open to inspection by representatives of the Protecting Power.

Article 124

Internees shall not in any case be transferred to penitentiary establishments (prisons, penitentiaries, convict prisons, etc.) to undergo disciplinary punishment therein.

The premises in which disciplinary punishments are undergone shall conform to sanitary requirements: they shall in particular be provided with adequate bedding. Internees undergoing punishment shall be enabled to keep themselves in a state of cleanliness.

Women internees undergoing disciplinary punishment shall be confined in separate quarters from male internees and shall be under the immediate supervision of women.

Article 125

Internees awarded disciplinary punishment shall be allowed to exercise and to stay in the open air at least two hours daily.

They shall be allowed, if they so request, to be present at the daily medical inspections. They shall receive the attention which their state of health requires and, if necessary, shall be removed to the infirmary of the place of internment or to a hospital.

They shall have permission to read and write, likewise to send and receive letters. Parcels and remittances of money, however, may be withheld from them until the completion of their punishment; such consignments shall meanwhile be entrusted to the Internee Committee, who will hand over to the infirmary the perishable goods contained in the parcels.

No internee given a disciplinary punishment may be deprived of the benefit of the provisions of Articles 107 and 143 of the present Convention.

Article 126

The provisions of Articles 71 to 76 inclusive shall apply, by analogy, to proceedings against internees who are in the national territory of the Detaining Power.

CHAPTER X: TRANSFERS OF INTERNEES

Article 127

The transfer of internees shall always be effected humanely. As a general rule, it shall be carried out by rail or other means of transport, and under conditions at least equal to those obtaining for the forces of the Detaining Power in their changes of station. If, as an exceptional measure, such removals have to be effected on foot, they may not take place unless the internees are in a fit state of health, and may not in any case expose them to excessive fatigue.

The Detaining Power shall supply internees during transfer with drinking water and food sufficient in quantity, quality and variety to maintain them in good health, and also with the necessary clothing, adequate shelter and the necessary medical attention. The Detaining Power shall take all suitable precautions to ensure their safety during transfer, and shall establish before their departure a complete list of all internees transferred.

Sick, wounded or infirm internees and maternity cases shall not be transferred if the journey would be seriously detrimental to them, unless their safety imperatively so demands.

If the combat zone draws close to a place of internment, the internees in the said place shall not be transferred unless their removal can be carried out in adequate conditions of safety, or unless they are exposed to greater risks by remaining on the spot than by being transferred.

When making decisions regarding the transfer of internees, the Detaining Power shall take their interests into account and, in particular, shall not do anything to increase the difficulties of repatriating them or returning them to their own homes.

Basic Documents about the Detainees

Article 128

In the event of transfer, internees shall be officially advised of their departure and of their new postal address. Such notification shall be given in time for them to pack their luggage and inform their next of kin.

They shall be allowed to take with them their personal effects, and the correspondence and parcels which have arrived for them. The weight of such baggage may be limited if the conditions of transfer so require, but in no case to less than twenty-five kilograms per internee.

Mail and parcels addressed to their former place of internment shall be forwarded to them without delay.

The commandant of the place of internment shall take, in agreement with the Internee Committee, any measures needed to ensure the transport of the internees' community property and of the luggage the internees are unable to take with them in consequence of restrictions imposed by virtue of the second paragraph.

CHAPTER XI: DEATHS

Article 129

The wills of internees shall be received for safe-keeping by the responsible authorities; and if the event of the death of an internee his will shall be transmitted without delay to a person whom he has previously designated.

Deaths of internees shall be certified in every case by a doctor, and a death certificate shall be made out, showing the causes of death and the conditions under which it occurred.

An official record of the death, duly registered, shall be drawn up in accordance with the procedure relating thereto in force in the territory where the place of internment is situated, and a duly certified copy of such record shall be transmitted without delay to the Protecting Power as well as to the Central Agency referred to in Article 140.

Article 130

The detaining authorities shall ensure that internees who die while interned are honourably buried, if possible according to the rites of the religion to which they belonged and that their graves are respected, properly maintained, and marked in such a way that they can always be recognized.

Deceased internees shall be buried in individual graves unless unavoidable circumstances require the use of collective graves. Bodies may be cremated only for imperative reasons of hygiene, on account of the religion of the deceased or in accordance with his expressed wish to this effect. In case of cremation, the fact shall be stated and the reasons given in the death certificate of the deceased. The ashes shall be retained for safe-keeping by the detaining authorities and shall be transferred as soon as possible to the next of kin on their request.

As soon as circumstances permit, and not later than the close of hostilities, the Detaining Power shall forward lists of graves of deceased internees to the Powers on whom deceased internees depended, through the Information Bureaux provided for in Article 136. Such lists shall include all particulars necessary for the identification of the deceased internees, as well as the exact location of their graves.

Article 131

Every death or serious injury of an internee, caused or suspected to have been caused by a sentry, another internee or any other person, as well as any death the cause of which is unknown, shall be immediately followed by an official enquiry by the Detaining Power.

A communication on this subject shall be sent immediately to the Protecting Power. The evidence of any witnesses shall be taken, and a report including such evidence shall be prepared and forwarded to the said Protecting Power.

If the enquiry indicates the guilt of one or more persons, the Detaining Power shall take all necessary steps to ensure the prosecution of the person or persons responsible.

CHAPTER XII: RELEASE, REPATRIATION AND ACCOMMODATION IN NEUTRAL COUNTRIES

Article 132

Each interned person shall be released by the Detaining Power as soon as the reasons which necessitated his internment no longer exist.

The Parties to the conflict shall, moreover, endeavour during the course of hostilities, to conclude agreements for the release, the repatriation, the return to places of residence or the accommodation in a neutral country of certain classes of internees, in particular children, pregnant women and mothers with infants and young children, wounded and sick, and internees who have been detained for a long time.

Article 133

Internment shall cease as soon as possible after the close of hostilities.

Internees in the territory of a Party to the conflict against whom penal proceedings are pending for offences not exclusively subject to disciplinary penalties, may be detained until the close of such proceedings and, if circumstances require, until the completion of the penalty. The same shall apply to internees who have been previously sentenced to a punishment depriving them of liberty.

BASIC DOCUMENTS ABOUT THE DETAINEES

By agreement between the Detaining Power and the Powers concerned, committees may be set up after the close of hostilities, or of the occupation of territories, to search for dispersed internees.

Article 134

The High Contracting Parties shall endeavour, upon the close of hostilities or occupation, to ensure the return of all internees to their last place of residence, or to facilitate their repatriation.

Article 135

The Detaining Power shall bear the expense of returning released internees to the places where they were residing when interned, or, if it took them into custody while they were in transit or on the high seas, the cost of completing their journey or of their return to their point of departure.

Where a Detaining Power refuses permission to reside in its territory to a released internee who previously had his permanent domicile therein, such Detaining Power shall pay the cost of the said internee's repatriation. If, however, the internee elects to return to his country on his own responsibility or in obedience to the Government of the Power to which he owes allegiance, the Detaining Power need not pay the expenses of his journey beyond the point of his departure from its territory. The Detaining Power need not pay the cost of repatriation of an internee who was interned at his own request.

If internees are transferred in accordance with Article 45, the transferring and receiving Powers shall agree on the portion of the above costs to be borne by each.

The foregoing shall not prejudice such special agreements as may be concluded between Parties to the conflict concerning the exchange and repatriation of their nationals in enemy hands.

SECTION V: Information Bureaux and Central Agency

Article 136

Upon the outbreak of a conflict and in all cases of occupation, each of the Parties to the conflict shall establish an official Information Bureau responsible for receiving and transmitting information in respect of the protected persons who are in its power.

Each of the Parties to the conflict shall, within the shortest possible period, give its Bureau information of any measure taken by it concerning any protected persons who are kept in custody for more than two weeks, who are subjected to assigned residence or who are interned. It shall, furthermore, require its various departments concerned with such matters to provide the aforesaid Bureau promptly with information concerning all changes pertaining to these protected persons, as, for example, transfers, releases, repatriations, escapes, admittances to hospitals, births and deaths.

Article 137

Each national Bureau shall immediately forward information concerning protected persons by the most rapid means to the Powers in whose territory they resided, through the intermediary of the Protecting Powers and likewise through the Central Agency provided for in Article 140. The Bureaux shall also reply to all enquiries which may be received regarding protected persons.

Information Bureaux shall transmit information concerning a protected person unless its transmission might be detrimental to the person concerned or to his or her relatives. Even in such a case, the information may not be withheld from the Central Agency which, upon being notified of the circumstances, will take the necessary precautions indicated in Article 140.

All communications in writing made by any Bureau shall be authenticated by a signature or a seal.

Article 138

The information received by the national Bureau and transmitted by it shall be of such a character as to make it possible to identify the protected person exactly and to advise his next of kin quickly. The information in respect of each person shall include at least his surname, first names, place and date of birth, nationality last residence and distinguishing characteristics, the first name of the father and the maiden name of the mother, the date, place and nature of the action taken with regard to the individual, the address at which correspondence may be sent to him and the name and address of the person to be informed.

Likewise, information regarding the state of health of internees who are seriously ill or seriously wounded shall be supplied regularly and if possible every week.

Article 139

Each national Information Bureau shall, furthermore, be responsible for collecting all personal valuables left by protected persons mentioned in Article 136, in particular those who have been repatriated or released, or who have escaped or died; it shall forward the said valuables to those concerned, either direct, or, if necessary, through the Central Agency. Such articles shall be sent by the Bureau in sealed packets which shall be accompanied by statements giving clear and full identity particulars of the person to whom the articles belonged, and by a complete list of the contents of the parcel. Detailed records shall be maintained of the receipt and despatch of all such valuables.

Article 140

A Central Information Agency for protected persons, in particular for internees, shall be created in a neutral country. The International Committee of the Red Cross shall, if it deems necessary, propose to the

Powers concerned the organization of such an Agency, which may be the same as that provided for in Article 123 of the Geneva Convention relative to the Treatment of Prisoners of War of 12 August 1949.

The function of the Agency shall be to collect all information of the type set forth in Article 136 which it may obtain through official or private channels and to transmit it as rapidly as possible to the countries of origin or of residence of the persons concerned, except in cases where such transmissions might be detrimental to the persons whom the said information concerns, or to their relatives. It shall receive from the Parties to the conflict all reasonable facilities for effecting such transmissions.

The High Contracting Parties, and in particular those whose nationals benefit by the services of the Central Agency, are requested to give the said Agency the financial aid it may require.

The foregoing provisions shall in no way be interpreted as restricting the humanitarian activities of the International Committee of the Red Cross and of the relief Societies described in Article 142.

Article 141

The national Information Bureaux and the Central Information Agency shall enjoy free postage for all mail, likewise the exemptions provided for in Article 110, and further, so far as possible, exemption from telegraphic charges or, at least, greatly reduced rates.

PART IV: EXECUTION OF THE CONVENTION

SECTION I: General Provisions

Article 142

Subject to the measures which the Detaining Powers may consider essential to ensure their security or to meet any other reasonable need, the representatives of religious organizations, relief societies, or any other organizations assisting the protected persons, shall receive from these Powers, for themselves or their duly accredited agents, all facilities for visiting the protected persons, for distributing relief supplies and material from any source, intended for educational, recreational or religious purposes, or for assisting them in organizing their leisure time within the places of internment. Such societies or organizations may be constituted in the territory of the Detaining Power, or in any other country, or they may have an international character.

The Detaining Power may limit the number of societies and organizations whose delegates are allowed to carry out their activities in its territory and under its supervision, on condition, however, that such limitation shall not hinder the supply of effective and adequate relief to all protected persons.

The special position of the International Committee of the Red Cross in this field shall be recognized and respected at all times.

Article 143

Representatives or delegates of the Protecting Powers shall have permission to go to all places where protected persons are, particularly to places of internment, detention and work.

They shall have access to all premises occupied by protected persons and shall be able to interview the latter without witnesses, personally or through an interpreter.

Such visits may not be prohibited except for reasons of imperative military necessity, and then only as an exceptional and temporary measure. Their duration and frequency shall not be restricted.

Such representatives and delegates shall have full liberty to select the places they wish to visit. The Detaining or Occupying Power, the Protecting Power and when occasion arises the Power of origin of the persons to be visited, may agree that compatriots of the internees shall be permitted to participate in the visits.

The delegates of the International Committee of the Red Cross shall also enjoy the above prerogatives. The appointment of such delegates shall be submitted to the approval of the Power governing the territories where they will carry out their duties.

Article 144

The High Contracting Parties undertake, in time of peace as in time of war, to disseminate the text of the present Convention as widely as possible in their respective countries, and, in particular, to include the study thereof in their programmes of military and, if possible, civil instruction, so that the principles thereof may become known to the entire population.

Any civilian, military, police or other authorities, who in time of war assume responsibilities in respect of protected persons, must possess the text of the Convention and be specially instructed as to its provisions.

Article 145

The High Contracting Parties shall communicate to one another through the Swiss Federal Council and, during hostilities, through the Protecting Powers, the official translations of the present Convention, as well as the laws and regulations which they may adopt to ensure the application thereof.

Article 146

The High Contracting Parties undertake to enact any legislation necessary to provide effective penal sanctions for persons committing, or ordering to be committed, any of the grave breaches of the present Convention defined in the following Article.

Each High Contracting Party shall be under the obligation to search for persons alleged to have committed, or to have ordered to be committed, such grave breaches, and shall bring such persons, regardless of their nationality, before its own courts. It may also, if it prefers, and in accordance with the provisions of its own legislation, hand such persons over for trial to another High Contracting Party concerned, provided such High Contracting Party has made out a prima facie case.

Each High Contracting Party shall take measures necessary for the suppression of all acts contrary to the provisions of the present Convention other than the grave breaches defined in the following Article.

In all circumstances, the accused persons shall benefit by safeguards of proper trial and defence, which shall not be less favourable than those provided by Article 105 and those following of the Geneva Convention relative to the Treatment of Prisoners of War of 12 August 1949. Article 147. Grave breaches to which the preceding Article relates shall be those involving any of the following acts, if committed against persons or property protected by the present Convention: wilful killing, torture or inhuman treatment, including biological experiments, wilfully causing great suffering or serious injury to body or health, unlawful deportation or transfer or unlawful confinement of a protected person, compelling a protected person to serve in the forces of a hostile Power, or wilfully depriving a protected person of the rights of fair and regular trial prescribed in the present Convention, taking of hostages and extensive destruction and appropriation of property, not justified by military necessity and carried out unlawfully and wantonly.

Article 148

No High Contracting Party shall be allowed to absolve itself or any other High Contracting Party of any liability incurred by itself or by another High Contracting Party in respect of breaches referred to in the preceding Article.

Article 149

At the request of a Party to the conflict, an enquiry shall be instituted, in a manner to be decided between the interested Parties, concerning any alleged violation of the Convention.

If agreement has not been reached concerning the procedure for the enquiry, the Parties should agree on the choice of an umpire who will decide upon the procedure to be followed.

Once the violation has been established, the Parties to the conflict shall put an end to it and shall repress it with the least possible delay.

SECTION II: Final Provisions

Article 150

The present Convention is established in English and in French. Both texts are equally authentic.

The Swiss Federal Council shall arrange for official translations of the Convention to be made in the Russian and Spanish languages.

Article 151

The present Convention, which bears the date of this day, is open to signature until 12 February 1950, in the name of the Powers represented at the Conference which opened at Geneva on 21 April 1949.

Article 152

The present Convention shall be ratified as soon as possible and the ratifications shall be deposited at Berne.

A record shall be drawn up of the deposit of each instrument of ratification and certified copies of this record shall be transmitted by the Swiss Federal Council to all the Powers in whose name the Convention has been signed, or whose accession has been notified.

Article 153

The present Convention shall come into force six months after not less than two instruments of ratification have been deposited.

Thereafter, it shall come into force for each High Contracting Party six months after the deposit of the instrument of ratification.

Article 154

In the relations between the Powers who are bound by the Hague Conventions respecting the Laws and Customs of War on Land, whether that of 29 July 1899, or that of 18 October 1907, and who are parties to the present Convention, this last Convention shall be supplementary to Sections II and III of the Regulations annexed to the above-mentioned Conventions of The Hague.

Article 155

From the date of its coming into force, it shall be open to any Power in whose name the present Convention has not been signed, to accede to this Convention.

Article 156

Accessions shall be notified in writing to the Swiss Federal Council, and shall take effect six months after the date on which they are received.

The Swiss Federal Council shall communicate the accessions to all the Powers in whose name the Convention has been signed, or whose accession has been notified.

Article 157

The situations provided for in Articles 2 and 3 shall effective immediate effect to ratifications deposited and accessions notified by the Parties to the conflict before or after the beginning of hostilities or occupation. The Swiss Federal Council shall communicate by the quickest method any ratifications or accessions received from Parties to the conflict.

Article 158

Each of the High Contracting Parties shall be at liberty to denounce the present Convention.

The denunciation shall be notified in writing to the Swiss Federal Council, which shall transmit it to the Governments of all the High Contracting Parties.

The denunciation shall take effect one year after the notification thereof has been made to the Swiss Federal Council. However, a denunciation of which notification has been made at a time when the denouncing Power is involved in a conflict shall not take effect until peace has been concluded, and until after operations connected with release, repatriation and re-establishment of the persons protected by the present Convention have been terminated.

The denunciation shall have effect only in respect of the denouncing Power. It shall in no way impair the obligations which the Parties to the conflict shall remain bound to fulfil by virtue of the principles of the law of nations, as they result from the usages established among civilized peoples, from the laws of humanity and the dictates of the public conscience.

Article 159

The Swiss Federal Council shall register the present Convention with the Secretariat of the United Nations. The Swiss Federal Council shall also inform the Secretariat of the United Nations of all ratifications, accessions and denunciations received by it with respect to the present Convention.

In witness whereof the undersigned, having deposited their respective full powers, have signed the present Convention.

Done at Geneva this twelfth day of August 1949, in the English and French languages. The original shall be deposited in the Archives of the Swiss Confederation. The Swiss Federal Council shall transmit certified copies thereof to each of the signatory and acceding States.

ANNEX I: DRAFT AGREEMENT RELATING TO HOSPITAL AND SAFETY ZONES AND LOCALITIES

Article 1

Hospital and safety zones shall be strictly reserved for the persons mentioned in Article 23 of the Geneva Convention for the Amelioration of the Condition of the Wounded and Sick in Armed Forces in the Field of 12 August 1949, and in Article 14 of the Geneva Convention relative to the Protection of Civilian Persons in Time of War of 12 August 1949, and for the personnel entrusted with the organization and administration of these zones and localities, and with the care of the persons therein assembled.

Nevertheless, persons whose permanent residence is within such zones shall have the right to stay there.

Article 2

No persons residing, in whatever capacity, in a hospital and safety zone shall perform any work, either within or without the zone, directly connected with military operations or the production of war material.

Article 3

The Power establishing a hospital and safety zone shall take all necessary measures to prohibit access to all persons who have no right of residence or entry therein.

Article 4

Hospital and safety zones shall fulfil the following conditions:

(a) they shall comprise only a small part of the territory governed by the Power which has established them

(b) they shall be thinly populated in relation to the possibilities of accommodation

(c) they shall be far removed and free from all military objectives, or large industrial or administrative establishments

(d) they shall not be situated in areas which, according to every probability, may become important for the conduct of the war.

Article 5

Hospital and safety zones shall be subject to the following obligations:

(a) the lines of communication and means of transport which they possess shall not be used for the transport of military personnel or material, even in transit

(b) they shall in no case be defended by military means.

Article 6

Hospital and safety zones shall be marked by means of oblique red bands on a white ground, placed on the buildings and outer precincts.

Zones reserved exclusively for the wounded and sick may be marked by means of the Red Cross (Red Crescent, Red Lion and Sun) emblem on a white ground.

They may be similarly marked at night by means of appropriate illumination.

Article 7

The Powers shall communicate to all the High Contracting Parties in peacetime or on the outbreak of hostilities, a list of the hospital and safety zones in the territories governed by them. They shall also give notice of any new zones set up during hostilities.

As soon as the adverse party has received the above-mentioned notification, the zone shall be regularly established.

If, however, the adverse party considers that the conditions of the present agreement have not been fulfilled, it may refuse to recognize the zone by giving immediate notice thereof to the Party responsible for the said zone, or may make its recognition of such zone dependent upon the institution of the control provided for in Article 8.

Article 8

Any Power having recognized one or several hospital and safety zones instituted by the adverse Party shall be entitled to demand control by one or more Special Commissions, for the purpose of ascertaining if the zones fulfil the conditions and obligations stipulated in the present agreement.

For this purpose, members of the Special Commissions shall at all times have free access to the various zones and may even reside there permanently. They shall be given all facilities for their duties of inspection.

Article 9

Should the Special Commissions note any facts which they consider contrary to the stipulations of the present agreement, they shall at once draw the attention of the Power governing the said zone to these facts, and shall fix a time limit of five days within which the matter should be rectified. They shall duly notify the Power which has recognized the zone.

If, when the time limit has expired, the Power governing the zone has not complied with the warning, the adverse Party may declare that it is no longer bound by the present agreement in respect of the said zone.

Article 10

Any Power setting up one or more hospital and safety zones, and the adverse Parties to whom their existence has been notified, shall nominate or have nominated by the Protecting Powers or by other neutral Powers, persons eligible to be members of the Special Commissions mentioned in Articles 8 and 9.

Article 11

In no circumstances may hospital and safety zones be the object of attack. They shall be protected and respected at all times by the Parties to the conflict.

Article 12

In the case of occupation of a territory, the hospital and safety zones therein shall continue to be respected and utilized as such.

Their purpose may, however, be modified by the Occupying Power, on condition that all measures are taken to ensure the safety of the persons accommodated.

Article 13

The present agreement shall also apply to localities which the Powers may utilize for the same purposes as hospital and safety zones.

ANNEX II: DRAFT REGULATIONS CONCERNING COLLECTIVE RELIEF

Article 1

The Internee Committees shall be allowed to distribute collective relief shipments for which they are responsible to all internees who are dependent for administration on the said Committee's place of internment, including those internees who are in hospitals, or in prison or other penitentiary establishments.

Article 2

The distribution of collective relief shipments shall be effected in accordance with the instructions of the donors and with a plan drawn up by the Internee Committees. The issue of medical stores shall, however, be made for preference in agreement with the senior medical officers, and the latter may, in hospitals and infirmaries, waive the said instructions, if the needs of their patients so demand. Within the limits thus defined, the distribution shall always be carried out equitably.

Article 3

Members of Internee Committees shall be allowed to go to the railway stations or other points of arrival of relief supplies near their places of internment so as to enable them to verify the quantity as well as the quality of the goods received and to make out detailed reports thereon for the donors.

Article 4

Internee Committees shall be given the facilities necessary for verifying whether the distribution of collective relief in all subdivisions and annexes of their places of internment has been carried out in accordance with their instructions.

Article 5

Internee Committees shall be allowed to complete, and to cause to be completed by members of the Internee Committees in labour detachments or by the senior medical officers of infirmaries and hospitals, forms or questionnaires intended for the donors, relating to collective relief supplies (distribution, requirements, quantities, etc.). Such forms and questionnaires, duly completed, shall be forwarded to the donors without delay.

Article 6

In order to secure the regular distribution of collective relief supplies to the internees in their place of internment, and to meet any needs that may arise through the arrival of fresh parties of internees, the Internee Committees shall be allowed to create and maintain sufficient reserve stocks of collective relief. For this purpose, they shall have suitable warehouses at their disposal; each warehouse shall be provided with two locks, the Internee Committee holding the keys of one lock, and the commandant of the place of internment the keys of the other.

Article 7

The High Contracting Parties, and the Detaining Powers in particular, shall, so far as is in any way possible and subject to the regulations governing the food supply of the population, authorize purchases of goods to be made in their territories for the distribution of collective relief to the internees. They shall likewise facilitate the transfer of funds and other financial measures of a technical or administrative nature taken for the purpose of making such purchases.

Article 8

The foregoing provisions shall not constitute an obstacle to the right of internees to receive collective relief before their arrival in a place of internment or in the course of their transfer, nor to the possibility of representatives of the Protecting Power, or of the International Committee of the Red Cross or any other humanitarian organization giving assistance to internees and responsible for forwarding such supplies, ensuring the distribution thereof to the recipients by any other means they may deem suitable.

[ANNEX III, illustrations of Internment Card, Letter, and Correspondence Card, not included]

Basic Documents about the Detainees

RASUL V. BUSH

Nimble Books

BASIC DOCUMENTS ABOUT THE DETAINEES

(Slip Opinion) OCTOBER TERM, 2003 1

Syllabus

> NOTE: Where it is feasible, a syllabus (headnote) will be released, as is being done in connection with this case, at the time the opinion is issued. The syllabus constitutes no part of the opinion of the Court but has been prepared by the Reporter of Decisions for the convenience of the reader. See *United States* v. *Detroit Timber & Lumber Co.*, 200 U. S. 321, 337.

SUPREME COURT OF THE UNITED STATES

Syllabus

RASUL ET AL. *v.* BUSH, PRESIDENT OF THE UNITED STATES, ET AL.

CERTIORARI TO THE UNITED STATES COURT OF APPEALS FOR THE DISTRICT OF COLUMIBA CIRCUIT

No. 03–334. Argued April 20, 2004—Decided June 28, 2004*

Pursuant to Congress' joint resolution authorizing the use of necessary and appropriate force against nations, organizations, or persons that planned, authorized, committed, or aided in the September 11, 2001, al Qaeda terrorist attacks, the President sent Armed Forces into Afghanistan to wage a military campaign against al Qaeda and the Taliban regime that had supported it. Petitioners, 2 Australians and 12 Kuwaitis captured abroad during the hostilities, are being held in military custody at the Guantanamo Bay, Cuba, Naval Base, which the United States occupies under a lease and treaty recognizing Cuba's ultimate sovereignty, but giving this country complete jurisdiction and control for so long as it does not abandon the leased areas. Petitioners filed suits under federal law challenging the legality of their detention, alleging that they had never been combatants against the United States or engaged in terrorist acts, and that they have never been charged with wrongdoing, permitted to consult counsel, or provided access to courts or other tribunals. The District Court construed the suits as habeas petitions and dismissed them for want of jurisdiction, holding that, under *Johnson* v. *Eisentrager,* 339 U. S. 763, aliens detained outside United States sovereign territory may not invoke habeas relief. The Court of Appeals affirmed.

Held: United States courts have jurisdiction to consider challenges to the legality of the detention of foreign nationals captured abroad in

---

*Together with No. 03–343, *Al Odah et al.* v. *United States et al.*, also on certiorari to the same court.

Syllabus

connection with hostilities and incarcerated at Guantanamo Bay. Pp. 4–17.

(a) The District Court has jurisdiction to hear petitioners' habeas challenges under 28 U. S. C. §2241, which authorizes district courts, "within their respective jurisdictions," to entertain habeas applications by persons claiming to be held "in custody in violation of the . . . laws . . . of the United States," §§2241(a), (c)(3). Such jurisdiction extends to aliens held in a territory over which the United States exercises plenary and exclusive jurisdiction, but not "ultimate sovereignty." Pp. 4–16.

(1) The Court rejects respondents' primary submission that these cases are controlled by *Eisentrager*'s holding that a District Court lacked authority to grant habeas relief to German citizens captured by U. S. forces in China, tried and convicted of war crimes by an American military commission headquartered in Nanking, and incarcerated in occupied Germany. Reversing a Court of Appeals judgment finding jurisdiction, the *Eisentrager* Court found six critical facts: The German prisoners were (a) enemy aliens who (b) had never been or resided in the United States, (c) were captured outside U. S. territory and there held in military custody, (d) were there tried and convicted by the military (e) for offenses committed there, and (f) were imprisoned there at all times. 339 U. S., at 777. Petitioners here differ from the *Eisentrager* detainees in important respects: They are not nationals of countries at war with the United States, and they deny that they have engaged in or plotted acts of aggression against this country; they have never been afforded access to any tribunal, much less charged with and convicted of wrongdoing; and for more than two years they have been imprisoned in territory over which the United States exercises exclusive jurisdiction and control. The *Eisentrager* Court also made clear that all six of the noted critical facts were relevant only to the question of the prisoners' *constitutional* entitlement to habeas review. *Ibid.* The Court's only statement on their *statutory* entitlement was a passing reference to its absence. *Id.*, at 768. This cursory treatment is explained by the Court's then-recent decision in *Ahrens* v. *Clark,* 335 U. S. 188, in which it held that the District Court for the District of Columbia lacked jurisdiction to entertain the habeas claims of aliens detained at Ellis Island because the habeas statute's phrase "within their respective jurisdictions" required the petitioners' presence within the court's territorial jurisdiction, *id.*, at 192. However, the Court later held, in *Braden* v. *30th Judicial Circuit Court of Ky.,* 410 U. S. 484, 494–495, that such presence is not "an invariable prerequisite" to the exercise of §2241 jurisdiction because habeas acts upon the person holding the prisoner, not the prisoner himself, so that the court acts "within [its] re-

spective jurisdiction" if the custodian can be reached by service of process. Because *Braden* overruled the statutory predicate to *Eisentrager*'s holding, *Eisentrager* does not preclude the exercise of §2241 jurisdiction over petitioners' claims. Pp. 6–11.

(2) Also rejected is respondents' contention that §2241 is limited by the principle that legislation is presumed not to have extraterritorial application unless Congress clearly manifests such an intent, *EEOC* v. *Arabian American Oil Co.*, 499 U. S. 244, 248. That presumption has no application to the operation of the habeas statute with respect to persons detained within "the [United States'] territorial jurisdiction." *Foley Bros., Inc.* v. *Filardo*, 336 U. S. 281, 285. By the express terms of its agreements with Cuba, the United States exercises complete jurisdiction and control over the Guantanamo Base, and may continue to do so permanently if it chooses. Respondents concede that the habeas statute would create federal-court jurisdiction over the claims of an American citizen held at the base. Considering that §2241 draws no distinction between Americans and aliens held in federal custody, there is little reason to think that Congress intended the statute's geographical coverage to vary depending on the detainee's citizenship. Aliens held at the base, like American citizens, are entitled to invoke the federal courts' §2241 authority. Pp. 12–15.

(3) Petitioners contend that they are being held in federal custody in violation of United States laws, and the District Court's jurisdiction over petitioners' custodians is unquestioned, cf. *Braden*, 410 U. S., at 495. Section 2241 requires nothing more and therefore confers jurisdiction on the District Court. Pp. 15–16.

(b) The District Court also has jurisdiction to hear the *Al Odah* petitioners' complaint invoking 28 U. S. C. §1331, the federal question statute, and §1350, the Alien Tort Statute. The Court of Appeals, again relying on *Eisentrager*, held that the District Court correctly dismissed these claims for want of jurisdiction because the petitioners lacked the privilege of litigation in U. S. courts. Nothing in *Eisentrager* or any other of the Court's cases categorically excludes aliens detained in military custody outside the United States from that privilege. United States courts have traditionally been open to nonresident aliens. Cf. *Disconto Gesellschaft* v. *Umbreit*, 208 U. S. 570, 578. And indeed, §1350 explicitly confers the privilege of suing for an actionable "tort . . . committed in violation of the law of nations or a treaty of the United States" on aliens alone. The fact that petitioners are being held in military custody is immaterial. Pp. 16–17.

(c) Whether and what further proceedings may become necessary after respondents respond to the merits of petitioners' claims are not here addressed. P. 17.

321 F. 3d 1134, reversed and remanded.

RASUL v. BUSH

Syllabus

STEVENS, J., delivered the opinion of the Court, in which O'CONNOR, SOUTER, GINSBURG, and BREYER, JJ., joined. KENNEDY, J., filed an opinion concurring in the judgment. SCALIA, J., filed a dissenting opinion, in which REHNQUIST, C. J., and THOMAS, J., joined.

Basic Documents about the Detainees

Cite as: 542 U. S. ____ (2004) 1

Opinion of the Court

NOTICE: This opinion is subject to formal revision before publication in the preliminary print of the United States Reports. Readers are requested to notify the Reporter of Decisions, Supreme Court of the United States, Washington, D. C. 20543, of any typographical or other formal errors, in order that corrections may be made before the preliminary print goes to press.

SUPREME COURT OF THE UNITED STATES

Nos. 03–334 and 03–343

SHAFIQ RASUL, ET AL., PETITIONERS
03–334   *v.*
GEORGE W. BUSH, PRESIDENT OF THE UNITED STATES, ET AL.

FAWZI KHALID ABDULLAH FAHAD AL ODAH, ET AL., PETITIONERS
03–343   *v.*
UNITED STATES ET AL.

ON WRITS OF CERTIORARI TO THE UNITED STATES COURT OF APPEALS FOR THE DISTRICT OF COLUMBIA CIRCUIT

[June 28, 2004]

JUSTICE STEVENS delivered the opinion of the Court.

These two cases present the narrow but important question whether United States courts lack jurisdiction to consider challenges to the legality of the detention of foreign nationals captured abroad in connection with hostilities and incarcerated at the Guantanamo Bay Naval Base, Cuba.

I

On September 11, 2001, agents of the al Qaeda terrorist network hijacked four commercial airliners and used them as missiles to attack American targets. While one of the four attacks was foiled by the heroism of the plane's passengers, the other three killed approximately 3,000 innocent civilians, destroyed hundreds of millions of dollars of property, and severely damaged the U. S. economy. In response to the attacks, Congress passed a joint resolution authorizing the President to use "all necessary and appropriate force against those nations, organizations, or persons he determines planned, authorized, committed, or aided the terrorist attacks . . . or harbored such organizations or persons." Authorization for Use of Military Force, Pub. L. 107–40, §§1–2, 115 Stat. 224. Acting pursuant to that authorization, the President sent U. S. Armed Forces into Afghanistan to wage a military campaign against al Qaeda and the Taliban regime that had supported it.

Petitioners in these cases are 2 Australian citizens and 12 Kuwaiti citizens who were captured abroad during hostilities between the United States and the Taliban.[1] Since early 2002, the U. S. military has held them—along with, according to the Government's estimate, approximately 640 other non-Americans captured abroad—at the Naval Base at Guantanamo Bay. Brief for United States 6. The United States occupies the Base, which comprises 45 square miles of land and water along the southeast coast of Cuba, pursuant to a 1903 Lease Agreement executed with the newly independent Republic of Cuba in the aftermath of the Spanish-American War. Under the Agreement, "the United States recognizes the continuance of the ultimate sovereignty of the Republic of Cuba over the [leased areas]," while "the Republic of Cuba consents that during the period of the occupation by the United States . . . the United States shall exercise complete jurisdiction and control over and within said areas."[2] In 1934,

---

[1] When we granted certiorari, the petitioners also included two British citizens, Shafiq Rasul and Asif Iqbal. These petitioners have since been released from custody.

[2] Lease of Lands for Coaling and Naval Stations, Feb. 23, 1903, U. S.-Cuba, Art. III, T. S. No. 418 (hereinafter 1903 Lease Agreement). A

the parties entered into a treaty providing that, absent an agreement to modify or abrogate the lease, the lease would remain in effect "[s]o long as the United States of America shall not abandon the . . . naval station of Guantanamo."[3]

In 2002, petitioners, through relatives acting as their next friends, filed various actions in the U. S. District Court for the District of Columbia challenging the legality of their detention at the Base. All alleged that none of the petitioners has ever been a combatant against the United States or has ever engaged in any terrorist acts.[4] They also alleged that none has been charged with any wrongdoing, permitted to consult with counsel, or provided access to the courts or any other tribunal. App. 29, 77, 108.[5]

The two Australians, Mamdouh Habib and David Hicks, each filed a petition for writ of habeas corpus, seeking release from custody, access to counsel, freedom from interrogations, and other relief. *Id.,* at 98–99, 124–126.

---

supplemental lease agreement, executed in July 1903, obligates the United States to pay an annual rent in the amount of "two thousand dollars, in gold coin of the United States" and to maintain "permanent fences" around the base. Lease of Certain Areas for Naval or Coaling Stations, July 2, 1903, U. S.-Cuba, Arts. I–II, T. S. No. 426.

[3] Treaty Defining Relations with Cuba, May 29, 1934, U. S.-Cuba, Art. III, 48 Stat. 1683, T. S. No. 866 (hereinafter 1934 Treaty).

[4] Relatives of the Kuwaiti detainees allege that the detainees were taken captive "by local villagers seeking promised bounties or other financial rewards" while they were providing humanitarian aid in Afghanistan and Pakistan, and were subsequently turned over to U. S. custody. App. 24–25. The Australian David Hicks was allegedly captured in Afghanistan by the Northern Alliance, a coalition of Afghan groups opposed to the Taliban, before he was turned over to the United States. *Id.,* at 84. The Australian Mamdouh Habib was allegedly arrested in Pakistan by Pakistani authorities and turned over to Egyptian authorities, who in turn transferred him to U. S. custody. *Id.,* at 110–111.

[5] David Hicks has since been permitted to meet with counsel. Brief for United States 9.

Opinion of the Court

Fawzi Khalid Abdullah Fahad Al Odah and the 11 other Kuwaiti detainees filed a complaint seeking to be informed of the charges against them, to be allowed to meet with their families and with counsel, and to have access to the courts or some other impartial tribunal. *Id.,* at 34. They claimed that denial of these rights violates the Constitution, international law, and treaties of the United States. Invoking the court's jurisdiction under 28 U. S. C. §§1331 and 1350, among other statutory bases, they asserted causes of action under the Administrative Procedure Act, 5 U. S. C. §§555, 702, 706; the Alien Tort Statute, 28 U. S. C. §1350; and the general federal habeas corpus statute, §§2241–2243. App. 19.

Construing all three actions as petitions for writs of habeas corpus, the District Court dismissed them for want of jurisdiction. The court held, in reliance on our opinion in *Johnson* v. *Eisentrager,* 339 U. S. 763 (1950), that "aliens detained outside the sovereign territory of the United States [may not] invok[e] a petition for a writ of habeas corpus." 215 F. Supp. 2d 55, 68 (DC 2002). The Court of Appeals affirmed. Reading *Eisentrager* to hold that "'the privilege of litigation' does not extend to aliens in military custody who have no presence in 'any territory over which the United States is sovereign,'" 321 F. 3d 1134, 1144 (CADC 2003) (quoting *Eisentrager,* 339 U. S., at 777–778), it held that the District Court lacked jurisdiction over petitioners' habeas actions, as well as their remaining federal statutory claims that do not sound in habeas. We granted certiorari, 540 U. S. 1003 (2003), and now reverse.

II

Congress has granted federal district courts, "within their respective jurisdictions," the authority to hear applications for habeas corpus by any person who claims to be held "in custody in violation of the Constitution or laws or treaties of the United States." 28 U. S. C. §§2241(a), (c)(3).

BASIC DOCUMENTS ABOUT THE DETAINEES

Cite as: 542 U. S. ____ (2004)

Opinion of the Court

The statute traces its ancestry to the first grant of federal court jurisdiction: Section 14 of the Judiciary Act of 1789 authorized federal courts to issue the writ of habeas corpus to prisoners "in custody, under or by colour of the authority of the United States, or committed for trial before some court of the same." Act of Sept. 24, 1789, ch. 20, §14, 1 Stat. 82. In 1867, Congress extended the protections of the writ to "all cases where any person may be restrained of his or her liberty in violation of the constitution, or of any treaty or law of the United States." Act of Feb. 5, 1867, ch. 28, 14 Stat. 385. See *Felker* v. *Turpin*, 518 U. S. 651, 659–660 (1996).

Habeas corpus is, however, "a writ antecedent to statute, . . . throwing its root deep into the genius of our common law." *Williams* v. *Kaiser*, 323 U. S. 471, 484, n. 2 (1945) (internal quotation marks omitted). The writ appeared in English law several centuries ago, became "an integral part of our common-law heritage" by the time the Colonies achieved independence, *Preiser* v. *Rodriguez*, 411 U. S. 475, 485 (1973), and received explicit recognition in the Constitution, which forbids suspension of "[t]he Privilege of the Writ of Habeas Corpus . . . unless when in Cases of Rebellion or Invasion the public Safety may require it," Art. I, §9, cl. 2.

As it has evolved over the past two centuries, the habeas statute clearly has expanded habeas corpus "beyond the limits that obtained during the 17th and 18th centuries." *Swain* v. *Pressley*, 430 U. S. 372, 380, n. 13 (1977). But "[a]t its historical core, the writ of habeas corpus has served as a means of reviewing the legality of Executive detention, and it is in that context that its protections have been strongest." *INS* v. *St. Cyr*, 533 U. S. 289, 301 (2001). See also *Brown* v. *Allen*, 344 U. S. 443, 533 (1953) (Jackson, J., concurring in result) ("The historic purpose of the writ has been to relieve detention by executive authorities without judicial trial"). As Justice Jackson wrote in an opinion respecting the availability of habeas corpus to aliens held in U. S. custody:

> "Executive imprisonment has been considered oppressive and lawless since John, at Runnymede, pledged that no free man should be imprisoned, dispossessed, outlawed, or exiled save by the judgment of his peers or by the law of the land. The judges of England developed the writ of habeas corpus largely to preserve these immunities from executive restraint." *Shaughnessy* v. *United States ex rel. Mezei,* 345 U. S. 206, 218–219 (1953) (dissenting opinion).

Consistent with the historic purpose of the writ, this Court has recognized the federal courts' power to review applications for habeas relief in a wide variety of cases involving Executive detention, in wartime as well as in times of peace. The Court has, for example, entertained the habeas petitions of an American citizen who plotted an attack on military installations during the Civil War, *Ex parte Milligan,* 4 Wall. 2 (1866), and of admitted enemy aliens convicted of war crimes during a declared war and held in the United States, *Ex parte Quirin,* 317 U. S. 1 (1942), and its insular possessions, *In re Yamashita,* 327 U. S. 1 (1946).

The question now before us is whether the habeas statute confers a right to judicial review of the legality of Executive detention of aliens in a territory over which the United States exercises plenary and exclusive jurisdiction, but not "ultimate sovereignty."[6]

III

Respondents' primary submission is that the answer to the jurisdictional question is controlled by our decision in *Eisentrager.* In that case, we held that a Federal District

---

[6] 1903 Lease Agreement, Art. III.

Court lacked authority to issue a writ of habeas corpus to 21 German citizens who had been captured by U. S. forces in China, tried and convicted of war crimes by an American military commission headquartered in Nanking, and incarcerated in the Landsberg Prison in occupied Germany. The Court of Appeals in *Eisentrager* had found jurisdiction, reasoning that "any person who is deprived of his liberty by officials of the United States, acting under purported authority of that Government, and who can show that his confinement is in violation of a prohibition of the Constitution, has a right to the writ." *Eisentrager* v. *Forrestal,* 174 F. 2d 961, 963 (CADC 1949). In reversing that determination, this Court summarized the six critical facts in the case:

> "We are here confronted with a decision whose basic premise is that these prisoners are entitled, as a constitutional right, to sue in some court of the United States for a writ of *habeas corpus*. To support that assumption we must hold that a prisoner of our military authorities is constitutionally entitled to the writ, even though he (a) is an enemy alien; (b) has never been or resided in the United States; (c) was captured outside of our territory and there held in military custody as a prisoner of war; (d) was tried and convicted by a Military Commission sitting outside the United States; (e) for offenses against laws of war committed outside the United States; (f) and is at all times imprisoned outside the United States." 339 U. S., at 777.

On this set of facts, the Court concluded, "no right to the writ of *habeas corpus* appears." *Id.,* at 781.

Petitioners in these cases differ from the *Eisentrager* detainees in important respects: They are not nationals of countries at war with the United States, and they deny that they have engaged in or plotted acts of aggression against the United States; they have never been afforded access to any tribunal, much less charged with and convicted of wrongdoing; and for more than two years they have been imprisoned in territory over which the United States exercises exclusive jurisdiction and control.

Not only are petitioners differently situated from the *Eisentrager* detainees, but the Court in *Eisentrager* made quite clear that all six of the facts critical to its disposition were relevant only to the question of the prisoners' *constitutional* entitlement to habeas corpus. *Id.*, at 777. The Court had far less to say on the question of the petitioners' *statutory* entitlement to habeas review. Its only statement on the subject was a passing reference to the absence of statutory authorization: "Nothing in the text of the Constitution extends such a right, nor does anything in our statutes." *Id.*, at 768.

Reference to the historical context in which *Eisentrager* was decided explains why the opinion devoted so little attention to question of statutory jurisdiction. In 1948, just two months after the *Eisentrager* petitioners filed their petition for habeas corpus in the U. S. District Court for the District of Columbia, this Court issued its decision in *Ahrens* v. *Clark,* 335 U. S. 188, a case concerning the application of the habeas statute to the petitions of 120 Germans who were then being detained at Ellis Island, New York, for deportation to Germany. The *Ahrens* detainees had also filed their petitions in the U. S. District Court for the District of Columbia, naming the Attorney General as the respondent. Reading the phrase "within their respective jurisdictions" as used in the habeas statute to require the petitioners' presence within the district court's territorial jurisdiction, the Court held that the District of Columbia court lacked jurisdiction to entertain the detainees' claims. *Id.*, at 192. *Ahrens* expressly reserved the question "of what process, if any, a person confined in an area not subject to the jurisdiction of any district court may employ to assert federal rights." *Id.,* 192, n. 4. But as the dissent noted, if the presence of the petitioner in the territorial jurisdiction of a federal district court were truly a jurisdictional requirement, there could be only one response to that question. *Id.,* at 209 (opinion of Rutledge, J.).[7]

When the District Court for the District of Columbia reviewed the German prisoners' habeas application in *Eisentrager,* it thus dismissed their action on the authority of *Ahrens.* See *Eisentrager,* 339 U. S., at 767, 790. Although the Court of Appeals reversed the District Court, it implicitly conceded that the District Court lacked jurisdiction under the habeas statute as it had been interpreted in *Ahrens.* The Court of Appeals instead held that petitioners had a constitutional right to habeas corpus secured by the Suspension Clause, U. S. Const., Art. I, §9, cl. 2, reasoning that "if a person has a right to a writ of habeas corpus, he cannot be deprived of the privilege by an omission in a federal jurisdictional statute." *Eisentrager* v. *Forrestal,* 174 F. 2d, at 965. In essence, the Court of Appeals concluded that the habeas statute, as construed in *Ahrens,* had created an unconstitutional gap that had to be filled by reference to "fundamentals." 174 F. 2d, at 963. In its review of that decision, this Court, like the Court of Appeals, proceeded from the premise that "nothing in our statutes" conferred federal-court jurisdiction, and accordingly evaluated the Court of Appeals' resort to "fundamentals" on its own terms. 339 U. S., at 768.[8]

---

[7] Justice Rutledge wrote:

"[I]f absence of the body detained from the territorial jurisdiction of the court having jurisdiction of the jailer creates a total and irremediable void in the court's capacity to act, . . . then it is hard to see how that gap can be filled by such extraneous considerations as whether there is no other court in the place of detention from which remedy might be had . . . ." 335 U. S., at 209.

[8] Although JUSTICE SCALIA disputes the basis for the Court of Appeals' holding, *post,* at 4, what is most pertinent for present purposes is that

Opinion of the Court

Because subsequent decisions of this Court have filled the statutory gap that had occasioned *Eisentrager*'s resort to "fundamentals," persons detained outside the territorial jurisdiction of any federal district court no longer need rely on the Constitution as the source of their right to federal habeas review. In *Braden* v. *30th Judicial Circuit Court of Ky.,* 410 U. S. 484, 495 (1973), this Court held, contrary to *Ahrens,* that the prisoner's presence within the territorial jurisdiction of the district court is not "an invariable prerequisite" to the exercise of district court jurisdiction under the federal habeas statute. Rather, because "the writ of habeas corpus does not act upon the prisoner who seeks relief, but upon the person who holds him in what is alleged to be unlawful custody," a district court acts "within [its] respective jurisdiction" within the meaning of §2241 as long as "the custodian can be reached by service of process." 410 U. S., at 494–495. *Braden* reasoned that its departure from the rule of *Ahrens* was warranted in light of developments that "had a profound impact on the continuing vitality of that decision." 410 U. S., at 497. These developments included, notably, decisions of this Court in cases involving habeas petitioners "confined overseas (and thus outside the territory of any district court)," in which the Court "held, if only implicitly, that the petitioners' absence from the district does not present a jurisdictional obstacle to the consideration of the claim." *Id.,* at 498 (citing *Burns* v. *Wilson,* 346 U. S.

---

this Court clearly understood the Court of Appeals' decision to rest on constitutional and not statutory grounds. *Eisentrager,* 339 U. S., at 767 ("[The Court of Appeals] concluded that any person, including an enemy alien, deprived of his liberty anywhere under any purported authority of the United States is entitled to the writ if he can show that extension to his case of any constitutional rights or limitations would show his imprisonment illegal; [and] that, *although no statutory jurisdiction of such cases is given,* courts must be held to possess it as part of the judicial power of the United States . . ." (emphasis added)).

137 (1953), rehearing denied, 346 U. S. 844, 851–852 (opinion of Frankfurter, J.); *United States ex rel. Toth* v. *Quarles,* 350 U. S. 11 (1955); *Hirota* v. *MacArthur,* 338 U. S. 197, 199 (1948) (Douglas, J., concurring)). *Braden* thus established that *Ahrens* can no longer be viewed as establishing "an inflexible jurisdictional rule," and is strictly relevant only to the question of the appropriate forum, not to whether the claim can be heard at all. 410 U. S., at 499–500.

Because *Braden* overruled the statutory predicate to *Eisentrager*'s holding, *Eisentrager* plainly does not preclude the exercise of §2241 jurisdiction over petitioners' claims.[9]

---

[9]The dissent argues that *Braden* did not overrule *Ahrens*' jurisdictional holding, but simply distinguished it. *Post,* at 7. Of course, *Braden* itself indicated otherwise, 410 U. S., at 495–500, and a long line of judicial and scholarly interpretations, beginning with then-JUSTICE REHNQUIST's dissenting opinion, have so understood the decision. See, *e.g., id.,* at 502 ("Today the Court overrules *Ahrens*"); *Moore* v. *Olson,* 368 F. 3d 757, 758 (CA7 2004) ("[A]fter *Braden* . . . , which overruled *Ahrens,* the location of a collateral attack is best understood as a matter of venue"); *Armentero* v. *INS,* 340 F. 3d 1058, 1063 (CA9 2003) ("[T]he Court in *[Braden]* declared that *Ahrens* was overruled" (citations omitted)); *Henderson* v. *INS,* 157 F. 3d 106, 126, n. 20 (CA2 1998) ("On the issue of territorial jurisdiction, *Ahrens* was subsequently overruled by *Braden*"); *Chatman-Bey* v. *Thornburgh,* 864 F. 2d 804, 811 (CADC 1988) (en banc) ("[I]n *Braden,* the Court cut back substantially on *Ahrens* (and indeed overruled its territorially-based jurisdictional holding)"). See also, *e.g., Patterson* v. *McLean Credit Union,* 485 U. S. 617, 618 (1988) *(per curiam);* Eskridge, Overruling Statutory Precedents, 76 Geo. L. J. 1361, App. A (1988).

The dissent also disingenuously contends that the continuing vitality of *Ahrens*' jurisdictional holding is irrelevant to the question presented in these cases, "inasmuch as *Ahrens* did not pass upon any of the statutory issues decided by *Eisentrager.*" *Post,* at 7. But what JUSTICE SCALIA describes as *Eisentrager*'s statutory holding—"that, unaided by the canon of constitutional avoidance, the statute did not confer jurisdiction over an alien detained outside the territorial jurisdiction of the courts of the United States," *post,* at 6—is little more than the rule of

Opinion of the Court

IV

Putting *Eisentrager* and *Ahrens* to one side, respondents contend that we can discern a limit on §2241 through application of the "longstanding principle of American law" that congressional legislation is presumed not to have extraterritorial application unless such intent is clearly manifested. *EEOC* v. *Arabian American Oil Co.*, 499 U. S. 244, 248 (1991). Whatever traction the presumption against extraterritoriality might have in other contexts, it certainly has no application to the operation of the habeas statute with respect to persons detained within "the territorial jurisdiction" of the United States. *Foley Bros., Inc.* v. *Filardo*, 336 U. S. 281, 285 (1949). By the express terms of its agreements with Cuba, the United States exercises "complete jurisdiction and control" over the Guantanamo Bay Naval Base, and may continue to exercise such control permanently if it so chooses. 1903 Lease Agreement, Art. III; 1934 Treaty, Art. III. Respondents themselves concede that the habeas statute would create federal-court jurisdiction over the claims of an American citizen held at the base. Tr. of Oral Arg. 27. Considering that the statute draws no distinction between Americans and aliens held in federal custody, there is little reason to think that Congress intended the geographical coverage of the statute to vary depending on the detainee's citizenship.[10] Aliens held at the

---

Ahrens cloaked in the garb of *Eisentrager*'s facts. To contend plausibly that this holding survived *Braden*, JUSTICE SCALIA at a minimum must find a textual basis for the rule other than the phrase "within their respective jurisdictions"—a phrase which, after *Braden*, can no longer be read to require the habeas petitioner's physical presence within the territorial jurisdiction of a federal district court. Two references to the district of confinement in provisions relating to recordkeeping and pleading requirements in proceedings before circuit judges hardly suffice in that regard. See *post*, at 2 (citing 28 U. S. C. §§2241(a), 2242).

[10] JUSTICE SCALIA appears to agree that neither the plain text of the statute nor his interpretation of that text provides a basis for treating

base, no less than American citizens, are entitled to invoke the federal courts' authority under §2241.

Application of the habeas statute to persons detained at the base is consistent with the historical reach of the writ of habeas corpus. At common law, courts exercised habeas jurisdiction over the claims of aliens detained within sovereign territory of the realm,[11] as well as the claims of persons detained in the so-called "exempt jurisdictions," where ordinary writs did not run,[12] and all other domin-

---

American citizens differently from aliens. *Post,* at 10. But resisting the practical consequences of his position, he suggests that he might nevertheless recognize an "atextual exception" to his statutory rule for citizens held beyond the territorial jurisdiction of the federal district courts. *Ibid.*

[11] See, *e.g., King* v. *Schiever,* 2 Burr. 765, 97 Eng. Rep. 551 (K. B. 1759) (reviewing the habeas petition of a neutral alien deemed a prisoner of war because he was captured aboard an enemy French privateer during a war between England and France); *Sommersett* v. *Stewart,* 20 How. St. Tr. 1, 79–82 (K. B. 1772) (releasing on habeas an African slave purchased in Virginia and detained on a ship docked in England and bound for Jamaica); *Case of the Hottentot Venus,* 13 East 195, 104 Eng. Rep. 344 (K. B. 1810) (reviewing the habeas petition of a "native of *South Africa*" allegedly held in private custody).

American courts followed a similar practice in the early years of the Republic. See, *e.g., United States* v. *Villato,* 2 Dall. 370 (CC Pa. 1797) (granting habeas relief to Spanish-born prisoner charged with treason on the ground that he had never become a citizen of the United States); *Ex parte D'Olivera,* 7 F. Cas. 853 (No, 3,967) (CC Mass. 1813) (Story, J., on circuit) (ordering the release of Portuguese sailors arrested for deserting their ship); *Wilson* v. *Izard,* 30 F. Cas. 131 (No. 17,810) (CC NY 1815) (Livingston, J., on circuit) (reviewing the habeas petition of enlistees who claimed that they were entitled to discharge because of their status as enemy aliens).

[12] See, *e.g., Bourn's Case,* Cro. Jac. 543, 79 Eng. Rep. 465 (K. B. 1619) (writ issued to the Cinque-Ports town of Dover); *Alder* v. *Puisy,* 1 Freeman 12, 89 Eng. Rep. 10 (K. B. 1671) (same); *Jobson's Case,* Latch 160, 82 Eng. Rep. 325 (K. B. 1626) (entertaining the habeas petition of a prisoner held in the County Palatine of Durham). See also 3 W. Blackstone, Commentaries on the Laws of England 79 (1769) (hereinafter Blackstone) ("[A]ll prerogative writs (as those of *habeas corpus,*

ions under the sovereign's control.¹³ As Lord Mansfield wrote in 1759, even if a territory was "no part of the realm," there was "no doubt" as to the court's power to issue writs of habeas corpus if the territory was "under the subjection of the Crown." *King* v. *Cowle,* 2 Burr. 834, 854–855, 97 Eng. Rep. 587, 598–599 (K. B.). Later cases confirmed that the reach of the writ depended not on formal notions of territorial sovereignty, but rather on the practical question of "the exact extent and nature of the jurisdiction or dominion exercised in fact by the Crown." *Ex parte Mwenya,* [1960] 1 Q. B. 241, 303 (C. A.) (Lord Evershed, M. R.).¹⁴

---

prohibition, *certiorari,* and *mandamus*) may issue ... to all these exempt jurisdictions; because the privilege, that the king's writ runs not, must be intended between party and party, for there can be no such privilege against the king" (footnotes omitted)); R. Sharpe, Law of Habeas Corpus 188–189 (2d ed. 1989) (describing the "extraordinary territorial ambit" of the writ at common law).

¹³ See, *e.g., King* v. *Overton,* 1 Sid. 387, 82 Eng. Rep. 1173 (K. B. 1668) (writ issued to Isle of Jersey); *King* v. *Salmon,* 2 Keble 450, 84 Eng. Rep. 282 (K. B. 1669) (same). See also 3 Blackstone 131 (habeas corpus "run[s] into all parts of the king's dominions: for the king is at all times [e]ntitled to have an account, why the liberty of any of his subjects is restrained, wherever that restraint may be inflicted" (footnotes omitted)); M. Hale, History of the Common Law 120–121 (C. Gray ed. 1971) (writ of habeas corpus runs to the Channel Islands, even though "they are not Parcel of the Realm of England").

¹⁴ *Ex parte Mwenya* held that the writ ran to a territory described as a "foreign country within which [the Crown] ha[d] power and jurisdiction by treaty, grant, usage, sufferance, and other lawful means." *Ex parte Mwenya,* 1 Q. B., at 265 (internal quotation marks omitted). See also *King* v. *The Earl of Crewe ex parte Sekgome,* [1910] 2 K. B. 576, 606 (C. A.) (Williams, L. J.) (concluding that the writ would run to such a territory); *id.,* at 618 (Farwell, L. J.) (same). As Lord Justice Sellers explained:

"Lord Mansfield gave the writ the greatest breadth of application which in the then circumstances could well be conceived. . . . 'Subjection' is fully appropriate to the powers exercised or exercisable by this country irrespective of territorial sovereignty or dominion, and it

Cite as: 542 U. S. ____ (2004)

Opinion of the Court

In the end, the answer to the question presented is clear. Petitioners contend that they are being held in federal custody in violation of the laws of the United States.[15] No party questions the District Court's jurisdiction over petitioners' custodians. Cf. *Braden,* 410 U. S., at 495. Section 2241, by its terms, requires nothing more. We therefore hold that §2241 confers on the District Court jurisdiction to hear petitioners' habeas corpus challenges to the legality of their detention at the Guantanamo Bay

───────────

embraces in outlook the power of the Crown in the place concerned.'" 1 Q. B., at 310.

JUSTICE SCALIA cites *In re Ning Yi-Ching,* 56 T. L. R. 3 (Vacation Ct. 1939), for the broad proposition that habeas corpus has been categorically unavailable to aliens held outside sovereign territory. *Post,* at 18. *Ex parte Mwenya,* however, casts considerable doubt on this narrow view of the territorial reach of the writ. See *Ex parte Mwenya,* 1 Q. B., at 295 (Lord Evershed, M. R.) (noting that *In re Ning Yi-Ching* relied on Lord Justice Kennedy's opinion in *Ex parte Sekgome* concerning the territorial reach of the writ, despite the opinions of two members of the court who "took a different view upon this matter"). And *In re Ning Yi-Ching* itself made quite clear that "the remedy of *habeas corpus* was not confined to British subjects," but would extend to "any person . . . detained" within reach of the writ. 56 T. L. R., at 5 (citing *Ex parte Sekgome,* 2 K. B., at 620 (Kennedy, L. J.)). Moreover, the result in that case can be explained by the peculiar nature of British control over the area where the petitioners, four Chinese nationals accused of various criminal offenses, were being held pending transfer to the local district court. Although the treaties governing the British Concession at Tientsin did confer on Britain "certain rights of administration and control," "the right to administer justice" to Chinese nationals was not among them. 56 T. L. R., at 4–6.

[15] Petitioners' allegations—that, although they have engaged neither in combat nor in acts of terrorism against the United States, they have been held in Executive detention for more than two years in territory subject to the long-term, exclusive jurisdiction and control of the United States, without access to counsel and without being charged with any wrongdoing—unquestionably describe "custody in violation of the Constitution or laws or treaties of the United States." 28 U. S. C. §2241(c)(3). Cf. *United States* v. *Verdugo-Urquidez,* 494 U. S. 259, 277–278 (1990) (KENNEDY, J., concurring), and cases cited therein.

Naval Base.

V

In addition to invoking the District Court's jurisdiction under §2241, the *Al Odah* petitioners' complaint invoked the court's jurisdiction under 28 U. S. C. §1331, the federal question statute, as well as §1350, the Alien Tort Statute. The Court of Appeals, again relying on *Eisentrager*, held that the District Court correctly dismissed the claims founded on §1331 and §1350 for lack of jurisdiction, even to the extent that these claims "deal only with conditions of confinement and do not sound in habeas," because petitioners lack the "privilege of litigation" in U. S. courts. 321 F. 3d, at 1144 (internal quotation marks omitted). Specifically, the court held that because petitioners' §1331 and §1350 claims "necessarily rest on alleged violations of the same category of laws listed in the habeas corpus statute," they, like claims founded on the habeas statute itself, must be "beyond the jurisdiction of the federal courts." *Id.*, at 1144–1145.

As explained above, *Eisentrager* itself erects no bar to the exercise of federal court jurisdiction over the petitioners' habeas corpus claims. It therefore certainly does not bar the exercise of federal-court jurisdiction over claims that merely implicate the "same category of laws listed in the habeas corpus statute." But in any event, nothing in *Eisentrager* or in any of our other cases categorically excludes aliens detained in military custody outside the United States from the "'privilege of litigation'" in U. S. courts. 321 F. 3d, at 1139. The courts of the United States have traditionally been open to nonresident aliens. Cf. *Disconto Gesellschaft* v. *Umbreit*, 208 U. S. 570, 578 (1908) ("Alien citizens, by the policy and practice of the courts of this country, are ordinarily permitted to resort to the courts for the redress of wrongs and the protection of their rights"). And indeed, 28 U. S. C. §1350 explicitly confers the privilege of suing for an actionable "tort . . . committed in violation of the law of nations or a treaty of the United States" on aliens alone. The fact that petitioners in these cases are being held in military custody is immaterial to the question of the District Court's jurisdiction over their nonhabeas statutory claims.

VI

Whether and what further proceedings may become necessary after respondents make their response to the merits of petitioners' claims are matters that we need not address now. What is presently at stake is only whether the federal courts have jurisdiction to determine the legality of the Executive's potentially indefinite detention of individuals who claim to be wholly innocent of wrongdoing. Answering that question in the affirmative, we reverse the judgment of the Court of Appeals and remand for the District Court to consider in the first instance the merits of petitioners' claims.

It is so ordered.

KENNEDY, J., concurring in judgment

SUPREME COURT OF THE UNITED STATES

Nos. 03–334 and 03–343

SHAFIQ RASUL, ET AL., PETITIONERS
03–334   *v.*
GEORGE W. BUSH, PRESIDENT OF THE UNITED STATES, ET AL.

FAWZI KHALID ABDULLAH FAHAD AL ODAH, ET AL., PETITIONERS
03–343   *v.*
UNITED STATES ET AL.

ON WRITS OF CERTIORARI TO THE UNITED STATES COURT OF APPEALS FOR THE DISTRICT OF COLUMBIA CIRCUIT

[June 28, 2004]

JUSTICE KENNEDY, concurring in the judgment.

The Court is correct, in my view, to conclude that federal courts have jurisdiction to consider challenges to the legality of the detention of foreign nationals held at the Guantanamo Bay Naval Base in Cuba. While I reach the same conclusion, my analysis follows a different course. JUSTICE SCALIA exposes the weakness in the Court's conclusion that *Braden* v. *30th Judicial Circuit Court of Ky.*, 410 U. S. 484 (1973), "overruled the statutory predicate to *Eisentrager*'s holding," *ante*, at 10–11. As he explains, the Court's approach is not a plausible reading of *Braden* or *Johnson* v. *Eisentrager*, 339 U. S. 763 (1950). In my view, the correct course is to follow the framework of *Eisentrager*.

Eisentrager considered the scope of the right to petition for a writ of habeas corpus against the backdrop of the constitutional command of the separation of powers. The issue before the Court was whether the Judiciary could

KENNEDY, J., concurring in judgment

exercise jurisdiction over the claims of German prisoners held in the Landsberg prison in Germany following the cessation of hostilities in Europe. The Court concluded the petition could not be entertained. The petition was not within the proper realm of the judicial power. It concerned matters within the exclusive province of the Executive, or the Executive and Congress, to determine.

The Court began by noting the "ascending scale of rights" that courts have recognized for individuals depending on their connection to the United States. *Id.*, at 770. Citizenship provides a longstanding basis for jurisdiction, the Court noted, and among aliens physical presence within the United States also "gave the Judiciary power to act." *Id.*, at 769, 771. This contrasted with the "essential pattern for seasonable Executive constraint of enemy aliens." *Id.*, at 773. The place of the detention was also important to the jurisdictional question, the Court noted. Physical presence in the United States "implied protection," *id.*, at 777–778, whereas in *Eisentrager* "th[e] prisoners at no relevant time were within any territory over which the United States is sovereign," *id.*, at 778. The Court next noted that the prisoners in *Eisentrager* "were actual enemies" of the United States, proven to be so at trial, and thus could not justify "a limited opening of our courts" to distinguish the "many [aliens] of friendly personal disposition to whom the status of enemy" was unproven. *Id.*, at 778. Finally, the Court considered the extent to which jurisdiction would "hamper the war effort and bring aid and comfort to the enemy." *Id.*, at 779. Because the prisoners in *Eisentrager* were proven enemy aliens found and detained outside the United States, and because the existence of jurisdiction would have had a clear harmful effect on the Nation's military affairs, the matter was appropriately left to the Executive Branch and there was no jurisdiction for the courts to hear the prisoner's claims.

KENNEDY, J., concurring in judgment

The decision in *Eisentrager* indicates that there is a realm of political authority over military affairs where the judicial power may not enter. The existence of this realm acknowledges the power of the President as Commander in Chief, and the joint role of the President and the Congress, in the conduct of military affairs. A faithful application of *Eisentrager*, then, requires an initial inquiry into the general circumstances of the detention to determine whether the Court has the authority to entertain the petition and to grant relief after considering all of the facts presented. A necessary corollary of *Eisentrager* is that there are circumstances in which the courts maintain the power and the responsibility to protect persons from unlawful detention even where military affairs are implicated. See also *Ex parte Milligan,* 4 Wall. 2 (1866).

The facts here are distinguishable from those in *Eisentrager* in two critical ways, leading to the conclusion that a federal court may entertain the petitions. First, Guantanamo Bay is in every practical respect a United States territory, and it is one far removed from any hostilities. The opinion of the Court well explains the history of its possession by the United States. In a formal sense, the United States leases the Bay; the 1903 lease agreement states that Cuba retains "ultimate sovereignty" over it. Lease of Lands for Coaling and Naval Stations, Feb. 23, 1903, U. S.-Cuba, Art. III, T. S. No. 418. At the same time, this lease is no ordinary lease. Its term is indefinite and at the discretion of the United States. What matters is the unchallenged and indefinite control that the United States has long exercised over Guantanamo Bay. From a practical perspective, the indefinite lease of Guantanamo Bay has produced a place that belongs to the United States, extending the "implied protection" of the United States to it. *Eisentrager, supra,* at 777–778.

The second critical set of facts is that the detainees at Guantanamo Bay are being held indefinitely, and without

RASUL v. BUSH

KENNEDY, J., concurring in judgment

benefit of any legal proceeding to determine their status. In *Eisentrager*, the prisoners were tried and convicted by a military commission of violating the laws of war and were sentenced to prison terms. Having already been subject to procedures establishing their status, they could not justify "a limited opening of our courts" to show that they were "of friendly personal disposition" and not enemy aliens. 339 U. S., at 778. Indefinite detention without trial or other proceeding presents altogether different considerations. It allows friends and foes alike to remain in detention. It suggests a weaker case of military necessity and much greater alignment with the traditional function of habeas corpus. Perhaps, where detainees are taken from a zone of hostilities, detention without proceedings or trial would be justified by military necessity for a matter of weeks; but as the period of detention stretches from months to years, the case for continued detention to meet military exigencies becomes weaker.

In light of the status of Guantanamo Bay and the indefinite pretrial detention of the detainees, I would hold that federal-court jurisdiction is permitted in these cases. This approach would avoid creating automatic statutory authority to adjudicate the claims of persons located outside the United States, and remains true to the reasoning of *Eisentrager*. For these reasons, I concur in the judgment of the Court.

SCALIA, J., dissenting

SUPREME COURT OF THE UNITED STATES

Nos. 03–334 and 03–343

SHAFIQ RASUL, ET AL., PETITIONERS
03–334 v.
GEORGE W. BUSH, PRESIDENT OF THE UNITED STATES, ET AL.

FAWZI KHALID ABDULLAH FAHAD AL ODAH, ET AL., PETITIONERS
03–343 v.
UNITED STATES ET AL.

ON WRITS OF CERTIORARI TO THE UNITED STATES COURT OF APPEALS FOR THE DISTRICT OF COLUMBIA CIRCUIT

[June 28, 2004]

JUSTICE SCALIA, with whom THE CHIEF JUSTICE and JUSTICE THOMAS join, dissenting.

The Court today holds that the habeas statute, 28 U. S. C. §2241, extends to aliens detained by the United States military overseas, outside the sovereign borders of the United States and beyond the territorial jurisdictions of all its courts. This is not only a novel holding; it contradicts a half-century-old precedent on which the military undoubtedly relied, *Johnson* v. *Eisentrager*, 339 U. S. 763 (1950). The Court's contention that *Eisentrager* was somehow negated by *Braden* v. *30th Judicial Circuit Court of Ky.*, 410 U. S. 484 (1973)—a decision that dealt with a different issue and did not so much as mention *Eisentrager*—is implausible in the extreme. This is an irresponsible overturning of settled law in a matter of extreme importance to our forces currently in the field. I would leave it to Congress to change §2241, and dissent

BASIC DOCUMENTS ABOUT THE DETAINEES

RASUL *v.* BUSH

SCALIA, J., dissenting

from the Court's unprecedented holding.

I

As we have repeatedly said: "Federal courts are courts of limited jurisdiction. They possess only that power authorized by Constitution and statute, which is not to be expanded by judicial decree. It is to be presumed that a cause lies outside this limited jurisdiction . . . ." *Kokkonen* v. *Guardian Life Ins. Co. of America,* 511 U. S. 375, 377 (1994) (citations omitted). The petitioners do not argue that the Constitution independently requires jurisdiction here.[1] Accordingly, this case turns on the words of §2241, a text the Court today largely ignores. Even a cursory reading of the habeas statute shows that it presupposes a federal district court with territorial jurisdiction over the detainee. Section 2241(a) states:

> "Writs of habeas corpus may be granted by the Supreme Court, any justice thereof, the district courts and any circuit judge *within their respective jurisdictions.*" (Emphasis added).

It further requires that "[t]he order of a circuit judge shall be entered in the records of *the* district court of *the district wherein the restraint complained of is had.*" 28 U. S. C. §2241(a) (emphases added). And §2242 provides that a petition "addressed to the Supreme Court, a justice thereof or a circuit judge . . . shall state the reasons for not making application to *the* district court of *the district in which the applicant is held.*" (Emphases added). No matter to whom the writ is directed, custodian or detainee, the statute could not be clearer that a necessary requirement for issuing the

---

[1] See Tr. of Oral Arg. 5 ("Question: And you don't raise the issue of any potential jurisdiction on the basis of the Constitution alone. We are here debating the jurisdiction under the Habeas Statute, is that right? [Answer]: That's correct. . .").

SCALIA, J., dissenting

writ is that *some* federal district court have territorial jurisdiction over the detainee. Here, as the Court allows, see *ante*, at 10, the Guantanamo Bay detainees are not located within the territorial jurisdiction of any federal district court. One would think that is the end of this case.

The Court asserts, however, that the decisions of this Court have placed a gloss on the phrase "within their respective jurisdictions" in §2241 which allows jurisdiction in this case. That is not so. In fact, the only case in point holds just the opposite (and just what the statute plainly says). That case is *Eisentrager*, but to fully understand its implications for the present dispute, I must also discuss our decisions in the earlier case of *Ahrens* v. *Clark*, 335 U. S. 188 (1948), and the later case of *Braden*.

In *Ahrens*, the Court considered "whether the presence within the territorial jurisdiction of the District Court of the person detained is prerequisite to filing a petition for a writ of habeas corpus." 335 U. S., at 189 (construing 28 U. S. C. §452, the statutory precursor to §2241). The *Ahrens* detainees were held at Ellis Island, New York, but brought their petitions in the District Court for the District of Columbia. Interpreting "within their respective jurisdictions," the Court held that a district court has jurisdiction to issue the writ only on behalf of petitioners detained within its territorial jurisdiction. It was "not sufficient . . . that the jailer or custodian alone be found in the jurisdiction." 335 U. S., at 190.

Ahrens explicitly reserved "the question of what process, if any, a person confined in an area not subject to the jurisdiction of any district court may employ to assert federal rights." *Id.*, at 192, n. 4. That question, the same question presented to this Court today, was shortly thereafter resolved in *Eisentrager* insofar as noncitizens are concerned. *Eisentrager* involved petitions for writs of habeas corpus filed in the District Court for the District of Columbia by German nationals imprisoned in Landsberg

SCALIA, J., dissenting

Prison, Germany. The District Court, relying on *Ahrens*, dismissed the petitions because the petitioners were not located within its territorial jurisdiction. The Court of Appeals reversed. According to the Court today, the Court of Appeals "implicitly conceded that the District Court lacked jurisdiction under the habeas statute as it had been interpreted in *Ahrens*," and "[i]n essence . . . concluded that the habeas statute, as construed in *Ahrens*, had created an unconstitutional gap that had to be filled by reference to 'fundamentals.'" *Ante*, at 9. That is not so. The Court of Appeals concluded that there *was* statutory jurisdiction. It arrived at that conclusion by applying the canon of constitutional avoidance: "[I]f the existing jurisdictional act be construed to deny the writ to a person entitled to it as a substantive right, the act would be unconstitutional. It should be construed, if possible, to avoid that result." *Eisentrager* v. *Forrestal*, 174 F. 2d 961, 966 (CADC 1949). In cases where there was no territorial jurisdiction over the detainee, the Court of Appeals held, the writ would lie at the place of a respondent with directive power over the detainee. "It is not too violent an interpretation of 'custody' to construe it as including those who have directive custody, as well as those who have immediate custody, where such interpretation is necessary to comply with constitutional requirements. . . . *The statute must be so construed*, lest it be invalid as constituting a suspension of the writ in violation of the constitutional provision." *Id.*, at 967 (emphasis added).[2]

---

[2]The parties' submissions to the Court in *Eisentrager* construed the Court of Appeals' decision as I do. See Pet. for Cert., O. T. 1949, No. 306, pp. 8–9 ("[T]he court felt constrained to construe the habeas corpus jurisdictional statute—despite its reference to the 'respective jurisdictions' of the various courts and the gloss put on that terminology in the *Ahrens* and previous decisions—to permit a petition to be filed in the district court with territorial jurisdiction over the officials who have

SCALIA, J., dissenting

This Court's judgment in *Eisentrager* reversed the Court of Appeals. The opinion was largely devoted to rejecting the lower court's constitutional analysis, since the doctrine of constitutional avoidance underlay its statutory conclusion. But the opinion *had* to pass judgment on whether the statute granted jurisdiction, since that was the basis for the judgments of both lower courts. A conclusion of no constitutionally conferred right would obviously not support reversal of a judgment that rested upon a statutorily conferred right.[3] And absence of a right to the writ under

---

directive authority over the immediate jailer in Germany"); Brief for Respondent, O. T. 1949, No. 306, p. 9 ("Respondent contends that the U. S. Court of Appeals . . . was correct in its holding that the statute, 28 U. S. C. 2241, provides that the U. S. District Court for the District of Columbia has jurisdiction to entertain the petition for a writ of habeas corpus in the case at bar"). Indeed, the briefing in *Eisentrager* was mainly devoted to the question of whether there was statutory jurisdiction. See, *e.g.*, Brief for Petitioner, O. T. 1949, No. 306, pp. 15–59; Brief for Respondent, O. T. 1949, No. 306, pp. 9–27, 38–49.

[3] The Court does not seriously dispute my analysis of the Court of Appeals' holding in *Eisentrager*. Instead, it argues that this Court in *Eisentrager* "understood the Court of Appeals' decision to rest on constitutional and not statutory grounds." *Ante*, at 10, n. 8. That is inherently implausible, given that the Court of Appeals' opinion clearly reached a statutory holding, and that both parties argued the case to this Court on that basis, see n. 2, *supra*. The only evidence of misunderstanding the Court adduces today is the *Eisentrager* Court's description of the Court of Appeals' reasoning as "that, although no statutory jurisdiction of such cases is given, courts must be held to possess it as part of the judicial power of the United States . . . ." 339 U. S., at 767. That is no misunderstanding, but an entirely accurate description of the Court of Appeals' reasoning—the penultimate step of that reasoning rather than its conclusion. The Court of Appeals went on to hold that, in light of the constitutional imperative, the statute should be interpreted as supplying jurisdiction. See *Eisentrager* v. *Forrestal*, 174 F. 2d 961, 965–967 (CADC 1949). This Court in *Eisentrager* undoubtedly understood that, which is why it immediately followed the foregoing description with a description of the Court of Appeals' *conclusion* tied to the language of the habeas statute: "[w]here deprivation of

the clear wording of the habeas statute is what the *Eisentrager* opinion held: "Nothing in the text of the Constitution extends such a right, *nor does anything in our statutes.*" 339 U. S., at 768 (emphasis added). "[T]hese prisoners at no relevant time were within any territory over which the United States is sovereign, and the scenes of their offense, their capture, their trial and their punishment *were all beyond the territorial jurisdiction of any court of the United States.*" *Id.*, at 777–778. See also *id.*, at 781 (concluding that "no right to the writ of *habeas corpus* appears"); *id.*, at 790 (finding "no basis for invoking federal judicial power in any district"). The brevity of the Court's statutory analysis signifies nothing more than that the Court considered it obvious (as indeed it is) that, unaided by the canon of constitutional avoidance, the statute did not confer jurisdiction over an alien detained outside the territorial jurisdiction of the courts of the United States.

Eisentrager's directly-on-point statutory holding makes it exceedingly difficult for the Court to reach the result it desires today. To do so neatly and cleanly, it must either argue that our decision in *Braden* overruled *Eisentrager*, or admit that *it* is overruling *Eisentrager*. The former course would not pass the laugh test, inasmuch as *Braden* dealt with a detainee held within the territorial jurisdiction of a district court, and never *mentioned Eisentrager*. And the latter course would require the Court to explain why our almost categorical rule of *stare decisis* in statutory cases should be set aside in order to complicate the present war, *and*, having set it aside, to explain why the habeas statute does not mean what it plainly says. So

---

liberty by an official act occurs outside the territorial jurisdiction of any District Court, the petition will lie in the District Court which has territorial jurisdiction over officials who have directive power over the immediate jailer." 339 U. S., at 767.

SCALIA, J., dissenting

instead the Court tries an oblique course: "*Braden*," it claims, "overruled *the statutory predicate* to *Eisentrager*'s holding," *ante*, at 11 (emphasis added), by which it means the statutory analysis of *Ahrens*. Even assuming, for the moment, that *Braden* overruled some aspect of *Ahrens*, inasmuch as *Ahrens* did not pass upon any of the statutory issues decided by *Eisentrager*, it is hard to see how any of that case's "statutory predicate" could have been impaired.

But in fact *Braden* did not overrule *Ahrens*; it distinguished *Ahrens*. *Braden* dealt with a habeas petitioner incarcerated in Alabama. The petitioner filed an application for a writ of habeas corpus in Kentucky, challenging an indictment that had been filed against him in that Commonwealth and naming as respondent the Kentucky court in which the proceedings were pending. This Court held that Braden was in custody because a detainer had been issued against him by Kentucky, and was being executed by Alabama, serving as an agent for Kentucky. We found that jurisdiction existed in Kentucky for Braden's petition challenging the Kentucky detainer, notwithstanding his physical confinement in Alabama. *Braden* was careful to *distinguish* that situation from the general rule established in *Ahrens*.

"A further, *critical* development since our decision in *Ahrens* is the emergence of *new classes of prisoners* who are able to petition for habeas corpus because of the adoption of a more expansive definition of the 'custody' requirement of the habeas statute. The overruling of *McNally* v. *Hill,* 293 U. S. 131 (1934), made it possible for prisoners in custody under one sentence to attack a sentence which they had not yet begun to serve. And it also enabled a petitioner held in one State to attack a detainer lodged against him by another State. In such a case, the State holding the prisoner in immediate confinement acts as agent for the

RASUL v. BUSH

SCALIA, J., dissenting

demanding State, and the custodian State is presumably indifferent to the resolution of the prisoner's attack on the detainer. Here, for example, the petitioner is confined in Alabama, but his dispute is with the Commonwealth of Kentucky, not the State of Alabama. *Under these circumstances*, it would serve no useful purpose to apply the *Ahrens* rule and require that the action be brought in Alabama." 410 U. S., at 498–499 (citations and footnotes omitted; emphases added).

This cannot conceivably be construed as an overturning of the *Ahrens* rule *in other circumstances*. See also *Braden, supra,* at 499–500 (noting that *Ahrens* does not establish "an inflexible jurisdictional rule dictating the choice of an inconvenient forum *even in a class of cases which could not have been foreseen at the time of that decision*" (emphasis added)). Thus, *Braden* stands for the proposition, and only the proposition, that where a petitioner is in custody in multiple jurisdictions within the United States, he may seek a writ of habeas corpus in a jurisdiction in which he suffers legal confinement, though not physical confinement, if his challenge is to that legal confinement. Outside that class of cases, *Braden* did not question the general rule of *Ahrens* (much less that of *Eisentrager*). Where, as here, present physical custody is at issue, *Braden* is inapposite, and *Eisentrager* unquestionably controls.[4]

---

[4]The Court points to Court of Appeals cases that have described *Braden* as "overruling" *Ahrens*. See *ante*, at 11, n. 9. Even if that description (rather than what I think the correct one, "distinguishing") is accepted, it would not support the Court's view that *Ahrens* was overruled *with regard to the point on which Eisentrager relied*. The *ratio decidendi* of *Braden* does not call into question the principle of *Ahrens* applied in *Eisentrager*: that habeas challenge to present physical confinement must be made in the district where the physical confinement exists. The Court is unable to produce a single authority that

SCALIA, J., dissenting

The considerations of forum convenience that drove the analysis in *Braden* do not call into question *Eisentrager*'s holding. The *Braden* opinion is littered with venue reasoning of the following sort: "The expense and risk of transporting the petitioner to the Western District of Kentucky, should his presence at a hearing prove necessary, would in all likelihood be outweighed by the difficulties of transporting records and witnesses from Kentucky to the district where petitioner is confined." 410 U. S., at 494. Of course nothing could be *more* inconvenient than what the Court (on the alleged authority of *Braden*) prescribes today: a domestic hearing for persons held abroad, dealing with events that transpired abroad.

Attempting to paint *Braden* as a refutation of *Ahrens* (and thereby, it is suggested, *Eisentrager*), today's Court imprecisely describes *Braden* as citing with approval post-*Ahrens* cases in which "habeas petitioners" located over-

---

agrees with its conclusion that *Braden* overruled *Eisentrager*.

JUSTICE KENNEDY recognizes that *Eisentrager* controls, *ante*, at 1 (opinion concurring in judgment), but misconstrues that opinion. He thinks it makes jurisdiction under the habeas statute turn on the circumstances of the detainees' confinement—including, apparently, the availability of legal proceedings and the length of detention, see *ante*, at 3–4. The *Eisentrager* Court mentioned those circumstances, however, only in the course of its *constitutional* analysis, and not in its application of the statute. It is quite impossible to read §2241 as conditioning its geographic scope upon them. Among the consequences of making jurisdiction turn upon circumstances of confinement are (1) that courts would *always* have authority to inquire into circumstances of confinement, and (2) that the Executive would be unable to know with certainty that any given prisoner-of-war camp is immune from writs of habeas corpus. And among the questions this approach raises: When does definite detention become indefinite? How much process will suffice to stave off jurisdiction? If there is a terrorist attack at Guantanamo Bay, will the area suddenly fall outside the habeas statute because it is no longer "far removed from any hostilities," *ante*, at 3? JUSTICE KENNEDY's approach provides enticing law-school-exam imponderables in an area where certainty is called for.

seas were allowed to proceed (without consideration of the jurisdictional issue) in the District Court for the District of Columbia. *Ante*, at 10. In fact, what *Braden* said is that "[w]here *American citizens* confined overseas (and thus outside the territory of any district court) have sought relief in habeas corpus, we have held, if only implicitly, that the petitioners' absence from the district does not present a jurisdictional obstacle to consideration of the claim." 410 U. S., at 498 (emphasis added). Of course "the existence of unaddressed jurisdictional defects has no precedential effect," *Lewis* v. *Casey,* 518 U. S. 343, 352, n. 2 (1996) (citing cases), but we need not "overrule" those implicit holdings to decide this case. Since *Eisentrager itself* made an exception for such cases, they in no way impugn its holding. "With the citizen," *Eisentrager* said, "we are now little concerned, except to set his case apart *as untouched by this decision* and to take measure of the difference between his status and that of all categories of aliens." 339 U. S., at 769. The constitutional doubt that the Court of Appeals in *Eisentrager* had erroneously attributed to the lack of habeas for an alien abroad might indeed exist with regard to a *citizen* abroad—justifying a strained construction of the habeas statute, or (more honestly) a determination of constitutional right to habeas. Neither party to the present case challenges the atextual extension of the habeas statute to United States citizens held beyond the territorial jurisdictions of the United States courts; but the possibility of one atextual exception thought to be required by the Constitution is no justification for abandoning the clear application of the text to a situation in which it raises no constitutional doubt.

The reality is this: Today's opinion, and today's opinion alone, overrules *Eisentrager;* today's opinion, and today's opinion alone, extends the habeas statute, for the first time, to aliens held beyond the sovereign territory of the United States and beyond the territorial jurisdiction of its courts. No reasons are given for this result; no acknowledgment of its consequences made. By spurious reliance on *Braden* the Court evades explaining why *stare decisis* can be disregarded, *and why Eisentrager was wrong.* Normally, we consider the interests of those who have relied on our decisions. Today, the Court springs a trap on the Executive, subjecting Guantanamo Bay to the oversight of the federal courts even though it has never before been thought to be within their jurisdiction—and thus making it a foolish place to have housed alien wartime detainees.

II

In abandoning the venerable statutory line drawn in *Eisentrager*, the Court boldly extends the scope of the habeas statute to the four corners of the earth. Part III of its opinion asserts that *Braden* stands for the proposition that "a district court acts 'within [its] respective jurisdiction' within the meaning of §2241 as long as 'the custodian can be reached by service of process.'" *Ante*, at 10. Endorsement of that proposition is repeated in Part IV. *Ante*, at 16 ("Section 2241, by its terms, requires nothing more [than the District Court's jurisdiction over petitioners' custodians]").

The consequence of this holding, as applied to aliens outside the country, is breathtaking. It permits an alien captured in a foreign theater of active combat to bring a §2241 petition against the Secretary of Defense. Over the course of the last century, the United States has held millions of alien prisoners abroad. See, *e.g.*, Department of Army, G. Lewis & J. Mewha, History of Prisoner of War Utilization by the United States Army 1776–1945, Pamphlet No. 20–213, p. 244 (1955) (noting that, "[b]y the end of hostilities [in World War II], U. S. forces had in custody approximately two million enemy soldiers"). A great many of these prisoners would no doubt have complained about the circumstances of their capture and the terms of their confinement. The military is currently detaining over 600 prisoners at Guantanamo Bay alone; each detainee undoubtedly has complaints—real or contrived—about those terms and circumstances. The Court's unheralded expansion of federal-court jurisdiction is not even mitigated by a comforting assurance that the legion of ensuing claims will be easily resolved on the merits. To the contrary, the Court says that the "[p]etitioners' allegations . . . unquestionably describe 'custody in violation of the Constitution or laws or treaties of the United States.'" *Ante,* at 15, n. 15 (citing *United States* v. *Verdugo-Urquidez,* 494 U. S. 259, 277–278 (1990) (KENNEDY, J., concurring)). From this point forward, federal courts will entertain petitions from these prisoners, and others like them around the world, challenging actions and events far away, and forcing the courts to oversee one aspect of the Executive's conduct of a foreign war.

Today's carefree Court disregards, without a word of acknowledgment, the dire warning of a more circumspect Court in *Eisentrager:*

> "To grant the writ to these prisoners might mean that our army must transport them across the seas for hearing. This would require allocation for shipping space, guarding personnel, billeting and rations. It might also require transportation for whatever witnesses the prisoners desired to call as well as transportation for those necessary to defend legality of the sentence. The writ, since it is held to be a matter of right, would be equally available to enemies during active hostilities as in the present twilight between war and peace. Such trials would hamper the war effort and bring aid and comfort to the enemy. They would diminish the prestige of our commanders, not only with enemies but with wavering neutrals. It

would be difficult to devise more effective fettering of a field commander than to allow the very enemies he is ordered to reduce to submission to call him to account in his own civil courts and divert his efforts and attention from the military offensive abroad to the legal defensive at home. Nor is it unlikely that the result of such enemy litigiousness would be conflict between judicial and military opinion highly comforting to enemies of the United States." 339 U. S., at 778–779.

These results should not be brought about lightly, and certainly not without a textual basis in the statute and on the strength of nothing more than a decision dealing with an Alabama prisoner's ability to seek habeas in Kentucky.

III

Part IV of the Court's opinion, dealing with the status of Guantanamo Bay, is a puzzlement. The Court might have made an effort (a vain one, as I shall discuss) to distinguish *Eisentrager* on the basis of a difference between the status of Landsberg Prison in Germany and Guantanamo Bay Naval Base. But Part III flatly rejected such an approach, holding that the place of detention of an alien has no bearing on the statutory availability of habeas relief, but "is strictly relevant only to the question of the appropriate forum." *Ante*, at 11. That rejection is repeated at the end of Part IV: "In the end, the answer to the question presented is clear. . . . No party questions the District Court's jurisdiction over petitioners' custodians. . . . Section 2241, by its terms, requires nothing more." *Ante*, at 15–16. Once that has been said, the status of Guantanamo Bay is entirely irrelevant to the issue here. The habeas statute is (according to the Court) being applied *domestically*, to "petitioners' custodians," and the doctrine that statutes are presumed to have no extraterritorial effect simply has no application.

14   RASUL *v.* BUSH

SCALIA, J., dissenting

Nevertheless, the Court spends most of Part IV rejecting respondents' invocation of that doctrine on the peculiar ground that it has no application to Guantanamo Bay. Of course if the Court is right about that, not only §2241 but presumably *all* United States law applies there—including, for example, the federal cause of action recognized in *Bivens* v. *Six Unknown Fed. Narcotics Agents,* 403 U. S. 388 (1971), which would allow prisoners to sue their captors for damages. Fortunately, however, the Court's irrelevant discussion also happens to be wrong.

The Court gives only two reasons why the presumption against extraterritorial effect does not apply to Guantanamo Bay. First, the Court says (without any further elaboration) that "the United States exercises 'complete jurisdiction and control' over the Guantanamo Bay Naval Base [under the terms of a 1903 lease agreement], and may continue to exercise such control permanently if it so chooses [under the terms of a 1934 Treaty]." *Ante,* at 12; see *ante,* at 2–3. But that lease agreement explicitly recognized "the continuance of the ultimate sovereignty of the Republic of Cuba over the [leased areas]," Lease of Lands for Coaling and Naval Stations, Feb. 23, 1903, U. S.-Cuba, Art. III, T. S. No. 418, and the Executive Branch—whose head is "exclusively responsible" for the "conduct of diplomatic and foreign affairs," *Eisentrager, supra,* at 789—affirms that the lease and treaty do not render Guantanamo Bay the sovereign territory of the United States, see Brief for Respondents 21.

The Court does not explain how "complete jurisdiction and control" without sovereignty causes an enclave to be part of the United States for purposes of its domestic laws. Since "jurisdiction and control" obtained through a lease is no different in effect from "jurisdiction and control" acquired by lawful force of arms, parts of Afghanistan and Iraq should logically be regarded as subject to our domestic laws. Indeed, if "jurisdiction and control" rather than

SCALIA, J., dissenting

sovereignty were the test, so should the Landsberg Prison in Germany, where the United States held the *Eisentrager* detainees.

The second and last reason the Court gives for the proposition that domestic law applies to Guantanamo Bay is the Solicitor General's concession that there would be habeas jurisdiction over a United States citizen in Guantanamo Bay. "Considering that the statute draws no distinction between Americans and aliens held in federal custody, there is little reason to think that Congress intended the geographical coverage of the statute to vary depending on the detainee's citizenship." *Ante*, at 12–13. But the reason the Solicitor General conceded there would be jurisdiction over a detainee who was a United States citizen had *nothing to do* with the special status of Guantanamo Bay: "Our answer to that question, Justice Souter, is that citizens of the United States, because of their constitutional circumstances, may have greater rights with respect to the scope and reach of the Habeas Statute as the Court has or would interpret it." Tr. of Oral Arg. 40. See also *id.*, at 27–28. And *that* position—the position that United States citizens throughout the world may be entitled to habeas corpus rights—is precisely the position that this Court adopted in *Eisentrager*, see 339 U. S., at 769–770, even while holding that aliens abroad *did not have* habeas corpus rights. Quite obviously, the Court's second reason has no force whatever.

The last part of the Court's Part IV analysis digresses from the point that the presumption against extraterritorial application does not apply to Guantanamo Bay. Rather, it is directed to the contention that the Court's approach to habeas jurisdiction—applying it to aliens abroad—is "consistent with the historical reach of the writ." *Ante*, at 13. None of the authorities it cites comes close to supporting that claim. Its first set of authorities involves claims by aliens detained in what is indisputably domestic territory. *Ante*, at 13, n. 11. Those cases are irrelevant because they do not purport to address the territorial reach of the writ. The remaining cases involve issuance of the writ to "'exempt jurisdictions'" and "other dominions under the sovereign's control." *Ante*, at 13–14, and nn. 12–13. These cases are inapposite for two reasons: Guantanamo Bay is not a sovereign dominion, and even if it were, jurisdiction would be limited to subjects.

"Exempt jurisdictions"—the Cinque Ports and Counties Palatine (located in modern-day England)—were local franchises granted by the Crown. See 1 W. Holdsworth, History of English Law 108, 532 (7th ed. rev. 1956); 3 W. Blackstone, Commentaries *78–*79 (hereinafter Blackstone). These jurisdictions were "exempt" in the sense that the Crown had ceded management of municipal affairs to local authorities, whose courts had exclusive jurisdiction over private disputes among residents (although review was still available in the royal courts by writ of error). See *id.*, at *79. Habeas jurisdiction nevertheless extended to those regions on the theory that the delegation of the King's authority did not include his own prerogative writs. *Ibid.*; R. Sharpe, Law of Habeas Corpus 188–189 (2d ed. 1989) (hereinafter Sharpe). Guantanamo Bay involves no comparable local delegation of pre-existing sovereign authority.

The cases involving "other dominions under the sovereign's control" fare no better. These cases stand only for the proposition that the writ extended to dominions of the Crown outside England proper. The authorities relating to Jersey and the other Channel Islands, for example, see *ante*, at 14, n. 13, involve territories that are "dominions of the crown of Great Britain" even though not "part of the kingdom of England," 1 Blackstone *102–*105, much as were the colonies in America, *id.*, at *104–*105, and Scotland, Ireland, and Wales, *id.*, at *93. See also *King* v. *Cowle*, 2 Burr. 834, 853–854, 97 Eng. Rep. 587, 598 (K. B.

SCALIA, J., dissenting

1759) (even if Berwick was "no part of the realm of England," it was still a "dominion of the Crown"). All of the dominions in the cases the Court cites—and all of the territories Blackstone lists as dominions, see 1 Blackstone *93–*106—are the sovereign territory of the Crown: colonies, acquisitions and conquests, and so on. It is an enormous extension of the term to apply it to installations merely leased for a particular use from another nation that still retains ultimate sovereignty.

The Court's historical analysis fails for yet another reason: To the extent the writ's "extraordinary territorial ambit" did extend to exempt jurisdictions, outlying dominions, and the like, that extension applied only to British *subjects*. The very sources the majority relies on say so: Sharpe explains the "broader ambit" of the writ on the ground that it is "said to depend not on the ordinary jurisdiction of the court for its effectiveness, but upon the authority of the sovereign over all her *subjects*." Sharpe, *supra*, at 188 (emphasis added). Likewise, Blackstone explained that the writ "run[s] into all parts of the king's dominions" because "the king is at all times entitled to have an account why the liberty of any of his *subjects* is restrained." 3 Blackstone *131 (emphasis added). *Ex parte Mwenya*, [1960] 1 Q. B. 241 (C. A.), which can hardly be viewed as evidence of the *historic* scope of the writ, only confirms the ongoing relevance of the sovereign-subject relationship to the scope of the writ. There, the question was whether "the Court of Queen's Bench can be debarred from making an order in favour of a British citizen unlawfully or arbitrarily detained" in Northern Rhodesia, which was at the time a protectorate of the Crown. *Id.*, at 300 (Lord Evershed M. R.). Each judge made clear that the detainee's status as a subject was material to the resolution of the case. See *id.*, at 300, 302 (Lord Evershed, M. R.); *id.*, at 305 (Romer, L. J.) ("[I]t is difficult to see why the sovereign should be deprived of her right to be in-

RASUL v. BUSH

SCALIA, J., dissenting

formed through her High Court as to the validity of the detention of her subjects in that territory"); *id.*, at 311 (Sellers, L. J.) ("I am not prepared to say, as we are solely asked to say on this appeal, that the English courts have no jurisdiction in any circumstances to entertain an application for a writ of habeas corpus ad subjiciendum in respect of an unlawful detention of a British subject in a British protectorate"). None of the exempt-jurisdiction or dominion cases the Court cites involves someone not a subject of the Crown.

The rule against issuing the writ to aliens in foreign lands was still the law when, in *In re Ning Yi-Ching*, 56 T. L. R. 3 (Vacation Ct. 1939), an English court considered the habeas claims of four Chinese subjects detained on criminal charges in Tientsin, China, an area over which Britain had by treaty acquired a lease and "therewith exercised certain rights of administration and control." *Id.*, at 4. The court held that Tientsin was a foreign territory, and that the writ would not issue to a foreigner detained there. The Solicitor-General had argued that "[t]here was no case on record in which a writ of *habeas corpus* had been obtained on behalf of a foreign subject on foreign territory," *id.*, at 5, and the court "listened in vain for a case in which the writ of *habeas corpus* had issued in respect of a foreigner detained in a part of the world which was not a part of the King's dominions or realm," *id.*, at 6.[5]

In sum, the Court's treatment of Guantanamo Bay, like

---

[5] The Court argues at some length that *Ex parte Mwenya*, [1960] 1 Q. B. 241 (C. A.), calls into question my reliance on *In re Ning Yi-Ching*. See *ante*, at 15, n. 14. But as I have explained, see *supra*, at 17–18, *Mwenya* dealt with a British subject and the court went out of its way to explain that its expansive description of the scope of the writ was premised on that fact. The Court cites not a single case holding that aliens held outside the territory of the sovereign were within reach of the writ.

SCALIA, J., dissenting

its treatment of §2241, is a wrenching departure from precedent.[6]

* * *

Departure from our rule of *stare decisis* in statutory cases is always extraordinary; it ought to be unthinkable when the departure has a potentially harmful effect upon the Nation's conduct of a war. The Commander in Chief and his subordinates had every reason to expect that the internment of combatants at Guantanamo Bay would not have the consequence of bringing the cumbersome machinery of our domestic courts into military affairs. Congress is in session. If it wished to change federal judges' habeas jurisdiction from what this Court had previously held that to be, it could have done so. And it could have done so by intelligent revision of the statute,[7] instead of by

---

[6] The Court grasps at two other bases for jurisdiction: the Alien Tort Statute (ATS), 28 U. S. C. §1350, and the federal-question statute, 28 U. S. C. §1331. The former is not presented to us. The ATS, while invoked below, was repudiated as a basis for jurisdiction by all petitioners, either in their petition for certiorari, in their briefing before this Court, or at oral argument. See Pet. for Cert. in No. 03–334, p. 2, n. 1 ("Petitioners withdraw any reliance on the Alien Tort Claims Act . . ."); Brief for Petitioners in No. 03–343, p. 13; Tr. of Oral Arg. 6.

With respect to §1331, petitioners assert a variety of claims arising under the Constitution, treaties, and laws of the United States. In *Eisentrager*, though the Court's holding focused on §2241, its analysis spoke more broadly: "We have pointed out that the privilege of litigation has been extended to aliens, whether friendly or enemy, only because permitting their presence in the country implied protection. No such basis can be invoked here, for these prisoners at no relevant time were within any territory over which the United States is sovereign, and the scenes of their offense, their capture, their trial and their punishment were all beyond the territorial jurisdiction of any court of the United States." 339 U. S., at 777–778. That reasoning dooms petitioners' claims under §1331, at least where Congress has erected a jurisdictional bar to their raising such claims in habeas.

[7] It could, for example, provide for jurisdiction by placing Guantanamo Bay within the territory of an existing district court; or by creating a

RASUL v. BUSH

SCALIA, J., dissenting

today's clumsy, countertextual reinterpretation that confers upon wartime prisoners greater habeas rights than domestic detainees. The latter must challenge their present physical confinement in the district of their confinement, see *Rumsfeld* v. *Padilla, ante,* whereas under today's strange holding Guantanamo Bay detainees can petition in any of the 94 federal judicial districts. The fact that extraterritorially located detainees lack the district of detention that the statute requires has been converted from a factor that precludes their ability to bring a petition at all into a factor that frees them to petition wherever they wish—and, as a result, to forum shop. For this Court to create such a monstrous scheme in time of war, and in frustration of our military commanders' reliance upon clearly stated prior law, is judicial adventurism of the worst sort. I dissent.

---

district court for Guantanamo Bay, as it did for the Panama Canal Zone, see 22 U. S. C. §3841(a) (repealed 1979).

NIMBLE BOOKS

BASIC DOCUMENTS ABOUT THE DETAINEES

HAMDI V. RUMSFELD

NIMBLE BOOKS

(Slip Opinion) OCTOBER TERM, 2003 1

Syllabus

NOTE: Where it is feasible, a syllabus (headnote) will be released, as is being done in connection with this case, at the time the opinion is issued. The syllabus constitutes no part of the opinion of the Court but has been prepared by the Reporter of Decisions for the convenience of the reader. See *United States* v. *Detroit Timber & Lumber Co.*, 200 U. S. 321, 337.

SUPREME COURT OF THE UNITED STATES

Syllabus

HAMDI ET AL. *v.* RUMSFELD, SECRETARY OF DEFENSE, ET AL.

CERTIORARI TO THE UNITED STATES COURT OF APPEALS FOR THE FOURTH CIRCUIT

No. 03–6696. Argued April 28, 2004—Decided June 28, 2004

After Congress passed a resolution—the Authorization for Use of Military Force (AUMF)—empowering the President to "use all necessary and appropriate force" against "nations, organizations, or persons" that he determines "planned, authorized, committed, or aided" in the September 11, 2001, al Qaeda terrorist attacks, the President ordered the Armed Forces to Afghanistan to subdue al Qaeda and quell the supporting Taliban regime. Petitioner Hamdi, an American citizen whom the Government has classified as an "enemy combatant" for allegedly taking up arms with the Taliban during the conflict, was captured in Afghanistan and presently is detained at a naval brig in Charleston, S. C. Hamdi's father filed this habeas petition on his behalf under 28 U. S. C. §2241, alleging, among other things, that the Government holds his son in violation of the Fifth and Fourteenth Amendments. Although the petition did not elaborate on the factual circumstances of Hamdi's capture and detention, his father has asserted in other documents in the record that Hamdi went to Afghanistan to do "relief work" less than two months before September 11 and could not have received military training. The Government attached to its response to the petition a declaration from Michael Mobbs (Mobbs Declaration), a Defense Department official. The Mobbs Declaration alleges various details regarding Hamdi's trip to Afghanistan, his affiliation there with a Taliban unit during a time when the Taliban was battling U. S allies, and his subsequent surrender of an assault rifle. The District Court found that the Mobbs Declaration, standing alone, did not support Hamdi's detention and ordered the Government to turn over numerous materials for *in camera* review. The Fourth Circuit reversed, stressing that, because it

Syllabus

was undisputed that Hamdi was captured in an active combat zone, no factual inquiry or evidentiary hearing allowing Hamdi to be heard or to rebut the Government's assertions was necessary or proper. Concluding that the factual averments in the Mobbs Declaration, if accurate, provided a sufficient basis upon which to conclude that the President had constitutionally detained Hamdi, the court ordered the habeas petition dismissed. The appeals court held that, assuming that express congressional authorization of the detention was required by 18 U. S. C. §4001(a)—which provides that "[n]o citizen shall be imprisoned or otherwise detained by the United States except pursuant to an Act of Congress"— the AUMF's "necessary and appropriate force" language provided the authorization for Hamdi's detention. It also concluded that Hamdi is entitled only to a limited judicial inquiry into his detention's legality under the war powers of the political branches, and not to a searching review of the factual determinations underlying his seizure.

Held: The judgment is vacated, and the case is remanded.

JUSTICE O'CONNOR, joined by THE CHIEF JUSTICE, JUSTICE KENNEDY, and JUSTICE BREYER, concluded that although Congress authorized the detention of combatants in the narrow circumstances alleged in this case, due process demands that a citizen held in the United States as an enemy combatant be given a meaningful opportunity to contest the factual basis for that detention before a neutral decisionmaker. Pp. 14–15.

JUSTICE SOUTER, joined by JUSTICE GINSBURG, concluded that Hamdi's detention is unauthorized, but joined with the plurality to conclude that on remand Hamdi should have a meaningful opportunity to offer evidence that he is not an enemy combatant. Pp. 2–3, 15.

O'CONNOR, J., announced the judgment of the Court and delivered an opinion, in which REHNQUIST, C. J., and KENNEDY and BREYER, JJ., joined. SOUTER, J., filed an opinion concurring in part, dissenting in part, and concurring in the judgment, in which GINSBURG, J., joined. SCALIA, J., filed a dissenting opinion, in which STEVENS, J., joined. THOMAS, J., filed a dissenting opinion.

Cite as: 542 U. S. ____ (2004)

Opinion of O'CONNOR, J.

NOTICE: This opinion is subject to formal revision before publication in the preliminary print of the United States Reports. Readers are requested to notify the Reporter of Decisions, Supreme Court of the United States, Washington, D. C. 20543, of any typographical or other formal errors, in order that corrections may be made before the preliminary print goes to press.

SUPREME COURT OF THE UNITED STATES

No. 03–6696

YASER ESAM HAMDI AND ESAM FOUAD HAMDI, AS NEXT FRIEND OF YASER ESAM HAMDI, PETITIONERS *v.* DONALD H. RUMSFELD, SECRETARY OF DEFENSE, ET AL.

ON WRIT OF CERTIORARI TO THE UNITED STATES COURT OF APPEALS FOR THE FOURTH CIRCUIT

[June 28, 2004]

JUSTICE O'CONNOR announced the judgment of the Court and delivered an opinion, in which THE CHIEF JUSTICE, JUSTICE KENNEDY, and JUSTICE BREYER join.

At this difficult time in our Nation's history, we are called upon to consider the legality of the Government's detention of a United States citizen on United States soil as an "enemy combatant" and to address the process that is constitutionally owed to one who seeks to challenge his classification as such. The United States Court of Appeals for the Fourth Circuit held that petitioner's detention was legally authorized and that he was entitled to no further opportunity to challenge his enemy-combatant label. We now vacate and remand. We hold that although Congress authorized the detention of combatants in the narrow circumstances alleged here, due process demands that a citizen held in the United States as an enemy combatant be given a meaningful opportunity to contest the factual basis for that detention before a neutral decisionmaker.

HAMDI v. RUMSFELD

Opinion of O'CONNOR, J.

I

On September 11, 2001, the al Qaeda terrorist network used hijacked commercial airliners to attack prominent targets in the United States. Approximately 3,000 people were killed in those attacks. One week later, in response to these "acts of treacherous violence," Congress passed a resolution authorizing the President to "use all necessary and appropriate force against those nations, organizations, or persons he determines planned, authorized, committed, or aided the terrorist attacks" or "harbored such organizations or persons, in order to prevent any future acts of international terrorism against the United States by such nations, organizations or persons." Authorization for Use of Military Force ("the AUMF"), 115 Stat. 224. Soon thereafter, the President ordered United States Armed Forces to Afghanistan, with a mission to subdue al Qaeda and quell the Taliban regime that was known to support it.

This case arises out of the detention of a man whom the Government alleges took up arms with the Taliban during this conflict. His name is Yaser Esam Hamdi. Born an American citizen in Louisiana in 1980, Hamdi moved with his family to Saudi Arabia as a child. By 2001, the parties agree, he resided in Afghanistan. At some point that year, he was seized by members of the Northern Alliance, a coalition of military groups opposed to the Taliban government, and eventually was turned over to the United States military. The Government asserts that it initially detained and interrogated Hamdi in Afghanistan before transferring him to the United States Naval Base in Guantanamo Bay in January 2002. In April 2002, upon learning that Hamdi is an American citizen, authorities transferred him to a naval brig in Norfolk, Virginia, where he remained until a recent transfer to a brig in Charleston, South Carolina. The Government contends that Hamdi is an "enemy combatant," and that this status

BASIC DOCUMENTS ABOUT THE DETAINEES

Cite as: 542 U. S. ____ (2004)   3

Opinion of O'CONNOR, J.

justifies holding him in the United States indefinitely—without formal charges or proceedings—unless and until it makes the determination that access to counsel or further process is warranted.

In June 2002, Hamdi's father, Esam Fouad Hamdi, filed the present petition for a writ of habeas corpus under 28 U. S. C. §2241 in the Eastern District of Virginia, naming as petitioners his son and himself as next friend. The elder Hamdi alleges in the petition that he has had no contact with his son since the Government took custody of him in 2001, and that the Government has held his son "without access to legal counsel or notice of any charges pending against him." App. 103, 104. The petition contends that Hamdi's detention was not legally authorized. *Id.*, at 105. It argues that, "[a]s an American citizen, . . . Hamdi enjoys the full protections of the Constitution," and that Hamdi's detention in the United States without charges, access to an impartial tribunal, or assistance of counsel "violated and continue[s] to violate the Fifth and Fourteenth Amendments to the United States Constitution." *Id.*, at 107. The habeas petition asks that the court, among other things, (1) appoint counsel for Hamdi; (2) order respondents to cease interrogating him; (3) declare that he is being held in violation of the Fifth and Fourteenth Amendments; (4) "[t]o the extent Respondents contest any material factual allegations in this Petition, schedule an evidentiary hearing, at which Petitioners may adduce proof in support of their allegations"; and (5) order that Hamdi be released from his "unlawful custody." *Id.*, at 108–109. Although his habeas petition provides no details with regard to the factual circumstances surrounding his son's capture and detention, Hamdi's father has asserted in documents found elsewhere in the record that his son went to Afghanistan to do "relief work," and that he had been in that country less than two months before September 11, 2001, and could not have received

Opinion of O'CONNOR, J.

military training. *Id.*, at 188–189. The 20-year-old was traveling on his own for the first time, his father says, and "[b]ecause of his lack of experience, he was trapped in Afghanistan once that military campaign began." *Id.*, at 188–189.

The District Court found that Hamdi's father was a proper next friend, appointed the federal public defender as counsel for the petitioners, and ordered that counsel be given access to Hamdi. *Id.*, at 113–116. The United States Court of Appeals for the Fourth Circuit reversed that order, holding that the District Court had failed to extend appropriate deference to the Government's security and intelligence interests. 296 F. 3d 278, 279, 283 (2002). It directed the District Court to consider "the most cautious procedures first," *id.*, at 284, and to conduct a deferential inquiry into Hamdi's status, *id.*, at 283. It opined that "if Hamdi is indeed an 'enemy combatant' who was captured during hostilities in Afghanistan, the government's present detention of him is a lawful one." *Ibid.*

On remand, the Government filed a response and a motion to dismiss the petition. It attached to its response a declaration from one Michael Mobbs (hereinafter "Mobbs Declaration"), who identified himself as Special Advisor to the Under Secretary of Defense for Policy. Mobbs indicated that in this position, he has been "substantially involved with matters related to the detention of enemy combatants in the current war against the al Qaeda terrorists and those who support and harbor them (including the Taliban)." App. 148. He expressed his "familiar[ity]" with Department of Defense and United States military policies and procedures applicable to the detention, control, and transfer of al Qaeda and Taliban personnel, and declared that "[b]ased upon my review of relevant records and reports, I am also familiar with the facts and circumstances related to the capture of ... Hamdi and his detention by U. S. military forces." *Ibid.*

BASIC DOCUMENTS ABOUT THE DETAINEES

Opinion of O'CONNOR, J.

Mobbs then set forth what remains the sole evidentiary support that the Government has provided to the courts for Hamdi's detention. The declaration states that Hamdi "traveled to Afghanistan" in July or August 2001, and that he thereafter "affiliated with a Taliban military unit and received weapons training." *Ibid.* It asserts that Hamdi "remained with his Taliban unit following the attacks of September 11" and that, during the time when Northern Alliance forces were "engaged in battle with the Taliban," "Hamdi's Taliban unit surrendered" to those forces, after which he "surrender[ed] his Kalishnikov assault rifle" to them. *Id.*, at 148–149. The Mobbs Declaration also states that, because al Qaeda and the Taliban "were and are hostile forces engaged in armed conflict with the armed forces of the United States," "individuals associated with" those groups "were and continue to be enemy combatants." *Id.*, at 149. Mobbs states that Hamdi was labeled an enemy combatant "[b]ased upon his interviews and in light of his association with the Taliban." *Ibid.* According to the declaration, a series of "U.S. military screening team[s]" determined that Hamdi met "the criteria for enemy combatants," and "a subsequent interview of Hamdi has confirmed that he surrendered and gave his firearm to Northern Alliance forces, which supports his classification as an enemy combatant." *Id.*, at 149–150.

After the Government submitted this declaration, the Fourth Circuit directed the District Court to proceed in accordance with its earlier ruling and, specifically, to "'consider the sufficiency of the Mobbs Declaration as an independent matter before proceeding further.'" 316 F. 3d at 450, 462 (2003). The District Court found that the Mobbs Declaration fell "far short" of supporting Hamdi's detention. App. 292. It criticized the generic and hearsay nature of the affidavit, calling it "little more than the government's 'say-so.'" *Id.*, at 298. It ordered the Government to turn over numerous materials for *in camera* review, including copies of all of Hamdi's statements and the notes taken from interviews with him that related to his reasons for going to Afghanistan and his activities therein; a list of all interrogators who had questioned Hamdi and their names and addresses; statements by members of the Northern Alliance regarding Hamdi's surrender and capture; a list of the dates and locations of his capture and subsequent detentions; and the names and titles of the United States Government officials who made the determinations that Hamdi was an enemy combatant and that he should be moved to a naval brig. *Id.*, at 185–186. The court indicated that all of these materials were necessary for "meaningful judicial review" of whether Hamdi's detention was legally authorized and whether Hamdi had received sufficient process to satisfy the Due Process Clause of the Constitution and relevant treaties or military regulations. *Id.*, at 291–292.

The Government sought to appeal the production order, and the District Court certified the question of whether the Mobbs Declaration, "'standing alone, is sufficient as a matter of law to allow meaningful judicial review of [Hamdi's] classification as an enemy combatant.'" 316 F. 3d, at 462. The Fourth Circuit reversed, but did not squarely answer the certified question. It instead stressed that, because it was "undisputed that Hamdi was captured in a zone of active combat in a foreign theater of conflict," no factual inquiry or evidentiary hearing allowing Hamdi to be heard or to rebut the Government's assertions was necessary or proper. *Id.*, at 459. Concluding that the factual averments in the Mobbs Declaration, "if accurate," provided a sufficient basis upon which to conclude that the President had constitutionally detained Hamdi pursuant to the President's war powers, it ordered the habeas petition dismissed. *Id.*, at 473. The Fourth Circuit emphasized that the "vital purposes" of the detention of uncharged enemy combatants—preventing those combatants

Opinion of O'CONNOR, J.

from rejoining the enemy while relieving the military of the burden of litigating the circumstances of wartime captures halfway around the globe—were interests "directly derived from the war powers of Articles I and II." *Id.*, at 465–466. In that court's view, because "Article III contains nothing analogous to the specific powers of war so carefully enumerated in Articles I and II," *id.*, at 463, separation of powers principles prohibited a federal court from "delv[ing] further into Hamdi's status and capture," *id.*, at 473. Accordingly, the District Court's more vigorous inquiry "went far beyond the acceptable scope of review." *Ibid.*

On the more global question of whether legal authorization exists for the detention of citizen enemy combatants at all, the Fourth Circuit rejected Hamdi's arguments that 18 U. S. C. §4001(a) and Article 5 of the Geneva Convention rendered any such detentions unlawful. The court expressed doubt as to Hamdi's argument that §4001(a), which provides that "[n]o citizen shall be imprisoned or otherwise detained by the United States except pursuant to an Act of Congress," required express congressional authorization of detentions of this sort. But it held that, in any event, such authorization was found in the post-September 11 Authorization for Use of Military Force. 316 F. 3d, at 467. Because "capturing and detaining enemy combatants is an inherent part of warfare," the court held, "the 'necessary and appropriate force' referenced in the congressional resolution necessarily includes the capture and detention of any and all hostile forces arrayed against our troops." *Ibid.*; see also *id.*, at 467–468 (noting that Congress, in 10 U. S. C. §956(5), had specifically authorized the expenditure of funds for keeping prisoners of war and persons whose status was determined "to be similar to prisoners of war," and concluding that this appropriation measure also demonstrated that Congress had "authorized [these individuals'] detention in the first instance"). The court likewise rejected Hamdi's Geneva Convention claim, concluding that the convention is not self-executing and that, even if it were, it would not preclude the Executive from detaining Hamdi until the cessation of hostilities. 316 F. 3d, at 468–469.

Finally, the Fourth Circuit rejected Hamdi's contention that its legal analyses with regard to the authorization for the detention scheme and the process to which he was constitutionally entitled should be altered by the fact that he is an American citizen detained on American soil. Relying on *Ex parte Quirin*, 317 U. S. 1 (1942), the court emphasized that "[o]ne who takes up arms against the United States in a foreign theater of war, regardless of his citizenship, may properly be designated an enemy combatant and treated as such." 316 F.3d, at 475. "The privilege of citizenship," the court held, "entitles Hamdi to a limited judicial inquiry into his detention, but only to determine its legality under the war powers of the political branches. At least where it is undisputed that he was present in a zone of active combat operations, we are satisfied that the Constitution does not entitle him to a searching review of the factual determinations underlying his seizure there." *Ibid.*

The Fourth Circuit denied rehearing en banc, 337 F. 3d 335 (2003), and we granted certiorari. 540 U. S. __ (2004). We now vacate the judgment below and remand.

II

The threshold question before us is whether the Executive has the authority to detain citizens who qualify as "enemy combatants." There is some debate as to the proper scope of this term, and the Government has never provided any court with the full criteria that it uses in classifying individuals as such. It has made clear, however, that, for purposes of this case, the "enemy combatant" that it is seeking to detain is an individual who, it

BASIC DOCUMENTS ABOUT THE DETAINEES

Cite as: 542 U. S. ____ (2004) 9

Opinion of O'CONNOR, J.

alleges, was "'part of or supporting forces hostile to the United States or coalition partners'" in Afghanistan and who "'engaged in an armed conflict against the United States'" there. Brief for Respondents 3. We therefore answer only the narrow question before us: whether the detention of citizens falling within that definition is authorized.

The Government maintains that no explicit congressional authorization is required, because the Executive possesses plenary authority to detain pursuant to Article II of the Constitution. We do not reach the question whether Article II provides such authority, however, because we agree with the Government's alternative position, that Congress has in fact authorized Hamdi's detention, through the AUMF.

Our analysis on that point, set forth below, substantially overlaps with our analysis of Hamdi's principal argument for the illegality of his detention. He posits that his detention is forbidden by 18 U. S. C. §4001(a). Section 4001(a) states that "[n]o citizen shall be imprisoned or otherwise detained by the United States except pursuant to an Act of Congress." Congress passed §4001(a) in 1971 as part of a bill to repeal the Emergency Detention Act of 1950, 50 U. S. C. §811 *et seq.*, which provided procedures for executive detention, during times of emergency, of individuals deemed likely to engage in espionage or sabotage. Congress was particularly concerned about the possibility that the Act could be used to reprise the Japanese internment camps of World War II. H. R. Rep. No. 92–116 (1971); *id.*, at 4 ("The concentration camp implications of the legislation render it abhorrent"). The Government again presses two alternative positions. First, it argues that §4001(a), in light of its legislative history and its location in Title 18, applies only to "the control of civilian prisons and related detentions," not to military detentions. Brief for Respondents 21. Second, it maintains that §4001(a) is satisfied,

Opinion of O'CONNOR, J.

because Hamdi is being detained "pursuant to an Act of Congress"—the AUMF. *Id.*, at 21–22. Again, because we conclude that the Government's second assertion is correct, we do not address the first. In other words, for the reasons that follow, we conclude that the AUMF is explicit congressional authorization for the detention of individuals in the narrow category we describe (assuming, without deciding, that such authorization is required), and that the AUMF satisfied §4001(a)'s requirement that a detention be "pursuant to an Act of Congress" (assuming, without deciding, that §4001(a) applies to military detentions).

The AUMF authorizes the President to use "all necessary and appropriate force" against "nations, organizations, or persons" associated with the September 11, 2001, terrorist attacks. 115 Stat. 224. There can be no doubt that individuals who fought against the United States in Afghanistan as part of the Taliban, an organization known to have supported the al Qaeda terrorist network responsible for those attacks, are individuals Congress sought to target in passing the AUMF. We conclude that detention of individuals falling into the limited category we are considering, for the duration of the particular conflict in which they were captured, is so fundamental and accepted an incident to war as to be an exercise of the "necessary and appropriate force" Congress has authorized the President to use.

The capture and detention of lawful combatants and the capture, detention, and trial of unlawful combatants, by "universal agreement and practice," are "important incident[s] of war." *Ex parte Quirin*, 317 U. S., at 28. The purpose of detention is to prevent captured individuals from returning to the field of battle and taking up arms once again. Naqvi, Doubtful Prisoner-of-War Status, 84 Int'l Rev. Red Cross 571, 572 (2002) ("[C]aptivity in war is 'neither revenge, nor punishment, but solely protective custody, the only purpose of which is to prevent the pris-

Basic Documents about the Detainees

Opinion of O'Connor, J.

oners of war from further participation in the war'" (quoting decision of Nuremberg Military Tribunal, reprinted in 41 Am. J. Int'l L. 172, 229 (1947)); W. Winthrop, Military Law and Precedents 788 (rev. 2d ed. 1920) ("The time has long passed when 'no quarter' was the rule on the battlefield.... It is now recognized that 'Captivity is neither a punishment nor an act of vengeance,' but 'merely a temporary detention which is devoid of all penal character.' ... 'A prisoner of war is no convict; his imprisonment is a simple war measure.'" (citations omitted); cf. *In re Territo*, 156 F. 2d 142, 145 (CA9 1946) ("The object of capture is to prevent the captured individual from serving the enemy. He is disarmed and from then on must be removed as completely as practicable from the front, treated humanely, and in time exchanged, repatriated, or otherwise released" (footnotes omitted)).

There is no bar to this Nation's holding one of its own citizens as an enemy combatant. In *Quirin*, one of the detainees, Haupt, alleged that he was a naturalized United States citizen. 317 U. S., at 20. We held that "[c]itizens who associate themselves with the military arm of the enemy government, and with its aid, guidance and direction enter this country bent on hostile acts, are enemy belligerents within the meaning of ... the law of war." *Id.*, at 37–38. While Haupt was tried for violations of the law of war, nothing in *Quirin* suggests that his citizenship would have precluded his mere detention for the duration of the relevant hostilities. See *id.*, at 30–31. See also Lieber Code, ¶153, Instructions for the Government of Armies of the United States in the Field, Gen. Order No. 100 (1863), reprinted in 2 Lieber, Miscellaneous Writings, p. 273 (contemplating, in code binding the Union Army during the Civil War, that "captured rebels" would be treated "as prisoners of war"). Nor can we see any reason for drawing such a line here. A citizen, no less than an alien, can be "part of or supporting forces hostile to the United States or coalition partners" and "engaged in an armed conflict against the United States," Brief for Respondents 3; such a citizen, if released, would pose the same threat of returning to the front during the ongoing conflict.

In light of these principles, it is of no moment that the AUMF does not use specific language of detention. Because detention to prevent a combatant's return to the battlefield is a fundamental incident of waging war, in permitting the use of "necessary and appropriate force," Congress has clearly and unmistakably authorized detention in the narrow circumstances considered here.

Hamdi objects, nevertheless, that Congress has not authorized the *indefinite* detention to which he is now subject. The Government responds that "the detention of enemy combatants during World War II was just as 'indefinite' while that war was being fought." *Id.*, at 16. We take Hamdi's objection to be not to the lack of certainty regarding the date on which the conflict will end, but to the substantial prospect of perpetual detention. We recognize that the national security underpinnings of the "war on terror," although crucially important, are broad and malleable. As the Government concedes, "given its unconventional nature, the current conflict is unlikely to end with a formal cease-fire agreement." *Ibid.* The prospect Hamdi raises is therefore not far-fetched. If the Government does not consider this unconventional war won for two generations, and if it maintains during that time that Hamdi might, if released, rejoin forces fighting against the United States, then the position it has taken throughout the litigation of this case suggests that Hamdi's detention could last for the rest of his life.

It is a clearly established principle of the law of war that detention may last no longer than active hostilities. See Article 118 of the Geneva Convention (III) Relative to the Treatment of Prisoners of War, Aug. 12, 1949, [1955] 6

Opinion of O'CONNOR, J.

U. S. T. 3316, 3406, T. I. A. S. No. 3364 ("Prisoners of war shall be released and repatriated without delay after the cessation of active hostilities"). See also Article 20 of the Hague Convention (II) on Laws and Customs of War on Land, July 29, 1899, 32 Stat. 1817 (as soon as possible after "conclusion of peace"); Hague Convention (IV), *supra*, Oct. 18, 1907, 36 Stat. 2301("conclusion of peace" (Art. 20)); Geneva Convention, *supra*, July 27, 1929, 47 Stat. 2055 (repatriation should be accomplished with the least possible delay after conclusion of peace (Art. 75)); Praust, Judicial Power to Determine the Status and Rights of Persons Detained without Trial, 44 Harv. Int'l L. J. 503, 510–511 (2003) (prisoners of war "can be detained during an armed conflict, but the detaining country must release and repatriate them 'without delay after the cessation of active hostilities,' unless they are being lawfully prosecuted or have been lawfully convicted of crimes and are serving sentences" (citing Arts. 118, 85, 99, 119, 129, Geneva Convention (III), 6 T. I .A. S., at 3384, 3392, 3406, 3418)).

Hamdi contends that the AUMF does not authorize indefinite or perpetual detention. Certainly, we agree that indefinite detention for the purpose of interrogation is not authorized. Further, we understand Congress' grant of authority for the use of "necessary and appropriate force" to include the authority to detain for the duration of the relevant conflict, and our understanding is based on long-standing law-of-war principles. If the practical circumstances of a given conflict are entirely unlike those of the conflicts that informed the development of the law of war, that understanding may unravel. But that is not the situation we face as of this date. Active combat operations against Taliban fighters apparently are ongoing in Afghanistan. See, *e.g.*, Constable, U. S. Launches New Operation in Afghanistan, Washington Post, Mar. 14, 2004, p. A22 (reporting that 13,500 United States troops remain in Afghanistan, including several thousand new arrivals); J. Abizaid, Dept. of Defense, Gen. Abizaid Central Command Operations Update Briefing, Apr. 30, 2004, http://www.defenselink.mil/transcripts/2004/tr20040430-1402.html (as visited June 8, 2004, and available in the Clerk of Court's case file) (media briefing describing ongoing operations in Afghanistan involving 20,000 United States troops). The United States may detain, for the duration of these hostilities, individuals legitimately determined to be Taliban combatants who "engaged in an armed conflict against the United States." If the record establishes that United States troops are still involved in active combat in Afghanistan, those detentions are part of the exercise of "necessary and appropriate force," and therefore are authorized by the AUMF.

Ex parte Milligan, 4 Wall. 2, 125 (1866), does not undermine our holding about the Government's authority to seize enemy combatants, as we define that term today. In that case, the Court made repeated reference to the fact that its inquiry into whether the military tribunal had jurisdiction to try and punish Milligan turned in large part on the fact that Milligan was not a prisoner of war, but a resident of Indiana arrested while at home there. *Id.,* at 118, 131. That fact was central to its conclusion. Had Milligan been captured while he was assisting Confederate soldiers by carrying a rifle against Union troops on a Confederate battlefield, the holding of the Court might well have been different. The Court's repeated explanations that Milligan was not a prisoner of war suggest that had these different circumstances been present he could have been detained under military authority for the duration of the conflict, whether or not he was a citizen.[1]

---

[1] Here the basis asserted for detention by the military is that Hamdi was carrying a weapon against American troops on a foreign battlefield;

Opinion of O'CONNOR, J.

Moreover, as JUSTICE SCALIA acknowledges, the Court in *Ex parte Quirin*, 317 U. S. 1 (1942), dismissed the language of *Milligan* that the petitioners had suggested prevented them from being subject to military process. *Post*, at 17–18 (dissenting opinion). Clear in this rejection was a disavowal of the New York State cases cited in *Milligan*, 4 Wall., at 128–129, on which JUSTICE SCALIA relies. *See id.*, at 128–129. Both *Smith* v. *Shaw*, 12 Johns. *257 (N. Y. 1815), and *M'Connell* v. *Hampton*, 12 Johns. *234 (N. Y. 1815), were civil suits for false imprisonment. Even accepting that these cases once could have been viewed as standing for the sweeping proposition for which JUSTICE SCALIA cites them—that the military does not have authority to try an American citizen accused of spying against his country during wartime—*Quirin* makes undeniably clear that this is not the law today. Haupt, like the citizens in *Smith* and *M'Connell*, was accused of being a spy. The Court in *Quirin* found him "subject to trial and punishment by [a] military tribunal[ ]" for those acts, and held that his citizenship did not change this result. 317 U. S., at 31, 37–38.

Quirin was a unanimous opinion. It both postdates and clarifies *Milligan*, providing us with the most apposite precedent that we have on the question of whether citizens may be detained in such circumstances. Brushing aside such precedent—particularly when doing so gives rise to a host of new questions never dealt with by this Court—is unjustified and unwise.

To the extent that JUSTICE SCALIA accepts the precedential value of *Quirin*, he argues that it cannot guide our inquiry here because "[i]n *Quirin* it was uncontested that

---

that is, that he was an enemy combatant. The legal category of enemy combatant has not been elaborated upon in great detail. The permissible bounds of the category will be defined by the lower courts as subsequent cases are presented to them.

the petitioners were members of enemy forces," while Hamdi challenges his classification as an enemy combatant. *Post*, at 19. But it is unclear why, in the paradigm outlined by JUSTICE SCALIA, such a concession should have any relevance. JUSTICE SCALIA envisions a system in which the only options are congressional suspension of the writ of habeas corpus or prosecution for treason or some other crime. *Post*, at 1. He does not explain how his historical analysis supports the addition of a third option—detention under some other process after concession of enemy-combatant status—or why a concession should carry any different effect than proof of enemy-combatant status in a proceeding that comports with due process. To be clear, our opinion only finds legislative authority to detain under the AUMF once it is sufficiently clear that the individual is, in fact, an enemy combatant; whether that is established by concession or by some other process that verifies this fact with sufficient certainty seems beside the point.

Further, JUSTICE SCALIA largely ignores the context of this case: a United States citizen captured in a *foreign* combat zone. JUSTICE SCALIA refers to only one case involving this factual scenario—a case in which a United States citizen-POW (a member of the Italian army) from World War II was seized on the battlefield in Sicily and then held in the United States. The court in that case held that the military detention of that United States citizen was lawful. See *In re Territo*, 156 F. 2d, at 148.

JUSTICE SCALIA's treatment of that case—in a footnote—suffers from the same defect as does his treatment of *Quirin:* Because JUSTICE SCALIA finds the fact of battlefield capture irrelevant, his distinction based on the fact that the petitioner "conceded" enemy combatant status is beside the point. See *supra*, at 15–16. JUSTICE SCALIA can point to no case or other authority for the proposition that those captured on a foreign battlefield (whether detained there or in U. S. territory) cannot be detained outside the criminal process.

Moreover, JUSTICE SCALIA presumably would come to a different result if Hamdi had been kept in Afghanistan or even Guantanamo Bay. See *post*, at 25 (SCALIA, J., dissenting). This creates a perverse incentive. Military authorities faced with the stark choice of submitting to the full-blown criminal process or releasing a suspected enemy combatant captured on the battlefield will simply keep citizen-detainees abroad. Indeed, the Government transferred Hamdi from Guantanamo Bay to the United States naval brig only after it learned that he might be an American citizen. It is not at all clear why that should make a determinative constitutional difference.

III

Even in cases in which the detention of enemy combatants is legally authorized, there remains the question of what process is constitutionally due to a citizen who disputes his enemy-combatant status. Hamdi argues that he is owed a meaningful and timely hearing and that "extrajudicial detention [that] begins and ends with the submission of an affidavit based on third-hand hearsay" does not comport with the Fifth and Fourteenth Amendments. Brief for Petitioners 16. The Government counters that any more process than was provided below would be both unworkable and "constitutionally intolerable." Brief for Respondents 46. Our resolution of this dispute requires a careful examination both of the writ of habeas corpus, which Hamdi now seeks to employ as a mechanism of judicial review, and of the Due Process Clause, which informs the procedural contours of that mechanism in this instance.

A

Though they reach radically different conclusions on the process that ought to attend the present proceeding, the parties begin on common ground. All agree that, absent suspension, the writ of habeas corpus remains available to every individual detained within the United States. U. S. Const., Art. I, §9, cl. 2 ("The Privilege of the Writ of Habeas Corpus shall not be suspended, unless when in Cases of Rebellion or Invasion the public Safety may require it"). Only in the rarest of circumstances has Congress seen fit to suspend the writ. See, *e.g.*, Act of Mar. 3, 1863, ch. 81, §1, 12 Stat. 755; Act of April 20, 1871, ch. 22, §4, 17 Stat. 14. At all other times, it has remained a critical check on the Executive, ensuring that it does not detain individuals except in accordance with law. See *INS* v. *St. Cyr,* 533 U. S. 289, 301 (2001). All agree suspension of the writ has not occurred here. Thus, it is undisputed that Hamdi was properly before an Article III court to challenge his detention under 28 U. S. C. §2241. Brief for Respondents 12. Further, all agree that §2241 and its companion provisions provide at least a skeletal outline of the procedures to be afforded a petitioner in federal habeas review. Most notably, §2243 provides that "the person detained may, under oath, deny any of the facts set forth in the return or allege any other material facts," and §2246 allows the taking of evidence in habeas proceedings by deposition, affidavit, or interrogatories.

The simple outline of §2241 makes clear both that Congress envisioned that habeas petitioners would have some opportunity to present and rebut facts and that courts in cases like this retain some ability to vary the ways in which they do so as mandated by due process. The Government recognizes the basic procedural protections required by the habeas statute, *Id.*, at 37–38, but asks us to hold that, given both the flexibility of the habeas mechanism and the circumstances presented in this case, the

Opinion of O'CONNOR, J.

presentation of the Mobbs Declaration to the habeas court completed the required factual development. It suggests two separate reasons for its position that no further process is due.

B

First, the Government urges the adoption of the Fourth Circuit's holding below—that because it is "undisputed" that Hamdi's seizure took place in a combat zone, the habeas determination can be made purely as a matter of law, with no further hearing or factfinding necessary. This argument is easily rejected. As the dissenters from the denial of rehearing en banc noted, the circumstances surrounding Hamdi's seizure cannot in any way be characterized as "undisputed," as "those circumstances are neither conceded in fact, nor susceptible to concession in law, because Hamdi has not been permitted to speak for himself or even through counsel as to those circumstances." 337 F. 3d 335, 357 (CA4 2003) (Luttig, J., dissenting from denial of rehearing en banc); see also *id.*, at 371–372 (Motz, J., dissenting from denial of rehearing en banc). Further, the "facts" that constitute the alleged concession are insufficient to support Hamdi's detention. Under the definition of enemy combatant that we accept today as falling within the scope of Congress' authorization, Hamdi would need to be "part of or supporting forces hostile to the United States or coalition partners" and "engaged in an armed conflict against the United States" to justify his detention in the United States for the duration of the relevant conflict. Brief for Respondents 3. The habeas petition states only that "[w]hen seized by the United States Government, Mr. Hamdi resided in Afghanistan." App. 104. An assertion that one *resided* in a country in which combat operations are taking place is not a concession that one was "*captured* in a zone of active combat operations in a foreign theater of war," 316 F. 3d, at 459 (emphasis added), and certainly is not a concession that one was "part of or supporting forces hostile to the United States or coalition partners" and "engaged in an armed conflict against the United States." Accordingly, we reject any argument that Hamdi has made concessions that eliminate any right to further process.

C

The Government's second argument requires closer consideration. This is the argument that further factual exploration is unwarranted and inappropriate in light of the extraordinary constitutional interests at stake. Under the Government's most extreme rendition of this argument, "[r]espect for separation of powers and the limited institutional capabilities of courts in matters of military decision-making in connection with an ongoing conflict" ought to eliminate entirely any individual process, restricting the courts to investigating only whether legal authorization exists for the broader detention scheme. Brief for Respondents 26. At most, the Government argues, courts should review its determination that a citizen is an enemy combatant under a very deferential "some evidence" standard. *Id.*, at 34 ("Under the some evidence standard, the focus is exclusively on the factual basis supplied by the Executive to support its own determination" (citing *Superintendent, Mass. Correctional Institution at Walpole v. Hill,* 472 U. S. 445, 455–457 (1985) (explaining that the some evidence standard "does not require" a "weighing of the evidence," but rather calls for assessing "whether there is any evidence in the record that could support the conclusion")). Under this review, a court would assume the accuracy of the Government's articulated basis for Hamdi's detention, as set forth in the Mobbs Declaration, and assess only whether that articulated basis was a legitimate one. Brief for Respondents 36; see also 316 F. 3d, at 473–474 (declining to address

Opinion of O'CONNOR, J.

whether the "some evidence" standard should govern the adjudication of such claims, but noting that "[t]he factual averments in the [Mobbs] affidavit, if accurate, are sufficient to confirm" the legality of Hamdi's detention).

In response, Hamdi emphasizes that this Court consistently has recognized that an individual challenging his detention may not be held at the will of the Executive without recourse to some proceeding before a neutral tribunal to determine whether the Executive's asserted justifications for that detention have basis in fact and warrant in law. See, *e.g., Zadvydas* v. *Davis,* 533 U. S. 678, 690 (2001); *Addington* v. *Texas,* 441 U. S. 418, 425–427 (1979). He argues that the Fourth Circuit inappropriately "ceded power to the Executive during wartime to define the conduct for which a citizen may be detained, judge whether that citizen has engaged in the proscribed conduct, and imprison that citizen indefinitely," Brief for Petitioners 21, and that due process demands that he receive a hearing in which he may challenge the Mobbs Declaration and adduce his own counter evidence. The District Court, agreeing with Hamdi, apparently believed that the appropriate process would approach the process that accompanies a criminal trial. It therefore disapproved of the hearsay nature of the Mobbs Declaration and anticipated quite extensive discovery of various military affairs. Anything less, it concluded, would not be "meaningful judicial review." App. 291.

Both of these positions highlight legitimate concerns. And both emphasize the tension that often exists between the autonomy that the Government asserts is necessary in order to pursue effectively a particular goal and the process that a citizen contends he is due before he is deprived of a constitutional right. The ordinary mechanism that we use for balancing such serious competing interests, and for determining the procedures that are necessary to ensure that a citizen is not "deprived of life, liberty, or property,

Opinion of O'CONNOR, J.

without due process of law," U. S. Const., Amdt. 5, is the test that we articulated in *Mathews* v. *Eldridge,* 424 U. S. 319 (1976). See, *e.g., Heller* v. *Doe,* 509 U. S. 312, 330–331 (1993); *Zinermon* v. *Burch,* 494 U. S. 113, 127–128 (1990); *United States* v. *Salerno,* 481 U. S. 739, 746 (1987); *Schall* v. *Martin,* 467 U. S. 253, 274–275 (1984); *Addington* v. *Texas, supra,* at 425. *Mathews* dictates that the process due in any given instance is determined by weighing "the private interest that will be affected by the official action" against the Government's asserted interest, "including the function involved" and the burdens the Government would face in providing greater process. 424 U. S., at 335. The *Mathews* calculus then contemplates a judicious balancing of these concerns, through an analysis of "the risk of an erroneous deprivation" of the private interest if the process were reduced and the "probable value, if any, of additional or substitute safeguards." *Ibid.* We take each of these steps in turn.

1

It is beyond question that substantial interests lie on both sides of the scale in this case. Hamdi's "private interest . . . affected by the official action," *ibid.,* is the most elemental of liberty interests—the interest in being free from physical detention by one's own government. *Foucha* v. *Louisiana,* 504 U. S. 71, 80 (1992) ("Freedom from bodily restraint has always been at the core of the liberty protected by the Due Process Clause from arbitrary governmental action"); see also *Parham* v. *J. R.,* 442 U. S. 584, 600 (1979) (noting the "substantial liberty interest in not being confined unnecessarily"). "In our society liberty is the norm," and detention without trial "is the carefully limited exception." *Salerno, supra,* at 755. "We have always been careful not to 'minimize the importance and fundamental nature' of the individual's right to liberty," *Foucha, supra,* at 80 (quoting *Salerno, supra,* at 750), and

BASIC DOCUMENTS ABOUT THE DETAINEES

Opinion of O'CONNOR, J.

we will not do so today.

Nor is the weight on this side of the *Mathews* scale offset by the circumstances of war or the accusation of treasonous behavior, for "[i]t is clear that commitment for *any* purpose constitutes a significant deprivation of liberty that requires due process protection," *Jones* v. *United States,* 463 U. S. 354, 361 (1983) (emphasis added; internal quotation marks omitted), and at this stage in the *Mathews* calculus, we consider the interest of the *erroneously* detained individual. *Carey* v. *Piphus,* 435 U. S. 247, 259 (1978) ("Procedural due process rules are meant to protect persons not from the deprivation, but from the mistaken or unjustified deprivation of life, liberty, or property"); see also *id.,* at 266 (noting "the importance to organized society that procedural due process be observed," and emphasizing that "the right to procedural due process is 'absolute' in the sense that it does not depend upon the merits of a claimant's substantive assertions"). Indeed, as *amicus* briefs from media and relief organizations emphasize, the risk of erroneous deprivation of a citizen's liberty in the absence of sufficient process here is very real. See Brief for AmeriCares et al. as *Amici Curiae* 13–22 (noting ways in which "[t]he nature of humanitarian relief work and journalism present a significant risk of mistaken military detentions"). Moreover, as critical as the Government's interest may be in detaining those who actually pose an immediate threat to the national security of the United States during ongoing international conflict, history and common sense teach us that an unchecked system of detention carries the potential to become a means for oppression and abuse of others who do not present that sort of threat. See *Ex parte Milligan,* 4 Wall., at 125 ("[The Founders] knew—the history of the world told them—the nation they were founding, be its existence short or long, would be involved in war; how often or how long continued, human foresight could not tell; and that unlimited power, wherever lodged at such a time, was especially hazardous to freemen"). Because we live in a society in which "[m]ere public intolerance or animosity cannot constitutionally justify the deprivation of a person's physical liberty," *O'Connor* v. *Donaldson,* 422 U. S. 563, 575 (1975), our starting point for the *Mathews* v. *Eldridge* analysis is unaltered by the allegations surrounding the particular detainee or the organizations with which he is alleged to have associated. We reaffirm today the fundamental nature of a citizen's right to be free from involuntary confinement by his own government without due process of law, and we weigh the opposing governmental interests against the curtailment of liberty that such confinement entails.

2

On the other side of the scale are the weighty and sensitive governmental interests in ensuring that those who have in fact fought with the enemy during a war do not return to battle against the United States. As discussed above, *supra,* at 10, the law of war and the realities of combat may render such detentions both necessary and appropriate, and our due process analysis need not blink at those realities. Without doubt, our Constitution recognizes that core strategic matters of warmaking belong in the hands of those who are best positioned and most politically accountable for making them. *Department of Navy* v. *Egan,* 484 U. S. 518, 530 (1988) (noting the reluctance of the courts "to intrude upon the authority of the Executive in military and national security affairs"); *Youngstown Sheet & Tube Co.* v. *Sawyer,* 343 U. S. 579, 587 (1952) (acknowledging "broad powers in military commanders engaged in day-to-day fighting in a theater of war").

The Government also argues at some length that its interests in reducing the process available to alleged enemy combatants are heightened by the practical diffi-

Opinion of O'CONNOR, J.

culties that would accompany a system of trial-like process. In its view, military officers who are engaged in the serious work of waging battle would be unnecessarily and dangerously distracted by litigation half a world away, and discovery into military operations would both intrude on the sensitive secrets of national defense and result in a futile search for evidence buried under the rubble of war. Brief for Respondents 46–49. To the extent that these burdens are triggered by heightened procedures, they are properly taken into account in our due process analysis.

3

Striking the proper constitutional balance here is of great importance to the Nation during this period of ongoing combat. But it is equally vital that our calculus not give short shrift to the values that this country holds dear or to the privilege that is American citizenship. It is during our most challenging and uncertain moments that our Nation's commitment to due process is most severely tested; and it is in those times that we must preserve our commitment at home to the principles for which we fight abroad. See *Kennedy* v. *Mendoza-Martinez,* 372 U. S. 144, 164–165 (1963) ("The imperative necessity for safeguarding these rights to procedural due process under the gravest of emergencies has existed throughout our constitutional history, for it is then, under the pressing exigencies of crisis, that there is the greatest temptation to dispense with guarantees which, it is feared, will inhibit government action"); see also *United States* v. *Robel,* 389 U. S. 258, 264 (1967) ("It would indeed be ironic if, in the name of national defense, we would sanction the subversion of one of those liberties . . . which makes the defense of the Nation worthwhile").

With due recognition of these competing concerns, we believe that neither the process proposed by the Government nor the process apparently envisioned by the District Court below strikes the proper constitutional balance when a United States citizen is detained in the United States as an enemy combatant. That is, "the risk of erroneous deprivation" of a detainee's liberty interest is unacceptably high under the Government's proposed rule, while some of the "additional or substitute procedural safeguards" suggested by the District Court are unwarranted in light of their limited "probable value" and the burdens they may impose on the military in such cases. *Mathews*, 424 U. S., at 335.

We therefore hold that a citizen-detainee seeking to challenge his classification as an enemy combatant must receive notice of the factual basis for his classification, and a fair opportunity to rebut the Government's factual assertions before a neutral decisionmaker. See *Cleveland Bd. of Ed.* v. *Loudermill,* 470 U. S. 532, 542 (1985) ("An essential principle of due process is that a deprivation of life, liberty, or property 'be preceded by notice and opportunity for hearing appropriate to the nature of the case'" (quoting *Mullane* v. *Central Hanover Bank & Trust Co.,* 339 U. S. 306, 313 (1950)); *Concrete Pipe & Products of Cal., Inc.* v. *Construction Laborers Pension Trust for Southern Cal.,* 508 U. S. 602, 617 (1993) ("due process requires a 'neutral and detached judge in the first instance'" (quoting *Ward* v. *Monroeville,* 409 U. S. 57, 61–62 (1972)). "For more than a century the central meaning of procedural due process has been clear: 'Parties whose rights are to be affected are entitled to be heard; and in order that they may enjoy that right they must first be notified.' It is equally fundamental that the right to notice and an opportunity to be heard 'must be granted at a meaningful time and in a meaningful manner.'" *Fuentes* v. *Shevin,* 407 U. S. 67, 80 (1972) (quoting *Baldwin* v. *Hale,* 1 Wall. 223, 233 (1864); *Armstrong* v. *Manzo,* 380 U. S. 545, 552 (1965) (other citations omitted)). These essential constitutional promises may not be eroded.

At the same time, the exigencies of the circumstances

may demand that, aside from these core elements, enemy combatant proceedings may be tailored to alleviate their uncommon potential to burden the Executive at a time of ongoing military conflict. Hearsay, for example, may need to be accepted as the most reliable available evidence from the Government in such a proceeding. Likewise, the Constitution would not be offended by a presumption in favor of the Government's evidence, so long as that presumption remained a rebuttable one and fair opportunity for rebuttal were provided. Thus, once the Government puts forth credible evidence that the habeas petitioner meets the enemy-combatant criteria, the onus could shift to the petitioner to rebut that evidence with more persuasive evidence that he falls outside the criteria. A burden-shifting scheme of this sort would meet the goal of ensuring that the errant tourist, embedded journalist, or local aid worker has a chance to prove military error while giving due regard to the Executive once it has put forth meaningful support for its conclusion that the detainee is in fact an enemy combatant. In the words of *Mathews*, process of this sort would sufficiently address the "risk of erroneous deprivation" of a detainee's liberty interest while eliminating certain procedures that have questionable additional value in light of the burden on the Government. 424 U. S., at 335.[2]

We think it unlikely that this basic process will have the dire impact on the central functions of warmaking that the Government forecasts. The parties agree that initial captures on the battlefield need not receive the process we have discussed here; that process is due only when the determination is made to *continue* to hold those who have

---

[2] Because we hold that Hamdi is constitutionally entitled to the process described above, we need not address at this time whether any treaty guarantees him similar access to a tribunal for a determination of his status.

been seized. The Government has made clear in its briefing that documentation regarding battlefield detainees already is kept in the ordinary course of military affairs. Brief for Respondents 3–4. Any factfinding imposition created by requiring a knowledgeable affiant to summarize these records to an independent tribunal is a minimal one. Likewise, arguments that military officers ought not have to wage war under the threat of litigation lose much of their steam when factual disputes at enemy-combatant hearings are limited to the alleged combatant's acts. This focus meddles little, if at all, in the strategy or conduct of war, inquiring only into the appropriateness of continuing to detain an individual claimed to have taken up arms against the United States. While we accord the greatest respect and consideration to the judgments of military authorities in matters relating to the actual prosecution of a war, and recognize that the scope of that discretion necessarily is wide, it does not infringe on the core role of the military for the courts to exercise their own time-honored and constitutionally mandated roles of reviewing and resolving claims like those presented here. Cf. *Korematsu* v. *United States*, 323 U. S. 214, 233–234 (1944) (Murphy, J., dissenting) ("[L]ike other claims conflicting with the asserted constitutional rights of the individual, the military claim must subject itself to the judicial process of having its reasonableness determined and its conflicts with other interests reconciled"); *Sterling* v. *Constantin*, 287 U. S. 378, 401 (1932) ("What are the allowable limits of military discretion, and whether or not they have been overstepped in a particular case, are judicial questions").

In sum, while the full protections that accompany challenges to detentions in other settings may prove unworkable and inappropriate in the enemy-combatant setting, the threats to military operations posed by a basic system of independent review are not so weighty as to trump a

Cite as: 542 U. S. ____ (2004)

Opinion of O'CONNOR, J.

citizen's core rights to challenge meaningfully the Government's case and to be heard by an impartial adjudicator.

D

In so holding, we necessarily reject the Government's assertion that separation of powers principles mandate a heavily circumscribed role for the courts in such circumstances. Indeed, the position that the courts must forgo any examination of the individual case and focus exclusively on the legality of the broader detention scheme cannot be mandated by any reasonable view of separation of powers, as this approach serves only to *condense* power into a single branch of government. We have long since made clear that a state of war is not a blank check for the President when it comes to the rights of the Nation's citizens. *Youngstown Sheet & Tube*, 343 U. S., at 587. Whatever power the United States Constitution envisions for the Executive in its exchanges with other nations or with enemy organizations in times of conflict, it most assuredly envisions a role for all three branches when individual liberties are at stake. *Mistretta* v. *United States,* 488 U. S. 361, 380 (1989) (it was "the central judgment of the Framers of the Constitution that, within our political scheme, the separation of governmental powers into three coordinate Branches is essential to the preservation of liberty"); *Home Building & Loan Assn.* v. *Blaisdell,* 290 U. S. 398, 426 (1934) (The war power "is a power to wage war successfully, and thus it permits the harnessing of the entire energies of the people in a supreme cooperative effort to preserve the nation. But even the war power does not remove constitutional limitations safeguarding essential liberties"). Likewise, we have made clear that, unless Congress acts to suspend it, the Great Writ of habeas corpus allows the Judicial Branch to play a necessary role in maintaining this delicate balance of governance, serving as an important judicial check on the Executive's discretion in the realm of detentions. See *St. Cyr*, 533 U. S., at 301 ("At its historical core, the writ of habeas corpus has served as a means of reviewing the legality of Executive detention, and it is in that context that its protections have been strongest"). Thus, while we do not question that our due process assessment must pay keen attention to the particular burdens faced by the Executive in the context of military action, it would turn our system of checks and balances on its head to suggest that a citizen could not make his way to court with a challenge to the factual basis for his detention by his government, simply because the Executive opposes making available such a challenge. Absent suspension of the writ by Congress, a citizen detained as an enemy combatant is entitled to this process.

Because we conclude that due process demands some system for a citizen detainee to refute his classification, the proposed "some evidence" standard is inadequate. Any process in which the Executive's factual assertions go wholly unchallenged or are simply presumed correct without any opportunity for the alleged combatant to demonstrate otherwise falls constitutionally short. As the Government itself has recognized, we have utilized the "some evidence" standard in the past as a standard of review, not as a standard of proof. Brief for Respondents 35. That is, it primarily has been employed by courts in examining an administrative record developed after an adversarial proceeding—one with process at least of the sort that we today hold is constitutionally mandated in the citizen enemy-combatant setting. See, *e.g.*, *St. Cyr, supra*; *Hill*, 472 U. S., at 455–457. This standard therefore is ill suited to the situation in which a habeas petitioner has received no prior proceedings before any tribunal and had no prior opportunity to rebut the Executive's factual assertions before a neutral decisionmaker.

Today we are faced only with such a case. Aside from unspecified "screening" processes, Brief for Respondents 3–4, and military interrogations in which the Government suggests Hamdi could have contested his classification, Tr. of Oral Arg. 40, 42, Hamdi has received no process. An interrogation by one's captor, however effective an intelligence-gathering tool, hardly constitutes a constitutionally adequate factfinding before a neutral decisionmaker. Compare Brief for Respondents 42–43 (discussing the "secure interrogation environment," and noting that military interrogations require a controlled "interrogation dynamic" and "a relationship of trust and dependency" and are "a critical source" of "timely and effective intelligence") with *Concrete Pipe,* 508 U. S., at 617–618 ("one is entitled as a matter of due process of law to an adjudicator who is not in a situation which would offer a possible temptation to the average man as a judge . . . which might lead him not to hold the balance nice, clear and true" (internal quotation marks omitted). That even purportedly fair adjudicators "are disqualified by their interest in the controversy to be decided is, of course, the general rule." *Tumey* v. *Ohio,* 273 U. S. 510, 522 (1927). Plainly, the "process" Hamdi has received is not that to which he is entitled under the Due Process Clause.

There remains the possibility that the standards we have articulated could be met by an appropriately authorized and properly constituted military tribunal. Indeed, it is notable that military regulations already provide for such process in related instances, dictating that tribunals be made available to determine the status of enemy detainees who assert prisoner-of-war status under the Geneva Convention. See Enemy Prisoners of War, Retained Personnel, Civilian Internees and Other Detainees, Army Regulation 190–8, §1–6 (1997). In the absence of such process, however, a court that receives a petition for a writ of habeas corpus from an alleged enemy combatant must itself ensure that the minimum requirements of due process are achieved. Both courts below recognized as much, focusing their energies on the question of whether Hamdi was due an opportunity to rebut the Government's case against him. The Government, too, proceeded on this assumption, presenting its affidavit and then seeking that it be evaluated under a deferential standard of review based on burdens that it alleged would accompany any greater process. As we have discussed, a habeas court in a case such as this may accept affidavit evidence like that contained in the Mobbs Declaration, so long as it also permits the alleged combatant to present his own factual case to rebut the Government's return. We anticipate that a District Court would proceed with the caution that we have indicated is necessary in this setting, engaging in a factfinding process that is both prudent and incremental. We have no reason to doubt that courts faced with these sensitive matters will pay proper heed both to the matters of national security that might arise in an individual case and to the constitutional limitations safeguarding essential liberties that remain vibrant even in times of security concerns.

IV

Hamdi asks us to hold that the Fourth Circuit also erred by denying him immediate access to counsel upon his detention and by disposing of the case without permitting him to meet with an attorney. Brief for Petitioners 19. Since our grant of certiorari in this case, Hamdi has been appointed counsel, with whom he has met for consultation purposes on several occasions, and with whom he is now being granted unmonitored meetings. He unquestionably has the right to access to counsel in connection with the proceedings on remand. No further consideration of this issue is necessary at this stage of the case.

* * *

Opinion of O'CONNOR, J.

The judgment of the United States Court of Appeals for the Fourth Circuit is vacated, and the case is remanded for further proceedings.

It is so ordered.

Cite as: 542 U. S. ____ (2004)

Opinion of SOUTER, J.

SUPREME COURT OF THE UNITED STATES

No. 03–6696

YASER ESAM HAMDI AND ESAM FOUAD HAMDI, AS NEXT FRIEND OF YASER ESAM HAMDI, PETITIONERS v. DONALD H. RUMSFELD, SECRETARY OF DEFENSE, ET AL.

ON WRIT OF CERTIORARI TO THE UNITED STATES COURT OF APPEALS FOR THE FOURTH CIRCUIT

[June 28, 2004]

JUSTICE SOUTER, with whom JUSTICE GINSBURG joins, concurring in part, dissenting in part, and concurring in the judgment.

According to Yaser Hamdi's petition for writ of habeas corpus, brought on his behalf by his father, the Government of the United States is detaining him, an American citizen on American soil, with the explanation that he was seized on the field of battle in Afghanistan, having been on the enemy side. It is undisputed that the Government has not charged him with espionage, treason, or any other crime under domestic law. It is likewise undisputed that for one year and nine months, on the basis of an Executive designation of Hamdi as an "enemy combatant," the Government denied him the right to send or receive any communication beyond the prison where he was held and, in particular, denied him access to counsel to represent him.[1] The Government asserts a right to hold Hamdi under these conditions indefinitely, that is, until the Government determines that the United States is no longer threatened

---

[1] The Government has since February 2004 permitted Hamdi to consult with counsel as a matter of policy, but does not concede that it has an obligation to allow this. Brief for Respondents 9, 39–46.

HAMDI v. RUMSFELD

Opinion of SOUTER, J.

by the terrorism exemplified in the attacks of September 11, 2001.

In these proceedings on Hamdi's petition, he seeks to challenge the facts claimed by the Government as the basis for holding him as an enemy combatant. And in this Court he presses the distinct argument that the Government's claim, even if true, would not implicate any authority for holding him that would satisfy 18 U. S. C. §4001(a) (Non-Detention Act), which bars imprisonment or detention of a citizen "except pursuant to an Act of Congress."

The Government responds that Hamdi's incommunicado imprisonment as an enemy combatant seized on the field of battle falls within the President's power as Commander in Chief under the laws and usages of war, and is in any event authorized by two statutes. Accordingly, the Government contends that Hamdi has no basis for any challenge by petition for habeas except to his own status as an enemy combatant; and even that challenge may go no further than to enquire whether "some evidence" supports Hamdi's designation, see Brief for Respondents 34–36; if there is "some evidence," Hamdi should remain locked up at the discretion of the Executive. At the argument of this case, in fact, the Government went further and suggested that as long as a prisoner could challenge his enemy combatant designation when responding to interrogation during incommunicado detention he was accorded sufficient process to support his designation as an enemy combatant. See Tr. of Oral Arg. 40; *id.*, at 42 ("[H]e has an opportunity to explain it in his own words" "[d]uring interrogation"). Since on either view judicial enquiry so limited would be virtually worthless as a way to contest detention, the Government's concession of jurisdiction to hear Hamdi's habeas claim is more theoretical than practical, leaving the assertion of Executive authority close to unconditional.

Opinion of SOUTER, J.

The plurality rejects any such limit on the exercise of habeas jurisdiction and so far I agree with its opinion. The plurality does, however, accept the Government's position that if Hamdi's designation as an enemy combatant is correct, his detention (at least as to some period) is authorized by an Act of Congress as required by §4001(a), that is, by the Authorization for Use of Military Force, 115 Stat. 224 (hereinafter Force Resolution). *Ante,* at 9–14. Here, I disagree and respectfully dissent. The Government has failed to demonstrate that the Force Resolution authorizes the detention complained of here even on the facts the Government claims. If the Government raises nothing further than the record now shows, the Non-Detention Act entitles Hamdi to be released.

I

The Government's first response to Hamdi's claim that holding him violates §4001(a), prohibiting detention of citizens "except pursuant to an Act of Congress," is that the statute does not even apply to military wartime detentions, being beyond the sphere of domestic criminal law. Next, the Government says that even if that statute does apply, two Acts of Congress provide the authority §4001(a) demands: a general authorization to the Department of Defense to pay for detaining "prisoners of war" and "similar" persons, 10 U. S. C. §956(5), and the Force Resolution, passed after the attacks of 2001. At the same time, the Government argues that in detaining Hamdi in the manner described, the President is in any event acting as Commander in Chief under Article II of the Constitution, which brings with it the right to invoke authority under the accepted customary rules for waging war. On the record in front of us, the Government has not made out a case on any theory.

HAMDI v. RUMSFELD

Opinion of SOUTER, J.

II

The threshold issue is how broadly or narrowly to read the Non-Detention Act, the tone of which is severe: "No citizen shall be imprisoned or otherwise detained by the United States except pursuant to an Act of Congress." Should the severity of the Act be relieved when the Government's stated factual justification for incommunicado detention is a war on terrorism, so that the Government may be said to act "pursuant" to congressional terms that fall short of explicit authority to imprison individuals? With one possible though important qualification, see *infra*, at 10–11, the answer has to be no. For a number of reasons, the prohibition within §4001(a) has to be read broadly to accord the statute a long reach and to impose a burden of justification on the Government.

First, the circumstances in which the Act was adopted point the way to this interpretation. The provision superseded a cold-war statute, the Emergency Detention Act of 1950 (formerly 50 U. S. C. §811 *et seq.* (1970 ed.)), which had authorized the Attorney General, in time of emergency, to detain anyone reasonably thought likely to engage in espionage or sabotage. That statute was repealed in 1971 out of fear that it could authorize a repetition of the World War II internment of citizens of Japanese ancestry; Congress meant to preclude another episode like the one described in *Korematsu* v. *United States*, 323 U. S. 214 (1944). See H. R. Rep. No. 92–116, pp. 2, 4–5 (1971). While Congress might simply have struck the 1950 statute, in considering the repealer the point was made that the existing statute provided some express procedural protection, without which the Executive would seem to be subject to no statutory limits protecting individual liberty. See *id.*, at 5 (mere repeal "might leave citizens subject to arbitrary executive action, with no clear demarcation of the limits of executive authority"); 117 Cong. Rec. 31544 (1971) (Emergency Detention Act "remains as the only

Opinion of SOUTER, J.

existing barrier against the future exercise of executive power which resulted in" the Japanese internment); cf. *id.*, at 31548 (in the absence of further procedural provisions, even §4001(a) "will virtually leave us stripped naked against the great power . . . which the President has"). It was in these circumstances that a proposed limit on Executive action was expanded to the inclusive scope of §4001(a) as enacted.

The fact that Congress intended to guard against a repetition of the World War II internments when it repealed the 1950 statute and gave us §4001(a) provides a powerful reason to think that §4001(a) was meant to require clear congressional authorization before any citizen can be placed in a cell. It is not merely that the legislative history shows that §4001(a) was thought necessary in anticipation of times just like the present, in which the safety of the country is threatened. To appreciate what is most significant, one must only recall that the internments of the 1940's were accomplished by Executive action. Although an Act of Congress ratified and confirmed an Executive order authorizing the military to exclude individuals from defined areas and to accommodate those it might remove, see *Ex parte Endo*, 323 U. S. 283, 285–288 (1944), the statute said nothing whatever about the detention of those who might be removed, *id.*, at 300–301; internment camps were creatures of the Executive, and confinement in them rested on assertion of Executive authority, see *id.*, at 287–293. When, therefore, Congress repealed the 1950 Act and adopted §4001(a) for the purpose of avoiding another *Korematsu*, it intended to preclude reliance on vague congressional authority (for example, providing "accommodations" for those subject to removal) as authority for detention or imprisonment at the discretion of the Executive (maintaining detention camps of American citizens, for example). In requiring that any Executive detention be "pursuant to an Act of Congress," then, Congress necessarily meant to require a congressional enactment that clearly authorized detention or imprisonment.

Second, when Congress passed §4001(a) it was acting in light of an interpretive regime that subjected enactments limiting liberty in wartime to the requirement of a clear statement and it presumably intended §4001(a) to be read accordingly. This need for clarity was unmistakably expressed in *Ex parte Endo, supra,* decided the same day as *Korematsu. Endo* began with a petition for habeas corpus by an interned citizen claiming to be loyal and law-abiding and thus "unlawfully detained." 323 U. S., at 294. The petitioner was held entitled to habeas relief in an opinion that set out this principle for scrutinizing wartime statutes in derogation of customary liberty:

> "In interpreting a wartime measure we must assume that [its] purpose was to allow for the greatest possible accommodation between . . . liberties and the exigencies of war. We must assume, when asked to find implied powers in a grant of legislative or executive authority, that the law makers intended to place no greater restraint on the citizen than was clearly and unmistakably indicated by the language they used." *Id.,* at 300.

Congress's understanding of the need for clear authority before citizens are kept detained is itself therefore clear, and §4001(a) must be read to have teeth in its demand for congressional authorization.

Finally, even if history had spared us the cautionary example of the internments in World War II, even if there had been no *Korematsu,* and *Endo* had set out no principle of statutory interpretation, there would be a compelling reason to read §4001(a) to demand manifest authority to detain before detention is authorized. The defining character of American constitutional government is its con-

Opinion of SOUTER, J.

stant tension between security and liberty, serving both by partial helpings of each. In a government of separated powers, deciding finally on what is a reasonable degree of guaranteed liberty whether in peace or war (or some condition in between) is not well entrusted to the Executive Branch of Government, whose particular responsibility is to maintain security. For reasons of inescapable human nature, the branch of the Government asked to counter a serious threat is not the branch on which to rest the Nation's entire reliance in striking the balance between the will to win and the cost in liberty on the way to victory; the responsibility for security will naturally amplify the claim that security legitimately raises. A reasonable balance is more likely to be reached on the judgment of a different branch, just as Madison said in remarking that "the constant aim is to divide and arrange the several offices in such a manner as that each may be a check on the other—that the private interest of every individual may be a sentinel over the public rights." The Federalist No. 51, p. 349 (J. Cooke ed. 1961). Hence the need for an assessment by Congress before citizens are subject to lockup, and likewise the need for a clearly expressed congressional resolution of the competing claims.

III

Under this principle of reading §4001(a) robustly to require a clear statement of authorization to detain, none of the Government's arguments suffices to justify Hamdi's detention.

A

First, there is the argument that §4001(a) does not even apply to wartime military detentions, a position resting on the placement of §4001(a) in Title 18 of the United States Code, the gathering of federal criminal law. The text of the statute does not, however, so limit its reach, and the legislative history of the provision shows its placement in Title 18 was not meant to render the statute more restricted than its terms. The draft of what is now §4001(a) as contained in the original bill prohibited only imprisonment unauthorized by Title 18. See H. R. Rep. No. 92–116, at 4. In response to the Department of Justice's objection that the original draft seemed to assume wrongly that all provisions for the detention of convicted persons would be contained in Title 18, the provision was amended by replacing a reference to that title with the reference to an "Act of Congress." *Id.*, at 3. The Committee on the Judiciary, discussing this change, stated that "[limiting] detention of citizens . . . to situations in which . . . an Act of Congres[s] exists" would "assure that no detention camps can be established without at least the acquiescence of the Congress." *Id.*, at 5. See also *supra*, at 4–6. This understanding, that the amended bill would sweep beyond imprisonment for crime and apply to Executive detention in furtherance of wartime security, was emphasized in an extended debate. Representative Ichord, chairman of the House Internal Security Committee and an opponent of the bill, feared that the redrafted statute would "deprive the President of his emergency powers and his most effective means of coping with sabotage and espionage agents in war-related crises." 117 Cong. Rec., at 31542. Representative Railsback, the bill's sponsor, spoke of the bill in absolute terms: "[I]n order to prohibit arbitrary executive action, [the bill] assures that no detention of citizens can be undertaken by the Executive without the prior consent of Congress." *Id.*, at 31551. This legislative history indicates that Congress was aware that §4001(a) would limit the Executive's power to detain citizens in wartime to protect national security, and it is fair to say that the prohibition was thus intended to extend not only to the exercise of power to vindicate the interests underlying domestic criminal law, but to statutorily unauthor-

Opinion of SOUTER, J.

ized detention by the Executive for reasons of security in wartime, just as Hamdi claims.[2]

B

Next, there is the Government's claim, accepted by the Court, that the terms of the Force Resolution are adequate to authorize detention of an enemy combatant under the circumstances described,[3] a claim the Government fails to support sufficiently to satisfy §4001(a) as read to require a clear statement of authority to detain. Since the Force Resolution was adopted one week after the attacks of September 11, 2001, it naturally speaks with some generality, but its focus is clear, and that is on the use of military power. It is fairly read to authorize the use of armies and weapons, whether against other armies or individual terrorists. But, like the statute discussed in *Endo*, it never so much as uses the word detention, and there is no reason to think Congress might have perceived any need to augment Executive power to deal with dangerous citizens within the United States, given the well-stocked

---

[2] Nor is it possible to distinguish between civilian and military authority to detain based on the congressional object of avoiding another *Korematsu* v. *United States,* 323 U. S. 214 (1944). See Brief for Respondents 21 (arguing that military detentions are exempt). Although a civilian agency authorized by Executive order ran the detention camps, the relocation and detention of American citizens was ordered by the military under authority of the President as Commander in Chief. See *Ex parte Endo*, 323 U. S. 283, 285–288 (1944). The World War II internment was thus ordered under the same Presidential power invoked here and the intent to bar a repetition goes to the action taken and authority claimed here.

[3] As noted, *supra*, at 3, the Government argues that a required Act of Congress is to be found in a statutory authorization to spend money appropriated for the care of prisoners of war and of other, similar prisoners, 10 U. S. C. §956(5). It is enough to say that this statute is an authorization to spend money if there are prisoners, not an authorization to imprison anyone to provide the occasion for spending money.

statutory arsenal of defined criminal offenses covering the gamut of actions that a citizen sympathetic to terrorists might commit. See, *e.g.*, 18 U. S. C. §2339A (material support for various terrorist acts); §2339B (material support to a foreign terrorist organization); §2332a (use of a weapon of mass destruction, including conspiracy and attempt); §2332b(a)(1) (acts of terrorism "transcending national boundaries," including threats, conspiracy, and attempt); 18 U. S. C. A. §2339C (Supp. 2004) (financing of certain terrorist acts); see also 18 U. S. C. §3142(e) (pretrial detention). See generally Brief for Janet Reno et al. as *Amici Curiae* in *Rumsfeld* v. *Padilla*, O. T. 2003, No. 03–1027, pp. 14–19, and n. 17 (listing the tools available to the Executive to fight terrorism even without the power the Government claims here); Brief for Louis Henkin et al. as *Amici Curiae* in *Rumsfeld* v. *Padilla*, O. T. 2003, No. 03–1027, p. 23, n. 27.[4]

C

Even so, there is one argument for treating the Force Resolution as sufficiently clear to authorize detention of a citizen consistently with §4001(a). Assuming the argument to be sound, however, the Government is in no position to claim its advantage.

Because the Force Resolution authorizes the use of military force in acts of war by the United States, the argument goes, it is reasonably clear that the military and its Commander in Chief are authorized to deal with enemy belligerents according to the treaties and customs known collectively as the laws of war. Brief for Respondents 20–

---

[4] Even a brief examination of the reported cases in which the Government has chosen to proceed criminally against those who aided the Taliban shows the Government has found no shortage of offenses to allege. See *United States* v. *Lindh*, 212 F. Supp. 2d 541, 547 (ED Va. 2002); *United States* v. *Khan*, 309 F. Supp. 2d 789, 796 (ED Va. 2004).

Opinion of SOUTER, J.

22; see *ante*, at 9–14 (accepting this argument). Accordingly, the United States may detain captured enemies, and *Ex parte Quirin,* 317 U. S. 1 (1942), may perhaps be claimed for the proposition that the American citizenship of such a captive does not as such limit the Government's power to deal with him under the usages of war. *Id.,* at 31, 37–38. Thus, the Government here repeatedly argues that Hamdi's detention amounts to nothing more than customary detention of a captive taken on the field of battle: if the usages of war are fairly authorized by the Force Resolution, Hamdi's detention is authorized for purposes of §4001(a).

There is no need, however, to address the merits of such an argument in all possible circumstances. For now it is enough to recognize that the Government's stated legal position in its campaign against the Taliban (among whom Hamdi was allegedly captured) is apparently at odds with its claim here to be acting in accordance with customary law of war and hence to be within the terms of the Force Resolution in its detention of Hamdi. In a statement of its legal position cited in its brief, the Government says that "the Geneva Convention applies to the Taliban detainees." Office of the White House Press Secretary, Fact Sheet, Status of Detainees at Guantanamo (Feb. 7, 2002), www.whitehouse.gov/news/releases/2002/02/20020207-13.html (as visited June 18, 2004, and available in Clerk of Court's case file) (hereinafter White House Press Release) (cited in Brief for Respondents 24, n. 9). Hamdi presumably is such a detainee, since according to the Government's own account, he was taken bearing arms on the Taliban side of a field of battle in Afghanistan. He would therefore seem to qualify for treatment as a prisoner of war under the Third Geneva Convention, to which the United States is a party. Article 4 of the Geneva Convention (III) Relative to the Treatment of Prisoners of War, Aug. 12, 1949, [1955] 6 U. S. T. 3316, 3320,

HAMDI v. RUMSFELD

Opinion of SOUTER, J.

T. I. A. S. No. 3364.

By holding him incommunicado, however, the Government obviously has not been treating him as a prisoner of war, and in fact the Government claims that no Taliban detainee is entitled to prisoner of war status. See Brief for Respondents 24; White House Press Release. This treatment appears to be a violation of the Geneva Convention provision that even in cases of doubt, captives are entitled to be treated as prisoners of war "until such time as their status has been determined by a competent tribunal." Art. 5, 6 U. S. T., at 3324. The Government answers that the President's determination that Taliban detainees do not qualify as prisoners of war is conclusive as to Hamdi's status and removes any doubt that would trigger application of the Convention's tribunal requirement. See Brief for Respondents 24. But reliance on this categorical pronouncement to settle doubt is apparently at odds with the military regulation, Enemy Prisoners of War, Retained Personnel, Civilian Internees and Other Detainees, Army Reg. 190–8, §§1–5, 1–6 (1997), adopted to implement the Geneva Convention, and setting out a detailed procedure for a military tribunal to determine an individual's status. See, *e.g.*, *id.*, §1–6 ("A competent tribunal shall be composed of three commissioned officers"; a "written record shall be made of proceedings"; "[p]roceedings shall be open" with certain exceptions; "[p]ersons whose status is to be determined shall be advised of their rights at the beginning of their hearings," "allowed to attend all open sessions," "allowed to call witnesses if reasonably available, and to question those witnesses called by the Tribunal," and to "have a right to testify"; and a tribunal shall determine status by a "[p]reponderance of evidence"). One of the types of doubt these tribunals are meant to settle is whether a given individual may be, as Hamdi says he is, an "[i]nnocent civilian who should be immediately returned to his home or released." *Id.*, 1–6e(10)(c). The

Opinion of SOUTER, J.

regulation, jointly promulgated by the Headquarters of the Departments of the Army, Navy, Air Force, and Marine Corps, provides that "[p]ersons who have been determined by a competent tribunal not to be entitled to prisoner of war status may not be executed, imprisoned, or otherwise penalized without further proceedings to determine what acts they have committed and what penalty should be imposed." *Id.*, §1–6g. The regulation also incorporates the Geneva Convention's presumption that in cases of doubt, "persons shall enjoy the protection of the . . . Convention until such time as their status has been determined by a competent tribunal." *Id.*, §1–6a. Thus, there is reason to question whether the United States is acting in accordance with the laws of war it claims as authority.

Whether, or to what degree, the Government is in fact violating the Geneva Convention and is thus acting outside the customary usages of war are not matters I can resolve at this point. What I can say, though, is that the Government has not made out its claim that in detaining Hamdi in the manner described, it is acting in accord with the laws of war authorized to be applied against citizens by the Force Resolution. I conclude accordingly that the Government has failed to support the position that the Force Resolution authorizes the described detention of Hamdi for purposes of §4001(a).

It is worth adding a further reason for requiring the Government to bear the burden of clearly justifying its claim to be exercising recognized war powers before declaring §4001(a) satisfied. Thirty-eight days after adopting the Force Resolution, Congress passed the statute entitled Uniting and Strengthening America by Providing Appropriate Tools Required to Intercept and Obstruct Terrorism Act of 2001 (USA PATRIOT ACT), 115 Stat. 272; that Act authorized the detention of alien terrorists for no more than seven days in the absence of criminal charges or deportation proceedings, 8 U. S. C. §1226a(a)(5)

(2000 ed., Supp. I). It is very difficult to believe that the same Congress that carefully circumscribed Executive power over alien terrorists on home soil would not have meant to require the Government to justify clearly its detention of an American citizen held on home soil incommunicado.

D

Since the Government has given no reason either to deflect the application of §4001(a) or to hold it to be satisfied, I need to go no further; the Government hints of a constitutional challenge to the statute, but it presents none here. I will, however, stray across the line between statutory and constitutional territory just far enough to note the weakness of the Government's mixed claim of inherent, extrastatutory authority under a combination of Article II of the Constitution and the usages of war. It is in fact in this connection that the Government developed its argument that the exercise of war powers justifies the detention, and what I have just said about its inadequacy applies here as well. Beyond that, it is instructive to recall Justice Jackson's observation that the President is not Commander in Chief of the country, only of the military. *Youngstown Sheet & Tube Co.* v. *Sawyer*, 343 U. S. 579, 643–644 (1952) (concurring opinion); see also *id.*, at 637–638 (Presidential authority is "at its lowest ebb" where the President acts contrary to congressional will).

There may be room for one qualification to Justice Jackson's statement, however: in a moment of genuine emergency, when the Government must act with no time for deliberation, the Executive may be able to detain a citizen if there is reason to fear he is an imminent threat to the safety of the Nation and its people (though I doubt there is any want of statutory authority, see *supra*, at 9–10). This case, however, does not present that question, because an emergency power of necessity must at least be limited by the emergency; Hamdi has been locked up for over two years. Cf. *Ex parte Milligan,* 4 Wall. 2, 127 (1866) (martial law justified only by "actual and present" necessity as in a genuine invasion that closes civilian courts).

Whether insisting on the careful scrutiny of emergency claims or on a vigorous reading of §4001(a), we are heirs to a tradition given voice 800 years ago by Magna Carta, which, on the barons' insistence, confined executive power by "the law of the land."

IV

Because I find Hamdi's detention forbidden by §4001(a) and unauthorized by the Force Resolution, I would not reach any questions of what process he may be due in litigating disputed issues in a proceeding under the habeas statute or prior to the habeas enquiry itself. For me, it suffices that the Government has failed to justify holding him in the absence of a further Act of Congress, criminal charges, a showing that the detention conforms to the laws of war, or a demonstration that §4001(a) is unconstitutional. I would therefore vacate the judgment of the Court of Appeals and remand for proceedings consistent with this view.

Since this disposition does not command a majority of the Court, however, the need to give practical effect to the conclusions of eight members of the Court rejecting the Government's position calls for me to join with the plurality in ordering remand on terms closest to those I would impose. See *Screws* v. *United States,* 325 U. S. 91, 134 (1945) (Rutledge, J., concurring in result). Although I think litigation of Hamdi's status as an enemy combatant is unnecessary, the terms of the plurality's remand will allow Hamdi to offer evidence that he is not an enemy combatant, and he should at the least have the benefit of that opportunity.

It should go without saying that in joining with the

plurality to produce a judgment, I do not adopt the plurality's resolution of constitutional issues that I would not reach. It is not that I could disagree with the plurality's determinations (given the plurality's view of the Force Resolution) that someone in Hamdi's position is entitled at a minimum to notice of the Government's claimed factual basis for holding him, and to a fair chance to rebut it before a neutral decision maker, see *ante*, at 26; nor, of course, could I disagree with the plurality's affirmation of Hamdi's right to counsel, see *ante*, at 32–33. On the other hand, I do not mean to imply agreement that the Government could claim an evidentiary presumption casting the burden of rebuttal on Hamdi, see *ante*, at 27, or that an opportunity to litigate before a military tribunal might obviate or truncate enquiry by a court on habeas, see *ante*, at 31–32.

Subject to these qualifications, I join with the plurality in a judgment of the Court vacating the Fourth Circuit's judgment and remanding the case.

Cite as: 542 U. S. ____ (2004) 1

SCALIA, J., dissenting

SUPREME COURT OF THE UNITED STATES

No. 03–6696

YASER ESAM HAMDI AND ESAM FOUAD HAMDI, AS NEXT FRIEND OF YASER ESAM HAMDI, PETITIONERS *v.* DONALD H. RUMSFELD, SECRETARY OF DEFENSE, ET AL.

ON WRIT OF CERTIORARI TO THE UNITED STATES COURT OF APPEALS FOR THE FOURTH CIRCUIT

[June 28, 2004]

JUSTICE SCALIA, with whom JUSTICE STEVENS joins, dissenting.

Petitioner, a presumed American citizen, has been imprisoned without charge or hearing in the Norfolk and Charleston Naval Brigs for more than two years, on the allegation that he is an enemy combatant who bore arms against his country for the Taliban. His father claims to the contrary, that he is an inexperienced aid worker caught in the wrong place at the wrong time. This case brings into conflict the competing demands of national security and our citizens' constitutional right to personal liberty. Although I share the Court's evident unease as it seeks to reconcile the two, I do not agree with its resolution.

Where the Government accuses a citizen of waging war against it, our constitutional tradition has been to prosecute him in federal court for treason or some other crime. Where the exigencies of war prevent that, the Constitution's Suspension Clause, Art. I, §9, cl. 2, allows Congress to relax the usual protections temporarily. Absent suspension, however, the Executive's assertion of military exigency has not been thought sufficient to permit detention without charge. No one contends that the congres-

HAMDI v. RUMSFELD

SCALIA, J., dissenting

sional Authorization for Use of Military Force, on which the Government relies to justify its actions here, is an implementation of the Suspension Clause. Accordingly, I would reverse the decision below.

I

The very core of liberty secured by our Anglo-Saxon system of separated powers has been freedom from indefinite imprisonment at the will of the Executive. Blackstone stated this principle clearly:

"Of great importance to the public is the preservation of this personal liberty: for if once it were left in the power of any, the highest, magistrate to imprison arbitrarily whomever he or his officers thought proper . . . there would soon be an end of all other rights and immunities. . . . To bereave a man of life, or by violence to confiscate his estate, without accusation or trial, would be so gross and notorious an act of despotism, as must at once convey the alarm of tyranny throughout the whole kingdom. But confinement of the person, by secretly hurrying him to gaol, where his sufferings are unknown or forgotten; is a less public, a less striking, and therefore a more dangerous engine of arbitrary government. . . .

"To make imprisonment lawful, it must either be, by process from the courts of judicature, or by warrant from some legal officer, having authority to commit to prison; which warrant must be in writing, under the hand and seal of the magistrate, and express the causes of the commitment, in order to be examined into (if necessary) upon a *habeas corpus*. If there be no cause expressed, the gaoler is not bound to detain the prisoner. For the law judges in this respect, . . . that it is unreasonable to send a prisoner, and not to signify withal the crimes alleged against him." 1 W. Blackstone, Commentaries on the Laws of England

132–133 (1765) (hereinafter Blackstone).

These words were well known to the Founders. Hamilton quoted from this very passage in The Federalist No. 84, p. 444 (G. Carey & J. McClellan eds. 2001). The two ideas central to Blackstone's understanding—due process as the right secured, and habeas corpus as the instrument by which due process could be insisted upon by a citizen illegally imprisoned—found expression in the Constitution's Due Process and Suspension Clauses. See Amdt. 5; Art. I, §9, cl. 2.

The gist of the Due Process Clause, as understood at the founding and since, was to force the Government to follow those common-law procedures traditionally deemed necessary before depriving a person of life, liberty, or property. When a citizen was deprived of liberty because of alleged criminal conduct, those procedures typically required committal by a magistrate followed by indictment and trial. See, *e.g.,* 2 & 3 Phil. & M., c. 10 (1555); 3 J. Story, Commentaries on the Constitution of the United States §1783, p. 661 (1833) (hereinafter Story) (equating "due process of law" with "due presentment or indictment, and being brought in to answer thereto by due process of the common law"). The Due Process Clause "in effect affirms the right of trial according to the process and proceedings of the common law." *Ibid.* See also T. Cooley, General Principles of Constitutional Law 224 (1880) ("When life and liberty are in question, there must in every instance be judicial proceedings; and that requirement implies an accusation, a hearing before an impartial tribunal, with proper jurisdiction, and a conviction and judgment before the punishment can be inflicted" (internal quotation marks omitted)).

To be sure, certain types of permissible *non*criminal detention—that is, those not dependent upon the contention that the citizen had committed a criminal act—did

HAMDI v. RUMSFELD

SCALIA, J., dissenting

not require the protections of criminal procedure. However, these fell into a limited number of well-recognized exceptions—civil commitment of the mentally ill, for example, and temporary detention in quarantine of the infectious. See *Opinion on the Writ of Habeas Corpus*, 97 Eng. Rep. 29, 36–37 (H. L. 1758) (Wilmot, J.). It is unthinkable that the Executive could render otherwise criminal grounds for detention noncriminal merely by disclaiming an intent to prosecute, or by asserting that it was incapacitating dangerous offenders rather than punishing wrongdoing. Cf. *Kansas* v. *Hendricks,* 521 U. S. 346, 358 (1997) ("A finding of dangerousness, standing alone, is ordinarily not a sufficient ground upon which to justify indefinite involuntary commitment").

These due process rights have historically been vindicated by the writ of habeas corpus. In England before the founding, the writ developed into a tool for challenging executive confinement. It was not always effective. For example, in *Darnel's Case*, 3 How. St. Tr. 1 (K. B. 1627), King Charles I detained without charge several individuals for failing to assist England's war against France and Spain. The prisoners sought writs of habeas corpus, arguing that without specific charges, "imprisonment shall not continue on for a time, but for ever; and the subjects of this kingdom may be restrained of their liberties perpetually." *Id.,* at 8. The Attorney General replied that the Crown's interest in protecting the realm justified imprisonment in "a matter of state . . . not ripe nor timely" for the ordinary process of accusation and trial. *Id.,* at 37. The court denied relief, producing widespread outrage, and Parliament responded with the Petition of Right, accepted by the King in 1628, which expressly prohibited imprisonment without formal charges, see 3 Car. 1, c. 1, §§5, 10.

The struggle between subject and Crown continued, and culminated in the Habeas Corpus Act of 1679, 31 Car. 2, c.

2, described by Blackstone as a "second *magna charta*, and stable bulwark of our liberties." 1 Blackstone 133. The Act governed all persons "committed or detained . . . for any crime." §3. In cases other than felony or treason plainly expressed in the warrant of commitment, the Act required release upon appropriate sureties (unless the commitment was for a nonbailable offense). *Ibid.* Where the commitment was for felony or high treason, the Act did not require immediate release, but instead required the Crown to commence criminal proceedings within a specified time. §7. If the prisoner was not "indicted some Time in the next Term," the judge was "required . . . to set at Liberty the Prisoner upon Bail" unless the King was unable to produce his witnesses. *Ibid.* Able or no, if the prisoner was not brought to trial by the *next* succeeding term, the Act provided that "he shall be discharged from his Imprisonment." *Ibid.* English courts sat four terms per year, see 3 Blackstone 275–277, so the practical effect of this provision was that imprisonment without indictment or trial for felony or high treason under §7 would not exceed approximately three to six months.

The writ of habeas corpus was preserved in the Constitution—the only common-law writ to be explicitly mentioned. See Art. I, §9, cl. 2. Hamilton lauded "the establishment of the writ of *habeas corpus*" in his Federalist defense as a means to protect against "the practice of arbitrary imprisonments . . . in all ages, [one of] the favourite and most formidable instruments of tyranny." The Federalist No. 84, *supra*, at 444. Indeed, availability of the writ under the new Constitution (along with the requirement of trial by jury in criminal cases, see Art. III, §2, cl. 3) was his basis for arguing that additional, explicit procedural protections were unnecessary. See The Federalist No. 83, at 433.

BASIC DOCUMENTS ABOUT THE DETAINEES

6   HAMDI *v.* RUMSFELD

SCALIA, J., dissenting

II

The allegations here, of course, are no ordinary accusations of criminal activity. Yaser Esam Hamdi has been imprisoned because the Government believes he participated in the waging of war against the United States. The relevant question, then, is whether there is a different, special procedure for imprisonment of a citizen accused of wrongdoing *by aiding the enemy in wartime*.

A

JUSTICE O'CONNOR, writing for a plurality of this Court, asserts that captured enemy combatants (other than those suspected of war crimes) have traditionally been detained until the cessation of hostilities and then released. *Ante*, at 10–11. That is probably an accurate description of wartime practice with respect to enemy *aliens*. The tradition with respect to American citizens, however, has been quite different. Citizens aiding the enemy have been treated as traitors subject to the criminal process.

As early as 1350, England's Statute of Treasons made it a crime to "levy War against our Lord the King in his Realm, or be adherent to the King's Enemies in his Realm, giving to them Aid and Comfort, in the Realm, or elsewhere." 25 Edw. 3, Stat. 5, c. 2. In his 1762 Discourse on High Treason, Sir Michael Foster explained:

> "With regard to Natural-born Subjects there can be no Doubt. They owe Allegiance to the Crown at all Times and in all Places.
>
> . . . . .
>
> "The joining with Rebels in an Act of Rebellion, or with Enemies in Acts of Hostility, will make a Man a Traitor: in the one Case within the Clause of Levying War, in the other within that of Adhering to the King's enemies.
>
> . . . . .

SCALIA, J., dissenting

"States in Actual Hostility with Us, though no War be solemnly Declared, are Enemies within the meaning of the Act. And therefore in an Indictment on the Clause of Adhering to the King's Enemies, it is sufficient to Aver that the Prince or State Adhered to *is an Enemy*, without shewing any War Proclaimed.... And if the Subject of a Foreign Prince in Amity with Us, invadeth the Kingdom without Commission from his Sovereign, He is an Enemy. And a Subject of *England* adhering to Him is a Traitor within this Clause of the Act." A Report of Some Proceedings on the Commission . . . for the Trial of the Rebels in the Year 1746 in the County of Surry, and of Other Crown Cases, Introduction, §1, p. 183; Ch. 2, §8, p. 216; §12, p. 219.

Subjects accused of levying war against the King were routinely prosecuted for treason. *E.g., Harding's Case*, 2 Ventris 315, 86 Eng. Rep. 461 (K. B. 1690); *Trial of Parkyns*, 13 How. St. Tr. 63 (K. B. 1696); *Trial of Vaughan*, 13 How. St. Tr. 485 (K. B. 1696); *Trial of Downie*, 24 How. St. Tr. 1 (1794). The Founders inherited the understanding that a citizen's levying war against the Government was to be punished criminally. The Constitution provides: "Treason against the United States, shall consist only in levying War against them, or in adhering to their Enemies, giving them Aid and Comfort"; and establishes a heightened proof requirement (two witnesses) in order to "convic[t]" of that offense. Art. III, §3, cl. 1.

In more recent times, too, citizens have been charged and tried in Article III courts for acts of war against the United States, even when their noncitizen co-conspirators were not. For example, two American citizens alleged to have participated during World War I in a spying conspiracy on behalf of Germany were tried in federal court. See *United States* v. *Fricke*, 259 F. 673 (SDNY 1919); *United*

States v. Robinson, 259 F. 685 (SDNY 1919). A German member of the same conspiracy was subjected to military process. See *United States ex rel. Wessels* v. *McDonald,* 265 F. 754 (EDNY 1920). During World War II, the famous German saboteurs of *Ex parte Quirin,* 317 U. S. 1 (1942), received military process, but the citizens who associated with them (with the exception of one citizen-saboteur, discussed below) were punished under the criminal process. See *Haupt* v. *United States,* 330 U. S. 631 (1947); L. Fisher, Nazi Saboteurs on Trial 80–84 (2003); see also *Cramer* v. *United States,* 325 U. S. 1 (1945).

The modern treason statute is 18 U. S. C. §2381; it basically tracks the language of the constitutional provision. Other provisions of Title 18 criminalize various acts of warmaking and adherence to the enemy. See, *e.g.,* §32 (destruction of aircraft or aircraft facilities), §2332a (use of weapons of mass destruction), §2332b (acts of terrorism transcending national boundaries), §2339A (providing material support to terrorists), §2339B (providing material support to certain terrorist organizations), §2382 (misprision of treason), §2383 (rebellion or insurrection), §2384 (seditious conspiracy), §2390 (enlistment to serve in armed hostility against the United States). See also 31 CFR §595.204 (2003) (prohibiting the "making or receiving of any contribution of funds, goods, or services" to terrorists); 50 U. S. C. §1705(b) (criminalizing violations of 31 CFR §595.204). The only citizen other than Hamdi known to be imprisoned in connection with military hostilities in Afghanistan against the United States *was* subjected to criminal process and convicted upon a guilty plea. See *United States* v. *Lindh,* 212 F. Supp. 2d 541 (ED Va. 2002) (denying motions for dismissal); Seelye, N. Y. Times, Oct. 5, 2002, p. A1, col. 5.

B

There are times when military exigency renders resort

SCALIA, J., dissenting

to the traditional criminal process impracticable. English law accommodated such exigencies by allowing legislative suspension of the writ of habeas corpus for brief periods. Blackstone explained:

> "And yet sometimes, when the state is in real danger, even this [*i.e.*, executive detention] may be a necessary measure. But the happiness of our constitution is, that it is not left to the executive power to determine when the danger of the state is so great, as to render this measure expedient. For the parliament only, or legislative power, whenever it sees proper, can authorize the crown, by suspending the *habeas corpus* act for a short and limited time, to imprison suspected persons without giving any reason for so doing.... In like manner this experiment ought only to be tried in case of extreme emergency; and in these the nation parts with it[s] liberty for a while, in order to preserve it for ever." 1 Blackstone 132.

Where the Executive has not pursued the usual course of charge, committal, and conviction, it has historically secured the Legislature's explicit approval of a suspension. In England, Parliament on numerous occasions passed temporary suspensions in times of threatened invasion or rebellion. *E.g.*, 1 W. & M., c. 7 (1688) (threatened return of James II); 7 & 8 Will. 3, c. 11 (1696) (same); 17 Geo. 2, c. 6 (1744) (threatened French invasion); 19 Geo. 2, c. 1 (1746) (threatened rebellion in Scotland); 17 Geo. 3, c. 9 (1777) (the American Revolution). Not long after Massachusetts had adopted a clause in its constitution explicitly providing for habeas corpus, see Mass. Const. pt. 2, ch. 6, art. VII (1780), reprinted in 3 Federal and State Constitutions, Colonial Charters and Other Organic Laws 1888, 1910 (F. Thorpe ed. 1909), it suspended the writ in order to deal with Shay's Rebellion, see Act for Suspending the Privilege of the Writ of Habeas Corpus, ch. 10, 1786 Mass.

Acts 510.

Our Federal Constitution contains a provision explicitly permitting suspension, but limiting the situations in which it may be invoked: "The privilege of the Writ of Habeas Corpus shall not be suspended, unless when in Cases of Rebellion or Invasion the public Safety may require it." Art. I, §9, cl. 2. Although this provision does not state that suspension must be effected by, or authorized by, a legislative act, it has been so understood, consistent with English practice and the Clause's placement in Article I. See *Ex parte Bollman,* 4 Cranch 75, 101 (1807); *Ex parte Merryman,* 17 F. Cas. 144, 151–152 (CD Md. 1861) (Taney, C. J., rejecting Lincoln's unauthorized suspension); 3 Story §1336, at 208–209.

The Suspension Clause was by design a safety valve, the Constitution's only "express provision for exercise of extraordinary authority because of a crisis," *Youngstown Sheet & Tube Co.* v. *Sawyer,* 343 U. S. 579, 650 (1952) (Jackson, J., concurring). Very early in the Nation's history, President Jefferson unsuccessfully sought a suspension of habeas corpus to deal with Aaron Burr's conspiracy to overthrow the Government. See 16 Annals of Congress 402–425 (1807). During the Civil War, Congress passed its first Act authorizing Executive suspension of the writ of habeas corpus, see Act of Mar. 3, 1863, 12 Stat. 755, to the relief of those many who thought President Lincoln's unauthorized proclamations of suspension (*e.g.*, Proclamation No. 1, 13 Stat. 730 (1862)) unconstitutional. Later Presidential proclamations of suspension relied upon the congressional authorization, *e.g.*, Proclamation No. 7, 13 Stat. 734 (1863). During Reconstruction, Congress passed the Ku Klux Klan Act, which included a provision authorizing suspension of the writ, invoked by President Grant in quelling a rebellion in nine South Carolina counties. See Act of Apr. 20, 1871, ch. 22, §4, 17 Stat. 14; A Proclamation [of Oct. 17, 1871], 7 Compilation of the Messages and Papers of the Presidents 136–138 (J. Richardson ed. 1899) (hereinafter Messages and Papers); *id.,* at 138–139.

Two later Acts of Congress provided broad suspension authority to governors of U. S. possessions. The Philippine Civil Government Act of 1902 provided that the Governor of the Philippines could suspend the writ in case of rebellion, insurrection, or invasion. Act of July 1, 1902, ch. 1369, §5, 32 Stat. 691. In 1905 the writ was suspended for nine months by proclamation of the Governor. See *Fisher* v. *Baker,* 203 U. S. 174, 179–181 (1906). The Hawaiian Organic Act of 1900 likewise provided that the Governor of Hawaii could suspend the writ in case of rebellion or invasion (or threat thereof). Ch. 339, §67, 31 Stat. 153.

III

Of course the extensive historical evidence of criminal convictions and habeas suspensions does not *necessarily* refute the Government's position in this case. When the writ is suspended, the Government is entirely free from judicial oversight. It does not claim such total liberation here, but argues that it need only produce what it calls "some evidence" to satisfy a habeas court that a detained individual is an enemy combatant. See Brief for Respondents 34. Even if suspension of the writ on the one hand, and committal for criminal charges on the other hand, have been the only *traditional* means of dealing with citizens who levied war against their own country, it is theoretically possible that the Constitution does not *require* a choice between these alternatives.

I believe, however, that substantial evidence does refute that possibility. First, the text of the 1679 Habeas Corpus Act makes clear that indefinite imprisonment on reasonable suspicion is not an available option of treatment for those accused of aiding the enemy, absent a suspension of the writ. In the United States, this Act was read as "enforc[ing] the common law," *Ex parte Watkins,* 3 Pet. 193,

202 (1830), and shaped the early understanding of the scope of the writ. As noted above, see *supra*, at 5, §7 of the Act specifically addressed those committed for high treason, and provided a remedy if they were not *indicted and tried* by the second succeeding court term. That remedy was *not* a bobtailed judicial inquiry into whether there were reasonable grounds to believe the prisoner had taken up arms against the King. Rather, if the prisoner was not indicted and tried within the prescribed time, "he shall be discharged from his Imprisonment." 31 Car. 2, c. 2, §7. The Act does not contain any exception for wartime. That omission is conspicuous, since §7 explicitly addresses the offense of "High Treason," which often involved offenses of a military nature. See cases cited *supra*, at 7.

Writings from the founding generation also suggest that, without exception, the only constitutional alternatives are to charge the crime or suspend the writ. In 1788, Thomas Jefferson wrote to James Madison questioning the need for a Suspension Clause in cases of rebellion in the proposed Constitution. His letter illustrates the constraints under which the Founders understood themselves to operate:

> "Why suspend the Hab. corp. in insurrections and rebellions? The parties who may be arrested may be charged instantly with a well defined crime. Of course the judge will remand them. If the publick safety requires that the government should have a man imprisoned on less probable testimony in those than in other emergencies; let him be taken and tried, retaken and retried, while the necessity continues, only giving him redress against the government for damages." 13 Papers of Thomas Jefferson 442 (July 31, 1788) (J. Boyd ed. 1956).

A similar view was reflected in the 1807 House debates over suspension during the armed uprising that came to be known as Burr's conspiracy:

> "With regard to those persons who may be implicated in the conspiracy, if the writ of habeas corpus be not suspended, what will be the consequence? When apprehended, they will be brought before a court of justice, who will decide whether there is any evidence that will justify their commitment for farther prosecution. From the communication of the Executive, it appeared there was sufficient evidence to authorize their commitment. Several months would elapse before their final trial, which would give time to collect evidence, and if this shall be sufficient, they will not fail to receive the punishment merited by their crimes, and inflicted by the laws of their country." 16 Annals of Congress, at 405 (remarks of Rep. Burwell).

The absence of military authority to imprison citizens indefinitely in wartime—whether or not a probability of treason had been established by means less than jury trial—was confirmed by three cases decided during and immediately after the War of 1812. In the first, *In re Stacy*, 10 Johns. *328 (N. Y. 1813), a citizen was taken into military custody on suspicion that he was "carrying provisions and giving information to the enemy." *Id.*, at *330 (emphasis deleted). Stacy petitioned for a writ of habeas corpus, and, after the defendant custodian attempted to avoid complying, Chief Justice Kent ordered attachment against him. Kent noted that the military was "without any color of authority in any military tribunal to try a citizen for that crime" and that it was "holding him in the closest confinement, and contemning the civil authority of the state." *Id.*, at *333–*334.

Two other cases, later cited with approval by this Court in *Ex parte Milligan*, 4 Wall. 2, 128–129 (1866), upheld verdicts for false imprisonment against military officers. In *Smith* v. *Shaw*, 12 Johns. *257 (N. Y. 1815), the court

HAMDI v. RUMSFELD

SCALIA, J., dissenting

affirmed an award of damages for detention of a citizen on suspicion that he was, among other things, "an enemy's spy in time of war." *Id.*, at *265. The court held that "[n]one of the offences charged against *Shaw* were cognizable by a court-martial, except that which related to his being a spy; and if he was an *American* citizen, he could not be charged with such an offence. He might be amenable to the civil authority for treason; but could not be punished, under martial law, as a spy." *Ibid.* "If the defendant was justifiable in doing what he did, every citizen of the *United States* would, in time of war, be equally exposed to a like exercise of military power and authority." *Id.*, at *266. Finally, in *M'Connell* v. *Hampton*, 12 Johns. *234 (N. Y. 1815), a jury awarded $9,000 for false imprisonment after a military officer confined a citizen on charges of treason; the judges on appeal did not question the verdict but found the damages excessive, in part because "it does not appear that [the defendant] . . . knew [the plaintiff] was a citizen." *Id.*, at *238 (Spencer, J.). See generally Wuerth, The President's Power to Detain "Enemy Combatants": Modern Lessons from Mr. Madison's Forgotten War, 98 Nw. U. L. Rev. (forthcoming 2004) (available in Clerk of Court's case file).

President Lincoln, when he purported to suspend habeas corpus without congressional authorization during the Civil War, apparently did not doubt that suspension was required if the prisoner was to be held without criminal trial. In his famous message to Congress on July 4, 1861, he argued only that he could suspend the writ, not that even without suspension, his imprisonment of citizens without criminal trial was permitted. See Special Session Message, 6 Messages and Papers 20–31.

Further evidence comes from this Court's decision in *Ex parte Milligan, supra.* There, the Court issued the writ to an American citizen who had been tried by military commission for offenses that included conspiring to overthrow

SCALIA, J., dissenting

the Government, seize munitions, and liberate prisoners of war. *Id.*, at 6–7. The Court rejected in no uncertain terms the Government's assertion that military jurisdiction was proper "under the 'laws and usages of war,'" *id.*, at 121:

> "It can serve no useful purpose to inquire what those laws and usages are, whence they originated, where found, and on whom they operate; they can never be applied to citizens in states which have upheld the authority of the government, and where the courts are open and their process unobstructed." *Ibid.*[1]

Milligan is not exactly this case, of course, since the petitioner was threatened with death, not merely imprisonment. But the reasoning and conclusion of *Milligan* logically cover the present case. The Government justifies imprisonment of Hamdi on principles of the law of war and admits that, absent the war, it would have no such authority. But if the law of war cannot be applied to citizens where courts are open, then Hamdi's imprisonment without criminal trial is no less unlawful than Milligan's trial by military tribunal.

Milligan responded to the argument, repeated by the Government in this case, that it is dangerous to leave suspected traitors at large in time of war:

> "If it was dangerous, in the distracted condition of affairs, to leave Milligan unrestrained of his liberty, because he 'conspired against the government, afforded aid and comfort to rebels, and incited the people to in-

---

[1] As I shall discuss presently, see *infra*, at 17–19, the Court purported to limit this language in *Ex parte Quirin*, 317 U. S. 1, 45 (1942). Whatever *Quirin*'s effect on *Milligan*'s precedential value, however, it cannot undermine its value as an indicator of original meaning. Cf. *Reid v. Covert*, 354 U. S. 1, 30 (1957) (plurality opinion) (*Milligan* remains "one of the great landmarks in this Court's history").

SCALIA, J., dissenting

surrection,' the *law* said arrest him, confine him closely, render him powerless to do further mischief; and then present his case to the grand jury of the district, with proofs of his guilt, and, if indicted, try him according to the course of the common law. If this had been done, the Constitution would have been vindicated, the law of 1863 enforced, and the securities for personal liberty preserved and defended." *Id.*, at 122.

Thus, criminal process was viewed as the primary means—and the only means absent congressional action suspending the writ—not only to punish traitors, but to incapacitate them.

The proposition that the Executive lacks indefinite wartime detention authority over citizens is consistent with the Founders' general mistrust of military power permanently at the Executive's disposal. In the Founders' view, the "blessings of liberty" were threatened by "those military establishments which must gradually poison its very fountain." The Federalist No. 45, p. 238 (J. Madison). No fewer than 10 issues of the Federalist were devoted in whole or part to allaying fears of oppression from the proposed Constitution's authorization of standing armies in peacetime. Many safeguards in the Constitution reflect these concerns. Congress's authority "[t]o raise and support Armies" was hedged with the proviso that "no Appropriation of Money to that Use shall be for a longer Term than two Years." U. S. Const., Art. 1, §8, cl. 12. Except for the actual command of military forces, all authorization for their maintenance and all explicit authorization for their use is placed in the control of Congress under Article I, rather than the President under Article II. As Hamilton explained, the President's military authority would be "much inferior" to that of the British King:

"It would amount to nothing more than the supreme command and direction of the military and naval forces, as first general and admiral of the confederacy: while that of the British king extends to the *declaring* of war, and to the *raising* and *regulating* of fleets and armies; all which, by the constitution under consideration, would appertain to the legislature." The Federalist No. 69, p. 357.

A view of the Constitution that gives the Executive authority to use military force rather than the force of law against citizens on American soil flies in the face of the mistrust that engendered these provisions.

IV

The Government argues that our more recent jurisprudence ratifies its indefinite imprisonment of a citizen within the territorial jurisdiction of federal courts. It places primary reliance upon *Ex parte Quirin,* 317 U. S. 1 (1942), a World War II case upholding the trial by military commission of eight German saboteurs, one of whom, Hans Haupt, was a U. S. citizen. The case was not this Court's finest hour. The Court upheld the commission and denied relief in a brief *per curiam* issued the day after oral argument concluded, see *id.*, at 18–19, unnumbered note; a week later the Government carried out the commission's death sentence upon six saboteurs, including Haupt. The Court eventually explained its reasoning in a written opinion issued several months later.

Only three paragraphs of the Court's lengthy opinion dealt with the particular circumstances of Haupt's case. See *id.*, at 37–38, 45–46. The Government argued that Haupt, like the other petitioners, could be tried by military commission under the laws of war. In agreeing with that contention, *Quirin* purported to interpret the language of *Milligan* quoted above (the law of war "can never be applied to citizens in states which have upheld the authority of the government, and where the courts are open and their process unobstructed") in the following manner:

> "Elsewhere in its opinion ... the Court was at pains to point out that Milligan, a citizen twenty years resident in Indiana, who had never been a resident of any of the states in rebellion, was not an enemy belligerent either entitled to the status of a prisoner of war or subject to the penalties imposed upon unlawful belligerents. We construe the Court's statement as to the inapplicability of the law of war to Milligan's case as having particular reference to the facts before it. From them the Court concluded that Milligan, not being a part of or associated with the armed forces of the enemy, was a non-belligerent, not subject to the law of war...." 317 U. S., at 45.

In my view this seeks to revise *Milligan* rather than describe it. *Milligan* had involved (among other issues) two separate questions: (1) whether the military trial of Milligan was justified by the laws of war, and if not (2) whether the President's suspension of the writ, pursuant to congressional authorization, prevented the issuance of habeas corpus. The Court's categorical language about the law of war's inapplicability to citizens where the courts are open (with no exception mentioned for citizens who were prisoners of war) was contained in its discussion of the first point. See 4 Wall., at 121. The factors pertaining to whether Milligan could reasonably be considered a belligerent and prisoner of war, while mentioned earlier in the opinion, see *id.*, at 118, were made relevant and brought to bear in the Court's later discussion, see *id.*, at 131, of whether Milligan came within the statutory provision that effectively made an exception to Congress's authorized suspension of the writ for (as the Court described it) "all parties, not prisoners of war, resident in their respective jurisdictions, ... who were citizens of states in which the administration of the laws in the Federal tribunals was

SCALIA, J., dissenting

unimpaired," *id.*, at 116. *Milligan* thus understood was in accord with the traditional law of habeas corpus I have described: Though treason often occurred in wartime, there was, absent provision for special treatment in a congressional suspension of the writ, no exception to the right to trial by jury for citizens who could be called "belligerents" or "prisoners of war."[2]

But even if *Quirin* gave a correct description of *Milligan*, or made an irrevocable revision of it, *Quirin* would still not justify denial of the writ here. In *Quirin* it was uncontested that the petitioners were members of enemy forces. They were "*admitted* enemy invaders," 317 U. S., at 47 (emphasis added), and it was "undisputed" that they had landed in the United States in service of German forces, *id.*, at 20. The specific holding of the Court was only that, "upon the *conceded* facts," the petitioners were "plainly within [the] boundaries" of military jurisdiction, *id.*, at 46 (emphasis added).[3] But where those jurisdic-

---

[2] Without bothering to respond to this analysis, the plurality states that *Milligan* "turned in large part" upon the defendant's lack of prisoner-of-war status, and that the *Milligan* Court explicitly and repeatedly *said* so. See *ante*, at 14. Neither is true. To the extent, however, that prisoner-of-war status was relevant in *Milligan*, it was only because prisoners of war *received different statutory treatment* under the conditional suspension then in effect.

[3] The only two Court of Appeals cases from World War II cited by the Government in which citizens were detained without trial likewise involved petitioners who were conceded to have been members of enemy forces. See *In re Territo*, 156 F. 2d 142, 143–145 (CA9 1946); *Colepaugh* v. *Looney*, 235 F. 2d 429, 432 (CA10 1956). The plurality complains that *Territo* is the only case I have identified in which "a United States citizen [was] captured in a *foreign* combat zone," *ante*, at 16. Indeed it is; such cases must surely be rare. But given the constitutional tradition I have described, the burden is not upon me to find cases in which the writ was *granted* to citizens in this country *who had been captured on foreign battlefields;* it is upon those who would carve out an exception for such citizens (as the plurality's complaint suggests it would) to find a single case (other than one where enemy status was

HAMDI v. RUMSFELD

SCALIA, J., dissenting

tional facts are *not* conceded—where the petitioner insists that he is *not* a belligerent—*Quirin* left the pre-existing law in place: Absent suspension of the writ, a citizen held where the courts are open is entitled either to criminal trial or to a judicial decree requiring his release.[4]

---

admitted) in which habeas was *denied*.

[4]The plurality's assertion that *Quirin* somehow "clarifies" *Milligan*, *ante*, at 15, is simply false. As I discuss *supra*, at 17–19, the *Quirin* Court propounded a mistaken understanding of *Milligan;* but nonetheless its holding was limited to "the case presented by the present record," and to "*the conceded facts*," and thus avoided conflict with the earlier case. See 317 U. S., at 45–46 (emphasis added). The plurality, ignoring this expressed limitation, thinks it "beside the point" whether belligerency is conceded or found "by some other process" (not necessarily a jury trial) "that verifies this fact with sufficient certainty." *Ante*, at 16. But the whole point of the procedural guarantees in the Bill of Rights is to limit the methods by which the Government can determine facts that the citizen disputes and on which the citizen's liberty depends. The plurality's claim that *Quirin*'s one-paragraph discussion of *Milligan* provides a "[c]lear . . . disavowal" of two false imprisonment cases from the War of 1812, *ante*, at 15, thus defies logic; unlike the plaintiffs in those cases, Haupt was concededly a member of an enemy force.

The Government also cites *Moyer* v. *Peabody,* 212 U. S. 78 (1909), a suit for damages against the Governor of Colorado, for violation of due process in detaining the alleged ringleader of a rebellion quelled by the state militia after the Governor's declaration of a state of insurrection and (he contended) suspension of the writ "as incident thereto." *Ex parte Moyer*, 35 Colo. 154, 157, 91 P. 738, 740 (1905). But the holding of *Moyer* v. *Peabody* (even assuming it is transferable from state-militia detention after state suspension to federal standing-army detention without suspension) is simply that "[s]o long as such arrests [were] made in good faith and in the honest belief that they [were] needed in order to head the insurrection off," 212 U. S., at 85, an action in damages could not lie. This "good-faith" analysis is a forebear of our modern doctrine of qualified immunity. Cf. *Scheuer* v. *Rhodes,* 416 U. S. 232, 247–248 (1974) (understanding *Moyer* in this way). Moreover, the detention at issue in *Moyer* lasted about two and a half months, see 212 U. S., at 85, roughly the length of time permissible under the 1679 Habeas Corpus Act, see *supra*, at 4–5.

SCALIA, J., dissenting

V

It follows from what I have said that Hamdi is entitled to a habeas decree requiring his release unless (1) criminal proceedings are promptly brought, or (2) Congress has suspended the writ of habeas corpus. A suspension of the writ could, of course, lay down conditions for continued detention, similar to those that today's opinion prescribes under the Due Process Clause. Cf. Act of Mar. 3, 1863, 12 Stat. 755. But there is a world of difference between the people's representatives' determining the need for that suspension (and prescribing the conditions for it), and this Court's doing so.

The plurality finds justification for Hamdi's imprisonment in the Authorization for Use of Military Force, 115 Stat. 224, which provides:

> "That the President is authorized to use all necessary and appropriate force against those nations, organizations, or persons he determines planned, authorized, committed, or aided the terrorist attacks that occurred on September 11, 2001, or harbored such organizations or persons, in order to prevent any future acts of international terrorism against the United States by such nations, organizations or persons." §2(a).

This is not remotely a congressional suspension of the writ, and no one claims that it is. Contrary to the plural-

---

In addition to *Moyer* v. *Peabody*, JUSTICE THOMAS relies upon *Luther* v. *Borden*, 7 How. 1 (1849), a case in which the state legislature had imposed martial law—a step even more drastic than suspension of the writ. See *post*, at 13–14 (dissenting opinion). But martial law has not been imposed here, and in any case is limited to "the theatre of active military operations, where war really prevails," and where therefore the courts are closed. *Ex parte Milligan*, 4 Wall. 2, 127 (1866); see also *id.*, at 129–130 (distinguishing *Luther*).

HAMDI *v.* RUMSFELD

SCALIA, J., dissenting

ity's view, I do not think this statute even authorizes detention of a citizen with the clarity necessary to satisfy the interpretive canon that statutes should be construed so as to avoid grave constitutional concerns, see *Edward J. DeBartolo Corp.* v. *Florida Gulf Coast Building & Constr. Trades Council,* 485 U. S. 568, 575 (1988); with the clarity necessary to comport with cases such as *Ex parte Endo,* 323 U. S. 283, 300 (1944), and *Duncan* v. *Kahanamoku,* 327 U. S. 304, 314–316, 324 (1946); or with the clarity necessary to overcome the statutory prescription that "[n]o citizen shall be imprisoned or otherwise detained by the United States except pursuant to an Act of Congress." 18 U. S. C. §4001(a).[5] But even if it did, I would not permit it to

---

[5] The plurality rejects any need for "specific language of detention" on the ground that detention of alleged combatants is a "fundamental incident of waging war." *Ante,* at 12. Its authorities do not support that holding in the context of the present case. Some are irrelevant because they do not address the detention of *American citizens. E.g.,* Naqvi, Doubtful Prisoner-of-War Status, 84 Int'l Rev. Red Cross 571, 572 (2002). The plurality's assertion that detentions of citizen and alien combatants are equally authorized has no basis in law or common sense. Citizens and noncitizens, even if equally dangerous, are not similarly situated. See, *e.g., Milligan, supra; Johnson* v. *Eisentrager,* 339 U. S. 763 (1950); Rev. Stat. 4067, 50 U. S. C. §21 (Alien Enemy Act). That captivity may be consistent with the principles of international law does not prove that it also complies with the restrictions that the Constitution places on the American Government's treatment of its own citizens. Of the authorities cited by the plurality that do deal with detention of citizens, *Quirin* and *Territo* have already been discussed and rejected. See *supra,* at 19–20, and n. 3. The remaining authorities pertain to U. S. detention of citizens during the Civil War, and are irrelevant for two reasons: (1) the Lieber Code was issued following a congressional authorization of suspension of the writ, see Instructions for the Government of Armies of the United States in the Field, Gen. Order No. 100 (1863), reprinted in 2 Lieber, Miscellaneous Writings, p. 246; Act of Mar. 3, 1863, 12 Stat. 755, §§1, 2; and (2) citizens of the Confederacy, while citizens of the United States, were also regarded as citizens of a hostile power.

overcome Hamdi's entitlement to habeas corpus relief. The Suspension Clause of the Constitution, which carefully circumscribes the conditions under which the writ can be withheld, would be a sham if it could be evaded by congressional prescription of requirements *other than the common-law requirement of committal for criminal prosecution* that render the writ, though available, unavailing. If the Suspension Clause does not guarantee the citizen that he will either be tried or released, unless the conditions for suspending the writ exist and the grave action of suspending the writ has been taken; if it merely guarantees the citizen that he will not be detained unless Congress by ordinary legislation says he can be detained; it guarantees him very little indeed.

It should not be thought, however, that the plurality's evisceration of the Suspension Clause augments, principally, the power of Congress. As usual, the major effect of its constitutional improvisation is to increase the power of the Court. Having found a congressional authorization for detention of citizens where none clearly exists; and having discarded the categorical procedural protection of the Suspension Clause; the plurality then proceeds, under the guise of the Due Process Clause, to prescribe what procedural protections *it* thinks appropriate. It "weigh[s] the private interest ... against the Government's asserted interest," *ante*, at 22 (internal quotation marks omitted), and—just as though writing a new Constitution—comes up with an unheard-of system in which the citizen rather than the Government bears the burden of proof, testimony is by hearsay rather than live witnesses, and the presiding officer may well be a "neutral" military officer rather than judge and jury. See *ante*, at 26–27. It claims authority to engage in this sort of "judicious balancing" from *Mathews v. Eldridge*, 424 U. S. 319 (1976), a case involving ... *the withdrawal of disability benefits!* Whatever the merits of this technique when newly recognized property rights are

HAMDI v. RUMSFELD

SCALIA, J., dissenting

at issue (and even there they are questionable), it has no place where the Constitution and the common law already supply an answer.

Having distorted the Suspension Clause, the plurality finishes up by transmogrifying the Great Writ—disposing of the present habeas petition by remanding for the District Court to "engag[e] in a factfinding process that is both prudent and incremental," *ante*, at 32. "In the absence of [the Executive's prior provision of procedures that satisfy due process], . . . a court that receives a petition for a writ of habeas corpus from an alleged enemy combatant must itself ensure that the minimum requirements of due process are achieved." *Ante*, at 31–32. This judicial remediation of executive default is unheard of. The role of habeas corpus is to determine the legality of executive detention, not to supply the omitted process necessary to make it legal. See *Preiser* v. *Rodriguez,* 411 U. S. 475, 484 (1973) ("[T]he essence of habeas corpus is an attack by a person in custody upon the legality of that custody, and . . . the traditional function of the writ is to secure release from illegal custody"); 1 Blackstone 132–133. It is not the habeas court's function to make illegal detention legal by supplying a process that the Government could have provided, but chose not to. If Hamdi is being imprisoned in violation of the Constitution (because without due process of law), then his habeas petition should be granted; the Executive may then hand him over to the criminal authorities, whose detention for the purpose of prosecution will be lawful, or else must release him.

There is a certain harmony of approach in the plurality's making up for Congress's failure to invoke the Suspension Clause and its making up for the Executive's failure to apply what it says are needed procedures—an approach that reflects what might be called a Mr. Fix-it Mentality. The plurality seems to view it as its mission to Make Everything Come Out Right, rather than merely to decree the consequences, as far as individual rights are concerned, of the other two branches' actions and omissions. Has the Legislature failed to suspend the writ in the current dire emergency? Well, we will remedy that failure by prescribing the reasonable conditions that a suspension should have included. And has the Executive failed to live up to those reasonable conditions? Well, we will ourselves make that failure good, so that this dangerous fellow (if he is dangerous) need not be set free. The problem with this approach is not only that it steps out of the courts' modest and limited role in a democratic society; but that by repeatedly doing what it thinks the political branches ought to do it encourages their lassitude and saps the vitality of government by the people.

VI

Several limitations give my views in this matter a relatively narrow compass. They apply only to citizens, accused of being enemy combatants, who are detained within the territorial jurisdiction of a federal court. This is not likely to be a numerous group; currently we know of only two, Hamdi and Jose Padilla. Where the citizen is captured outside and held outside the United States, the constitutional requirements may be different. Cf. *Johnson* v. *Eisentrager,* 339 U. S. 763, 769–771 (1950); *Reid* v. *Covert,* 354 U. S. 1, 74–75 (1957) (Harlan, J., concurring in result); *Rasul* v. *Bush, ante,* at 15–17 (SCALIA, J., dissenting). Moreover, even within the United States, the accused citizen-enemy combatant may lawfully be detained once prosecution is in progress or in contemplation. See, *e.g., County of Riverside* v. *McLaughlin,* 500 U. S. 44 (1991) (brief detention pending judicial determination after warrantless arrest); *United States* v. *Salerno,* 481 U. S. 739 (1987) (pretrial detention under the Bail Reform Act). The Government has been notably successful in securing conviction, and hence long-term custody or execution, of those who have waged

HAMDI v. RUMSFELD

SCALIA, J., dissenting

war against the state.

I frankly do not know whether these tools are sufficient to meet the Government's security needs, including the need to obtain intelligence through interrogation. It is far beyond my competence, or the Court's competence, to determine that. But it is not beyond Congress's. If the situation demands it, the Executive can ask Congress to authorize suspension of the writ—which can be made subject to whatever conditions Congress deems appropriate, including even the procedural novelties invented by the plurality today. To be sure, suspension is limited by the Constitution to cases of rebellion or invasion. But whether the attacks of September 11, 2001, constitute an "invasion," and whether those attacks still justify suspension several years later, are questions for Congress rather than this Court. See 3 Story §1336, at 208–209.[6] If civil rights are to be curtailed during wartime, it must be done openly and democratically, as the Constitution requires, rather than by silent erosion through an opinion of this Court.

* * *

The Founders well understood the difficult tradeoff between safety and freedom. "Safety from external danger," Hamilton declared,

> "is the most powerful director of national conduct. Even the ardent love of liberty will, after a time, give way to its dictates. The violent destruction of life and property incident to war; the continual effort and

---

[6] JUSTICE THOMAS worries that the constitutional conditions for suspension of the writ will not exist "during many . . . emergencies during which . . . detention authority might be necessary," *post*, at 16. It is difficult to imagine situations in which security is so seriously threatened as to justify indefinite imprisonment without trial, and yet the constitutional conditions of rebellion or invasion are not met.

alarm attendant on a state of continual danger, will compel nations the most attached to liberty, to resort for repose and security to institutions which have a tendency to destroy their civil and political rights. To be more safe, they, at length, become willing to run the risk of being less free." The Federalist No. 8, p. 33.

The Founders warned us about the risk, and equipped us with a Constitution designed to deal with it.

Many think it not only inevitable but entirely proper that liberty give way to security in times of national crisis—that, at the extremes of military exigency, *inter arma silent leges*. Whatever the general merits of the view that war silences law or modulates its voice, that view has no place in the interpretation and application of a Constitution designed precisely to confront war and, in a manner that accords with democratic principles, to accommodate it. Because the Court has proceeded to meet the current emergency in a manner the Constitution does not envision, I respectfully dissent.

SUPREME COURT OF THE UNITED STATES

No. 03–6696

YASER ESAM HAMDI AND ESAM FOUAD HAMDI, AS NEXT FRIEND OF YASER ESAM HAMDI, PETITIONERS *v.* DONALD H. RUMSFELD, SECRETARY OF DEFENSE, ET AL.

ON WRIT OF CERTIORARI TO THE UNITED STATES COURT OF APPEALS FOR THE FOURTH CIRCUIT

[June 28, 2004]

JUSTICE THOMAS, dissenting.

The Executive Branch, acting pursuant to the powers vested in the President by the Constitution and with explicit congressional approval, has determined that Yaser Hamdi is an enemy combatant and should be detained. This detention falls squarely within the Federal Government's war powers, and we lack the expertise and capacity to second-guess that decision. As such, petitioners' habeas challenge should fail, and there is no reason to remand the case. The plurality reaches a contrary conclusion by failing adequately to consider basic principles of the constitutional structure as it relates to national security and foreign affairs and by using the balancing scheme of *Mathews* v. *Eldridge,* 424 U. S. 319 (1976). I do not think that the Federal Government's war powers can be balanced away by this Court. Arguably, Congress could provide for additional procedural protections, but until it does, we have no right to insist upon them. But even if I were to agree with the general approach the plurality takes, I could not accept the particulars. The plurality utterly fails to account for the Government's compelling interests and for our own institutional inability to weigh competing concerns correctly. I respectfully dissent.

THOMAS, J., dissenting

I

"It is 'obvious and unarguable' that no governmental interest is more compelling than the security of the Nation." *Haig v. Agee,* 453 U. S. 280, 307 (1981) (quoting *Aptheker v. Secretary of State,* 378 U. S. 500, 509 (1964)). The national security, after all, is the primary responsibility and purpose of the Federal Government. See, *e.g., Youngstown Sheet & Tube Co. v. Sawyer,* 343 U. S. 579, 662 (1952) (Clark, J., concurring in judgment); The Federalist No. 23, pp. 146–147 (J. Cooke ed. 1961) (A. Hamilton) ("The principle purposes to be answered by Union are these—The common defence of the members—the preservation of the public peace as well against internal convulsions as external attacks"). But because the Founders understood that they could not foresee the myriad potential threats to national security that might later arise, they chose to create a Federal Government that necessarily possesses sufficient power to handle any threat to the security of the Nation. The power to protect the Nation

> "ought to exist without limitation . . . *[b]ecause it is impossible to foresee or define the extent and variety of national exigencies, or the correspondent extent & variety of the means which may be necessary to satisfy them.* The circumstances that endanger the safety of nations are infinite; and for this reason no constitutional shackles can wisely be imposed on the power to which the care of it is committed." *Id.,* at 147.

See also The Federalist Nos. 34 and 41.

The Founders intended that the President have primary responsibility—along with the necessary power—to protect the national security and to conduct the Nation's foreign relations. They did so principally because the structural advantages of a unitary Executive are essential in these domains. "Energy in the executive is a leading character in the definition of good government. It is essential to

Basic Documents about the Detainees

Thomas, J., dissenting

the protection of the community against foreign attacks." The Federalist No. 70, p. 471 (A. Hamilton). The principle "ingredien[t]" for "energy in the executive" is "unity." *Id.,* at 472. This is because "[d]ecision, activity, secrecy, and dispatch will generally characterise the proceedings of one man, in a much more eminent degree, than the proceedings of any greater number." *Ibid.*

These structural advantages are most important in the national-security and foreign-affairs contexts. "Of all the cares or concerns of government, the direction of war most peculiarly demands those qualities which distinguish the exercise of power by a single hand." The Federalist No. 74, p. 500 (A. Hamilton). Also for these reasons, John Marshall explained that "[t]he President is the sole organ of the nation in its external relations, and its sole representative with foreign nations." 10 Annals of Cong. 613 (1800); see *id.,* at 613–614. To this end, the Constitution vests in the President "[t]he executive Power," Art. II, §1, provides that he "shall be Commander in Chief of the" armed forces, §2, and places in him the power to recognize foreign governments, §3.

This Court has long recognized these features and has accordingly held that the President has *constitutional* authority to protect the national security and that this authority carries with it broad discretion.

> "If a war be made by invasion of a foreign nation, the President is not only authorized but bound to resist force by force. He does not initiate the war, but is bound to accept the challenge without waiting for any special legislative authority.... Whether the President in fulfilling his duties, as Commander in-chief, in suppressing an insurrection, has met with such armed hostile resistance ... is a question to be decided *by him.*" *Prize Cases,* 2 Black 635, 668, 670 (1863).

The Court has acknowledged that the President has the

THOMAS, J., dissenting

authority to "employ [the Nation's Armed Forces] in the manner he may deem most effectual to harass and conquer and subdue the enemy." *Fleming* v. *Page,* 9 How. 603, 615 (1850). With respect to foreign affairs as well, the Court has recognized the President's independent authority and need to be free from interference. See, *e.g., United States* v. *Curtiss-Wright Export Corp.,* 299 U. S. 304, 320 (1936) (explaining that the President "has his confidential sources of information. He has his agents in the form of diplomatic, consular and other officials. Secrecy in respect of information gathered by them may be highly necessary, and the premature disclosure of it productive of harmful results"); *Chicago & Southern Air Lines, Inc.* v. *Waterman S. S. Corp.,* 333 U. S. 103, 111 (1948).

Congress, to be sure, has a substantial and essential role in both foreign affairs and national security. But it is crucial to recognize that *judicial* interference in these domains destroys the purpose of vesting primary responsibility in a unitary Executive. I cannot improve on Justice Jackson's words, speaking for the Court:

> "The President, both as Commander-in-Chief and as the Nation's organ for foreign affairs, has available intelligence services whose reports are not and ought not to be published to the world. It would be intolerable that courts, without the relevant information, should review and perhaps nullify actions of the Executive taken on information properly held secret. Nor can courts sit *in camera* in order to be taken into executive confidences. But even if courts could require full disclosure, the very nature of executive decisions as to foreign policy is political, not judicial. Such decisions are wholly confided by our Constitution to the political departments of the government, Executive and Legislative. They are delicate, com-

THOMAS, J., dissenting

plex, and involve large elements of prophecy. They are and should be undertaken only by those directly responsible to the people whose welfare they advance or imperil. They are decisions of a kind for which the Judiciary has neither aptitude, facilities nor responsibility and which has long been held to belong in the domain of political power not subject to judicial intrusion or inquiry." *Ibid.*

Several points, made forcefully by Justice Jackson, are worth emphasizing. First, with respect to certain decisions relating to national security and foreign affairs, the courts simply lack the relevant information and expertise to second-guess determinations made by the President based on information properly withheld. Second, even if the courts could compel the Executive to produce the necessary information, such decisions are simply not amenable to judicial determination because "[t]hey are delicate, complex, and involve large elements of prophecy." *Ibid.* Third, the Court in *Chicago & Southern Air Lines* and elsewhere has correctly recognized the primacy of the political branches in the foreign-affairs and national-security contexts.

For these institutional reasons and because "Congress cannot anticipate and legislate with regard to every possible action the President may find it necessary to take or every possible situation in which he might act," it should come as no surprise that "[s]uch failure of Congress . . . does not, 'especially . . . in the areas of foreign policy and national security,' imply 'congressional disapproval' of action taken by the Executive." *Dames & Moore* v. *Regan,* 453 U. S. 654, 678 (1981) (quoting *Agee,* 453 U. S., at 291). Rather, in these domains, the fact that Congress has provided the President with broad authorities does not imply—and the Judicial Branch should not infer—that Congress intended to deprive him of particular powers not

THOMAS, J., dissenting

specifically enumerated. See *Dames & Moore,* 453 U. S., at 678. As far as the courts are concerned, "the enactment of legislation closely related to the question of the President's authority in a particular case which evinces legislative intent to accord the President broad discretion may be considered to 'invite' 'measures on independent presidential responsibility.'" *Ibid.* (quoting *Youngstown,* 343 U. S., at 637 (Jackson, J., concurring)).

Finally, and again for the same reasons, where "the President acts pursuant to an express or implied authorization from Congress, he exercises not only his powers but also those delegated by Congress[, and i]n such a case the executive action 'would be supported by the strongest of presumptions and the widest latitude of judicial interpretation, and the burden of persuasion would rest heavily upon any who might attack it.'" *Dames & Moore, supra,* at 668 (quoting *Youngstown, supra,* at 637 (Jackson, J., concurring)). That is why the Court has explained, in a case analogous to this one, that "the detention[,] ordered by the President in the declared exercise of his powers as Commander in Chief of the Army in time of war and of grave public danger[, is] not to be set aside by the courts without the clear conviction that [it is] in conflict with the Constitution or laws of Congress constitutionally enacted." *Ex parte Quirin,* 317 U. S. 1, 25 (1942). See also *Ex parte Milligan,* 4 Wall. 2, 133 (1866) (Chase, C. J., concurring in judgment) (stating that a sentence imposed by a military commission "must not be set aside except upon the clearest conviction that it cannot be reconciled with the Constitution and the constitutional legislation of Congress"). This deference extends to the President's determination of all the factual predicates necessary to conclude that a given action is appropriate. See *Quirin, supra,* at 25 ("We are not here concerned with any question of the guilt or innocence of petitioners"). See also *Hirabayashi* v. *United States,* 320 U. S. 81, 93 (1943); *Prize Cases,* 2 Black, at

670; *Martin* v. *Mott,* 12 Wheat. 19, 29–30 (1827).

To be sure, the Court has at times held, in specific circumstances, that the military acted beyond its warmaking authority. But these cases are distinguishable in important ways. In *Ex parte Endo,* 323 U. S. 283 (1944), the Court held unlawful the detention of an admittedly law-abiding and loyal American of Japanese ancestry. It did so because the Government's asserted reason for the detention had nothing to do with the congressional and executive authorities upon which the Government relied. Those authorities permitted detention for the purpose of preventing espionage and sabotage and thus could not be pressed into service for detaining a loyal citizen. See *id.,* at 301–302. Further, the Court "stress[ed] the silence . . . of the [relevant] Act *and the Executive Orders.*" *Id.,* at 301 (emphasis added); see also *id.,* at 301–304. The Court sensibly held that the Government could not detain a loyal citizen pursuant to executive and congressional authorities that could not conceivably be implicated given the Government's factual allegations. And in *Youngstown,* Justice Jackson emphasized that "Congress ha[d] not left seizure of private property an open field but ha[d] covered it by three statutory policies inconsistent with th[e] seizure." 343 U. S., at 639 (concurring opinion). See also *Milligan, supra,* at 134 (Chase, C. J., concurring in judgment) (noting that the Government failed to comply with statute directly on point).

I acknowledge that the question whether Hamdi's executive detention is lawful is a question properly resolved by the Judicial Branch, though the question comes to the Court with the strongest presumptions in favor of the Government. The plurality agrees that Hamdi's detention is lawful if he is an enemy combatant. But the question whether Hamdi is actually an enemy combatant is "of a kind for which the Judiciary has neither aptitude, facilities nor responsibility and which has long been held to

THOMAS, J., dissenting

belong in the domain of political power not subject to judicial intrusion or inquiry." *Chicago & Southern Air Lines*, 333 U. S., at 111. That is, although it is appropriate for the Court to determine the judicial question whether the President has the asserted authority, see, *e.g., Ex parte Endo, supra,* we lack the information and expertise to question whether Hamdi is actually an enemy combatant, a question the resolution of which is committed to other branches.[1] In the words of then-Judge Scalia:

> "In Old Testament days, when judges ruled the people of Israel and led them into battle, a court professing the belief that it could order a halt to a military operation in foreign lands might not have been a startling phenomenon. But in modern times, and in a country where such governmental functions have been committed to elected delegates of the people, such an assertion of jurisdiction is extraordinary. The [C]ourt's decision today reflects a willingness to extend judicial power into areas where we do not know, and have no way of finding out, what serious harm we may be doing." *Ramirez de Arellano* v. *Weinberger,* 745 F. 2d 1500, 1550–1551 (CADC 1984) (en banc) (dissenting opinion) (footnote omitted).

See also *id.,* at 1551, n. 1 (noting that "[e]ven the ancient Israelites eventually realized the shortcomings of judicial commanders-in-chief"). The decision whether someone is an enemy combatant is, no doubt, "delicate, complex, and involv[es] large elements of prophecy," *Chicago & South-*

---

[1] Although I have emphasized national-security concerns, the President's foreign-affairs responsibilities are also squarely implicated by this case. The Government avers that Northern Alliance forces captured Hamdi, and the District Court demanded that the Government turn over information relating to statements made by members of the Northern Alliance. See 316 F. 3d 450, 462 (CA4 2003).

THOMAS, J., dissenting

ern *Air Lines, supra,* at 111, which, incidentally might in part explain why "the Government has never provided any court with the full criteria that it uses in classifying individuals as such," *ante,* at 8. See also *infra,* at 18–20 (discussing other military decisions).

II

"The war power of the national government is 'the power to wage war successfully.'" *Lichter* v. *United States,* 334 U. S. 742, 767, n. 9 (1948) (quoting Hughes, War Powers Under the Constitution, 42 A. B. A. Rep. 232, 238). It follows that this power "is not limited to victories in the field, but carries with it the inherent power to guard against the immediate renewal of the conflict," *In re Yamashita,* 327 U. S. 1, 12 (1946); see also *Stewart* v. *Kahn,* 11 Wall. 493, 507 (1871), and quite obviously includes the ability to detain those (even United States citizens) who fight against our troops or those of our allies, see, *e.g., Quirin,* 317 U. S., at 28–29, 30–31; *id.,* at 37–39; *Duncan* v. *Kahanamoku,* 327 U. S. 304, 313–314 (1946); W. Winthrop, Military Law and Precedents 788 (2d ed. 1920); W. Whiting, War Powers Under the Constitution of the United States 167 (43d ed. 1871); *id.,* at 44–46 (noting that Civil War "rebels" may be treated as foreign belligerents); see also *ante,* at 10–12.

Although the President very well may have inherent authority to detain those arrayed against our troops, I agree with the plurality that we need not decide that question because Congress has authorized the President to do so. See *ante,* at 9. The Authorization for Use of Military Force (AUMF), 115 Stat. 224, authorizes the President to "use all necessary and appropriate force against those nations, organizations, or persons he determines planned, authorized, committed, or aided the terrorist attacks" of September 11, 2001. Indeed, the Court has previously concluded that language materially identical to

HAMDI v. RUMSFELD

THOMAS, J., dissenting

the AUMF authorizes the Executive to "make the ordinary use of the soldiers . . . ; that he may kill persons who resist and, of course, that he may use the milder measure of seizing [and detaining] the bodies of those whom he considers to stand in the way of restoring peace." *Moyer* v. *Peabody,* 212 U. S. 78, 84 (1909).

The plurality, however, qualifies its recognition of the President's authority to detain enemy combatants in the war on terrorism in ways that are at odds with our precedent. Thus, the plurality relies primarily on Article 118 of the Geneva Convention (III) Relative to the Treatment of Prisoners of War, Aug. 12, 1949, [1955] 6 U. S. T. 3406, T. I. A. S. No. 3364, for the proposition that "[i]t is a clearly established principle of the law of war that detention may last no longer than active hostilities." *Ante,* at 12–13. It then appears to limit the President's authority to detain by requiring that the record establis[h] that United States troops are still involved in active combat in Afghanistan because, in that case, detention would be "part of the exercise of 'necessary and appropriate force.'" *Ante,* at 14. But I do not believe that we may diminish the Federal Government's war powers by reference to a treaty and certainly not to a treaty that does not apply. See n. 6, *infra.* Further, we are bound by the political branches' determination that the United States is at war. See, *e.g., Ludecke* v. *Watkins,* 335 U. S. 160, 167–170 (1948); *Prize Cases,* 2 Black, at 670; *Mott,* 12 Wheat., at 30. And, in any case, the power to detain does not end with the cessation of formal hostilities. See, *e.g., Madsen* v. *Kinsella,* 343 U. S. 341, 360 (1952); *Johnson* v. *Eisentrager,* 339 U. S. 763, 786 (1950); cf. *Moyer, supra,* at 85.

Accordingly, the President's action here is "supported by the strongest of presumptions and the widest latitude of judicial interpretation." *Dames & Moore,* 453 U. S., at 668

THOMAS, J., dissenting

(internal quotation marks omitted).[2] The question becomes whether the Federal Government (rather than the President acting alone) has power to detain Hamdi as an enemy combatant. More precisely, we must determine whether the Government may detain Hamdi given the procedures that were used.

III

I agree with the plurality that the Federal Government has power to detain those that the Executive Branch determines to be enemy combatants. See *ante*, at 10. But I do not think that the plurality has adequately explained the breadth of the President's authority to detain enemy combatants, an authority that includes making virtually conclusive factual findings. In my view, the structural considerations discussed above, as recognized in our precedent, demonstrate that we lack the capacity and responsibility to second-guess this determination.

This makes complete sense once the process that is due Hamdi is made clear. As an initial matter, it is possible that the Due Process Clause requires only "that our Government must proceed according to the 'law of the land'— that is, according to written constitutional and statutory provisions." *In re Winship*, 397 U. S. 358, 382 (1970) (Black, J., dissenting). I need not go this far today because the Court has already explained the nature of due process in this context.

In a case strikingly similar to this one, the Court addressed a Governor's authority to detain for an extended

---

[2] It could be argued that the habeas statutes are evidence of congressional intent that enemy combatants are entitled to challenge the factual basis for the Government's determination. See, *e.g.*, 28 U. S. C. §§2243, 2246. But factual development is needed only to the extent necessary to resolve the legal challenge to the detention. See, *e.g.*, *Walker* v. *Johnston*, 312 U. S. 275, 284 (1941).

period a person the executive believed to be responsible, in part, for a local insurrection. Justice Holmes wrote for a unanimous Court:

> "When it comes to a decision by the head of the State upon a matter involving its life, the ordinary rights of individuals must yield to what *he deems* the necessities of the moment. Public danger warrants the substitution of executive process for judicial process. This was admitted with regard to killing men in the actual clash of arms, and we think it obvious, although it was disputed, that the same is true of temporary detention to prevent apprehended harm." *Moyer*, 212 U. S., at 85 (citation omitted; emphasis added).

The Court answered Moyer's claim that he had been denied due process by emphasizing that

> "it is familiar that what is due process of law depends on circumstances. It varies with the subject-matter and the necessities of the situation. Thus summary proceedings suffice for taxes, and executive decisions for exclusion from the country.... Such arrests are not necessarily for punishment, but are by way of precaution to prevent the exercise of hostile power." *Id.,* at 84–85 (citations omitted).

In this context, due process requires nothing more than a good-faith executive determination.[3] To be clear: The Court has held that an executive, acting pursuant to statutory and constitutional authority may, consistent with the Due Process Clause, unilaterally decide to detain an individual if the executive deems this necessary for the public

---

[3] Indeed, it is not even clear that the Court required good faith. See *Moyer,* 212 U. S., at 85 ("It is not alleged that [the Governor's] judgment was not honest, if that be material, or that [Moyer] was detained after fears of the insurrection were at an end").

safety *even if he is mistaken.*

Moyer is not an exceptional case. In *Luther* v. *Borden,* 7 How. 1 (1849), the Court discussed the President's constitutional and statutory authority, in response to a request from a state legislature or executive, "'to call forth such number of the militia of any other State or States, as may be applied for, as he may judge sufficient to suppress [an] insurrection.'" *Id.,* at 43 (quoting Act of Feb. 28, 1795). The Court explained that courts could not review the President's decision to recognize one of the competing legislatures or executives. See 7 How., at 43. If a court could second-guess this determination, "it would become the duty of the court (provided it came to the conclusion that the President had decided incorrectly) to discharge those who were arrested or detained by the troops in the service of the United States." *Ibid.* "If the judicial power extends so far," the Court concluded, "the guarantee contained in the Constitution of the United States [referring to Art. IV, §4] is a guarantee of anarchy, and not of order." *Ibid.* The Court clearly contemplated that the President had authority to detain as he deemed necessary, and such detentions evidently comported with the Due Process Clause as long as the President correctly decided to call forth the militia, a question the Court said it could not review.

The Court also addressed the natural concern that placing "this power in the President is dangerous to liberty, and may be abused." *Id.,* at 44. The Court noted that "[a]ll power may be abused if placed in unworthy hands," and explained that "it would be difficult ... to point out any other hands in which this power would be more safe, and at the same time equally effectual." *Ibid.* Putting that aside, the Court emphasized that this power "is conferred upon him by the Constitution and laws of the United States, and must therefore be respected and enforced in its judicial tribunals." *Ibid.* Finally, the Court explained that if the President abused this power "it would be in the power of

THOMAS, J., dissenting

Congress to apply the proper remedy. But the courts must administer the law as they find it." *Id.,* at 45.

Almost 140 years later, in *United States* v. *Salerno,* 481 U. S. 739, 748 (1987), the Court explained that the Due Process Clause "lays down [no] categorical imperative." The Court continued:

> "We have repeatedly held that the Government's regulatory interest in community safety can, in appropriate circumstances, outweigh an individual's liberty interest. For example, in times of war or insurrection, when society's interest is at its peak, the Government may detain individuals whom the Government believes to be dangerous." *Ibid.*

The Court cited *Ludecke* v. *Watkins,* 335 U. S. 160 (1948), for this latter proposition even though *Ludecke* actually involved detention of enemy aliens. See also *Selective Draft Law Cases,* 245 U. S. 366 (1918); *Jacobson* v. *Massachusetts,* 197 U. S. 11, 27–29 (1905) (upholding legislated mass vaccinations and approving of forced quarantines of Americans even if they show no signs of illness); cf. *Kansas* v. *Hendricks,* 521 U. S. 346 (1997); *Juragua Iron Co.* v. *United States,* 212 U. S. 297 (1909).

The Government's asserted authority to detain an individual that the President has determined to be an enemy combatant, at least while hostilities continue, comports with the Due Process Clause. As these cases also show, the Executive's decision that a detention is necessary to protect the public need not and should not be subjected to judicial second-guessing. Indeed, at least in the context of enemy-combatant determinations, this would defeat the unity, secrecy, and dispatch that the Founders believed to be so important to the warmaking function. See Part I, *supra.*

I therefore cannot agree with JUSTICE SCALIA's conclusion that the Government must choose between using

THOMAS, J., dissenting

standard criminal processes and suspending the writ. See *ante*, at 26 (dissenting opinion). JUSTICE SCALIA relies heavily upon *Ex parte Milligan,* 4 Wall. 2 (1866), see *ante*, at 14–16, 17–20, and three cases decided by New York state courts in the wake of the War of 1812, see *ante*, at 13–14. I admit that *Milligan* supports his position. But because the Executive Branch there, unlike here, did not follow a specific statutory mechanism provided by Congress, the Court did not need to reach the broader question of Congress' power, and its discussion on this point was arguably dicta, see 4 Wall., at 122, as four Justices believed, see *id.*, at 132, 134–136 (Chase, C. J., joined by Wayne, Swayne, and Miller, JJ., concurring in judgment).

More importantly, the Court referred frequently and pervasively to the criminal nature of the proceedings instituted against Milligan. In fact, this feature serves to distinguish the state cases as well. See *In re Stacy*, 10 Johns. *328, *334 (N. Y. 1813) ("A military commander is here assuming *criminal jurisdiction* over a private citizen" (emphasis added)); *Smith* v. *Shaw*, 12 Johns. *257, *265 (N. Y. 1815) (Shaw "might be amenable to the civil authority for treason; but could not *be punished*, under martial law, as a spy" (emphasis added)); *M'Connell* v. *Hampton*, 12 Johns. *234 (N. Y. 1815) (same for treason).

Although I do acknowledge that the reasoning of these cases might apply beyond criminal punishment, the punishment-nonpunishment distinction harmonizes all of the precedent. And, subsequent cases have at least implicitly distinguished *Milligan* in just this way. See, *e.g., Moyer*, 212 U. S., at 84–85 ("Such arrests are not necessarily for punishment, but are by way of precaution"). Finally, *Quirin* overruled *Milligan* to the extent that those cases are inconsistent. See *Quirin*, 317 U. S., at 45 (limiting *Milligan* to its facts). Because the Government does not detain Hamdi in order to punish him, as the plurality acknowledges, see *ante*, at 10–11, *Milligan* and the New

York cases do not control.

JUSTICE SCALIA also finds support in a letter Thomas Jefferson wrote to James Madison. See *ante,* at 12. I agree that this provides some evidence for his position. But I think this plainly insufficient to rebut the authorities upon which I have relied. In any event, I do not believe that JUSTICE SCALIA's evidence leads to the necessary "clear conviction that [the detention is] in conflict with the Constitution or laws of Congress constitutionally enacted," *Quirin, supra,* at 25, to justify nullifying the President's wartime action.

Finally, JUSTICE SCALIA's position raises an additional concern. JUSTICE SCALIA apparently does not disagree that the Federal Government has all power necessary to protect the Nation. If criminal processes do not suffice, however, JUSTICE SCALIA would require Congress to suspend the writ. See *ante,* at 26. But the fact that the writ may not be suspended "unless when in Cases of Rebellion or Invasion the public Safety may require it," Art. I, §9, cl. 2, poses two related problems. First, this condition might not obtain here or during many other emergencies during which this detention authority might be necessary. Congress would then have to choose between acting unconstitutionally[4] and depriving the President of the tools he needs to protect the Nation. Second, I do not see how suspension would make constitutional otherwise unconstitutional detentions ordered by the President. It simply removes a remedy. JUSTICE SCALIA's position might therefore require one or both of the political branches to act unconstitutionally in order to protect the Nation. But the power to protect the Nation must be the power to do so lawfully.

---

[4] I agree with JUSTICE SCALIA that this Court could not review Congress' decision to suspend the writ. See *ante,* at 26.

THOMAS, J., dissenting

Accordingly, I conclude that the Government's detention of Hamdi as an enemy combatant does not violate the Constitution. By detaining Hamdi, the President, in the prosecution of a war and authorized by Congress, has acted well within his authority. Hamdi thereby received all the process to which he was due under the circumstances. I therefore believe that this is no occasion to balance the competing interests, as the plurality unconvincingly attempts to do.

IV

Although I do not agree with the plurality that the balancing approach of *Mathews* v. *Eldridge,* 424 U. S. 319 (1976), is the appropriate analytical tool with which to analyze this case,[5] I cannot help but explain that the plurality misapplies its chosen framework, one that if applied correctly would probably lead to the result I have reached. The plurality devotes two paragraphs to its discussion of the Government's interest, though much of those two paragraphs explain why the Government's concerns are misplaced. See *ante*, at 24–25. But: "It is 'obvious and unarguable' that no governmental interest is more compelling than the security of the Nation." *Agee,* 453 U. S., at 307 (quoting *Aptheker,* 378 U. S., at 509). In *Moyer,* the Court recognized the paramount importance of the Governor's interest in the tranquility of a Colorado town. At issue here is the far more significant interest of the security of the Nation. The Government seeks to further that interest by detaining an enemy soldier not only to prevent him from rejoining the ongoing fight. Rather, as the Government explains, detention can serve to gather critical intelligence regarding the intentions and capabilities of our adversaries, a function that the Gov-

---

[5] Evidently, neither do the parties, who do not cite *Mathews* even once.

ernment avers has become all the more important in the war on terrorism. See Brief for Respondents 15; App. 347–351.

Additional process, the Government explains, will destroy the intelligence gathering function. Brief for Respondents 43–45. It also does seem quite likely that, under the process envisioned by the plurality, various military officials will have to take time to litigate this matter. And though the plurality does not say so, a meaningful ability to challenge the Government's factual allegations will probably require the Government to divulge highly classified information to the purported enemy combatant, who might then upon release return to the fight armed with our most closely held secrets.

The plurality manages to avoid these problems by discounting or entirely ignoring them. After spending a few sentences putatively describing the Government's interests, the plurality simply assures the Government that the alleged burdens "are properly taken into account in our due process analysis." *Ante,* at 25. The plurality also announces that "the risk of erroneous deprivation of a detainee's liberty interest is unacceptably high under the Government's proposed rule." *Ante,* at 26 (internal quotation marks omitted). But there is no particular reason to believe that the federal courts have the relevant information and expertise to make this judgment. And for the reasons discussed in Part I, *supra,* there is every reason to think that courts cannot and should not make these decisions.

The plurality next opines that "[w]e think it unlikely that this basic process will have the dire impact on the central functions of warmaking that the Government forecasts." *Ante,* at 27. Apparently by limiting hearings "to the alleged combatant's acts," such hearings "meddl[e] little, if at all, in the strategy or conduct of war." *Ante,* at 28. Of course, the meaning of the combatant's acts may

THOMAS, J., dissenting

become clear only after quite invasive and extensive inquiry. And again, the federal courts are simply not situated to make these judgments.

Ultimately, the plurality's dismissive treatment of the Government's asserted interests arises from its apparent belief that enemy-combatant determinations are not part of "the actual prosecution of a war," *ibid.*, or one of the "central functions of warmaking," *ante,* at 27. This seems wrong: Taking *and holding* enemy combatants is a quintessential aspect of the prosecution of war. See, *e.g., ante*, at 10–11; *Quirin,* 317 U. S., at 28. Moreover, this highlights serious difficulties in applying the plurality's balancing approach here. First, in the war context, we know neither the strength of the Government's interests nor the costs of imposing additional process.

Second, it is at least difficult to explain why the result should be different for other military operations that the plurality would ostensibly recognize as "central functions of warmaking." As the plurality recounts:

> "Parties whose rights are to be affected are entitled to be heard; and in order that they may enjoy that right they must first be notified. It is equally fundamental that the right to notice and an opportunity to be heard must be granted at a meaningful time and in a meaningful manner." *Ante,* at 26 (internal quotation marks omitted).

See also *ibid.* ("notice" of the Government's factual assertions and "a fair opportunity to rebut [those] assertions before a neutral decisionmaker" are essential elements of due process). Because a decision to bomb a particular target might extinguish *life* interests, the plurality's analysis seems to require notice to potential targets. To take one more example, in November 2002, a Central Intelligence Agency (CIA) Predator drone fired a Hellfire missile at a vehicle in Yemen carrying an al Qaeda leader, a citizen of

THOMAS, J., dissenting

the United States, and four others. See Priest, CIA Killed U. S. Citizen In Yemen Missile Strike, Washington Post, Nov. 8, 2002, p. A1. It is not clear whether the CIA knew that an American was in the vehicle. But the plurality's due process would seem to require notice and opportunity to respond here as well. Cf. *Tennessee* v. *Garner,* 471 U. S. 1 (1985). I offer these examples not because I think the plurality would demand additional process in these situations but because it clearly would not. The result here should be the same.

I realize that many military operations are, in some sense, necessary. But many, if not most, are merely expedient, and I see no principled distinction between the military operation the plurality condemns today (the holding of an enemy combatant based on the process given Hamdi) from a variety of other military operations. In truth, I doubt that there is any sensible, bright-line distinction. It could be argued that bombings and missile strikes are an inherent part of war, and as long as our forces do not violate the laws of war, it is of no constitutional moment that civilians might be killed. But this does not serve to distinguish this case because it is also consistent with the laws of war to detain enemy combatants exactly as the Government has detained Hamdi.[6] This, in fact, bolsters my argument in Part III to the extent that the laws of war show that the power to detain is part of a sovereign's war powers.

Undeniably, Hamdi has been deprived of a serious interest, one actually protected by the Due Process Clause. Against this, however, is the Government's overriding interest in protecting the Nation. If a deprivation of lib-

---

[6] Hamdi's detention comports with the laws of war, including the Geneva Convention (III) Relative to the Treatment of Prisoners of War, Aug. 12, 1949, [1955] 6 U. S. T. 3406, T. I. A. S. No. 3364. See Brief for Respondents 22–24.

THOMAS, J., dissenting

erty can be justified by the need to protect a town, the protection of the Nation, *a fortiori*, justifies it.

I acknowledge that under the plurality's approach, it might, at times, be appropriate to give detainees access to counsel and notice of the factual basis for the Government's determination. See *ante*, at 25–27. But properly accounting for the Government's interests also requires concluding that access to counsel and to the factual basis would not always be warranted. Though common sense suffices, the Government thoroughly explains that counsel would often destroy the intelligence gathering function. See Brief for Respondents 42–43. See also App. 347–351 (affidavit of Col. D. Woolfolk). Equally obvious is the Government's interest in not fighting the war in its own courts, see, *e.g.*, *Johnson* v. *Eisentrager*, 339 U. S., at 779, and protecting classified information, see, *e.g.*, *Department of Navy* v. *Egan*, 484 U. S. 518, 527 (1988) (President's "authority to classify and control access to information bearing on national security and to determine" who gets access "flows primarily from [the Commander-in-Chief Clause] and exists quite apart from any explicit congressional grant"); *Agee*, 453 U. S., at 307 (upholding revocation of former CIA employee's passport in large part by reference to the Government's need "to protect the secrecy of [its] foreign intelligence operations").[7]

---

[7] These observations cast still more doubt on the appropriateness and usefulness of *Mathews* v. *Eldridge*, 424 U. S. 319 (1976), in this context. It is, for example, difficult to see how the plurality can insist that Hamdi unquestionably has the right to access to counsel in connection with the proceedings on remand, when new information could become available to the Government showing that such access would pose a grave risk to national security. In that event, would the Government need to hold a hearing before depriving Hamdi of his newly acquired right to counsel even if that hearing would itself pose a grave threat?

THOMAS, J., dissenting

* * *

For these reasons, I would affirm the judgment of the Court of Appeals.

Basic Documents about the Detainees

RUMSFELD V. PADILLA

Nimble Books

(Slip Opinion) OCTOBER TERM, 2003 1

Syllabus

NOTE: Where it is feasible, a syllabus (headnote) will be released, as is being done in connection with this case, at the time the opinion is issued. The syllabus constitutes no part of the opinion of the Court but has been prepared by the Reporter of Decisions for the convenience of the reader. See *United States* v. *Detroit Timber & Lumber Co.*, 200 U. S. 321, 337.

SUPREME COURT OF THE UNITED STATES

Syllabus

RUMSFELD, SECRETARY OF DEFENSE v. PADILLA ET AL.

CERTIORARI TO THE UNITED STATES COURT OF APPEALS FOR THE SECOND CIRCUIT

No. 03–1027. Argued April 28, 2004—Decided June 28, 2004

Respondent Padilla, a United States citizen, was brought to New York for detention in federal criminal custody after federal agents apprehended him while executing a material witness warrant issued by the District Court for the Southern District of New York (Southern District) in connection with its grand jury investigation into the September 11, 2001, al Qaeda terrorist attacks. While his motion to vacate the warrant was pending, the President issued an order to Secretary of Defense Rumsfeld designating Padilla an "enemy combatant" and directing that he be detained in military custody. Padilla was later moved to a Navy brig in Charleston, S. C., where he has been held ever since. His counsel then filed in the Southern District a habeas petition under 28 U. S. C. §2241, which, as amended, alleged that Padilla's military detention violates the Constitution, and named as respondents the President, the Secretary, and Melanie Marr, the brig's commander. The Government moved to dismiss, arguing, *inter alia,* that Commander Marr, as Padilla's immediate custodian, was the only proper respondent, and that the District Court lacked jurisdiction over her because she is located outside the Southern District. That court held that the Secretary's personal involvement in Padilla's military custody rendered him a proper respondent, and that it could assert jurisdiction over the Secretary under New York's long-arm statute, notwithstanding his absence from the District. On the merits, the court accepted the Government's contention that the President has authority as Commander in Chief to detain as enemy combatants citizens captured on American soil during a time of war. The Second Circuit agreed that the Secretary was a proper respondent and that the Southern District had jurisdiction over the Secretary under New

Syllabus

York's long-arm statute. The appeals court reversed on the merits, however, holding that the President lacks authority to detain Padilla militarily.

Held:

1. Because this Court answers the jurisdictional question in the negative, it does not reach the question whether the President has authority to detain Padilla militarily. P. 1.

2. The Southern District lacks jurisdiction over Padilla's habeas petition. Pp. 5–23.

(a) Commander Marr is the only proper respondent to Padilla's petition because she, not Secretary Rumsfeld, is Padilla's custodian. The federal habeas statute straightforwardly provides that the proper respondent is "the person" having custody over the petitioner. §§2242, §2243. Its consistent use of the definite article indicates that there is generally only one proper respondent, and the custodian is "the person" with the ability to produce the prisoner's body before the habeas court, see *Wales* v. *Whitney,* 114 U. S. 564, 574. In accord with the statutory language and *Wales*' immediate custodian rule, long-standing federal-court practice confirms that, in "core" habeas challenges to present physical confinement, the default rule is that the proper respondent is the warden of the facility where the prisoner is being held, not the Attorney General or some other remote supervisory official. No exceptions to this rule, either recognized or proposed, apply here. Padilla does not deny the immediate custodian rule's general applicability, but argues that the rule is flexible and should not apply on the unique facts of this case. The Court disagrees. That the Court's understanding of custody has broadened over the years to include restraints short of physical confinement does nothing to undermine the rationale or statutory foundation of the *Wales* rule where, in core proceedings such as the present, physical custody *is* at issue. Indeed, that rule has consistently been applied in this core context. The Second Circuit erred in taking the view that this Court has relaxed the immediate custodian rule with respect to prisoners detained for other than federal criminal violations, and in holding that the proper respondent is the person exercising the "legal reality of control" over the petitioner. The statute itself makes no such distinction, nor does the Court's case law support a deviation from the immediate custodian rule here. Rather, the cases Padilla cites stand for the simple proposition that the immediate physical custodian rule, by its terms, does not apply when a habeas petitioner challenges something other than his present physical confinement. See, *e.g., Braden* v. *30th Judicial Circuit Court of Ky.,* 410 U. S. 484; *Strait* v. *Laird,* 406 U. S. 341. That is not the case here: Marr exercises day-to-day control over Padilla's physical cus-

BASIC DOCUMENTS ABOUT THE DETAINEES

Cite as: 542 U. S. ____ (2004)

Syllabus

tody. The petitioner cannot name someone else just because Padilla's physical confinement stems from a military order by the President. Identification of the party exercising legal control over the detainee only comes into play when there is no immediate physical custodian. *Ex parte Endo*, 323 U. S. 283, 304–305, distinguished. Although Padilla's detention is unique in many respects, it is at bottom a simple challenge to physical custody imposed by the Executive. His detention is thus not unique in any way that would provide arguable basis for a departure from the immediate custodian rule. Pp. 5–13.

(b) The Southern District does not have jurisdiction over Commander Marr. Section §2241(a)'s language limiting district courts to granting habeas relief "within their respective jurisdictions" requires "that the court issuing the writ have jurisdiction over the custodian," *Braden, supra,* at 495. Because Congress added the "respective jurisdictions" clause to prevent judges anywhere from issuing the Great Writ on behalf of applicants far distantly removed, *Carbo* v. *United States,* 364 U. S. 611, 617, the traditional rule has always been that habeas relief is issuable only in the district of confinement, *id.,* at 618. This commonsense reading is supported by other portions of the habeas statute, *e.g.,* §2242, and by Federal Rule of Appellate Procedure 22(a). Congress has also legislated against the background of the "district of confinement" rule by fashioning explicit exceptions: *E.g.,* when a petitioner is serving a state criminal sentence in a State containing more than one federal district, "the district . . . wherein [he] is in custody" and "the district . . . within which the State court was held which convicted and sentenced him" have "concurrent jurisdiction," §2241(d). Such exceptions would have been unnecessary if, as the Second Circuit believed, §2241 permits a prisoner to file outside the district of confinement. Despite this ample statutory and historical pedigree, Padilla urges that, under *Braden* and *Strait,* jurisdiction lies in any district in which the respondent is amenable to service of process. The Court disagrees, distinguishing those two cases. Padilla seeks to challenge his present physical custody in South Carolina. Because the immediate-custodian rule applies, the proper respondent is Commander Marr, who is present in South Carolina. There is thus no occasion to designate a "nominal" custodian and determine whether he or she is "present" in the same district as petitioner. The habeas statute's "respective jurisdictions" proviso forms an important corollary to the immediate custodian rule in challenges to present physical custody under §2241. Together they compose a simple rule that has been consistently applied in the lower courts, including in the context of military detentions: Whenever a §2241 habeas petitioner seeks to challenge his present physical custody within the United States, he should name his warden as respon-

RUMSFELD v. PADILLA

Syllabus

dent and file the petition in the district of confinement. This rule serves the important purpose of preventing forum shopping by habeas petitioners. The District of South Carolina, not the Southern District of New York, was where Padilla should have brought his habeas petition. Pp. 13–19.

(c) The Court rejects additional arguments made by the dissent in support of the mistaken view that exceptions exist to the immediate custodian and district of confinement rules whenever exceptional, special, or unusual cases arise. Pp. 19–23.

352 F. 3d 695, reversed and remanded.

REHNQUIST, C. J., delivered the opinion of the Court, in which O'CONNOR, SCALIA, KENNEDY, and THOMAS, JJ., joined. KENNEDY, J., filed a concurring opinion, in which O'CONNOR, J., joined. STEVENS, J., filed a dissenting opinion, in which SOUTER, GINSBURG, and BREYER, JJ., joined.

BASIC DOCUMENTS ABOUT THE DETAINEES

Cite as: 542 U. S. ____ (2004)

Opinion of the Court

NOTICE: This opinion is subject to formal revision before publication in the preliminary print of the United States Reports. Readers are requested to notify the Reporter of Decisions, Supreme Court of the United States, Washington, D. C. 20543, of any typographical or other formal errors, in order that corrections may be made before the preliminary print goes to press.

SUPREME COURT OF THE UNITED STATES

No. 03–1027

DONALD H. RUMSFELD, SECRETARY OF DEFENSE, PETITIONER *v.* JOSE PADILLA AND DONNA R. NEWMAN, AS NEXT FRIEND OF JOSE PADILLA

ON WRIT OF CERTIORARI TO THE UNITED STATES COURT OF APPEALS FOR THE SECOND CIRCUIT

[June 28, 2004]

CHIEF JUSTICE REHNQUIST delivered the opinion of the Court.

Respondent Jose Padilla is a United States citizen detained by the Department of Defense pursuant to the President's determination that he is an "enemy combatant" who conspired with al Qaeda to carry out terrorist attacks in the United States. We confront two questions: First, did Padilla properly file his habeas petition in the Southern District of New York; and second, did the President possess authority to detain Padilla militarily. We answer the threshold question in the negative and thus do not reach the second question presented.

Because we do not decide the merits, we only briefly recount the relevant facts. On May 8, 2002, Padilla flew from Pakistan to Chicago's O'Hare International Airport. As he stepped off the plane, Padilla was apprehended by federal agents executing a material witness warrant issued by the United States District Court for the Southern District of New York (Southern District) in connection with its grand jury investigation into the September 11th terrorist attacks. Padilla was then transported to New York, where he was held in federal criminal custody. On May 22, acting through appointed counsel, Padilla moved to vacate the material witness warrant.

Padilla's motion was still pending when, on June 9, the President issued an order to Secretary of Defense Donald H. Rumsfeld designating Padilla an "enemy combatant" and directing the Secretary to detain him in military custody. App. D to Brief for Petitioner 5a (June 9 Order). In support of this action, the President invoked his authority as "Commander in Chief of the U. S. armed forces" and the Authorization for Use of Military Force Joint Resolution, Pub. L. 107–40, 115 Stat. 224 (AUMF),[1] enacted by Congress on September 18, 2001. June 9 Order 5a. The President also made several factual findings explaining his decision to designate Padilla an enemy combatant.[2] Based on these findings, the President concluded that it is "consistent with U. S. law and the laws of war for the Secretary of Defense to detain Mr. Padilla as

---

[1] The AUMF provides in relevant part: "[T]he President is authorized to use all necessary and appropriate force against those nations, organizations, or persons he determines planned, authorized, committed, or aided the terrorist attacks that occurred on September 11, 2001, or harbored such organizations or persons, in order to prevent any future acts of international terrorism against the United States by such nations, organizations or persons." 115 Stat. 224.

[2] In short, the President "[d]etermine[d]" that Padilla (1) "is closely associated with al Qaeda, an international terrorist organization with which the United States is at war;" (2) that he "engaged in . . . hostile and war-like acts, including . . . preparation for acts of international terrorism" against the United States; (3) that he "possesses intelligence" about al Qaeda that "would aid U. S. efforts to prevent attacks by al Qaeda on the United States"; and finally, (4) that he "represents a continuing, present and grave danger to the national security of the United States," such that his military detention "is necessary to prevent him from aiding al Qaeda in its efforts to attack the United States." June 9 Order 5a–6a.

an enemy combatant." *Id.*, at 6a.

That same day, Padilla was taken into custody by Department of Defense officials and transported to the Consolidated Naval Brig in Charleston, South Carolina.[3] He has been held there ever since.

On June 11, Padilla's counsel, claiming to act as his next friend, filed in the Southern District a habeas corpus petition under 28 U. S. C. §2241. The petition, as amended, alleged that Padilla's military detention violates the Fourth, Fifth, and Sixth Amendments and the Suspension Clause, Art. I, §9, cl. 2, of the United States Constitution. The amended petition named as respondents President Bush, Secretary Rumsfeld, and Melanie A. Marr, Commander of the Consolidated Naval Brig.

The Government moved to dismiss, arguing that Commander Marr, as Padilla's immediate custodian, is the only proper respondent to his habeas petition, and that the District Court lacks jurisdiction over Commander Marr because she is located outside the Southern District. On the merits, the Government contended that the President has authority to detain Padilla militarily pursuant to the Commander in Chief Clause of the Constitution, Art. II, §2, cl. 1, the congressional AUMF, and this Court's decision in *Ex parte Quirin*, 317 U. S. 1 (1942).

The District Court issued its decision in December 2002. *Padilla ex rel. Newman* v. *Bush*, 233 F. Supp. 2d 564. The court held that the Secretary's "personal involvement" in Padilla's military custody renders him a proper respon-

---

[3] Also on June 9, the Government notified the District Court *ex parte* of the President's Order; informed the court that it was transferring Padilla into military custody in South Carolina and that it was consequently withdrawing its grand jury subpoena of Padilla; and asked the court to vacate the material witness warrant. *Padilla ex rel Newman* v. *Rumsfeld*, 233 F. Supp. 2d 564, 671 (SDNY 2002). The court vacated the warrant. *Ibid.*

Opinion of the Court

dent to Padilla's habeas petition, and that it can assert jurisdiction over the Secretary under New York's long-arm statute, notwithstanding his absence from the Southern District.[4] *Id.,* at 581–587. On the merits, however, the court accepted the Government's contention that the President has authority to detain as enemy combatants citizens captured on American soil during a time of war. *Id.,* at 587–599.[5]

The Court of Appeals for the Second Circuit reversed. 352 F. 3d 695 (2003). The court agreed with the District Court that Secretary Rumsfeld is a proper respondent, reasoning that in cases where the habeas petitioner is detained for "other than federal criminal violations, the Supreme Court has recognized exceptions to the general practice of naming the immediate physical custodian as respondent." *Id.,* at 704–708. The Court of Appeals concluded that on these "unique" facts Secretary Rumsfeld is Padilla's custodian because he exercises "the legal reality of control" over Padilla and because he was personally involved in Padilla's military detention. *Id.,* at 707–708. The Court of Appeals also affirmed the District Court's holding that it has jurisdiction over the Secretary under

---

[4]The court dismissed Commander Marr, Padilla's immediate custodian, reasoning that she would be obliged to obey any order the court directed to the Secretary. 233 F. Supp. 2d, at 583 The court also dismissed President Bush as a respondent, a ruling Padilla does not challenge. *Id.,* at 582–583.

[5]Although the District Court upheld the President's authority to detain domestically captured enemy combatants, it rejected the Government's contentions that Padilla has no right to challenge the factual basis for his detention and that he should be denied access to counsel. Instead, the court held that the habeas statute affords Padilla the right to controvert alleged facts, and granted him monitored access to counsel to effectuate that right. *Id.,* at 599–605. Finally, the court announced that after it received Padilla's factual proffer, it would apply a deferential "some evidence" standard to determine whether the record supports the President's designation of Padilla as an enemy combatant. *Id.,* at 605–608.

Basic Documents about the Detainees

Cite as: 542 U. S. ____ (2004)

Opinion of the Court

New York's long-arm statute. *Id.*, at 708–710.

Reaching the merits, the Court of Appeals held that the President lacks authority to detain Padilla militarily. *Id.*, at 710–724. The court concluded that neither the President's Commander-in-Chief power nor the AUMF authorizes military detentions of American citizens captured on American soil. *Id.*, at 712–718, 722–723. To the contrary, the Court of Appeals found in both our case law and in the Non-Detention Act, 18 U. S. C. §4001(a),[6] a strong presumption against domestic military detention of citizens absent explicit congressional authorization. 352 F. 3d, at 710–722. Accordingly, the court granted the writ of habeas corpus and directed the Secretary to release Padilla from military custody within 30 days. *Id.*, at 724.

We granted the Government's petition for certiorari to review the Court of Appeals' rulings with respect to the jurisdictional and the merits issues, both of which raise important questions of federal law. 540 U. S. ____ (2004).[7]

The question whether the Southern District has jurisdiction over Padilla's habeas petition breaks down into two related subquestions. First, who is the proper respondent to that petition? And second, does the Southern District have jurisdiction over him or her? We address these questions in turn.

I

The federal habeas statute straightforwardly provides that the proper respondent to a habeas petition is "the person who has custody over [the petitioner]." 28 U. S. C.

---

[6] Section 4001(a) provides that "[n]o citizen shall be imprisoned or otherwise detained by the United States except pursuant to an Act of Congress."

[7] The word "jurisdiction," of course, is capable of different interpretations. We use it in the sense that it is used in the habeas statute, 28 U. S. C. §2241(a), and not in the sense of subject-matter jurisdiction of the District Court.

§ 2242; see also § 2243 ("The writ, or order to show cause shall be directed to the person having custody of the person detained"). The consistent use of the definite article in reference to the custodian indicates that there is generally only one proper respondent to a given prisoner's habeas petition. This custodian, moreover, is "the person" with the ability to produce the prisoner's body before the habeas court. *Ibid.* We summed up the plain language of the habeas statute over 100 years ago in this way: "[T]hese provisions contemplate a proceeding against some person who has the *immediate custody* of the party detained, with the power to produce the body of such party before the court or judge, that he may be liberated if no sufficient reason is shown to the contrary." *Wales v. Whitney,* 114 U. S. 564, 574 (1885) (emphasis added); see also *Braden v. 30th Judicial Circuit Court of Ky.,* 410 U. S. 484, 494–495 (1973) ("The writ of habeas corpus" acts upon "the person who holds [the detainee] in what is alleged to be unlawful custody," citing *Wales, supra,* at 574); *Braden, supra,* at 495 ("'[T]his writ . . . is directed to . . . [the] jailer,'" quoting *In the Matter of Jackson,* 15 Mich. 417, 439–440 (1867)).

In accord with the statutory language and *Wales'* immediate custodian rule, longstanding practice confirms that in habeas challenges to present physical confinement— "core challenges"—the default rule is that the proper respondent is the warden of the facility where the prisoner is being held, not the Attorney General or some other remote supervisory official. See, *e.g., Hogan v. Hanks,* 97 F. 3d 189, 190 (CA7 1996), *Brittingham v. United States,* 982 F. 2d 378, 379 (CA9 1992); *Blango v. Thornburgh,* 942 F. 2d 1487, 1491–1492 (CA10 1991) *(per curiam); Brennan v. Cunningham,* 813 F. 2d 1, 12 (CA1 1987); *Guerra v. Meese,* 786 F. 2d 414, 416 (CADC 1986); *Billiteri v. United States Bd. of Parole,* 541 F. 2d 938, 948 (CA2 1976); *Sand-*

ers v. *Bennett*, 148 F. 2d 19, 20 (CADC 1945); *Jones* v. *Biddle*, 131 F. 2d 853, 854 (CA8 1942).[8] No exceptions to this rule, either recognized[9] or proposed, see *post*, at 4–5 (KENNEDY, J., concurring), apply here.

If the *Wales* immediate custodian rule applies in this case, Commander Marr—the equivalent of the warden at the military brig—is the proper respondent, not Secretary Rumsfeld. See *Al-Marri* v. *Rumsfeld*, 360 F. 3d 707, 708–709 (CA7 2004) (holding in the case of an alleged enemy combatant detained at the Consolidated Naval Brig, the proper respondent is Commander Marr, not Secretary Rumsfeld); *Monk* v. *Secretary of the Navy*, 793 F. 2d 364, 369 (CADC 1986) (holding that the proper respondent in a habeas action brought by a military prisoner is the commandant of the military detention facility, not the Secre-

---

[8] In *Ahrens* v. *Clark*, 335 U. S. 188 (1948), we left open the question whether the Attorney General is a proper respondent to a habeas petition filed by an alien detained pending deportation. *Id.*, at 189, 193. The lower courts have divided on this question, with the majority applying the immediate custodian rule and holding that the Attorney General is not a proper respondent. Compare *Robledo-Gonzales* v. *Ashcroft*, 342 F. 3d 667 (CA7 2003) (Attorney General is not proper respondent); *Roman* v. *Ashcroft*, 340 F. 3d 314 (CA6 2003) (same); *Vasquez* v. *Reno*, 233 F. 3d 688 (CA1 2000) (same); *Yi* v. *Maugans*, 24 F. 3d 500 (CA3 1994) (same), with *Armentero* v. *INS*, 340 F. 3d 1058 (CA9 2003) (Attorney General is proper respondent). The Second Circuit discussed the question at some length, but ultimately reserved judgment in *Henderson* v. *INS*, 157 F. 3d 106 (1998). Because the issue is not before us today, we again decline to resolve it.

[9] We have long implicitly recognized an exception to the immediate custodian rule in the military context where an American citizen is detained outside the territorial jurisdiction of any district court. *Braden* v. *30th Judicial Circuit Court of Ky.*, 410 U. S. 484, 498 (1973) (discussing the exception); *United States ex rel. Toth* v. *Quarles*, 350 U. S. 11 (1955) (court-martial convict detained in Korea named Secretary of the Air Force as respondent); *Burns* v. *Wilson*, 346 U. S. 137 (1953) (court-martial convicts detained in Guam named Secretary of Defense as respondent).

Opinion of the Court

tary of the Navy); cf. 10 U. S. C. §951(c) (providing that the Commanding Officer of a military correctional facility "shall have custody and control" of the prisoners confined therein). Neither Padilla, nor the courts below, nor JUSTICE STEVENS' dissent deny the general applicability of the immediate custodian rule to habeas petitions challenging physical custody. *Post*, at 4. They argue instead that the rule is flexible and should not apply on the "unique facts" of this case. Brief for Respondents 44. We disagree.

First, Padilla notes that the substantive holding of *Wales*—that a person released on his own recognizance is not "in custody" for habeas purposes—was disapproved in *Hensley* v. *Municipal Court, San Jose-Milpitas Judicial Dist., Santa Clara Cty.*, 411 U. S. 345, 350, n. 8 (1973), as part of this Court's expanding definition of "custody" under the habeas statute.[10] Padilla seems to contend, and the dissent agrees, *post*, at 7, that because we no longer require physical detention as a prerequisite to habeas relief, the immediate custodian rule, too, must no longer bind us, even in challenges to physical custody. That argument, as the Seventh Circuit aptly concluded, is a "non sequitur." *Al-Marri, supra*, at 711. That our understanding of custody has broadened to include restraints short of physical confinement does nothing to undermine the rationale or statutory foundation of *Wales*' immediate custodian rule where physical custody *is* at issue. Indeed, as the cases cited above attest, it has consistently been applied in this core habeas context within the United States.[11]

---

[10] For other landmark cases addressing the meaning of "in custody" under the habeas statute, see *Garlotte* v. *Fordice*, 515 U. S. 39 (1995); *Carafas* v. *LaVallee*, 391 U. S. 234 (1968); *Peyton* v. *Rowe*, 391 U. S. 54 (1968); *Jones* v. *Cunningham*, 371 U. S. 236 (1963).

[11] Furthermore, Congress has not substantively amended in more

The Court of Appeals' view that we have relaxed the immediate custodian rule in cases involving prisoners detained for "other than federal criminal violations," and that in such cases the proper respondent is the person exercising the "legal reality of control" over the petitioner, suffers from the same logical flaw. 352 F. 3d, at 705, 707. Certainly the statute itself makes no such distinction based on the source of the physical detention. Nor does our case law support a deviation from the immediate custodian rule here. Rather, the cases cited by Padilla stand for the simple proposition that the immediate physical custodian rule, by its terms, does not apply when a habeas petitioner challenges something other than his present physical confinement.

In *Braden*, for example, an Alabama prisoner filed a habeas petition in the Western District of Kentucky. He did not contest the validity of the Alabama conviction for which he was confined, but instead challenged a detainer lodged against him in Kentucky state court. Noting that petitioner sought to challenge a "confinement that would be imposed in the future," we held that petitioner was "in custody" in Kentucky by virtue of the detainer. 410 U. S., at 488–489. In these circumstances, the Court held that the proper respondent was not the prisoner's immediate physical custodian (the Alabama warden), but was instead the Kentucky court in which the detainer was lodged. This made sense because the Alabama warden was not "the person who [held] him in what [was] alleged to be unlawful custody." *Id.*, at 494–495 (citing *Wales*, 114 U. S., at 574); *Hensley, supra*, at 351, n. 9 (observing that the petitioner in *Braden* "was in the custody of Kentucky

---

than 130 years the relevant portions of the habeas statute on which *Wales* based its immediate custodian rule, despite uniform case law embracing the *Wales* rule in challenges to physical custody.

officials for purposes of his habeas corpus action"). Under *Braden*, then, a habeas petitioner who challenges a form of "custody" other than present physical confinement may name as respondent the entity or person who exercises legal control with respect to the challenged "custody." But nothing in *Braden* supports departing from the immediate custodian rule in the traditional context of challenges to present physical confinement. See *Al-Marri, supra*, at 711–712; *Monk, supra*, at 369. To the contrary, *Braden* cited *Wales* favorably and reiterated the traditional rule that a prisoner seeking release from confinement must sue his "jailer." 410 U. S., at 495 (internal quotation marks omitted).

For the same reason, *Strait* v. *Laird*, 406 U. S. 341 (1972), does not aid Padilla. *Strait* involved an inactive reservist domiciled in California who filed a §2241 petition seeking relief from his military obligations. We noted that the reservist's "nominal" custodian was a commanding officer in Indiana who had charge of petitioner's Army records. *Id.*, at 344. As in *Braden*, the immediate custodian rule had no application because petitioner was not challenging any present physical confinement.

In *Braden* and *Strait*, the immediate custodian rule did not apply because *there was no* immediate physical custodian with respect to the "custody" being challenged. That is not the case here: Commander Marr exercises day-to-day control over Padilla's physical custody. We have never intimated that a habeas petitioner could name someone other than his immediate physical custodian as respondent simply because the challenged physical custody does not arise out of a criminal conviction. Nor can we do so here just because Padilla's physical confinement stems from a military order by the President.

It follows that neither *Braden* nor *Strait* supports the Court of Appeals' conclusion that Secretary Rumsfeld is the proper respondent because he exercises the "legal reality of control" over Padilla.[12] As we have explained, identification of the party exercising legal control only comes into play when there is no immediate physical custodian with respect to the challenged "custody." In challenges to present physical confinement, we reaffirm that the immediate custodian, not a supervisory official who exercises legal control, is the proper respondent. If the "legal control" test applied to physical-custody challenges, a convicted prisoner would be able to name the State or the Attorney General as a respondent to a §2241 petition. As the statutory language, established practice, and our precedent demonstrate, that is not the case.[13]

At first blush *Ex parte Endo*, 323 U. S. 283 (1944), might seem to lend support to Padilla's "legal control" argument. There, a Japanese-American citizen interned in California by the War Relocation Authority (WRA) sought relief by filing a §2241 petition in the Northern District of California, naming as a respondent her immediate custodian. After she filed the petition, however, the Government moved her to Utah. Thus, the prisoner's

---

[12] The Court of Appeals reasoned that "only [the Secretary]—not Commander Marr—could inform the President that further restraint of Padilla as an enemy combatant is no longer necessary." 352 F. 3d 695, 707 (CA2 2003). JUSTICE STEVENS' dissent echoes this argument. *Post*, at 7–8.

[13] Even less persuasive is the Court of Appeals' and the dissent's belief that Secretary Rumsfeld's "unique" and "pervasive" personal involvement in authorizing Padilla's detention justifies naming him as the respondent. 352 F. 3d, at 707–708 (noting that the Secretary "was charged by the President in the June 9 Order with detaining Padilla" and that the Secretary "determined that Padilla would be sent to the brig in South Carolina"); *post*, at 8. If personal involvement were the standard, "then the prosecutor, the trial judge, or the governor would be named as respondents" in criminal habeas cases. *Al-Marri* v. *Rumsfeld*, 360 F. 3d 707, 711 (CA7 2004). As the Seventh Circuit correctly held, the proper respondent is the person responsible for maintaining—not authorizing—the custody of the prisoner. *Ibid.*

immediate physical custodian was no longer within the jurisdiction of the District Court. We held, nonetheless, that the Northern District "acquired jurisdiction in this case and that [Endo's] removal . . . did not cause it to lose jurisdiction where a person in whose custody she is remains within the district." 323 U. S., at 306. We held that, under these circumstances, the assistant director of the WRA, who resided in the Northern District, would be an "appropriate respondent" to whom the District Court could direct the writ. *Id.*, at 304–305.

While *Endo* did involve a petitioner challenging her present physical confinement, it did not, as Padilla and JUSTICE STEVENS contend, hold that such a petitioner may properly name as respondent someone other than the immediate physical custodian. *Post*, at 7–8 (citing *Endo* as supporting a "more functional approach" that allows habeas petitioners to name as respondent an individual with "control" over the petitioner). Rather, the Court's holding that the writ could be directed to a supervisory official came not in our holding that the District Court initially acquired jurisdiction—it did so because Endo properly named her immediate custodian and filed in the district of confinement—but in our holding that the District Court could effectively grant habeas relief despite the Government-procured absence of petitioner from the Northern District.[14] Thus, *Endo* stands for the important but limited proposition that when the Government moves a habeas petitioner after she properly files a petition naming her immediate custodian, the District Court re-

---

[14] As we explained: "Th[e] objective [of habeas relief] may be in no way impaired or defeated by the removal of the prisoner from the territorial jurisdiction of the District Court. That end may be served and the decree of the court made effective if a respondent who has custody of the [petitioner] is within reach of the court's process." 323 U. S., at 307.

tains jurisdiction and may direct the writ to any respondent within its jurisdiction who has legal authority to effectuate the prisoner's release.

Endo's holding does not help respondents here. Padilla was moved from New York to South Carolina before his lawyer filed a habeas petition on his behalf. Unlike the District Court in *Endo*, therefore, the Southern District never acquired jurisdiction over Padilla's petition.

Padilla's argument reduces to a request for a new exception to the immediate custodian rule based upon the "unique facts" of this case. While Padilla's detention is undeniably unique in many respects, it is at bottom a simple challenge to physical custody imposed by the Executive—the traditional core of the Great Writ. There is no indication that there was any attempt to manipulate behind Padilla's transfer—he was taken to the same facility where other al Qaeda members were already being held, and the Government did not attempt to hide from Padilla's lawyer where it had taken him. *Infra*, at 20–21 and n. 17; *post*, at 5 (KENNEDY, J., concurring). His detention is thus not unique in any way that would provide arguable basis for a departure from the immediate custodian rule. Accordingly, we hold that Commander Marr, not Secretary Rumsfeld, is Padilla's custodian and the proper respondent to his habeas petition.

II

We turn now to the second subquestion. District courts are limited to granting habeas relief "within their respective jurisdictions." 28 U. S. C. §2241(a). We have interpreted this language to require "nothing more than that the court issuing the writ have jurisdiction over the custodian." *Braden*, 410 U. S., at 495. Thus, jurisdiction over Padilla's habeas petition lies in the Southern District only if it has jurisdiction over Commander Marr. We conclude it does not.

Congress added the limiting clause—"within their respective jurisdictions"—to the habeas statute in 1867 to avert the "inconvenient [and] potentially embarrassing" possibility that "every judge anywhere [could] issue the Great Writ on behalf of applicants far distantly removed from the courts whereon they sat." *Carbo* v. *United States*, 364 U. S. 611, 617 (1961). Accordingly, with respect to habeas petitions "designed to relieve an individual from oppressive confinement," the traditional rule has always been that the Great Writ is "issuable only in the district of confinement." *Id.,* at 618.

Other portions of the habeas statute support this commonsense reading of §2241(a). For example, if a petitioner seeks habeas relief in the court of appeals, or from this Court or a Justice thereof, the petition must "state the reasons for not making application to *the* district court of the district *in which the applicant is held."* 28 U. S. C. §2242 (emphases added). Moreover, the court of appeals, this Court, or a Justice thereof "may decline to entertain an application for a writ of habeas corpus and may transfer the application . . . to *the* district court having jurisdiction to entertain it." §2241(b) (emphasis added). The Federal Rules similarly provide that an "application for a writ of habeas corpus must be made to *the* appropriate district court." Fed. Rule App. Proc. 22(a) (emphasis added).

Congress has also legislated against the background of the "district of confinement" rule by fashioning explicit exceptions to the rule in certain circumstances. For instance, §2241(d) provides that when a petitioner is serving a state criminal sentence in a State that contains more than one federal district, he may file a habeas petition not only "in the district court for the district wherein [he] is in custody," but also "in the district court for the district within which the State court was held which convicted and sentenced him;" and "each of such district courts shall have concurrent jurisdiction to entertain the application." Similarly, until Congress directed federal criminal prisoners to file certain postconviction petitions in the sentencing courts by adding §2255 to the habeas statute, federal prisoners could litigate such collateral attacks only in the district of confinement. See *United States* v. *Hayman,* 342 U. S. 205, 212–219 (1952). Both of these provisions would have been unnecessary if, as the Court of Appeals believed, §2241's general habeas provisions permit a prisoner to file outside the district of confinement.

The plain language of the habeas statute thus confirms the general rule that for core habeas petitions challenging present physical confinement, jurisdiction lies in only one district: the district of confinement. Despite this ample statutory and historical pedigree, Padilla contends, and the Court of Appeals held, that the district of confinement rule no longer applies to core habeas challenges. Rather, Padilla, as well as today's dissenters, *post,* at 8–10, urge that our decisions in *Braden* and *Strait* stand for the proposition that jurisdiction will lie in any district in which the respondent is amenable to service of process. We disagree.

Prior to *Braden,* we had held that habeas jurisdiction depended on the presence of both the petitioner and his custodian within the territorial confines of the district court. See *Ahrens* v. *Clark,* 335 U. S. 188, 190–192 (1948). By allowing an Alabama prisoner to challenge a Kentucky detainer in the Western District of Kentucky, *Braden* changed course and held that habeas jurisdiction requires only "that the court issuing the writ have jurisdiction over the custodian." 410 U. S., at 495.

But we fail to see how *Braden*'s requirement of jurisdiction over the respondent alters the district of confinement rule for challenges to present physical custody. *Braden* itself did not involve such a challenge; rather, Braden challenged his future confinement in Kentucky by suing his Kentucky custodian. We reasoned that "[u]nder these circumstances it would serve no useful purpose to apply the *Ahrens* rule and require that the action be brought in Alabama." *Id.,* at 499. In habeas challenges to *present* physical confinement, by contrast, the district of confinement is *synonymous* with the district court that has territorial jurisdiction over the proper respondent. This is because, as we have held, the immediate custodian rule applies to core habeas challenges to present physical custody. By definition, the immediate custodian and the prisoner reside in the same district.

Rather than focusing on the holding and historical context of *Braden,* JUSTICE STEVENS, *post,* at 8, like the Court of Appeals, seizes on dicta in which we referred to "service of process" to contend that the Southern District could assert jurisdiction over Secretary Rumsfeld under New York's long-arm statute. See *Braden,* 410 U. S., at 495 ("So long as the custodian can be reached by service of process, the court can issue a writ 'within its jurisdiction' . . . even if the prisoner himself is confined outside the court's territorial jurisdiction"). But that dicta did not indicate that a custodian may be served with process *outside* of the district court's territorial jurisdiction. To the contrary, the facts and holding of *Braden* dictate the opposite inference. Braden served his Kentucky custodian in Kentucky. Accordingly, we concluded that the Western District of Kentucky had jurisdiction over the petition "since the respondent was properly served *in that district.*" *Id.,* at 500 (emphasis added); see also *Endo, supra,* at 304–305 (noting that the court could issue the writ to a WRA official "whose office is at San Francisco, which is within the jurisdiction of the [Northern District of California]"). Thus, *Braden* in no way authorizes district courts to employ long-arm statutes to gain jurisdiction over custodians who are outside of their territorial jurisdiction. See *Al-Marri,* 360 F. 3d, at 711; *Guerra,* 786 F. 2d, at 417. Indeed, in stating its holding, *Braden* favorably cites *Schlanger* v. *Seamans*, 401 U. S. 487 (1971), a case squarely holding that the custodian's absence from the territorial jurisdiction of the district court is fatal to habeas jurisdiction. 410 U. S., at 500. Thus, *Braden* does not derogate from the traditional district of confinement rule for core habeas petitions challenging present physical custody.

The Court of Appeals also thought *Strait* supported its long-arm approach to habeas jurisdiction. But *Strait* offers even less help than *Braden*. In *Strait,* we held that the Northern District of California had jurisdiction over Strait's "nominal" custodian—the commanding officer of the Army records center—even though he was physically located in Indiana. We reasoned that the custodian was "present" in California "through the officers in the hierarchy of the command who processed [Strait's] application for discharge." 406 U. S., at 345. The *Strait* Court contrasted its broad view of "presence" in the case of a nominal custodian with a "'commanding officer who is responsible for the day to day control of his subordinates,'" who would be subject to habeas jurisdiction only in the district where he physically resides. *Ibid.* (quoting *Arlen* v. *Laird*, 451 F. 2d 684, 687 (CA2 1971)).

The Court of Appeals, much like JUSTICE STEVENS' dissent, reasoned that Secretary Rumsfeld, in the same way as Strait's commanding officer, was "present" in the Southern District through his subordinates who took Padilla into military custody. 352 F. 3d, at 709–710; *post*, at 8. We think not.

Strait simply has no application to the present case. *Strait* predated *Braden*, so the then-applicable *Ahrens* rule required that both the petitioner and his custodian be present in California. Thus, the only question was whether Strait's commanding officer was present in California notwithstanding his physical absence from the district. Distinguishing *Schlanger, supra,* we held that it would "exalt fiction over reality" to require Strait to sue his "nominal custodian" in Indiana when Strait had always resided in California and had his only meaningful contacts with the Army there. 406 U. S., at 344–346. Only under these limited circumstances did we invoke concepts of personal jurisdiction to hold that the custodian was "present" in California through the actions of his agents. *Id.,* at 345.

Here, by contrast, Padilla seeks to challenge his present physical custody in South Carolina. Because the immediate-custodian rule applies to such habeas challenges, the proper respondent is Commander Marr, who is also present in South Carolina. There is thus no occasion to designate a "nominal" custodian and determine whether he or she is "present" in the same district as petitioner.[15] Under *Braden* and the district of confinement rule, as we have explained, Padilla must file his habeas action in South Carolina. Were we to extend *Strait*'s limited exception to the territorial nature of habeas jurisdiction to the context of physical-custody challenges, we would undermine, if not negate, the purpose of Congress in amending the habeas statute in 1867.

The proviso that district courts may issue the writ only "within their respective jurisdictions" forms an important corollary to the immediate custodian rule in challenges to present physical custody under §2241. Together they compose a simple rule that has been consistently applied in the lower courts, including in the context of military detentions: Whenever a §2241 habeas petitioner seeks to challenge his present physical custody within the United

---

[15] In other words, Commander Marr is the equivalent of the "commanding officer with day to day control" that we distinguished in *Strait.* 406 U. S., at 345 (internal quotation marks omitted).

States, he should name his warden as respondent and file the petition in the district of confinement. See *Al-Marri, supra,* at 710, 712 (alleged enemy combatant detained at Consolidated Naval Brig must file petition in the District of South Carolina; collecting cases dismissing §2241 petitions filed outside the district of confinement); *Monk,* 793 F. 2d, at 369 (court-martial convict must file in district of confinement).[16]

This rule, derived from the terms of the habeas statute, serves the important purpose of preventing forum shopping by habeas petitioners. Without it, a prisoner could name a high-level supervisory official as respondent and then sue that person wherever he is amenable to long-arm jurisdiction. The result would be rampant forum shopping, district courts with overlapping jurisdiction, and the very inconvenience, expense, and embarrassment Congress sought to avoid when it added the jurisdictional limitation 137 years ago.

III

JUSTICE STEVENS' dissent, not unlike the Court of Appeals' decision, rests on the mistaken belief that we have made various exceptions to the immediate custodian and district of confinement rules whenever "exceptional,"

---

[16] As a corollary to the previously referenced exception to the immediate custodian rule, n. 8, *supra,* we have similarly relaxed the district of confinement rule when "Americans citizens confined overseas (and thus outside the territory of any district court) have sought relief in habeas corpus." *Braden,* 410 U. S., at 498 (citing cases). In such cases, we have allowed the petitioner to name as respondent a supervisory official and file the petition in the district where the respondent resides. *Burns v. Wilson,* 346 U. S. 137 (1953) (court-martial convicts held in Guam sued Secretary of Defense in the District of Columbia); *United States ex rel. Toth v. Quarles,* 350 U. S. 11 (1955) (court-martial convict held in Korea sued Secretary of the Air Force in the District of Columbia).

Opinion of the Court

"special," or "unusual" cases have arisen. *Post*, at 1, 4, 8, n. 5. We have addressed most of his contentions in the foregoing discussion, but we briefly touch on a few additional points.

Apparently drawing a loose analogy to *Endo*, JUSTICE STEVENS asks us to pretend that Padilla and his immediate custodian were present in the Southern District at the time counsel filed the instant habeas petition, thus rendering jurisdiction proper. *Post*, at 4–5. The dissent asserts that the Government "depart[ed] from the time-honored practice of giving one's adversary fair notice of an intent to present an important motion to the court," when on June 9 it moved *ex parte* to vacate the material witness warrant and allegedly failed to immediately inform counsel of its intent to transfer Padilla to military custody in South Carolina. *Ibid.*; cf. n. 3, *supra*. Constructing a hypothetical "scenario," the dissent contends that if counsel had been immediately informed, she "would have filed the habeas petition then and there," while Padilla remained in the Southern District, "rather than waiting two days." *Post*, at 4–5. Therefore, JUSTICE STEVENS concludes, the Government's alleged misconduct "justifies treating the habeas petition as the functional equivalent of one filed two days earlier." *Post*, at 5 ("[W]e should not permit the Government to obtain a tactical advantage as a consequence of an *ex parte* proceeding").

The dissent cites no authority whatsoever for its extraordinary proposition that a district court can exercise statutory jurisdiction based on a series of events that did not occur, or that jurisdiction might be premised on "punishing" alleged Government misconduct. The lower courts—unlike the dissent—did not perceive any hint of Government misconduct or bad faith that would warrant extending *Endo* to a case where both the petitioner and his immediate custodian were outside of the district at the time of filing. Not surprisingly, then, neither Padilla nor the lower courts relied on the dissent's counterfactual theory to argue that habeas jurisdiction was proper. Finding it contrary to our well-established precedent, we are not persuaded either.[17]

The dissent contends that even if we do not indulge its hypothetical scenario, the Court has made "numerous exceptions" to the immediate custodian and district of confinement rules, rendering our bright-line rule "far from bright." *Post*, at 6. Yet the dissent cannot cite *a single case* in which we have deviated from the longstanding rule we reaffirm today—that is, a case in which we allowed a habeas petitioner challenging his present physical custody within the United States to name as respondent someone

---

[17] On a related note, the dissent argues that the facts as they actually existed at the time of filing should not matter, because "what matters for present purposes are the facts available to [counsel] at the time of filing." *Post*, at 4–5, n. 3. According to the dissent, because the Government "shrouded . . . in secrecy" the location of Padilla's military custody, counsel was entitled to file in the district where Padilla's presence was "last officially confirmed." *Ibid.* As with the argument addressed above, neither Padilla nor the District Court—which was much closer to the facts of the case than we are—or the Court of Appeals ever suggested that the Government concealed Padilla's whereabouts from counsel, much less contended that such concealment was the basis for habeas jurisdiction in the Southern District. And even if this were a valid legal argument, the record simply does not support the dissent's inference of Government secrecy. The dissent relies solely on a letter written by Padilla's counsel. In that same letter, however, counsel states that she "was informed [on June 10]" that her client had been taken into custody by the Department of Defense and "detain[ed] at a naval military prison." App. 66. When counsel filed Padilla's habeas petition on June 11, she averred that "Padilla is being held in segregation at the high-security Consolidated Naval Brig in Charleston, South Carolina." Pet. for Writ of Habeas Corpus, June 11, 2002, p. 2. The only reasonable inference, particularly in light of Padilla's failure to argue to the contrary, is that counsel was well aware of Padilla's presence in South Carolina when she filed the habeas petition, not that the Government "shrouded" Padilla's whereabouts in secrecy.

other than the immediate custodian and to file somewhere other than the district of confinement.[18] If JUSTICE STEVENS' view were accepted, district courts would be consigned to making ad hoc determinations as to whether the circumstances of a given case are "exceptional," "special," or "unusual" enough to require departure from the jurisdictional rules this Court has consistently applied. We do not think Congress intended such a result.

Finally, the dissent urges us to bend the jurisdictional

---

[18] Instead, JUSTICE STEVENS, like the Court of Appeals, relies heavily on *Braden, Strait,* and other cases involving challenges to something other than present physical custody. *Post,* at 7–10; *post,* at 7–8, n. 4 (citing *Garlotte* v. *Fordice,* 515 U. S. 39 (1995) (habeas petitioner challenging expired sentence named Governor as respondent; immediate custodian issue not addressed); *Middendorf* v. *Henry,* 425 U. S. 25 (1976) (putative habeas class action challenging court-martial procedures throughout the military; immediate custodian issue not addressed)); *post,* at 9–10 (citing *Eisel* v. *Secretary of the Army,* 477 F. 2d 1251 (CADC 1973) (allowing an inactive reservist challenging his military status to name the Secretary of the Army as respondent)). *Demjanjuk* v. *Meese,* 784 F. 2d 1114 (CADC 1986), on which the dissent relies, *post,* at 4, is similarly unhelpful: When, as in that case, a prisoner is held in an undisclosed location by an unknown custodian, it is impossible to apply the immediate custodian and district of confinement rules. That is not the case here, where the identity of the immediate custodian and the location of the appropriate district court are clear.

The dissent also cites two cases in which a state prisoner proceeding under 28 U. S. C. §2254 named as respondent the State's officer in charge of penal institutions. *Post,* at 7, n. 4 (citing *California Dept. of Corrections* v. *Morales,* 514 U. S. 499 (1995); *Wainwright* v. *Greenfield,* 474 U. S. 284 (1986)). But such cases do not support Padilla's cause. First of all, the respondents did not challenge their designation as inconsistent with the immediate custodian rule. More to the point, Congress has authorized §2254 petitioners challenging present physical custody to name either the warden *or* the chief state penal officer as a respondent. Rule 2(a) of the Rules Governing Section 2254 Cases in the United States District Courts; Advisory Committee Note to Rule 2(a), 28 U. S. C. pp. 469–470 (adopted in 1976). Congress has made no such provision for §2241 petitioners like Padilla.

rules because the merits of this case are indisputably of "profound importance," *post,* at 1, 7. But it is surely just as necessary in important cases as in unimportant ones that courts take care not to exceed their "respective jurisdictions" established by Congress.

The District of South Carolina, not the Southern District of New York, was the district court in which Padilla should have brought his habeas petition. We therefore reverse the judgment of the Court of Appeals and remand the case for entry of an order of dismissal without prejudice.

It is so ordered.

Cite as: 542 U. S. ____ (2004) 1

KENNEDY, J., concurring

SUPREME COURT OF THE UNITED STATES

No. 03–1027

DONALD H. RUMSFELD, SECRETARY OF DEFENSE, PETITIONER *v.* JOSE PADILLA AND DONNA R. NEWMAN, AS NEXT FRIEND OF JOSE PADILLA

ON WRIT OF CERTIORARI TO THE UNITED STATES COURT OF APPEALS FOR THE SECOND CIRCUIT

[June 28, 2004]

JUSTICE KENNEDY, with whom JUSTICE O'CONNOR joins, concurring.

Though I join the opinion of the Court, this separate opinion is added to state my understanding of how the statute should be interpreted in light of the Court's holding. The Court's analysis relies on two rules. First, the habeas action must be brought against the immediate custodian. Second, when an action is brought in the district court, it must be filed in the district court whose territorial jurisdiction includes the place where the custodian is located.

These rules, however, are not jurisdictional in the sense of a limitation on subject-matter jurisdiction. *Ante,* at 5, n. 7. That much is clear from the many cases in which petitions have been heard on the merits despite their noncompliance with either one or both of the rules. See, *e.g. Braden* v. *30th Judicial Circuit Court of Ky.,* 410 U. S. 484, 495 (1973); *Strait* v. *Laird,* 406 U. S. 341, 345 (1972); *United States ex rel. Toth* v. *Quarles,* 350 U. S. 11 (1955); *Burns* v. *Wilson,* 346 U. S. 137 (1953); *Ex parte Endo,* 323 U. S. 283 (1944).

In my view, the question of the proper location for a habeas petition is best understood as a question of per-

RUMSFELD v. PADILLA

KENNEDY, J., concurring

sonal jurisdiction or venue. This view is more in keeping with the opinion in *Braden,* and its discussion explaining the rules for the proper forum for habeas petitions. 410 U. S., at 493, 500 (indicating that the analysis is guided by "traditional venue considerations" and "traditional principles of venue"); see also *Moore* v. *Olson,* 368 F. 3d 757, 759–760 (CA7 2004) (suggesting that the territorial-jurisdiction rule is a venue rule, and the immediate-custodian rule is a personal jurisdiction rule). This approach is consistent with the reference in the statute to the "respective jurisdictions" of the district court. 28 U. S. C. §2241. As we have noted twice this Term, the word "jurisdiction" is susceptible of different meanings, not all of which refer to the power of a federal court to hear a certain class of cases. *Kontrick* v. *Ryan,* 540 U. S. ___ (2004); *Scarborough* v. *Principi,* 541 U. S. ___ (2004). The phrase "respective jurisdictions" does establish a territorial restriction on the proper forum for habeas petitions, but does not of necessity establish that the limitation goes to the power of the court to hear the case.

Because the immediate-custodian and territorial-jurisdiction rules are like personal jurisdiction or venue rules, objections to the filing of petitions based on those grounds can be waived by the Government. *Moore, supra,* at 759; cf. *Endo, supra,* at 305 ("The fact that no respondent was ever served with process or appeared in the proceedings is not important. The United States resists the issuance of a writ. A cause exists in that state of the proceedings and an appeal lies from denial of a writ without the appearance of a respondent"). For the same reason, the immediate-custodian and territorial rules are subject to exceptions, as acknowledged in the Court's opinion. *Ante,* at 7, n. 9, 9–13, 16–18. This does not mean that habeas petitions are governed by venue rules and venue considerations that apply to other sorts of civil lawsuits. Although habeas actions are civil cases, they are not automatically subject to all of the Federal Rules of Civil Procedure. See Fed. Rule Civ. Proc. 81(a)(2) ("These rules are applicable to proceedings for . . . habeas corpus . . . to the extent that the practice in such proceedings is not set forth in statutes of the United States, the Rules Governing Section 2254 Cases, or the Rules Governing Section 2255 Proceedings"). Instead, these forum-location rules for habeas petitions are based on the habeas statutes and the cases interpreting them. Furthermore, the fact that these habeas rules are subject to exceptions does not mean that, in the exceptional case, a petition may be properly filed in any one of the federal district courts. When an exception applies, see, *e.g.*, *Rasul* v. *Bush*, *post*, p. ___, courts must still take into account the considerations that in the ordinary case are served by the immediate custodian rule, and, in a similar fashion, limit the available forum to the one with the most immediate connection to the named custodian.

I would not decide today whether these habeas rules function more like rules of personal jurisdiction or rules of venue. It is difficult to describe the precise nature of these restrictions on the filing of habeas petitions, as an examination of the Court's own opinions in this area makes clear. Compare, *e.g.*, *Ahrens* v. *Clark*, 335 U. S. 188 (1948), with *Schlanger* v. *Seamans*, 401 U. S. 487, 491 (1971), and *Braden*, *supra*, at 495. The precise question of how best to characterize the statutory direction respecting where the action must be filed need not be resolved with finality in this case. Here there has been no waiver by the Government; there is no established exception to the immediate-custodian rule or to the rule that the action must be brought in the district court with authority over the territory in question; and there is no need to consider some further exception to protect the integrity of the writ or the rights of the person detained.

For the purposes of this case, it is enough to note that,

RUMSFELD *v.* PADILLA

KENNEDY, J., concurring

even under the most permissive interpretation of the habeas statute as a venue provision, the Southern District of New York was not the proper place for this petition. As the Court concludes, in the ordinary case of a single physical custody within the borders of the United States, where the objection has not been waived by the Government, the immediate-custodian and territorial-jurisdiction rules must apply. *Ante*, at 23. I also agree with the arguments from statutory text and case law that the Court marshals in support of these two rules. *Ante*, at 5–6, 13–14. Only in an exceptional case may a court deviate from those basic rules to hear a habeas petition filed against some person other than the immediate custodian of the prisoner, or in some court other than the one in whose territory the custodian may be found.

The Court has made exceptions in the cases of nonphysical custody, see, *e.g, Strait*, 406 U. S., at 345, of dual custody, see, *e.g., Braden*, 410 U. S., at 500, and of removal of the prisoner from the territory of a district after a petition has been filed, see, *e.g., Endo*, 323 U. S., at 306; see also *ante*, at 11–12, 15–16. In addition, I would acknowledge an exception if there is an indication that the Government's purpose in removing a prisoner were to make it difficult for his lawyer to know where the habeas petition should be filed, or where the Government was not forthcoming with respect to the identity of the custodian and the place of detention. In cases of that sort, habeas jurisdiction would be in the district court from whose territory the petitioner had been removed. In this case, if the Government had removed Padilla from the Southern District of New York but refused to tell his lawyer where he had been taken, the District Court would have had jurisdiction over the petition. Or, if the Government did inform the lawyer where a prisoner was being taken but kept moving him so a filing could not catch up to the prisoner, again, in my view, habeas jurisdiction would lie

KENNEDY, J., concurring

in the district or districts from which he had been removed.

None of the exceptions apply here. There is no indication that the Government refused to tell Padilla's lawyer where he had been taken. The original petition demonstrates that the lawyer knew where Padilla was being held at that time. *Ante*, at 21, n. 17. In these circumstances, the basic rules apply, and the District of South Carolina was the proper forum. The present case demonstrates the wisdom of those rules.

Both Padilla's change in location and his change of custodian reflected a change in the Government's rationale for detaining him. He ceased to be held under the authority of the criminal justice system, see 18 U. S. C. §3144, and began to be held under that of the military detention system. Rather than being designed to play games with forums, the Government's removal of Padilla reflected the change in the theory on which it was holding him. Whether that theory is a permissible one, of course, is a question the Court does not reach today.

The change in custody, and the underlying change in rationale, should be challenged in the place the Government has brought them to bear and against the person who is the immediate representative of the military authority that is detaining him. That place is the District of South Carolina, and that person is Commander Marr. The Second Circuit erred in holding that the Southern District of New York was a proper forum for Padilla's petition. With these further observations, I join the opinion and judgment of the Court.

BASIC DOCUMENTS ABOUT THE DETAINEES

Cite as: 542 U. S. ____ (2004)

STEVENS, J., dissenting

SUPREME COURT OF THE UNITED STATES

No. 03–1027

DONALD H. RUMSFELD, SECRETARY OF DEFENSE, PETITIONER *v.* JOSE PADILLA AND DONNA R. NEWMAN, AS NEXT FRIEND OF JOSE PADILLA

ON WRIT OF CERTIORARI TO THE UNITED STATES COURT OF APPEALS FOR THE SECOND CIRCUIT

[June 28, 2004]

JUSTICE STEVENS, with whom JUSTICE SOUTER, JUSTICE GINSBURG, and JUSTICE BREYER join, dissenting.

The petition for a writ of habeas corpus filed in this case raises questions of profound importance to the Nation. The arguments set forth by the Court do not justify avoidance of our duty to answer those questions. It is quite wrong to characterize the proceeding as a "simple challenge to physical custody," *ante*, at 13, that should be resolved by slavish application of a "bright-line rule," *ante*, at 21, designed to prevent "rampant forum shopping" by litigious prison inmates, *ante*, at 19. As the Court's opinion itself demonstrates, that rule is riddled with exceptions fashioned to protect the high office of the Great Writ. This is an exceptional case that we clearly have jurisdiction to decide.

I

In May 2002, a grand jury convened in the Southern District of New York was conducting an investigation into the September 11, 2001, terrorist attacks. In response to an application by the Department of Justice, the Chief Judge of the District issued a material witness warrant authorizing Padilla's arrest when his plane landed in

RUMSFELD v. PADILLA

STEVENS, J., dissenting

Chicago on May 8.[1] Pursuant to that warrant, agents of the Department of Justice took Padilla (hereinafter respondent) into custody and transported him to New York City, where he was detained at the Metropolitan Correctional Center. On May 15, the court appointed Donna R. Newman, a member of the New York bar, to represent him. She conferred with respondent in person and filed motions on his behalf, seeking his release on the ground that his incarceration was unauthorized and unconstitutional. The District Court scheduled a hearing on those motions for Tuesday, June 11, 2002.

On Sunday, June 9, 2002, before that hearing could occur, the President issued a written command to the Secretary of Defense concerning respondent. "Based on the information available to [him] from all sources," the President determined that respondent is an "enemy combatant," that he is "closely associated with al Qaeda, an international terrorist organization with which the United States is at war," and that he possesses intelligence that, "if communicated to the U. S., would aid U. S. efforts to prevent attacks by al Qaeda" on U. S. targets. App. A to Pet. for Cert. 57a. The command stated that "it is in the interest of the United States" and "consistent with U. S. law and the laws of war for the Secretary of Defense to detain Mr. Padilla as an enemy combatant." *Id.*, at 58a. The President's order concluded: "Accordingly, you are

---

[1] As its authority for detaining respondent as a material witness, the Government relied on a federal statute that provides: "If it appears from an affidavit filed by a party that the testimony of a person is material in a criminal proceeding, and if it is shown that it may become impracticable to secure the presence of the person by subpoena, a judicial officer may order the arrest of the person and treat the person in accordance with the provisions of section 3142 . . . . Release of a material witness may be delayed for a reasonable period of time until the deposition of the witness can be taken pursuant to the Federal Rules of Criminal Procedure." 18 U. S. C. §3144.

BASIC DOCUMENTS ABOUT THE DETAINEES

Cite as: 542 U. S. ____ (2004) 3

STEVENS, J., dissenting

directed to receive Mr. Padilla from the Department of Justice and to detain him as an enemy combatant." *Ibid.*

On the same Sunday that the President issued his order, the Government notified the District Court in an *ex parte* proceeding that it was withdrawing its grand jury subpoena, and it asked the court to enter an order vacating the material witness warrant. *Padilla ex rel. Newman v. Bush*, 233 F. Supp. 2d 564, 571 (SDNY 2002). In that proceeding, in which respondent was not represented, the Government informed the court that the President had designated respondent an enemy combatant and had directed the Secretary of Defense, petitioner Donald Rumsfeld, to detain respondent. *Ibid.* The Government also disclosed that the Department of Defense would take custody of respondent and immediately transfer him to South Carolina. The District Court complied with the Government's request and vacated the warrant.[2]

On Monday, June 10, 2002, the Attorney General publicly announced respondent's detention and transfer "to the custody of the Defense Department," which he called "a significant step forward in the War on Terrorism." Amended Pet. for Writ of Habeas Corpus, Exh. A, p. 1, Record, Doc. 4. On June 11, 2002, presumably in response to that announcement, Newman commenced this proceeding by filing a petition for a writ of habeas corpus in the Southern District of New York. 233 F. Supp. 2d, at

---

[2] The order vacating the material witness warrant that the District Court entered in the *ex parte* proceeding on June 9 terminated the Government's lawful custody of respondent. After that order was entered, Secretary Rumsfeld's agents took custody of respondent. The authority for that action was based entirely on the President's command to the Secretary—a document that, needless to say, would not even arguably qualify as a valid warrant. Thus, whereas respondent's custody during the period between May 8 and June 9, 2002, was pursuant to a judicially authorized seizure, he has been held ever since—for two years—pursuant to a warrantless arrest.

STEVENS, J., dissenting

571. At a conference on that date, which had been originally scheduled to address Newman's motion to vacate the material witness warrant, the Government conceded that Defense Department personnel had taken custody of respondent in the Southern District of New York. *Id.*, at 571–572.

II

All Members of this Court agree that the immediate custodian rule should control in the ordinary case and that habeas petitioners should not be permitted to engage in forum shopping. But we also all agree with Judge Bork that "special circumstances" can justify exceptions from the general rule. *Demjanjuk* v. *Meese,* 784 F.2d 1114, 1116 (CADC 1986). See *ante,* at 22, n. 18. Cf. *ante,* at 2 (KENNEDY, J., concurring). More narrowly, we agree that if jurisdiction was proper when the petition was filed, it cannot be defeated by a later transfer of the prisoner to another district. *Ex parte Endo,* 323 U. S. 283, 306 (1944). See *ante,* at 12–13.

It is reasonable to assume that if the Government had given Newman, who was then representing respondent in an adversary proceeding, notice of its intent to ask the District Court to vacate the outstanding material witness warrant and transfer custody to the Department of Defense, Newman would have filed the habeas petition then and there, rather than waiting two days.[3] Under that

---

[3]The record indicates that the Government had not *officially* informed Newman of her client's whereabouts at the time she filed the habeas petition on June 11. Pet. for Writ of Habeas Corpus 2, ¶4 ("On information and belief, Padilla is being held in segregation at the high-security Consolidated Naval Brig in Charleston, South Carolina"); Letter from Donna R. Newman to General Counsel of the Department of Defense, June 17, 2002 ("I understand *from the media* that my client is being held in Charleston, South Carolina in the military brig" (emphasis added)), Amended Pet. for Writ of Habeas Corpus, Exh. A, p. 4,

STEVENS, J., dissenting

scenario, respondent's immediate custodian would then have been physically present in the Southern District of New York carrying out orders of the Secretary of Defense. Surely at that time Secretary Rumsfeld, rather than the lesser official who placed the handcuffs on petitioner, would have been the proper person to name as a respondent to that petition.

The difference between that scenario and the secret transfer that actually occurred should not affect our decision, for we should not permit the Government to obtain a tactical advantage as a consequence of an *ex parte* proceeding. The departure from the time-honored practice of giving one's adversary fair notice of an intent to present an important motion to the court justifies treating the habeas application as the functional equivalent of one filed two days earlier. See *Baldwin* v. *Hale,* 1 Wall. 223, 233

Record, Doc. 4. Thus, while it is true, as the Court observes, that "Padilla was moved from New York to South Carolina before his lawyer filed a habeas petition on his behalf," *ante*, at 13, what matters for present purposes are the facts available to Newman at the time of filing. When the Government shrouded those facts in secrecy, Newman had no option but to file immediately in the district where respondent's presence was last officially confirmed.

Moreover, Newman was appointed to represent respondent by the District Court for the Southern District of New York. Once the Government removed her client, it did not permit her to counsel him until February 11, 2004. Consultation thereafter has been allowed as a matter of the Government's grace, not as a matter of right stemming from the Southern District of New York appointment. Cf. *ante*, at 4–5 (KENNEDY, J., concurring). Further, it is not apparent why the District of South Carolina, rather than the Southern District of New York, should be regarded as the proper forum to determine the validity of the "change in the Government's rationale for detaining" respondent. *Ante*, at 5. If the Government's theory is not "a permissible one," *ibid.*, then the New York federal court would remain the proper forum in this case. Why should the New York court not have the authority to determine the legitimacy of the Government's removal of respondent beyond that court's borders?

STEVENS, J., dissenting

(1864) ("Common justice requires that no man shall be condemned in his person or property without notice and an opportunity to make his defence"). "The very nature of the writ demands that it be administered with the initiative and flexibility essential to insure that miscarriages of justice within its reach are surfaced and corrected." *Harris* v. *Nelson,* 394 U. S. 286, 291 (1969). But even if we treat respondent's habeas petition as having been filed in the Southern District after the Government removed him to South Carolina, there is ample precedent for affording special treatment to this exceptional case, both by recognizing Secretary Rumsfeld as the proper respondent and by treating the Southern District as the most appropriate venue.

Although the Court purports to be enforcing a "brightline rule" governing district courts' jurisdiction, *ante,* at 21, an examination of its opinion reveals that the line is far from bright. Faced with a series of precedents emphasizing the writ's "scope and flexibility," *Harris,* 394 U. S., at 291, the Court is forced to acknowledge the numerous exceptions we have made to the immediate custodian rule. The rule does not apply, the Court admits, when physical custody is not at issue, *ante,* at 8, or when American citizens are confined overseas, *ante,* at 19, n. 16, or when the petitioner has been transferred after filing, *ante,* at 12–13, or when the custodian is "'present'" in the district through his agents' conduct, *ante,* at 17. In recognizing exception upon exception and corollaries to corollaries, the Court itself persuasively demonstrates that the rule is not ironclad. It is, instead, a workable general rule that frequently gives way outside the context of "'core challenges'" to Executive confinement. *Ante,* at 6.

In the Court's view, respondent's detention falls within the category of "'core challenges'" because it is "not unique in any way that would provide arguable basis for a departure from the immediate custodian rule." *Ante,* at 13. It

STEVENS, J., dissenting

is, however, disingenuous at best to classify respondent's petition with run-of-the-mill collateral attacks on federal criminal convictions. On the contrary, this case is singular not only because it calls into question decisions made by the Secretary himself, but also because those decisions have created a unique and unprecedented threat to the freedom of every American citizen.

"[W]e have consistently rejected interpretations of the habeas corpus statute that would suffocate the writ in stifling formalisms or hobble its effectiveness with the manacles of arcane and scholastic procedural requirements." *Hensley* v. *Municipal Court, San Jose-Milpitas Judicial Dist., Santa Clara Cty.*, 411 U. S. 345, 350 (1973). With respect to the custody requirement, we have declined to adopt a strict reading of *Wales* v. *Whitney,* 114 U. S. 564 (1885), see *Hensley,* 411 U. S., at 350, n. 8, and instead have favored a more functional approach that focuses on the person with the power to produce the body. See *Endo,* 323 U. S., at 306–307.[4] In this case, the President entrusted the

---

[4]For other cases in which the immediate custodian rule has not been strictly applied, see *Garlotte* v. *Fordice,* 515 U. S. 39 (1995) (prisoner named Governor of Mississippi, not warden, as respondent); *California Dept. of Corrections* v. *Morales,* 514 U. S. 499 (1995) (prisoner named Department of Corrections, not warden, as respondent); *Wainwright* v. *Greenfield,* 474 U. S. 284 (1986) (prisoner named Secretary of Florida Department of Corrections, not warden, as respondent); *Middendorf* v. *Henry,* 425 U. S. 25 (1976) (persons convicted or ordered to stand trial at summary courts-martial named Secretary of the Navy as respondent); *Strait* v. *Laird,* 406 U. S. 341, 345–346 (1972) ("The concepts of 'custody' and 'custodian' are sufficiently broad to allow us to say that the commanding officer in Indiana, operating through officers in California in processing petitioner's claim, is in California for the limited purposes of habeas corpus jurisdiction"); *Burns* v. *Wilson,* 346 U. S. 137 (1953) (service members convicted and held in military custody in Guam named Secretary of Defense as respondent); *United States ex rel. Toth* v. *Quarles,* 350 U. S. 11 (1955) (next friend of ex-service member in military custody in Korea named Secretary of the Air Force as respondent); *Ex parte Endo,*

STEVENS, J., dissenting

Secretary of Defense with control over respondent. To that end, the Secretary deployed Defense Department personnel to the Southern District with instructions to transfer respondent to South Carolina. Under the President's order, only the Secretary—not a judge, not a prosecutor, not a warden—has had a say in determining respondent's location. As the District Court observed, Secretary Rumsfeld has publicly shown "both his familiarity with the circumstances of Padilla's detention, and his personal involvement in the handling of Padilla's case." 233 F. Supp. 2d, at 574. Having "emphasized and jealously guarded" the Great Writ's "ability to cut through barriers of form and procedural mazes," *Harris*, 394 U. S., at 291, surely we should acknowledge that the writ reaches the Secretary as the relevant custodian in this case.

Since the Secretary is a proper custodian, the question whether the petition was appropriately filed in the Southern District is easily answered. "So long as the custodian can be reached by service of process, the court can issue a writ 'within its jurisdiction' requiring that the prisoner be brought before the court for a hearing on his claim . . . even if the prisoner himself is confined outside the court's territorial jurisdiction." *Braden* v. *30th Judicial Circuit Court of Ky.*, 410 U. S. 484, 495 (1973).[5] See also *Endo*, 323 U. S., at 306 ("[T]he court may act if there is a respondent

---

323 U. S. 283, 304 (1944) (California District Court retained jurisdiction over Japanese-American's habeas challenge to her internment, despite her transfer to Utah, noting absence of any "suggestion that there is no one within the jurisdiction of the District Court who is responsible for the detention of appellant and who would be an appropriate respondent").

[5] Although, as the Court points out, *ante*, at 16, the custodian in *Braden* was served within the territorial jurisdiction of the District Court, the salient point is that *Endo* and *Braden* decoupled the District Court's jurisdiction from the detainee's place of confinement and adopted for unusual cases a functional analysis that does not depend on the physical location of any single party.

STEVENS, J., dissenting

within reach of its process who has custody of the petitioner"). In this case, Secretary Rumsfeld no doubt has sufficient contacts with the Southern District properly to be served with process there. The Secretary, after all, ordered military personnel to that forum to seize and remove respondent.

It bears emphasis that the question of the proper forum to determine the legality of Padilla's incarceration is not one of federal subject-matter jurisdiction. See *ante*, at 5, n. 7; *ante*, at 1 (KENNEDY, J., concurring). Federal courts undoubtedly have the authority to issue writs of habeas corpus to custodians who can be reached by service of process "within their respective jurisdictions." 28 U. S. C. §2241(a). Rather, the question is one of venue, *i.e.*, in which federal court the habeas inquiry may proceed.[6] The Government purports to exercise complete control, free from judicial surveillance, over that placement. Venue principles, however, center on the most convenient and efficient forum for resolution of a case, see *Braden*, 410 U. S., at 493–494, 499–500 (considering those factors in allowing Alabama prisoner to sue in Kentucky), and on the placement most likely to minimize forum shopping by either party, see *Eisel* v. *Secretary of the Army*, 477 F. 2d

---

[6] Although the Court makes no reference to venue principles, it is clear that those principles, not rigid jurisdictional rules, govern the forum determination. In overruling *Ahrens* v. *Clark*, 335 U. S. 188 (1948), the Court in *Braden* v. *30th Judicial Circuit Court of Ky.*, 410 U. S. 484 (1973), clarified that the place of detention pertains only to the question of venue. See *id.*, at 493–495 (applying "traditional venue considerations" and rejecting a stricter jurisdictional approach); *id.*, at 502 (REHNQUIST, J., dissenting) ("Today the Court overrules *Ahrens*"); *Moore* v. *Olson*, 368 F. 3d 757, 758 (CA7 2004) ("[A]fter *Braden* . . . , which overruled *Ahrens*, the location of a collateral attack is best understood as a matter of venue"); *Armentero* v. *INS*, 340 F. 3d 1058, 1070 (CA9 2003) ("District courts may use traditional venue considerations to control where detainees bring habeas petitions" (citing *Braden*, 410 U. S., at 493–494)).

STEVENS, J., dissenting

1251, 1254 (CADC 1973) (preferring such functional considerations to "blind incantation of words with implied magical properties, such as 'immediate custodian'").[7] Cf. *Ex parte Bollman,* 4 Cranch 75, 136 (1807) ("It would . . . be extremely dangerous to say, that because the prisoners were apprehended, not by a civil magistrate, but by the military power, there could be given by law a right to try the persons so seized in any place which the general might select, and to which he might direct them to be carried").

When this case is analyzed under those traditional venue principles, it is evident that the Southern District of New York, not South Carolina, is the more appropriate place to litigate respondent's petition. The Government sought a material witness warrant for respondent's detention in the Southern District, indicating that it would be convenient for its attorneys to litigate in that forum. As a result of the Government's initial forum selection, the District Judge and counsel in the Southern District were familiar with the legal and factual issues surrounding respondent's detention both before and after he was transferred to the Defense Department's custody. Accordingly, fairness and efficiency counsel in favor of preserving venue in the Southern District. In sum, respondent properly filed his petition against Secretary Rumsfeld in the Southern District of New York.

III

Whether respondent is entitled to immediate release is a question that reasonable jurists may answer in different ways.[8] There is, however, only one possible answer to the

---

[7] If, upon consideration of traditional venue principles, the district court in which a habeas petition is filed determines that venue is inconvenient or improper, it of course has the authority to transfer the petition. See 28 U. S. C. §§1404(a), 1406(a).

[8] Consistent with the judgment of the Court of Appeals, I believe that

BASIC DOCUMENTS ABOUT THE DETAINEES

STEVENS, J., dissenting

question whether he is entitled to a hearing on the justification for his detention.[9]

At stake in this case is nothing less than the essence of a free society. Even more important than the method of selecting the people's rulers and their successors is the character of the constraints imposed on the Executive by the rule of law. Unconstrained Executive detention for the purpose of investigating and preventing subversive activity is the hallmark of the Star Chamber.[10] Access to counsel for the purpose of protecting the citizen from official mistakes and mistreatment is the hallmark of due process.

Executive detention of subversive citizens, like detention of enemy soldiers to keep them off the battlefield, may sometimes be justified to prevent persons from launching or becoming missiles of destruction. It may not, however, be justified by the naked interest in using unlawful procedures to extract information. Incommunicado detention for months on end is such a procedure. Whether the information so procured is more or less reliable than that acquired by more extreme forms of torture is of no conse-

---

the Non-Detention Act, 18 U. S. C. §4001(a), prohibits—and the Authorization for Use of Military Force Joint Resolution, 115 Stat. 224, adopted on September 18, 2001, does not authorize—the protracted, incommunicado detention of American citizens arrested in the United States.

[9] Respondent's custodian has been remarkably candid about the Government's motive in detaining respondent: "'[O]ur interest really in his case is not law enforcement, it is not punishment because he was a terrorist or working with the terrorists. Our interest at the moment is to try and find out everything he knows so that hopefully we can stop other terrorist acts.'" 233 F. Supp. 2d 564, 573–574 (SDNY 2002) (quoting News Briefing, Dept. of Defense (June 12, 2002), 2002 WL 22026773).

[10] See *Watts* v. *Indiana,* 338 U. S. 49, 54 (1949) (opinion of Frankfurter, J.). "There is torture of mind as well as body; the will is as much affected by fear as by force. And there comes a point where this Court should not be ignorant as judges of what we know as men." *Id.,* at 52.

quence. For if this Nation is to remain true to the ideals symbolized by its flag, it must not wield the tools of tyrants even to resist an assault by the forces of tyranny.

I respectfully dissent.

Basic Documents about the Detainees

Colophon

This book was produced using Microsoft Word and Adobe Acrobat. The cover was produced using The Gimp 2.0.2 with Ghostscript.

The cover font and display fonts inside the book are Copperplate Gothic Black. Body text is Goudy Old Style.

The cover was designed by Kelsey Zimmerman.

The American Heritage® Dictionary of the English Language, Fourth Edition, copyright © 2000 by Houghton Mifflin Company defines col·o·phon as follows:

> An ancient Greek city of Asia Minor northwest of Ephesus. It was famous for its cavalry.

Along the same lines, Webster's Revised Unabridged, copyright 1996, 1998, MICRA, Inc.:

> \Col"o*phon\ (k[o^]l"[-o]*f[o^]n), n. [L. colophon finishing stroke, Gr. kolofw`n; cf. L. culmen top, collis hill. Cf. Holm.] An inscription, monogram, or cipher, containing the place and date of publication, printer's name, etc., formerly placed on the last page of a book.

If in doubt – go to the source!

NIMBLE BOOKS

BASIC DOCUMENTS ABOUT THE DETAINEES

NIMBLE BOOKS

Basic Documents about the Detainees

NIMBLE BOOKS

Basic Documents about the Detainees

NIMBLE BOOKS

www.ingramcontent.com/pod-product-compliance
Lightning Source LLC
Chambersburg PA
CBHW081838230426
43669CB00018B/2752